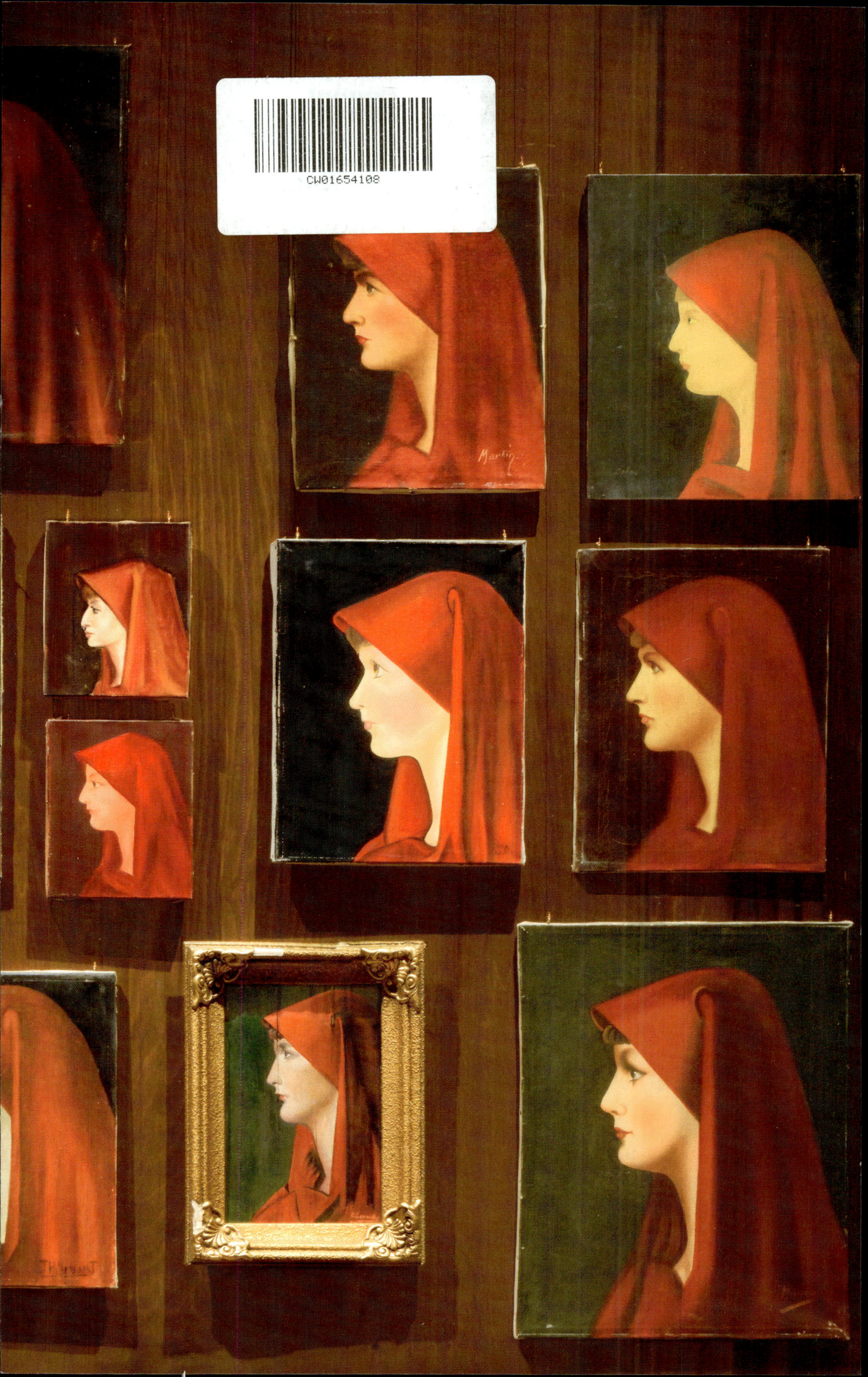
Martin

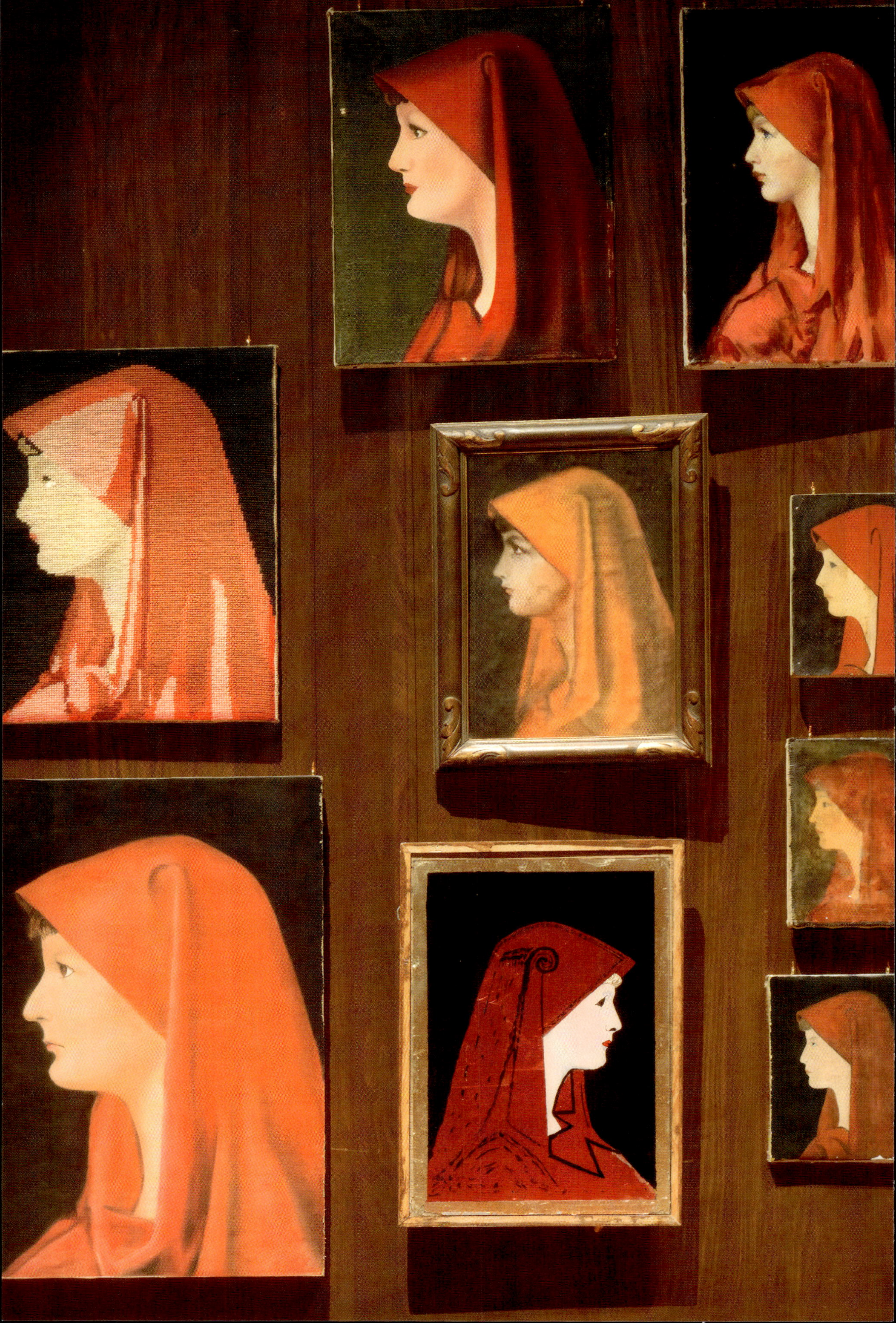

Francis Alÿs

Fabiola: An Investigation

Francis Alÿs

Fabiola: An Investigation

Dia Art Foundation, New York
Distributed by Yale University Press,
New Haven and London
2008

This book was published on the occasion of the exhibition "Francis Alÿs: Fabiola," organized by Dia Art Foundation, New York.
The publication is made possible by the Colección Patricia Phelps de Cisneros.
The exhibition, public programs, and publication are made possible by Brown Foundation, Peter Norton Family Foundation, The Juliet Lea Hillman Simonds Foundation, New York City Department of Cultural Affairs, New York City Councilmember Robert Jackson, New York State Council on the Arts, a State agency, and Erica and Joseph Samuels.

Designed by Filiep Tacq, Madrid
Editors, Karen Kelly and Lynne Cooke, with Bettina Funcke
Editorial and Research Assistant, Jeanne Dreskin
Proofreading by Barbara Schröder and Richard Gallin

535 West 22nd Street, New York, New York 10011
www.diaart.org

ISBN 978-0-300-13916-7 (Yale University Press)

Library of Congress Cataloging-in-Publication Data

Alÿs, Francis, 1959-
Francis Alÿs : Fabiola : an investigation / with essays by Stephen Bann ... [et al.].
p. cm.
Published on the occasion of an exhibition organized by Dia Art Foundation, New York.
Includes bibliographical references.
ISBN 978-0-300-13916-7
1. Alÿs, Francis, 1959—-Exhibitions. 2. Installations (Art)—New York (State)—New York—Exhibitions. 3. Fabiola, Saint, d. 399 or 400—Art—Exhibitions. 4. Painting—Copying—Exhibitions. I. Bann, Stephen. II. Dia Art Foundation. III. Title.
N6973.A45A4 2008
755′.63—dc22
2008008139

Front and back covers and endpapers, photographs by Cathy Carver
Catalogue of Works, photographs by Francesca Esmay. Reproduced courtesy of Francis Alÿs.

Saint Jerome's "Letter 77, To Oceanus on the Death of Fabiola," is reprinted from *Select Letters of St. Jerome*, trans. F. A. Wright (1933; repr. Cambridge, Mass.: Harvard University Press, 1991), pp. 308–37.

Distributed by Yale University Press, New Haven and London

Yale University Press
302 Temple Street
P.O. Box 209040
New Haven, CT 06520-9040
www.yalebooks.com

Printed and bound in Belgium.

CONTENTS

ACKNOWLEDGMENTS

There are many to acknowledge with regard to both this exhibition and book. First and foremost, of course, our gratitude goes to Francis Alÿs, for his dedication to the singular investigation of the Fabiola phenomenon and his thoughtful and perceptive approach to this collaboration.

We conceptualized this book in dialogue with the artist to examine the Fabiola project and its implications in a wider cultural context. Bettina Funcke's sensitive, critical voice was crucial throughout the book's development. The authors—Stephen Bann, Martha Buskirk, Susan Laningham, and David Morgan—embraced the project with enthusiasm and spirit, contributing essays that together shape this multifaceted book. Dia's conservator and registrar Francesca Esmay, along with Heidie Giannotti, meticulously produced the detailed descriptive catalogue of the collection. Jeanne Dreskin, assistant editor, joined Dia's staff as this book came into being, and it benefited from her devoted research. In Alÿs's studio, we were fortunate to have the assistance of Raúl Ortega Ayala. The book's designer, Filiep Tacq, proved a perfect complement to the concept; his insight and precision have been highly valued. We also would like to thank our distributor, Yale University Press, for helping us to reach a wider audience.

The professional and dedicated staff at Dia has been, as usual, a pleasure to work with and, equally, critical to the realization of the exhibition. In particular, we would like to thank curatorial assistants Kristin Poor and Armelle Pradalier, who skillfully and assiduously managed, over the course of several years, the countless aspects of transporting and caring for these works. John Bowsher, Dia's former exhibitions manager, organized the handling and installation of the project.

Mitchell A. Codding, director of the Hispanic Society of America, has been a generous partner in this, the first of several projects that Dia will produce in the spaces of the society's building on Audubon Terrace. The Hispanic Society's board of trustees and its staff have been most cooperative, and we could not be more grateful for such a smooth collaboration between our two institutions.

We thank Jeffrey Weiss, Dia's former director; Laura Raicovich, Dia's deputy director; and Dia's board of trustees for their unwavering trust, encouragement, and support. Both David Zwirner and Bellatrix Hubert, at the David Zwirner gallery, which represents the artist, have lent significant support to this project. Our thanks are also extended to Dia's former director Michael Govan, now director of the Los Angeles County Museum of Art, and Sandy Nairne, director of the National Portrait Gallery in London, the two institutions to which the show will travel after it closes in New York.

ACKNOWLEDGMENTS

The publication is made possible by support from the Colección Patricia Phelps de Cisneros. The exhibition, public programs, and publication were generously supported by the Brown Foundation; the Peter Norton Family Foundation; The Juliet Lea Hillman Simonds Foundation; the New York City Department of Cultural Affairs; New York City Councilmember Robert Jackson; the New York State Council on the Arts, a State agency; and by Erica and Joseph Samuels. Their generosity has made it possible for us to realize the Alÿs Fabiola project, and they have our sincerest gratitude.

Lynne Cooke, curator and editor, and Karen Kelly, editor

Thanks to Louise, Edith, Frederic, Nicolas, and all the friends
who helped me in collecting Fabiolas,
to Cuauhtémoc Medina,
to Karen, Kristin, and Filiep,
to the writers,
to Lynne,
and special thanks to Thierry Leclercq.

Francis Alÿs

Francis Alÿs was born in Antwerp, Belgium, in 1959. He studied architecture at the Institut d'Architecture, Tournai, Belgium, and the Istituto Universitario di Architettura, Venice, Italy. He began to work as an artist in the late eighties after moving to Mexico City and had his first one-person exhibition there in 1990. Major exhibitions of his work have been presented at such venues as Artangel, London (2005); Kunstmuseum Wolfsburg, Germany, and touring (2004), and the Israel Museum in Jerusalem (2005). He participated in the Habana Bienal in 1994, São Paulo Bienal in 1998, Istanbul Biennial in 1999 and 2001, Venice Biennale in 1999, 2001, and 2007, Lima Bienal in 2002, Sydney Biennale in 2004 and the Carnegie International in 2004.

Stephen Bann is professor of art history at the University of Bristol and was president of the Comité International d'Histoire de l'Art from 2000 to 2004. His books include *Ways Around Modernism* (2007), *Parallel Lines: Printmakers, Painters, and Photographers in 19th-Century France* (2001), *Paul Delaroche: History Painted* (1997), and *The True Vine: On Visual Representation and the Western Tradition* (1989).

Martha Buskirk is professor of art history and criticism at Montserrat College of Art in Beverly, Massachusetts. She is author of *The Contingent Object of Contemporary Art* (2003) and also co-editor of *The Duchamp Effect* (1996), with Mignon Nixon, and *The Destruction of Tilted Arc: Documents* (1990), with Clara Weyergraf-Serra. She is currently working on a new book, *Seeing through the Museum: Art, Life, Commerce*, which examines intersections between museum history and contemporary artistic practices that evoke conventions associated with the collection, souvenir, relic, and archive.

Lynne Cooke has been curator at Dia Art Foundation since 1991. Co-curator of the 1991 Carnegie International, and artistic director of the 1996 Sydney Biennale, she has also curated exhibitions in numerous venues in North America, Europe, and elsewhere. In addition to teaching at Columbia University in the graduate fine arts department, she is on the faculty for curatorial studies at Bard College. Among her numerous publications are recent essays on the works of Rodney Graham, Jorge Pardo, Richard Serra, and Agnes Martin.

Karen Kelly, editor, is director of publications at Dia Art Foundation, where she has worked since 1989. At Dia, she has edited, with curator Lynne Cooke, numerous books, including *Joan Jonas: The Shape, the Scent, the Feel of Things* (2006), *Robert Smithson: Spiral Jetty* (2005), and *Robert Whitman: Playback* (2003), among many others. In addition to publishing, she has produced a series of audio CDs, and has organized and coordinated film screenings, performance events, and symposia at Dia. Previously, she served as a senior editor at the literary journal *Conjunctions* and as an assistant editor at the art magazine *Parkett.*

Susan Laningham is associate professor of history at Tennessee Tech University. She specializes in medieval and early modern European history, with an emphasis in religious history and the history of the body. Her most recent monograph, "Maladies Up Her Sleeve? Clerical Interpretation of a Suffering Female Body in Counter-Reformation Spain," appeared in the 2006 inaugural issue of *Early Modern Women: An Interdisciplinary Journal*, and her essay, "Making a Saint out of a Sibling," on family and the construction of holy reputations in Spain, is included in *Sibling Relations and Gender in the Early Modern World* (2006). Currently, she is completing the editing and introduction for a new translation of the *vita* of the sixteenth-century Spanish nun and mystic, Maria Vela, for the University of Chicago Press's *Other Voices* Series.

David Morgan is professor of religion at Duke University. Author of several books, including *Visual Piety* (1998), *Protestants and Pictures* (1999), and *The Sacred Gaze* (2005), Morgan's latest book is *The Lure of Images: A History of Religion and Visual Media in America* (2007). Morgan is co-founder and editor of the scholarly journal, *Material Religion.* He is also very interested in contemporary art and has written essays on a number of leading artists such as Bill Viola, Kimsooja, Ed Paschke, and Magdalena Abakanowicz. He is currently editing a book of essays entitled *Keywords in Religion, Media, and Culture.*

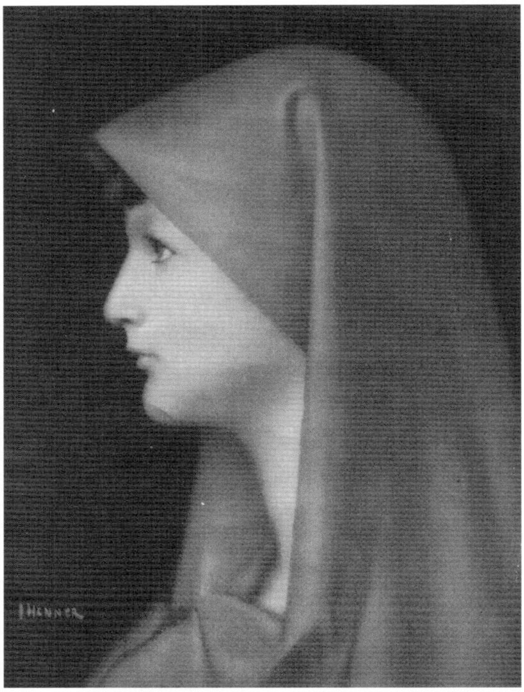

Fig. 1
Jean-Jacques Henner,
Fabiola, 1885.
13 x 16 ½ inches
(33.02 x 41.91 cm).
Location unknown.

FINDING FABIOLA

David Morgan

Fabiola has long taught the lessons of forgiveness and charity, but her many images also have something to teach about the nature and structure of human cognition in popular piety. Empiricists are fond of asserting that knowledge is founded on concrete experience—that facts are built from the ground up, tailored to the particularities of sensation. But Fabiola in her prosaic multiplicity, in the endless iteration of her spare, quiet imagery says otherwise. Consider her many pictures. Who are we looking at when we gaze upon any one of her many portraits? The sheer number of them destabilizes the prospect of a settled referent. Where is the fourth-century Roman lady of patrician status, befriended by Jerome and eulogized by him at her death? Finding Fabiola may not be possible, but who can resist trying when faced with so many portraits?

Fabiola and Jerome

The impulse to see images as grounded ultimately in facts is an important place to begin thinking about how pictures of Fabiola may be said to show her to the faithful. Perhaps the first thing one sees when looking at her images is not her, but what Jerome said about her. We look through the picture to the text of the bishop's eulogy, and a couple of other letters that may refer to her indirectly. This assumes, of course, that his words limned her reliably. But what's reliable? His letters can no longer be read in his handwriting, but they are corroborated by contemporaries and they bear the signature of his style and the verification of historical circumstances. Assuming that Jean-Jacques Henner started there in order to compose his lost portrait of 1885, *fig. 1* we, too, go to the letters to find Fabiola, the *real* Fabiola, seeking in the imagery correspondences to what Jerome said of her. But like the generations of Christians and scholars who have sought the historical Jesus in the documents of the New Testament, we find what the letters have constructed and we lack anything against which to test them. Jerome's Epistles, like the Gospels, are not indifferent transcripts, but accounts with a purpose, rooted in the communities and circumstances that birthed them. If they are "faithful" descriptions, they are faithful to the purpose and the needs of the writer and his correspondents. Hagiography, the writing of saints' lives, is far less a description of the dead than it is the edification of the living.

Matching word to image, we see the portraits as pictorial hagiography whose message is that a sinner experienced regeneration through the regimen of penitence and contrition. Fabiola was received back into the embrace of the Church after falling away. She put aside the desire and option for marriage and undertook the work of charity. Her heavy red mantle and hood, covering her bosom and clinging like a nun's habit to all but a sliver of her fair face and long neck, signal both her penitent denial of the flesh and her patrician status. The red attire recalls the iconographical tradition of portraying Jerome in the cardinal's red robe and hat. And, since Henner also painted a portrait of Jerome (1881), the connection is even more suggestive. What the two shared was a dedication to monastic self-denial. Signaling Fabiola's asceticism was important: it mattered that the elite of her day were penitent because their rank elevated the Christian community, reaffirming its principal bonds as deeper and surer than social status, but also conferring on the group the capacity to include Rome's finest. The Christian community was happy to recognize such privilege in a society where rank meant everything.

It is a double message—one of penance and submission, to be sure. But Fabiola's
fig. 3 beauty belies another. Let us choose one for closer inspection—no. 164. Her classical profile, as Henner and his faithful copyist, Francis Huys, have imagined it, is etched clearly against the dark ground, rendering the ideal of grace in a long Roman nose, a Hellenic chin, and a neck that remembers the languor of a privileged life even as it vanishes modestly into the scarlet fullness of the lady's tunic. It is the contour of an imperial face on coin or medallion. So one might call it an aquiline beauty, evoking the eagle (*aquila*) in imperial insignia, echoed in the beaklike prominence of Fabiola's nose, the sharp contour of her upper lip, and especially in the determined brow that sternly descends in some images. Does it remember the hauteur of patrician rank? Or has it been baptized into the austerity of self-denial so prized by Jerome among Rome's new vestal virgins?

But this is to read the imagery in a strictly historical manner, as if the scores of images collected by Francis Alÿs at flea markets, garage sales, and thrift stores hailed from the distant past. They don't. Their lost origin is Henner's portrait. Yet in the dimmest way they remember something about worlds no longer present. "Remember" may be pushing it. But vaguely encoded in the profile, in the hood and its folds, is iconography that can be traced backward some distance, though not all the way back to shadowy Fabiola. What did Henner consult as he conceived his image? In the world of ancient Rome one thinks of funerary sculpture or portrait busts in which the piety of noble Roman women was registered by their gracefully covered heads.
fig. 2 When viewed from the side, the marble bust of Livia, second wife of Augustus, observes the restrained and solemn demeanor still at work in Fabiola's countless portraits. Did Henner see Livia's bust or one of hundreds like it? He must have asked himself how Fabiola would look. She was from the upper crust, she was a person of means, one of several we know Jerome sought out to form a powerful circle of high-born women dedicated to his cause. Like each of them, Fabiola modestly put the life of privilege aside for the sake of piety. Henner would have recognized the countenance of nobility that suited Fabiola in the ancient face of Livia or any one of dozens

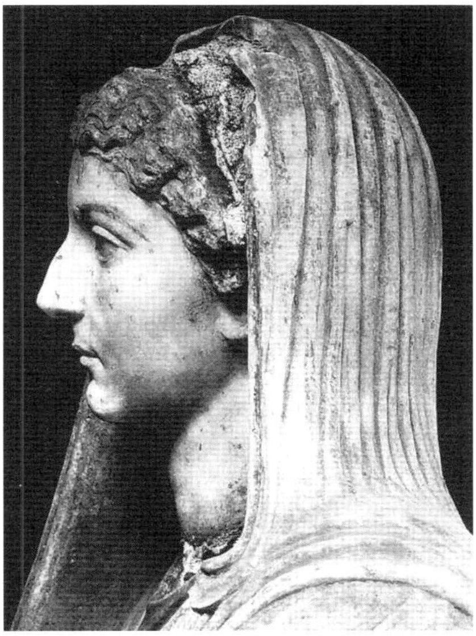

Fig. 2
Livia, 20 CE, marble.
Antiquarium, Pompeii.

painted during the Renaissance such as Piero della Francesca's impassive Battista Sforza (1472) or Domenico Ghirlandaio's charming portrait of Giovanna Tornabuoni (1488), or in his own day, Anselm Feuerbach's *Iphegenia* (1871). After all, she had to look the part if she were to be recognized by the devout. It was a matter of probability, of the saint looking the role.

The Nature of Recognition

Ever since Plato, recognition has been linked to epistemology, the study of how we know. Plato contended that to know is to recognize—that is, to remember what we already knew. But if no one ever recorded a portrait of Fabiola, how are we to know it's really her? Whom do we recognize as Fabiola when we gaze upon her portrait? The cult of the saints will help us understand what people see. One Catholic web site states that Saint Fabiola is patroness of "difficult marriages, divorced people, victims of abuse, victims of adultery, victims of unfaithfulness, widows."[1] Those are powerful connections for the faithful who seek consolation or counsel. Fabiola is said to have suffered these difficulties: Jerome (Letter 55) seems to indicate that her first husband was "an adulterer and sodomite."[2] She divorced him but was "compelled to

1. "Fabiola," Patron Saints Index, http://www.catholic-forum.com/saints/saintf20.htm (accessed November 14, 2007).

2. Saint Jerome, "Letter 55, to Amandus," http://www.newadvent.org/fathers/2001055.htm (accessed November 14, 2007).

take another," presumably by her family, the prominent Fabia clan. When the second husband died, she undertook public penance and was allowed to participate in Holy Communion once again. She never remarried and devoted herself to philanthropic enterprises, founding a hospital in Rome. Every saint is good for something: she will respond to petitions from the faithful precisely because she herself suffered as they do. She is inclined by sympathy to hear their prayers because she shares with them the pain and tribulation from which they seek relief.

People recognize in Fabiola what they bring to her and what they need from her. One powerful function of hagiography is to establish the basis of connection with the saint. Jerome offers bits of her story in his eulogy (Letter 77); what is lacking there, tradition makes up for by virtue of attribution. We have no evidence whatsoever that Jerome, in another epistolary exchange (Letter 55), is in fact referring to Fabiola when he writes to his correspondent, "I find joined to your letter of inquiries a short paper containing the following words: 'ask him, (that is me), whether a woman who has left her husband on the ground that he is an adulterer and sodomite and has found herself compelled to take another may in the lifetime of him whom she first left be in communion with the church without doing penance for her fault.'"[3] Jerome answered unambiguously: No, she could not. And he groused about her words: "I have not been able quite to determine what it is that she means by the words 'has found herself compelled' to marry again. What is this compulsion of which she speaks?" If she does not wish "to be accounted an adulterous," he ruled, "let her do penance."[4] Jerome could be a demanding, aggressive man. A fighter as scrappy as Augustine had suffered his famous invective.[5] Whoever she was, the woman whose query Amandus conveyed kept her name out of the public discourse of a prominent and prickly bishop's official correspondence. Assuming it was she, Fabiola clearly knew that the penance Jerome ordered was not the discreet sort, uttered quietly and privately in the pastor's study or the confidence of the confessional. It meant sackcloth and ashes in the front row on Sunday morning. Not the sort of thing a highborn Fabia took on lightly.

It requires no faith to want to recognize Fabiola. One is tugged by the pleasure of scandal in her story (if it is hers): Roman noblewoman married to a bestial lout who can't control his appetites, she walks out and divorces him. Ever cognizant of public perceptions, Fabiola's family compels her to remarry, resulting in her ostracism in the Christian community and her inadmissibility at the Lord's Table. No Eucharist meant no assurance of forgiveness of sins and therefore no salvation. Exclusion

3. Ibid.
4. Ibid.
5. Peter Brown, *Augustine of Hippo* (Berkeley: University of California Press, 1969), pp. 274–75.

meant a metaphysical bust. Hardliners like Jerome and Augustine rigorously policed the boundaries of membership. The privileges of belonging were enforced by the agony of being kept out. The resistance made the story better, which mattered since, among other things, sainthood consists of a story and an image. Hagiography and iconography are the media whereby the devout connect to the sacred. Fueled by need and encouraged by the fit, they discern between their story and the saint's; devotees solicit the saint's help. They focus their need and hope on the cult image, which commonly bears the traces of the saint's story. They recognize her because they know her story. The hole in their heart takes the shape of Fabiola's virtues.

Copy and Effigy: The Cultural Work of Iteration

One might regard the innumerable iterations of Fabiola's image as each painter's tailoring of the saint to him or herself. She appears now angry, now nymphlike, glamorous, then unassuming, valorous, then meek, solemn, then spry. Compare nos. 164 and 144: the latter woman looks like she comes from an afternoon television *figs. 3 & 4*

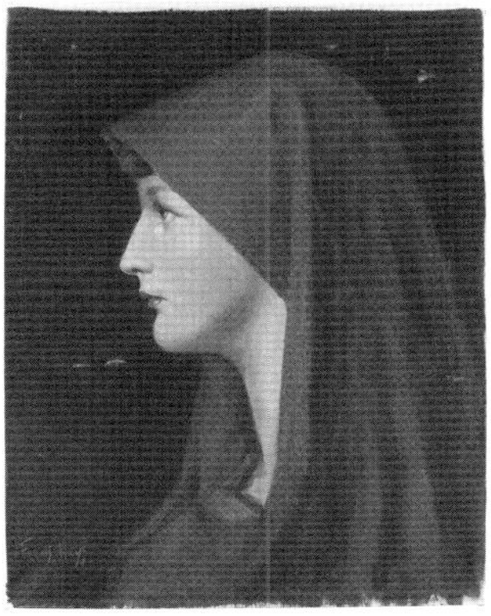

Fig. 3 Fabiola, no. 164.

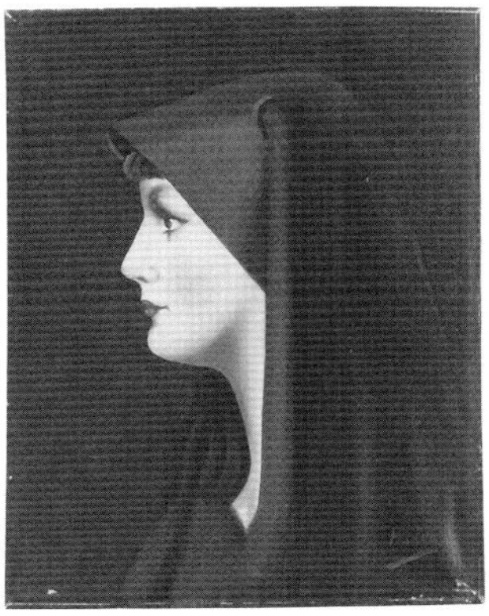

Fig. 4 Fabiola, no. 144.

commercial selling dishwashing soap in the 1960s, whereas no. 164 might be a publicity still from a 1940s bathrobe epic about the Bible. The suggestion is not so ludicrous when we consider the striking resemblance of many versions of Fabiola to the study of a woman from the early 1890s by Henner. The artist may have used the *fig. 5* same model for the two portraits. All the versions of Fabiola differ more or less from one another and the difference—grounded in more than just the painters' technical abilities—corresponds to the many reasons people must have for painting Fabiola. Perhaps it is in fulfillment of a vow, an ex-voto, a retablo meant to be displayed in gratitude for her assistance in resolving the difficulties of domestic affairs. Her small,

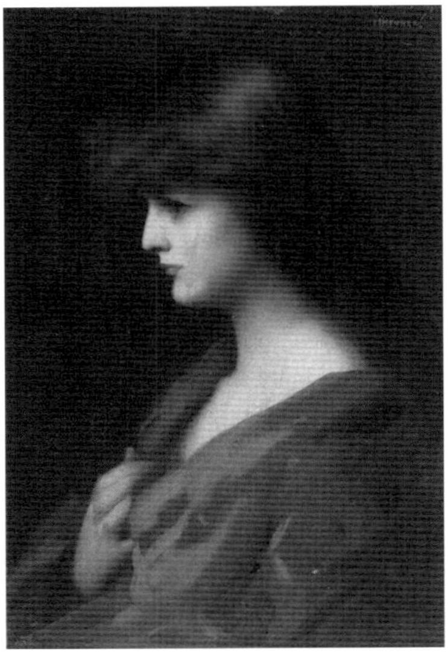

Fig. 5
Jean-Jacques Henner,
Study of a Woman in Red,
early 1890s.
The State Hermitage Museum,
St. Petersburg, Russia.

framed portrait is ideal for domestic display, where it celebrates victory over abusive husbands or a broken marriage. Buddhists received karmic merit for bathing images of Buddha and for copying important sutras. Hindus trace elaborate yantras on the steps of their homes or on pavement in temples in order to invoke the blessing of goddesses. Latino Catholics purchase small tin paintings portraying their miraculous deliverance from harm or illness by the blessing of the Virgin, then deposit them at pilgrimage sites. Pictures and copies do important religious work.[6] The very act of a layperson's making an image produces good karma, attracts blessing, conveys thanks, engages benevolent forces. This is not about art, not about personal expression, not about disinterested aesthetic contemplation, not about refined taste. Making copies is about the power of images. People make copies for the same reason they watch movies and television commercials: the lure of images lies in what they promise.

What's in a copy? Recently I visited a well-known Catholic pilgrimage site at Kevelaer, Germany, where a miraculous image of the Virgin and Child is displayed behind glass in an ornate Baroque shrine. The image is an engraving titled *fig. 6* *Miraculous Picture of the Comforter of the Afflicted* and dates to 1640. It is not a paint-

6. See Robert H. Scharf, "The Scripture on the Production of Buddha Images," in *Religions of China in Practice*, ed. Donald S. Lopez, Jr. (Princeton: Princeton University Press, 1996), pp. 261–67; Daniel Boucher, "Sūtra on the Merit of Bathing the Buddha," in *Religions of China in Practice*, pp. 59–68; Stephen P. Huyler, *Meeting God: Elements of Hindu Devotion* (New Haven: Yale University Press, 1999), pp. 52–53, 67, 205; Jorge Durand and Douglas S. Massey, *Miracles on the Border: Retablos of Mexican Migrants to the United States* (Tucson: University of Arizona Press, 1995).

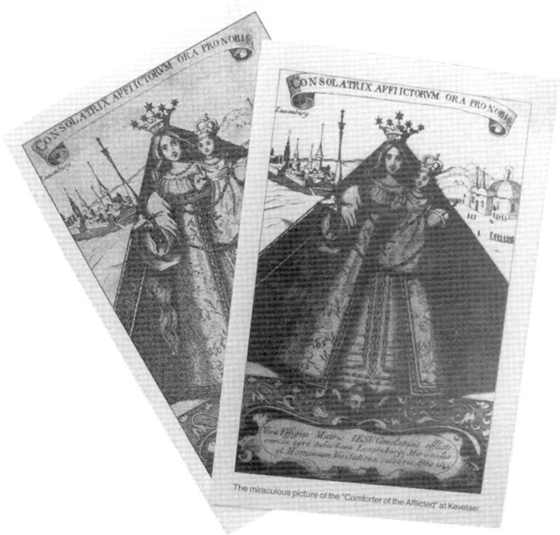

Fig. 6
Illustrated tracts of the *Comforter of the Afflicted*, Kevelaer, Germany, 2007.

ing or an icon but a print produced in multiple and infused with the power to heal those who petition Our Lady, who is pictured in the print. In a famous essay, Walter Benjamin once contended that the aura, the authoritative uniqueness of an image, was lost in mechanical reproduction in modern visual media. The picture at Kevelaer argues otherwise. The faithful line up to pass before the engraving. Sometimes they bring along an illustrated prayer card or a tract sold on-site explaining the history of the image and its shrine. On the cover of the tract appears the miraculous image of the Virgin and Child. I was struck when I watched a pilgrim press her copy of the tract against the pane protecting the engraving. She paused to pray as she held the tract in place, as if charging it with the blessing of the Virgin. This colloquy of images did not operate as a copy meeting original. There was no original, but two versions of the same thing meeting one another, as if like would recognize like in a bond cemented by the fervor of the pilgrim and sealed by prayer.

Plato long tutored Western philosophical thought regarding the loss of reality in the copy. A reproduction, he insisted, is never equal to its exemplar. A copy is no more than a shadow of its cause, a trace blunted and blurred, half forgotten. But the pilgrim woman might not agree. Images infused with the blessing of the Virgin are powerful media, suffering no loss of her presence. They are not copies, but iterations—one might say, "goings forth" of the sacred person to meet with the devout in the medium of her true effigies, her "vera effigies," as the Kevelaer engraving states in an ornate caption beneath the image. *Effigy* may be the word of choice, since it derives from the Latin verb *effingere*, to fashion or make, with the hand or finger, as the etymology suggests. An effigy is a making or rendering, not simply a copy. But even the word *copy* has a promising past: the word derives from *copia*, meaning abundance or multitude in the modern sense of copious. Medieval Latin used *copia* to designate the transcript. From there it was not far to the *carbon copy* of modern transcription. But *effigy* captures even more. It bodies forth the person. It is a version or rendition of the person, or a version of all its other versions. The better comparison might be to performing a musical score. The performance is not a facsimile of the composition but a rendition—one among an infinitude of possible renditions. The need for thinking beyond the paradigm of the copy, with its long metaphysical baggage, is important to bear in mind. Plato saw images as captive to the senses and therefore bound to the lower parts of the soul. Uninformed by ideas, by the true form of thought, whose higher life arced through the mind of God, images were delusions, deceptions, and nothing more.

The wily Socrates would like to work us into an interminable debate over what is true and false. More important, at least more useful, it seems to me, is careful attention to what believers do before images. What they do, in a word, is make the sacred present. Those who fashion a portrait of Fabiola offer her a flattering gift and in the act conjure a relationship she is obliged to honor. Or they give her picture to another who needs the tender commiseration of one who knows what intractable husbands are like. Devotees look to her image in order to find her present in their time of need. But this returns us to the issue of likeness. If the portrait is not a copy of her face, but a true effigy, what do we see when we look at any one or any number of the images of Fabiola? What sort of recognition occurs if the image is not a copy of the *real* thing?

Image and Epistemology

Looking at the breadth and number of Fabiola iterations, one is reminded of a number of more or less apposite types that stretch from the hallowed to the patently profane: icons of the Virgin Mary; holy cards with saints' images; portraits of Monica, mother of Saint Augustine; ceremonial portraiture, such as graduation pictures or official identification portraits; illustrations of Little Red Riding Hood; and Hollywood publicity head shots. As different as these are from one another, they bear at least a few compelling similarities. In every case, the image belongs to a class of images that asserts such canonical authority that what we recognize is a collective likeness rather than a portrait of a discrete person. The pictures forming the group, in other words, resemble one another, not a sitter limned long ago by a dutiful artist. Of course, there are powerful legends that assert the contrary. Saint Luke was said to have been a painter as well as a physician, and to have practiced his art on the Virgin and Child (even though the first verse of his Gospel indicates quite clearly that his understanding of the life of Jesus was based not on firsthand observation but the literary accounts of several other writers). Veronica's Veil purports to be a kind of sacred photocopy of the face of Jesus, and therefore a portrait par excellence. The many stories recounting the Mandylion or cloth that bears Christ's features tell of different kinds of origins, some involving the painter's art perfected by angels or by Jesus himself.[7] Medieval Catholic and Byzantine Christianity issued many stories like these, each of them able to warrant not only the authenticity of an original image but the countless versions of the image in circulation, venerated in shrines from Constantinople to Rome. They were not copies of one another but *copia*, transcripts in abundance, a multitude of images that each transmitted the honor and blessing of the sacred.

The large body of images of Saint Fabiola collected by Alÿs shows us this with unparalleled clarity. Examining them, one is struck by the visual fact that there is no original, no single image that emerges as authoritative, as the genesis and model of all, the grandparent from which the rest have descended. Yet, one senses that there is a referent, albeit elusive, never fully present in any single image, but there nonetheless. The nearly two hundred images vary considerably but almost never so much that one does not immediately associate each with the whole (though the images that invert the profile or use green or blue instead of red put one in the mind of another type such as the Virgin or Monica). Such variations only make the recognition stronger: we see the same face through the veil of each image's peculiarities. What we see is a juxtaposition of a consistently observed pictorial formula, virtually an eidetic schema, a mnemonic device branded on the surface of the neocortex. In virtually every instance, the angle of Fabiola's hood descends from the upper left at an angle of forty-five degrees to intersect with a vertical fold located at nearly the center of the image, leaning slightly to the right. The same intense red cloth meets in a crisp contour with pale flesh. The sinuous ribbon of Fabiola's profile breaks from the red enclosure to trace itself against the dark ground of the painting. Her profile staunchly parallels the picture plane. Her lips are pursed to a plump point; her eye is watchful. A concealed hand may hold the red mantle at her chest, corralling the circumscribed flesh into a shape that almost wants to inscribe a monogram but contenting itself instead with describing the peculiar schema that viewers will not forget. Such a schema is an eidetic image insofar as it imprints itself vividly on the mind and is easily recalled by virtue of its beguiling clarity. No. 58 gathers most of the essential features into a spare template. *fig. 7*

7. See Hans Belting, *A History of the Image before the Era of Art*, trans. Edmund Jephcott (Chicago: University of Chicago Press, 1994); David Freedberg, *The Power of Images: Studies in the History and Theory of Response* (Chicago: University of Chicago Press, 1989); Ewa Kuryluk, *Veronica and Her Cloth* (Cambridge: Basil Blackwell, 1991). I have discussed the issue of Luke as painter and writer in *The Sacred Gaze: Religious Visual Culture in Theory and Practice* (Berkeley: University of California Press, 2005), pp. 15–21.

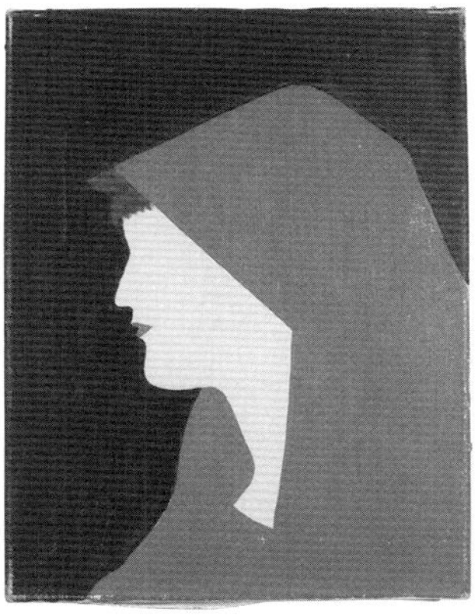

Fig. 7 Fabiola, no. 58.

If we see something often enough, we form a sort of mental average from the multitude, a cognitive norm that subsumes each individual manifestation—like no. 58. This is what Immanuel Kant argued in his *Critique of Judgment* (1790): "The imagination can . . . let one image glide into another, and thus, by the concurrence of several of the same kind come by an average, which serves as the common measure of all."[8] The stature of a beautiful man, Kant argued, was the average taken from a thousand individuals. This norm was the basis of judgment. "It is the image for the whole race, which floats among all the variously different intuitions of individuals, which nature takes as archetype in her productions of the same species, but which appears not to be fully reached in any individual case."[9] Kant wished to understand how aesthetic judgment operates as an intuitive form of cognition, capable of making determinations that are not rational in nature, that is, do not operate in the deductive nature of rules. Instead, he contended that aesthetic judgment is grounded in forms of apprehension that are shared by everyone and can order perception from the basis of an original faculty called taste.

Without engaging Kant's intricate arguments, we might apply his epistemology of intuition to popular religious images, since it accommodates the multiplicity or *copia* we face with Fabiola, as well as other ubiquitous images of saints and religious figures.[10] Where do we find Fabiola? Jerome remembers her, but the faithful find her in the covenants they form through her images and in the devotional practice of fashioning her effigy. Word and image work together. Her story draws a character, a

8. Immanuel Kant, *Critique of Judgment*, trans. J. H. Bernard (New York: Hafner Publishing Company, 1951), p. 70 (§ 17).
9. Ibid., p. 71.
10. For more on the epistemology of recognition and mass-produced images of Jesus, see my *Visual Piety: A History and Theory of Popular Religious Images* (Berkeley: University of California Press, 1998), pp. 34–50.

plot; her image answers the need people bring to the story. By itself, what Jerome has to tell the faithful is not enough. They need more. They need to find the one spoken of, and that is where her imagery arises. The multitude of Fabiola's portraits suggests that their referent is actually the idea in the mind of the devout, which is nourished and reaffirmed each time they see Fabiola's image. To paraphrase Kant, she floats among the many different versions as the elusive model that binds them together but is never fully, finally present in any one. Hence the need for many, for an ongoing flow or cascade of images. Each iteration incants her, calls her to the moment, shaped by the peculiar requirements of those who summon the saint in the portrait they paint or display.

PAINTING FABIOLA: THE HAGIOGRAPHER AS LITERARY ARTIST

Susan Laningham

How can a woman become a Christian saint and icon if she abandons a perfectly suitable husband, remarries in the face of religious censure, wails publicly in the city streets when her second husband dies, and spends the rest of her life dismantling her fortune? Easily, a scholar of religious history would say, for this is the stuff of which saints are made. On paper, the transition from sin to sanctity is fairly formulaic, no more so than in the written life of Saint Fabiola, the fourth-century Roman patrician woman whose marital history alienated her from the early Christian church and whose later repentance shocked the Christian faithful into acclaiming her holiness.

A dramatic religious conversion like that of Fabiola is typical of men and women accorded sainthood in late antiquity and the Middle Ages. Breathtaking in its dramatic appeal, the route from sinner to saint is replayed hundreds of times in the literary genre developed in late antiquity known as hagiography, or saints' vitae (lives of the saints). Hagiography is biography with a spiritual agenda. The subject's life is dramatized, sometimes in a completely fictional manner, so that into the story can be woven elements of Christian theology and instruction, for hagiography is, by its very nature, didactic—it must teach and encourage.

Since most early and medieval Christians were illiterate and ingested the stories of the saints either aurally or through visual media such as images and stained glass, doctrinal points in hagiography were made entertaining and thus more memorable. For instance, the vita of Saint Mary of Egypt tells the tale of a fifth-century repentant prostitute who spent nearly fifty years in the desert east of the Jordan River trying to make amends for her sins. Mary of Egypt's life story includes the requisite supernatural: three loaves of bread that last for decades, figures that walk on water, and a lion that helps dig a grave, but the most important elements of Mary of Egypt's vita are the subtle, or not-so-subtle, affirmations and endorsements of such fundamentals as holy shrines and relics, the cult of the Virgin Mary, baptism, the Eucharist, and the male hierarchy of the Church. On its surface, hagiographies appear quite melodramatic, but the sensationalized episodes in the life of the holy person, complete with commentary, ensure that listeners, particularly those who have no training in and often no capacity for complex theology, can at least imbibe, even subconsciously, the tenets of Christianity.

Hagiography, then, was perhaps one of the most effective tools, if not *the* most effective, in the Christianization of Europe. It supplied the populace with an inexhaustible supply of "written testimonies to God's perpetual intervention in human affairs."[1] These "testimonies" were flexible in content and could be utilized and altered as the need arose. An excellent example of the modifiable saint is Mary Magdalene, who, according to three of the four Gospels, was the first to witness the resurrected Christ.[2] The writer of the Gospel of Mark refers to her as the woman from whom Jesus cast out seven demons. Nothing else is said about her life, except that she was among the group of women who followed Jesus throughout his ministry, witnessed the crucifixion, and went to the tomb, where she encountered a man raised from the dead who was familiar enough with her to call her by name. But through the literary efforts of popes, monks, and abbots, Mary Magdalene had become, by the tenth century, a reformed prostitute: the consummate symbol of repentance in the Middle Ages. As early as 591 CE, Pope Gregory the Great welded together the Magdalene's sparse mention in the resurrection accounts with the stories of another Mary, sister of Lazarus, and the account of an unnamed female sinner who washed Jesus's feet with her tears of repentance. This "composite" Mary received a specifically titillating past when a ninth-century hagiographer meshed what was already Mary's multiple personality with the aforementioned hagiography of the converted prostitute, Saint Mary of Egypt.[3] Thus, Mary Magdalene became the quintessential reformed saint. Against her refashioned colorful past, theologians of the later Middle Ages discussed the issue of reclaimed virginity. Mary Magdalene, they argued, may not have been a virgin of the flesh, but she was certainly a "virgin of the mind" and therefore worthy of the same heavenly reward as the virgin saints.[4]

Like that of Mary Magdalene, Fabiola's image, reception, and popularity depended upon the pen of the hagiographer. It was the theologian Saint Jerome, Fabiola's personal friend and mentor, who introduced her to Christian readers and smoothed her path into the world of saints and saint making when he wrote her vita in the form of a eulogy after hearing of her death in 399 CE. Jerome, often called the "doctor of virginity" for his stand on the superiority of chastity over marriage, had some explaining to do with respect to the twice-married Fabiola.[5] Since Fabiola's second husband had died, Jerome was able to focus upon her widowhood, which, according to him, ranked as "the second degree of chastity," next to virginity.[6] Once freed

1. Lynda L. Coon, *Sacred Fictions: Holy Women and Hagiography in Late Antiquity* (Philadelphia: University of Pennsylvania Press, 1997), p. 27.
2. Matthew 28.1–10; Mark 16.9–11; John 20.14–18.
3. See Katherine Ludwig Jansen, *The Making of the Magdalen: Preaching and Popular Devotion in the Later Middle Ages* (Princeton: Princeton University Press, 2000), pp. 36–46.
4. Jansen, p. 293.
5. Jerome, "Letter LXXVII, The Eulogy of Fabiola: To Oceanus on the Death of Fabiola," in *Select Letters of St. Jerome*, trans. F. A. Wright (1933; repr., Cambridge, Mass.: Harvard University Press, 1991), pp. 308–37. See reprint in this book, pp. 81–90.
6. Jerome, "Letter XXII, The Virgin's Profession, to Eustochium," in *Select Letters of St. Jerome*, p. 83.

from marriage, Fabiola embarked on a life of profound penance after publicly confessing her sins in the courtyard of what is today the Basilica of Saint John Lateran in Rome. For the rest of her life, she personally tended to the sick and impoverished of the city and used her wealth to found what is generally believed to be the first hospital in the Western world.

Jerome's task in preparing Fabiola's vita was twofold, to dramatize (in the manner of all good hagiographers) both her exemplary penitential charity and the fleshly weakness that preceded her change of heart. In his account of her life, Fabiola's postrepentance largesse and compassion for others figures only slightly more conspicuously than her unfortunate marriages. Jerome is at pains to induce his readers into empathizing with the natural impulses that entice a woman like Fabiola to the marriage bed, while also assuring his audience that celibacy is not only more godly but also less bitter, particularly when there is spousal abuse, such as Fabiola experienced in her first marriage. Jerome subtly lets his audience know that Fabiola's rejection of virginity did not go unpunished: her first husband was an adulterer, her second husband died, and she never bore children. Thus, his depiction of Fabiola's self-inflicted penance is all the more poignant, in that she atoned for the rest of her life for a virginity lost in vain.

The vita of Fabiola is not just about Fabiola, however. Her vita is a platform for Jerome, just as all hagiography is a vehicle through which the hagiographer can express his own concerns and agenda. In Fabiola's vita, Jerome argues against those who advocate marriage over virginity; laments a government that cannot protect its own borders; establishes his credentials as a close confidant of illustrious Roman patricians; and lets slip some of those sentiments that have led scholars through the ages to brand him a misogynist. Indeed, in praising Fabiola, Jerome manages to remind his readers that a woman of such caliber is the exception to the rule. Fabiola is not like other women. She is, to her credit, "forgetful of her sex," to use Jerome's words.[7] In short, Fabiola does the sort of thing men do all the time. In fact, a significant portion of Fabiola's vita is given to extolling the virtues of Pammachius, Fabiola's male counterpart, who, as Jerome points out, matched Fabiola in founding hostels and distributing alms.

Fabiola, in the hands of her master hagiographer, aided in the dissemination of his version of Christian doctrine and practice, far beyond the fourth century. Her life story, as Jerome intended, could generate discussion on topics such as celibacy, repentance, obedience, Church hierarchy, charity, personal responsibility, and exclusion from the Church triumphant. Jerome, through the medium of widely disseminated correspondence, fashioned this all-too-human woman into something quite

7. Jerome, "Letter LXXVII," p. 333.

useful to humans struggling for a place in the celestial realm. Christians and would-be Christians could read the drama of her life, find the parts relative to their own experience, and amend themselves, accordingly. In laying Fabiola's strengths and weaknesses side by side, Jerome also set the tone that would ultimately render the Roman matron into the patron saint of married women, abused women, widows, and nurses well into the modern age, when she became the subject of countless pictorial representations in the nineteenth and twentieth centuries.

The number of Fabiola portraits inspired in the modern era by Jean-Jacques Henner's 1885 original suggests that Fabiola's mass popularity is long-standing, when, in fact, she is one of the most unexamined saints in history. Her name appears briefly in sermons throughout the Middle Ages, always coupled with that of Jerome, her hagiographer. A quick search of the *Patrologia Latina*, which lists all theological treatises and collections of sermons between 200–1216 CE, finds her name appearing fewer than forty times.[8] The emphasis, in the sermons, is on her status as a wealthy Roman matron who unstintingly gave to the Church; yet it remains the case that no church in Rome, where she founded her first hospital, is dedicated to her memory.

That the lovely eulogy written by one of the foremost theologians in late antiquity failed to spawn a significant cult in the Middle Ages need not imply indifference to the penitential life of a twice-married Roman matron. On the contrary, Fabiola, whose experiences encompassed almost every possible option available to the female sex, seems to have been far more useful to men than women. Historians and anthropologists recognize that women have always been good "to think with."[9] In the hands of the great scholars of the early Church, women and the lives they led were part of what scholar Peter Brown calls "the imaginative economy of the Church."[10] Just as late medieval theologians pondered the issue of nonvirginal purity by focusing on Mary Magdalene, the Church in the sixteenth century countered the Protestant denunciation of pilgrimage to holy places by pointing out that Fabiola, and many other pious Roman women, journeyed to Bethlehem in demonstration of their faith and penance.[11] Wealthy Roman widows like Fabiola who turned over their "unholy mammon" to the men of the Church were the instruments through which God funded his Church and reinforced its sexual hierarchy.

---

8. *Patrologiae Cursus Completus, Series Latina*, ed. Jacques-Paul Migne, 221 vols. (Paris, 1857–66).
9. See Peter Brown, *The Body and Society: Men, Women, and Sexual Renunciation in Early Christianity* (New York: Columbia University Press, 1988), p. 153. Brown (n. 57) admits that he borrows the phrase from the anthropologist, Claude Lévi-Strauss, but Brown's use of the term applied to the patristic age of the Church has defined the scholarship of the period.
10. Ibid., p. 150.
11. See Carolyn Valone, "Roman Matrons as Patrons: Various Views of the Cloister Wall," in *The Crannied Wall: Women, Religion, and the Arts in Early Modern Europe*, ed. Craig A. Monson (Ann Arbor: University of Michigan Press, 1992), p. 66.

Hagiographers were often concerned to maintain the status quo, particularly in the area of relations between the sexes, but the vitae could also work to invert the norm. Jerome's vita of Fabiola is representative of numerous hagiographies studied by Lynda L. Coon in which the pious acts of elite Christian women work to undermine the very society from which they claim descent.[12] In typical fashion, Jerome details the illustrious ancestry of Fabiola, so that when she dons sackcloth and appears in public with unwashed body and undressed hair, she is immediately marked as one who is now outside the world of privilege, a world to which she most definitely belonged only a day earlier. Fabiola's refutation of the role of classic Roman matron is revealed not only in her dress but also in the disassembling of her fortune. Her chastity, her poverty, and her exit from Rome render Fabiola the antithesis of the Roman matron: she is childless, poor, and homeless. Yet, in becoming the converse of classical womanhood, she became a more fortunate bride, wed not to a soldier, as Jerome puts it, but to a King.[13]

While Jerome allows Fabiola the empowerment that comes from rejecting the past and unwaveringly focusing on the next world, he is careful, as were all authors of female vitae, to stress her submission to the male hierarchy of the Church. Only by placing his female squarely under the control of men could the hagiographer expect the vita to be timeless—relevant, even in the twenty-first century. A woman may have loosened herself from the bonds of aristocratic obligation, but she could not free herself from the sexual hierarchy. She had to serve a new set of masters—still male, still the sex of the incarnate deity. In this, Fabiola imitates biblical women who served sacred males: the Samaritan woman, Martha of Bethany, and, most tellingly, the ubiquitous sinful woman who washes Jesus's feet with her tears of repentance.[14]

Church fathers acquired female protégés as a matter of course. Fabiola was only one woman who put herself at the service of the Church and the men who defined its theology. Her mentor, Jerome, was a prolific writer, who penned not only a number of vitae of holy women but also copious theological treatises and a translation of the Bible that would be the official text of the Roman church for nearly two thousand years—the Vulgate. He carefully chose his female pupils, it seems, drawing largely from the senatorial families of Rome. The women were well educated, making them particularly receptive to his role as teacher. They were also wealthy and independent, either widows or the daughters of widows, and able to spend their fortunes as they wished. What they wished to do, quite often, was to sponsor holy men like Jerome. Thus, the women not only provided Jerome and his learned male

12. See Coon, *Sacred Lives*, pp. 104–9.
13. See Jerome, "Letter LXXVII."
14. See Coon, p. 119. Coon points out that the conscious act of imitating female biblical models served to "temper the iconoclastic power of Christian women." Coon uses Jerome's better-known protégé to make her point: Saint Paula.

contemporaries with female subjects "to think with," they also, quite literally, provided for them.

Holy women, in the hagiographies, were clearly gendered according to social mores, in that they submitted to the authority of men. But the process to sanctification had the remarkable effect of rendering these same women "male," both mentally and physically. Like the vestal virgins of imperial Rome, female saints were considered "desexed" women. Their bodies, like the bodies of men, were impenetrable fortresses.[15] As perpetual virgins or women who reclaimed their virginity, as in the case of Fabiola (or Mary Magdalene), they became "honorary men." The mantle of holiness donned by the holy woman ensured that her impenetrability was not limited to her body but also was, as Kathleen Kelly says of Joan of Arc, "realized in the realm of the social as a force capable of dampening the potential ardor of the men around her."[16] Ideally, and potentially, men looked at a holy virgin no longer as a "sex object" but treated her as an equal, as a man.

Hagiography provides for a flexible application of its subject. Jerome fashioned his portrait of Fabiola in such a way that she could become many things to many people: a married woman who reclaimed her virginity; an indulged patrician who chose to give away her bounty; a housewife who became a student of theology, studying at the feet of renowned scholars, such as himself. Little wonder, then, that Fabiola functions as the patron saint of several special-interest groups: married women, abused women, divorced women, and nurses. Often, historical events determined *which* of the many Fabiolas moved to center stage. In the mid-nineteenth century, the role played by Florence Nightingale in the Crimean War (1853–56) brought about a renewed interest in the saint who founded the first hospital in the West, who personally nursed those whom Jerome labels as "human disasters." Not surprisingly, the new nurses of the nineteenth century saw Fabiola as the forerunner of their craft.

To Jerome, the hagiographer, goes the credit for Fabiola's longevity as a "usable" saint. He painted a lasting literary portrait, only augmented by the Henner-inspired art of the modern age. When Jerome's Fabiola forsook her religious vocation to marry, divorce, and marry again, she became a woman with whom the bulk of the female population could relate, perhaps even envy, certainly censure; when she repented and made amends by dedicating herself to a life of self-abnegation and the

15. For more on the vestal virgins as impenetrable men, see David Fredrick, "Mapping Penetrability in Late Republican and Early Imperial Rome," in *The Roman Gaze: Vision, Power, and the Body*, ed. Fredrick (Baltimore: Johns Hopkins University Press, 2002), pp. 236–64.

16. Kathleen Coyne Kelly, *Performing Virginity and Testing Chastity in the Middle Ages* (New York: Routledge, 2000), p. 40. See, also, Marina Warner, *Joan of Arc: The Image of Female Heroism* (Berkeley: University of California Press, 1981), pp. 17–18.

depleting of her fortune through the founding of hospitals and the care of the destitute, she became a woman less imitable, perhaps, but thoroughly inspiring. Fabiola represented, in fact, the possibility of salvation for those who had been kicked around a bit in life.

The nursing renaissance of the nineteenth century; Cardinal Nicholas Wiseman's best-selling 1854 novel, *Fabiola, or the Church of the Catacombs* (whose title character shared little with the saint of late antiquity other than the name); and the Henner portrait of 1885 brought Fabiola back into the lives of working people, but it was the hagiographer who created the much-copied original. Lacking Jerome, Fabiola would have likely remained just another aristocratic Roman matron with a complicated marital history and enough money to found a hospital or two. Hagiographers breathe the breath of life; saints cannot live without them.

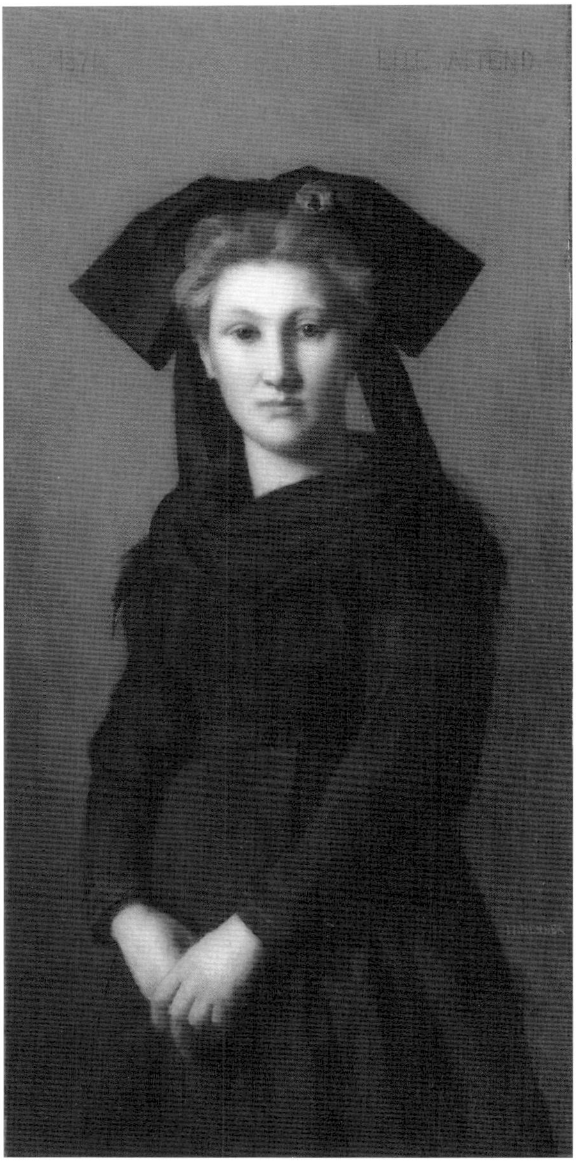

Fig. 1
Jean-Jacques Henner,
L'Alsace. Elle attend, 1871.
Musée Jean-Jacques Henner.
Réunion des musées nationaux /
Art Resource, New York.

BEYOND *FABIOLA*: HENNER IN AND OUT OF HIS NINETEENTH-CENTURY CONTEXT

Stephen Bann

The French nineteenth-century artist Jean-Jacques Henner painted two works that particularly established his reputation throughout his native country. The small picture, *L'Alsace. Elle attend*, dated 1871 and first exhibited the succeeding year at the Salon of the Académie des Beaux-Arts in Paris, displays a young woman of Alsace. She confronts us, full face, in her sober regional costume, a large black bow in her hair sporting a tricolor. As a result of the Franco-Prussian War of 1870–71, France had been obliged to make a treaty ceding the historic provinces of Alsace and Lorraine to the resurgent German Empire. Henner's title—*Alsace. She waits*—thus conveyed a message that was poignant and powerful in its simplicity. The women of the small town of Thann, in southern Alsace, commissioned the painting from Henner for presentation to the politician and future statesman Léon Gambetta, who as deputy for the department of Bas-Rhin had fiercely opposed the treaty. As the critic Jules-Antoine Castagnary wrote of it at the time, "This is not a woman of Alsace, it is Alsace." Reproduced in the form of an engraving by the prominent printmaker Léopold Flameng, the work carried its message of defiance to every corner of France.[1] *fig. 1*

This is indeed the image that best portrays one aspect of Henner's identity as an artist. He was born in 1829 to a family of farmers in the small community of Bernwiller in southern Alsace. He had begun his serious study of art in the studio of Gabriel Guérin at Strasbourg, and aided by local funds he proceeded on to Paris, where he joined successively the studios of the academicians Michel-Martin Drolling and François-Édouard Picot. His success in winning the Prix de Rome in 1858 opened up the possibility of a career that would emulate that of his masters—both also recipients of the Prix de Rome in their time. Henner remained in Rome until 1864, having assimilated both the classic examples of Raphael and Caravaggio and the Northern Italian schools, from which he selected, above all, the painterly styles of Correggio and Titian. The work that he sent back from Rome as official

1. See *Jean-Jacques Henner: Face à l'Impressionnisme, le dernier des romantiques* (Paris: Musée de la Vie romantique, in association with Réunion des musées nationaux, 2007), pp. 25–27; in particular, Catherine de Bourgoing's "Aide à la visite," p. 2. The details of Henner's career that I have summarized are mostly taken from this helpful new source.

evidence of his progress, *La Chaste Suzanne* (1864), was castigated by the Academy since it contained only two figures, whereas a minimum of three were required for a history painting. But this quibble did not prevent the work from being awarded a medal at the 1865 Salon, where it was bought by the French state for the Musée du Luxembourg.

L'Alsace. Elle attend was therefore the achievement of an artist who had already made his mark and was well set for membership in the exclusive company of the Academy, to which he was finally elected in 1889. His timely reference to his Alsatian roots was not just a flash in the pan, as he maintained regular contact with family and friends in the occupied province. As has been rightly emphasized, he took care to establish this double identity—Alsatian and Parisian, provincial and international. In this sense, he gave an especially contemporary resonance to the traditional aim of the French academic system, which was precisely to expand the horizons of the French national school by steeping its brightest prospects at their most formative stage in the incomparably rich artistic patrimony of Rome.

It is to this Roman allegiance, in particular, that we must credit the second emblematic picture created by Henner, which is also the prototype for those assembled in the pages of this book: his *Fabiola*, which was initially exhibited at the Salon of 1885. The original of this work appears to have been lost.[2] No trace of it can be found in the catalogue of works by the artist now housed by the Musée Henner in Paris. With reference to this source, the painting closest to the original would seem *fig. 2* to be the *Tête de femme au voile rouge* (*Head of a Woman with a Red Veil*), circa 1890, exhibited in Paris in 2007.[3] But a brief trawl through Emmanuel Bénézit's dictionary suggests that this must have been a painting often copied by others. The Musée des Beaux-Arts in Reims claims to own a *Fabiola.* Attributed to Henner in sales catalogues are a *Blue Fabiola* (sold in Paris in 1901 four years before the artist's death), and three *Fabiola*s without further specification (Paris, 1906; Paris, 1923; and The Hague, 1946). Kindred works are *Head in Profile with Blue Drapery* (Paris, 1921), *Profile of a Young Girl* (New York, 1929), *Young Woman with a Red Shawl* *fig. 3* (Saint-Dié, 1990) and *Woman with Red Veil* (New York, 2001).[4] In effect, they form

2. After the Salon of 1885, Henner's *Fabiola* was sold to an American collector through the international dealer Knoedler. After the collector's death in 1886, the work was auctioned and exhibited once again in Paris in 1889 before disappearing. Henner promised not to make replicas after the work, which was already much copied, probably after a photo by Braun. This information was kindly provided by Isabelle de Lannoy, author of *Jean-Jacques Henner (1829–1905) Catalogue Raisonné*, which is forthcoming.
3. See ibid., p. 146, for *Tête de femme au voile rouge*, which is also illustration no. 460 in *Musée National Jean-Jacques Henner—Catalogue des peintures*, ed. Isabelle de Lannoy (Paris: Réunion des musées nationaux, 1990), p. 220.
4. See Emmanuel Bénézit, *Dictionary of Artists* (1911; repr. Paris: Gründ, 2006).

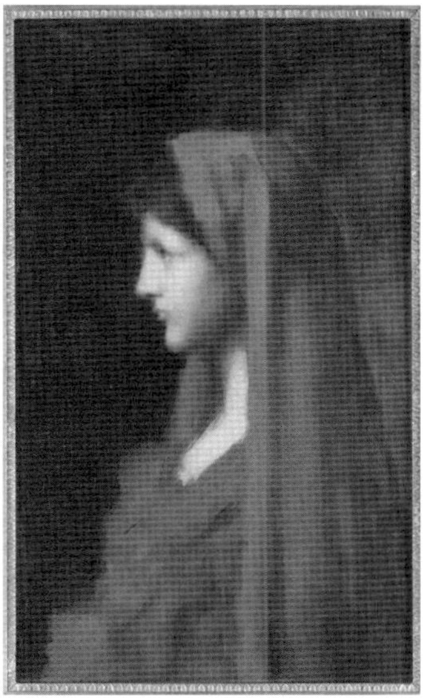

Fig. 2
Jean-Jacques Henner,
Tête de femme au voile rouge, c. 1890.
Musée Jean-Jacques Henner, Paris, France.
Photo: Franck Raux. Courtesy Réunion des musées nationaux / Art Resource, New York.

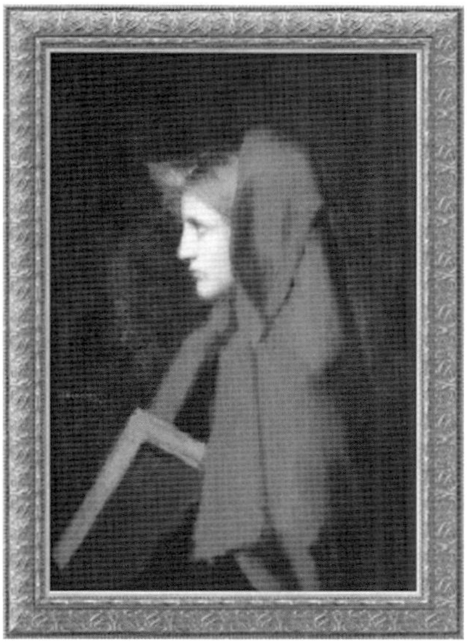

Fig. 3
Woman with Red Veil,
formerly attributed to
Jean-Jacques Henner.
Date and location unknown.

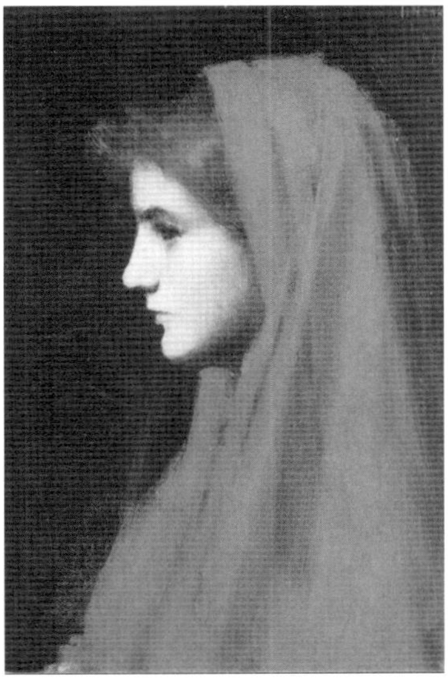

Fig. 4
Fabiola,
formerly attributed to
Jean-Jacques Henner.
Date and location unknown.

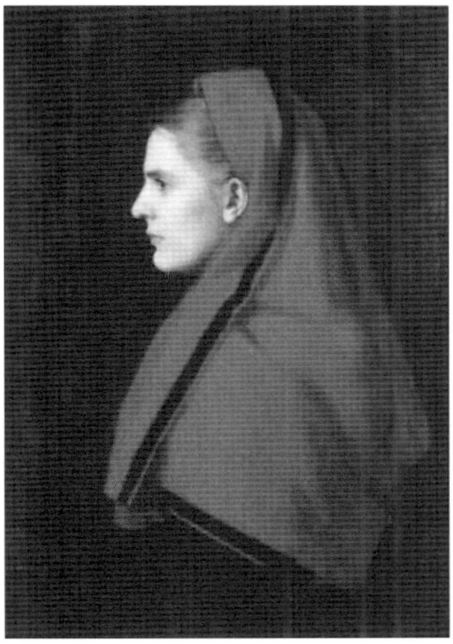

Fig. 5
Fabiola,
formerly attributed to
Jean-Jacques Henner.
Date and location unknown.

the largest single category of works attributed to Henner to pass through the sale rooms. However, according to the author of Henner's forthcoming catalogue raisonné, Isabelle de Lannoy, the oeuvre of this artist is marked by many contested attributions, including several paintings titled or strongly resembling *Fabiola*.

figs. 4 & 5

It would be foolhardy to speculate on the connection of these paintings with the works in this book. Suffice it to say that the image has indeed proved enduringly popular, and the line between an authenticated copy and the work of an amateur is not always an easy one to draw. But we can examine with more confidence the geneaology of Henner's work, since 2007 was also the year of the first major exhibition of Henner's work for many years, held at the Musée de la Vie romantique. It has to be admitted that the strategy for presenting this almost-forgotten painter to a contemporary audience owes as much to current prejudices as to historical veracity. The label "the last of the Romantics" may simply have been a tactful explanation for his presence in the charming little museum that jointly contains the legacies of the painter Ary Scheffer and the writer Georges Sand. The other slogan that was attached to his name in the text of posters and catalogues was *Face à l'impressionnisme*. Yet any idea of Henner "facing Impressionism" in his work is surely no more than a mirage of present-day retrospection, appropriate to an age that views Impressionism as the unique visual achievement of French painting in the later nineteenth century.[5] The terms "Romantic" and "Impressionist" seem to have been used in relation to Henner by publicists who sought primarily to avert the grim possibility that the word "academic" might be applied. The idea that such an artist might be thought academic is, of course, the surest way of killing an exhibition. Yet it is in Henner's Roman, and precisely academic, experience that the origins of the vanished *Fabiola* must be sought.

Academic French art in the nineteenth century was in no sense a merely mindless copying of previous masters. In effect, academic practice bound the artist to a sequence of precise moves and tactical adjustments that often gained their significance from challenging the codes that were laid down by the Academy.[6] Henner's earlier, considered decision to break the convention governing the number of figures in history painting proved no real obstacle to his success. As a general rule, a

5. There is, in fact, a specific sense in which Henner's work can be placed in parallel with that of an artist who today might be regarded the archetypal Impressionist, Edgar Degas: like Henner, he immersed himself for years, at his own expense, in the culture of the French Academy in Rome. See Richard Thompson, "Degas et Henner: comparaisons et contrastes," *La revue du Musée d'Orsay*, no. 24 (Spring 2007), pp. 6–19.

6. See Stephen Bann, "Questions of Genre in Early Nineteenth-Century French Painting," *New Literary History* 34, no. 3 (2003), pp. 501–11; also Paul Duro, "Giving Up On History: Challenges to the Hierarchy of the Genres in Early Nineteenth-Century France," in *About Stephen Bann*, ed. Deborah Cherry (Oxford: Blackwell, 2006), pp. 117–39.

prescriptive genre system governed academic art in the nineteenth century, but this element of regulation had the effect of stimulating new approaches that departed, by a perceptible margin, from the existing practice. Such approaches were incorporated, in turn, into a modified system. Intense critical debate in periodicals and the popular acclaim won by artists at the Salon moved this process of revisionism along.

One of the most significant instances of this process was the move of French painters studying in Rome in the 1820s toward the depiction of contemporary Roman folklore. Following the example of the Swiss artist Louis-Léopold Robert, who had studied with Jacques-Louis David and later proceeded to Rome, these painters employed the picturesque costumes of *contadini* and *banditti* to animate compositions that combined the attraction of vivid local color with the ambition of traditional history painting. One of the most dedicated artists to take this direction was Jean-Victor Schnetz (1787–1870), who fascinated critics of the Salon of 1831 with his monumental work: *Une famille de contadini surprise par un prompt débordement du Tibre se sauve à travers des eaux* (*A Family of Country Folk Surprised by a Sudden Flooding of the Tiber Escapes through the Waters*). Schnetz had already widened the boundaries of what might be taken for a "history painting" in a more traditional manner when he completed in 1827 *Les Adieux du consul Boetius à sa famille* (*The Farewell of Consul Boethius to His Family*). While the later work gave peasants of the modern world an antique flavor, the earlier focused on the grieving family of the late Roman philosopher who did not feature in the habitual classical vocabulary, though his writings under persecution were highly valued throughout the Christian Middle Ages.

These two works by Schnetz thus touched upon new possibilities of expanding the traditions of the genre. History painting in France had, since the seventeenth century, been essentially confined to two sources of subject matter: on the one hand, classical history and mythology and, on the other, stories from the Bible. The notion of late antiquity or Christian Rome being a major source of material was not prominent at the turn of the nineteenth century. Nicolas Poussin's two monumental series of works from the mid-seventeenth century on the theme of the Seven Sacraments had already made use of recently discovered archaeological materials to ensure accurate details of environment and dress in the depiction of the early Christian church. But the restrained classicism of Poussin did not appeal to the generation that arose prior to the French Revolution. Schnetz was appealing to a new vein of sentiment in his depictions of Christian Rome. Having varied the formula of historical genre painting in the two examples given above, he went on to exhibit at the Salon of 1848 a work that further tested its boundaries by vividly representing authentic contemporary dress in a scene depicting the pathos of martyrdom: *Funérailles d'une jeune martyre dans les catacombes à Rome* (*Funeral of a Young Martyr in the Catacombs of Rome during the Time of Persecutions*). *fig. 6*

Fig. 6
Jean-Victor Schnetz,
Funérailles d'une jeune martyre dans les catacombes à Rome, 1848.
Musee des Beaux-Arts, Nantes.
Réunion des musées nationaux / Art Resource, New York.
Photo: Gérard Blot.

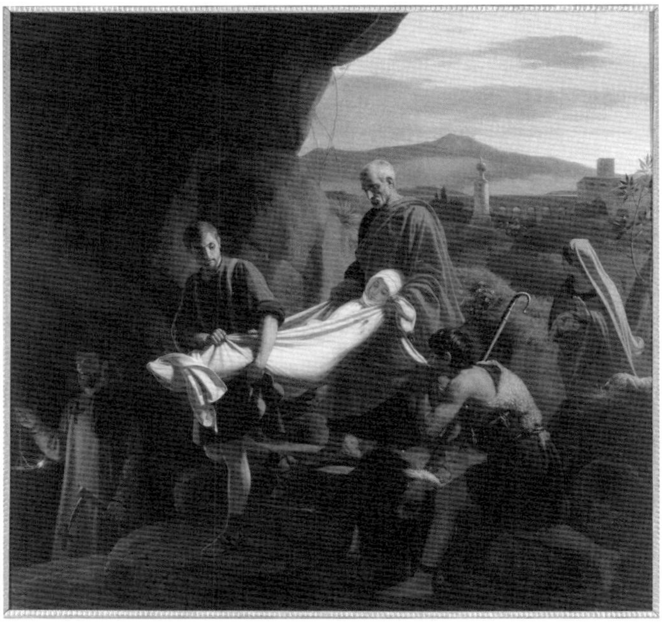

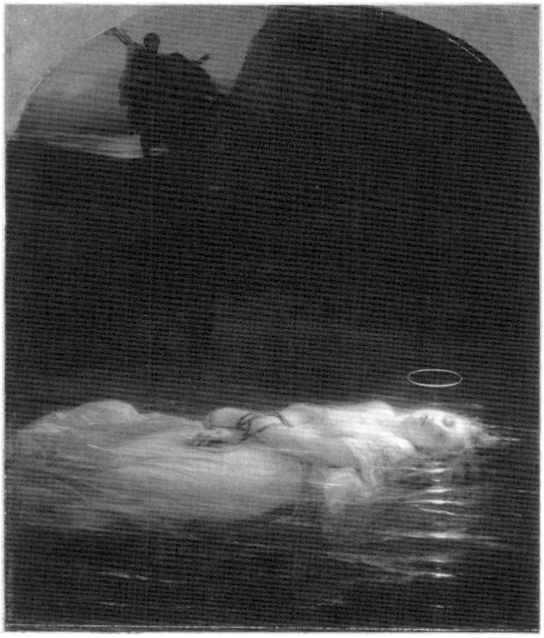

Fig. 7
Paul Delaroche,
La Jeune Martyre, 1854–55.
Louvre, Paris. Réunion des musées nationaux / Art Resource, New York.
Photo: Hervé Lewandowski.

Henner's *Fabiola* undoubtedly relates to this evolving academic tradition. But to isolate its special originality, it is necessary to mention a second painter who was a colleague of Schnetz in the Academy, Paul Delaroche. There is little doubt that Delaroche held major responsibility for revivifying history painting during the Romantic period through his procedure of infiltrating a series of modern (that is, postclassical) historical subjects such as *Joan of Arc* (Salon of 1824), *Princes in the Tower* (Salon of 1831), and *The Execution of Lady Jane Grey* (Salon of 1834). His most significant works of the 1820s and 1830s chiefly portrayed innocent victims, typically children or young women. The point at which he began to depict similar subjects from the early Christian period remains unclear. Recently a series of small drawings has come to light that adopt Schnetz's arresting motif of the philosopher Boethius glimpsed behind the iron grille of his prison and apply it to the case of an imprisoned female saint, probably the Carthaginian Saint Perpetua, from the third century AD. Delaroche may well have studied the moving autobiographical record of her imprisonment written by Perpetua and, so, completed several versions of the saint greeting members of her despairing family from behind the bars. Yet he never completed a full-scale painting on this theme, preferring to develop his own variant on Schnetz's prison motif in the major enterprise of his large painting *Strafford* (Salon of 1837), where the imprisoned Archbishop Laud extends his hands in blessing through the grille, through which he is unable to see the condemned man kneeling.[7]

Delaroche reserved for the end of his career his most memorable evocation of Christian antiquity: *La Jeune Martyre* (*The Young Female Martyr*) of 1854–55. In this *fig. 7* haunting work, completed the year before his death, Delaroche depicted an anonymous martyr thrown into the Tiber, her hands still bound together as she floats on the green tide, during the time of the persecutions of the emperor Diocletian. The comparison with John Everett Millais's *Ophelia* (1851–52), shown at the Paris Exposition universelle of 1855, is superficially striking, but evidence of earlier drawings suggests that Delaroche was unaware of this precedent when he commenced what he termed "the most sad and the most holy of all [his] compositions."[8] It is inconceivable that Henner would not have seen this work in the major retrospective devoted to Delaroche at the École des Beaux-Arts in 1857—the year before he achieved his own early success in the competition for the Prix de Rome. It also seems likely that he would have taken note of comparisons made by contemporary critics—Charles Blanc, remarking on the work's affinities to works by Pierre-Paul

7. See Stephen Bann, *Paul Delaroche: History Painted* (Princeton: Princeton University Press, 1997), pp. 146–51.
8. Delaroche, quoted in ibid., p. 262.

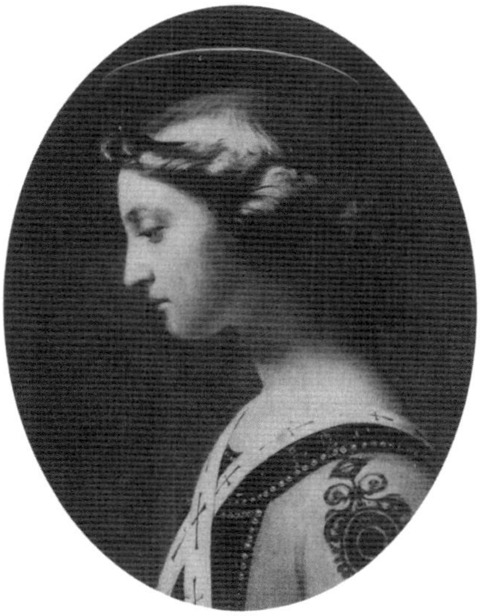

Fig. 8
Paul Delaroche,
Angel's Head, 1835.
Location unknown.
Photo: British Library, London.

Prud'hon, and Théophile Gautier, on its "Corregesque grace"[9]—since Prud'hon and Correggio were the very artists who would later be invoked in relation to Henner's own pictorial style.

There is no obvious formal link between *La Jeune Martyre* and the radically simplified image of *Fabiola*; however, Delaroche had already, by the stage of his *Jeune Martyre*, radically pared the scenographic apparatus of history painting, as compared with Schnetz's *Jeune Martyre* of 1848 or even Delaroche's own *The Execution of Lady Jane Grey*. There is no classical decor to be seen, no hint of Roman architecture, and the solitary witness who appears in the background in silhouette is barely identifiable from his dress. In this respect, Delaroche anticipates the simple, even severe, image of sanctity conveyed by Henner's *Fabiola*.

In Henner's development, what must be taken into account is the way in which he progressively refined the genre of portraiture. While Delaroche had utilized the portrait format with head and shoulders in profile for a number of religious works, *fig. 8* including *Angel's Head* (1835), which was engraved and shown in the 1857 retrospective, and he had employed the medallion format in several drawings, including the striking profile of his young wife, Louise Vernet,[10] Henner's use of the profile is at once more consistent and (it would seem) related dialectically to his parallel

9. Théophile Gautier, quoted in ibid.; and Charles Blanc, quoted in *Paul Delaroche: Un peintre dans l'histoire* (Nantes: Musée des Beaux-Arts, in association with Réunion des musées nationaux, Paris, 2000), p. 327.

10. The portrait of Louise Vernet was editioned as a print by Alphonse François after her death in 1845. See Stephen Bann, "Remembering Louise Vernet," *Art History* 26, no. 1 (February 2003), pp. 1–25.

portrayal of subjects in full face. In 1869–70, shortly before the runaway success of the full-face *L'Alsace. Elle attend*, he painted his young niece in Alsatian costume, her pretty features firmly outlined in profile against the olive green background. In some of his most distinctive female portraits, a brightly illuminated head emerges from a dark ground, effectively to confront the viewer, as in *Portrait de Madame Jeantaud* (1875) and *La Comtesse Kessler* (1886). The firm profile and averted gaze of the original *Fabiola* is recalled, though with a longer format, in *Tête de femme au voile rouge* and in the powerful image of his pupil Germaine Dawis, *Portrait de jeune femme* (*Portrait of a Young Woman*), 1892.[11]

Yet the most significant point of contact between Delaroche and Henner lies, no doubt, in another feature altogether: The fact that the work of both artists initiated a torrent of reproductions. The afterlife of Delaroche's *La Jeune Martyre* may be tracked through the archives of the Maison Goupil. This art gallery and print publisher, which held exclusive rights to his work, was at the forefront of the international trade in reproductive images that achieved unprecedented volume and diffusion in the second half of the nineteenth century. The collection of the Musée Goupil in Bordeaux thus contains no less than seven types of reproduction of this painting, issued successively and at difference price levels: a photograph by Robert Bingham (1858); an engraving by Hermann Eichens (1861); another example of the engraving by Eichens, hand colored in gouache (1861); a photograph after a drawing by Émile Rousseau (1863–64); an engraving by Rousseau (1872), no doubt based on the previous drawing; a photograph after an anonymous drawing (detail of the work), 1875; and a photogravure after the well-used drawing by Rousseau—described as a "miniature print" (1886).[12] It is an appropriate footnote to the history of this much-reproduced painting that (by anecdotal evidence) the postcard image sold in the Louvre currently ranks as the most in demand at that establishment.

What is more, the *La Jeune Martyre* was also reproduced in other media, as were many of Delaroche's works. One of his earliest religious designs was for a stained-glass window in the Orléans family chapel at the Château d'Eu in Normandy. His *Finding of Moses* (1853) was copied as a design on porcelain. No full account could possibly be given of the many drawings and paintings after his work that were completed both by approved pupils and by more or less gifted amateurs. The remarkable proliferation of afterimages of Henner's *Fabiola* begins in the very period when the publishing repertoire of the Maison Goupil had been fully extended in creating types of reproduction to suit every pocket—setting a precedent in the thirst for

11. See *Jean-Jacques Henner: Face à l'Impressionnisme*, pp. 120, 121, 136, 146, 147.
12. *Paul Delaroche: Un peintre dans l'histoire*, pp. 327–28. See, also, Pierre-Lin Renié, "Œuvres de Paul Delaroche reproduites et éditées par la maison Goupil," in *Paul Delaroche: Un peintre dans l'histoire*, pp. 200–18.

reproductions, which would continue to increase exponentially throughout the second half of the nineteenth century, and also offering wide variations in level of craft, facture, and medium, which would certainly distinguish reproductions made during the twentieth.

However, the collection of Fabiolas in this book is not in any way a historical footnote. Looking back beyond the immediate context of the original *Fabiola*'s production, one can indeed appreciate that a special significance lies in the story of Henner's development as an academic artist. It is not a question of whether he may be viewed as "the last Romantic," or if he achieves success in "facing Impressionism." What is significant, surely, is the fact that *Fabiola* and her progeny offer an especially interesting context in which to view the long-term implications of the phenomenon of image reproduction. In the case of *L'Alsace. Elle attend*, Henner relied for his popularity on the public success of Léopold Flameng's engraving. In this respect, he was following a precedent that dated back at least to the seventeenth century in France. But *Fabiola* appears to have achieved its fame in a distinctively new historical context. The various notations of the sale of related works recorded by Bénézit are like the seismic records of a movement that may never be satisfactorily tracked. The multiple copies collected by Francis Alÿs all testify, however remotely, to this ongoing process.

We have become inured to hearing the echoes of a theory popularized by Walter Benjamin, in respect of which the work of art loses its "aura" in an age of "mechanical" (or, more precisely, "technical") reproduction. It is worth remembering that Benjamin himself was thinking primarily of media, such as photography and film, where no "original" exists, for hardly would amateur artists have crossed Benjamin's mind. In the case of *Fabiola*, we have a prime example of a lost original, complemented by a vast array of heterogenous reproductions. Instead of lamenting the loss of aura, we can use this particular example to emphasize the essential *productivity* of the process of reproduction.[13] These multifarious Fabiolas may not, in the last resort, be recuperated by art history, but in testifying to the resilience of a historically grounded image they also enhance our awareness of the dynamics of contemporary visual culture.

13. For further discussion of this point, see Stephen Bann, "In the Age of Reproduction," in *Parallel Lines—Painters, Printmakers and Photographers in Nineteenth-Century France* (New Haven: Yale University Press, 2001), pp. 15–41.

CONSUMPTION AS PRODUCTION

Martha Buskirk

Artists have long been collectors, acquiring works by other artists through purchase and trade, and bringing together varieties of objects, certain of which may serve as source material for their own creations. Some of these accumulations are better known than others, often owing to accidents of fate: Rembrandt's collection is well documented in the 1656 inventory made when his possessions were sold as a result of bankruptcy; the scope of Andy Warhol's acquisitiveness was revealed by the 1988 auction sale of his voluminous hoard; and more than one scholar has seen fit to publish the list of books in Robert Smithson's library at the time of his unexpected death. Such collections are of particular interest when important connections can be drawn to the artist's work, or for the evidence of preoccupations that cut across the artist's production and consumption. A process of collecting also lies behind twentieth-century collage and assemblage practices, which involve fairly direct interaction with found material that is nonetheless transformed in the process, while the readymade emphasizes the unaltered status of the singular object.

Yet, there is another version of artist-as-collector, where the process of collecting, rather than serving as an adjunct to the artistic endeavor, forms the work of art. This shift in art making is deeply enmeshed in the role of the museum as site for display and, over the course of the twentieth century, increasingly for the production of art as well. The collection of objects that the artist simply assembled, but did not rework, introduces an ambiguous area of overlap between the roles of artist and curator as well as artist and collector. In addition, the activities of hunting down, researching, classifying, and ultimately assembling groupings of objects characterize popular collecting practices unrelated to artistic production, and the ways in which a collection itself can be authored poses further zones of ambiguity. With his focus on handmade copies of a nineteenth-century painting of a fourth-century saint, Francis Alÿs has chosen a specific subset within this field of activity. A full consideration of his collection of Fabiola paintings—which may or may not itself actually enjoy the status of a work of art by the artist known as Alÿs—requires an examination of the many points of intersection among the activities of artist, collector, and curator, as well as between the mass-produced and the handmade.

One aspect of this context is the trajectory leading from the archival bent in Conceptual practices of the 1960s and 1970s through to various forms of institutional critique, and further to a renewed attention to the objects collected in such contexts. A group of projects exhibited at Documenta 5 in Kassel in 1972 under the heading "Museen von Künstlern" provides a focused demonstration of the potential for overlap between artistic and curatorial activity. Then-recent projects by Marcel Broodthaers, Herbert Distel, Claes Oldenburg, Daniel Spoerri, and Ben Vautier were shown alongside Marcel Duchamp's 1941 *Box in a Valise*, the miniature museum of his own work assembled by the pioneer of the readymade.

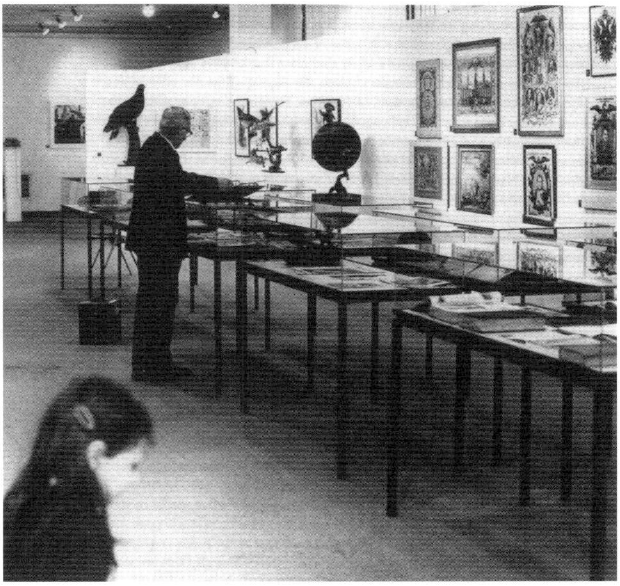

Fig. 1
Marcel Broodthaers,
Musée d'art moderne, Département des Aigles.
Installation at the Kunsthalle Düsseldorf, 1970.

fig. 1 Broodthaers's *Musée d'art moderne, Département des Aigles*, which celebrated its official "closing" at Documenta, figured in two parts of the exhibition, with a display of photographs, frames, plastic plaques, and assorted documents in the section devoted to museums by artists, and a second text-based installation in a section devoted to personal mythologies. This closing marked the end of a project that had gone through multiple permutations following its inauguration in 1968 as the *Musée d'art moderne, Département des Aigles, Section XIXème Siècle* with a display of packing crates and postcards of artworks in the artist's Brussels apartment, before moving backward to the seventeenth century for a brief 1969 appearance in Antwerp, also structured around packing crates and postcards. After that, it returned to the nineteenth century, incorporating actual historical paintings on loan, as Broodthaers's 1970 contribution to a group exhibition at the Städtische Kunsthalle in Düsseldorf. Three offshoots followed—involving, respectively, a temporary beach installation, a play with the cinematic, and a declaration of bankruptcy—prior to its most elaborate incarnation in 1972, again in Düsseldorf, with a broader focus on the eagle from the Oligocene to the present, realized through a display of more than three hundred objects, many on loan from forty-three different museums and private collectors.

If indeed, as he claimed, Broodthaers became an artist because he didn't have the resources to become a collector, then the creation of a work based on loans further confused an issue already ambiguous at the outset, when he turned his own space from a site of production to that of reception for the first incarnation of the museum.[1] There is a telling echo of the cabinet of curiosities, whose heterogeneous groupings of objects are arranged according to the dictates of the generally aristocratic collector. Broodthaers's motif of the eagle provides both the illusory unity of the display and the framework for its assembly, which absorbs everything from works of art to natural history specimens, originals to mass-produced objects and reproductions. Broodthaers's museum is not only the work of the artist *as* curator—one operating *through* the other rather than divided identities—but it also anticipates the ever-increasing tendency, in contemporary practices, for artistic authorship to provide the framework for introducing a range of object types once excluded from the art museum as part of its very definition.

Another kind of diversity held sway in Oldenburg's *Mouse Museum*, with its intermix of found, produced, and altered objects assembled by the artist in a mouse-shaped room. At the time of its Documenta appearance, the museum included a subset that was later split off and, for the project's 1977–78 incarnation, put on display in a separate *Ray Gun Wing*, appended to a refashioned version of the mouse-shaped main building. The removal of the ray gun collection left the *Mouse Museum* with divisions by object type that largely superseded the aforementioned distinctions between found and self-made: "Landscapes; Human beings; Food; Body parts; Clothing, make-up and adornment; Tools, simple to complex; Animals; Buildings, monuments and souvenirs; Money containers and practical systems; Smoking articles; Studio remnants and fragments; Objects added to the collection since 1972, not arranged according to the categories above."[2]

This somewhat incongruous list is reminiscent of Jorge Luis Borges's oft-quoted Chinese encyclopedia, where animals are divided according to such asymmetrical categories as "belonging to the emperor," "embalmed," "tame," et cetera. Of course Borges himself was no stranger to the play between found and invented, as evident in "The Analytical Language of John Wilkins," where the encyclopedia entry makes

1. On Marcel Broodthaers's claim that he became a creator because he lacked the means to be a collector, see Douglas Crimp, "This Is Not a Museum of Art," in *Marcel Broodthaers* (New York: Rizzoli, in association with Walker Art Center, Minneapolis, 1989), p. 71, and see this same publication for a general chronology of the different stages of the museum project, pp. 180–93. On the play between the sites of production and reception, see Benjamin H. D. Buchloh, "The Museum Fictions of Marcel Broodthaers," in *Museums by Artists*, ed. A. A. Bronson and Peggy Gale (Toronto: Art Metropole, 1983), p. 55.
2. *The Mouse Museum / The Ray Gun Wing: Two Collections / Two Buildings, by Claes Oldenburg* (Chicago: Museum of Contemporary Art, 1977), p. 18.

its appearance.[3] Its renown also derives from the opening paragraph of *The Order of Things*, where Michel Foucault posits the absurdity of Borges's list as a challenge, which he resolves by emphasizing its discursive status, as a series of juxtapositions that can only exist "in the non-place of language."[4] The fact that Oldenburg's categories are applied to physical objects does not, however, make them any more probable, given the groupings that result from these divisions. In this respect, the work plays off earlier taxonomies, without contesting their obsolescence, in much the same way that contemporary artists have given renewed attention to the cabinet of curiosities, with its intermix of objects, but have done so from the vantage point of their later division among different types of museum collections. Another interesting phe- *fig. 2* nomenon appears in Oldenburg's collection of ray guns, which ultimately expanded to include not just an already-eclectic mix of mass-produced, handmade (by himself as well as others), and happenstance objects (almost any sort of right-angle fragment that thus resembles a gun), but also ray guns "too fragile to move or fixed to sites," which appeared in a portfolio of photographs.[5]

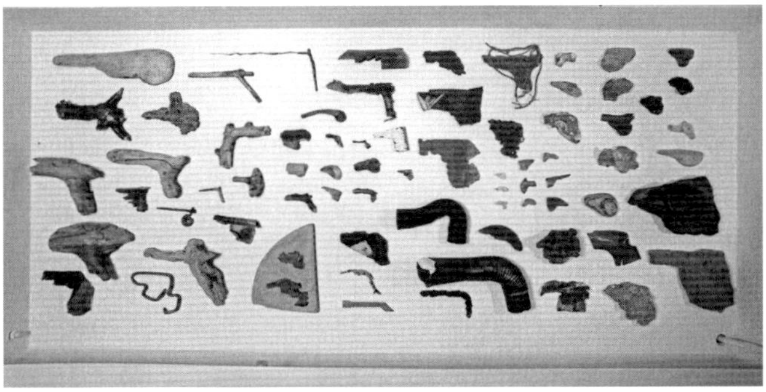

Fig. 2
Claes Oldenburg,
Mouse Museum / Ray Gun Wing, Unnumbered fragments in a right angle form resembling guns, 1977–78.
Courtesy Oldenburg van Bruggen Foundation.

3. Jorge Luis Borges, "The Analytical Language of John Wilkins," in *Other Inquisitions, 1937–1952*, trans. Ruth L. C. Simms (Austin: University of Texas Press, 1964). Citing Wilkins's *An Essay Toward a Real Character, and a Philosophical Language*, which does exist though Borges claims not to have had access to it, Borges compares Wilkins's division of the universe to a Chinese encyclopedia entry that is apparently Borges's invention, despite its attribution to Franz Kuhn, an actual sinologist. The entry, in full (as translated in Michel Foucault's preface), divides animals into "(a) belonging to the Emperor, (b) embalmed, (c) tame, (d) sucking pigs, (e) sirens, (f) fabulous, (g) stray dogs, (h) included in the present classification, (i) frenzied, (j) innumerable, (k) drawn with a very fine camelhair brush, (l) et cetera, (m) having just broken the water pitcher, (n) that from a long way off look like flies." Borges, quoted in preface to Michel Foucault, (*The Order of Things: An Archaeology of the Human Sciences* [New York: Pantheon, 1971], p. XVI.)
4. Foucault, p. XVII.
5. See *The Mouse Museum / The Ray Gun Wing*, pp. 50–51.

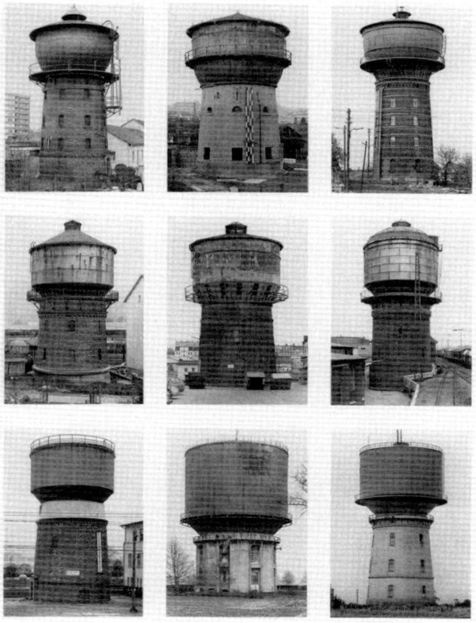

Fig. 3
Bernd and Hilla Becher,
Water Towers, 1963–88.
Courtesy Sonnabend Gallery.

The idea that material forms might be collected photographically, as well as physically, is an important point of intersection with projects oriented in relation to the archive—evident, perhaps most notably, in the sustained attention to different typologies of vernacular architecture within the expansive compendium of photographs by Bernd and Hilla Becher. A number of other issues meet here as well. One *fig. 3* is the interchange between private (already at play in artistic acts of collecting that refer to the earlier privileged form of the cabinet) and public (in their intended destination for display). Stressing the intimate relationship between collector and object, Walter Benjamin described a double dynamic of private and public engagement, via the historical artifact: while the artifact seemingly provides access or a sense of connection to the era of its origin, it is also inseparable from individual memories related to its acquisition and assimilation into the collection. Arguing that the "phenomenon of collecting loses its meaning as it loses its personal owner," Benjamin posits public access, despite the would-be social good, as accompanied by an inevitable loss.[6]

Important in distinguishing a collector from an obsessive hoarder is the collector's tendency to acquire according to specific categories, rather than randomly. Certain collectors focus their efforts on a single vein, however obscure (swizzle sticks and souvenir buildings are examples that figure in one book on popular collecting habits),

6. Walter Benjamin, "Unpacking My Library" (1931), in *Illuminations*, trans. Hannah Arendt (New York: Schocken, 1969), p. 67.

whereas others operate on multiple fronts; but even for collectors with interests in more than one area, the pursuit of specific sets of object types helps differentiate their actions from the more indiscriminate accumulator.[7] Marilynn Gelfman Karp's documentation of her astonishing array of collecting activities demonstrates the potentially arbitrary nature of such divisions, given that she has gun-shaped objects—potential ray guns, in other words—under glass candy containers, figural pencil sharpeners, as well as caps and cap guns. She has furthermore extended her collecting reach in similar fashion to Oldenburg, with a category of lists and mental collections for things observed but not available for removal—some of which, including certain signs, leaf impressions in New York City cement, and objects embedded in asphalt pavement, appear as photographs in her book.[8]

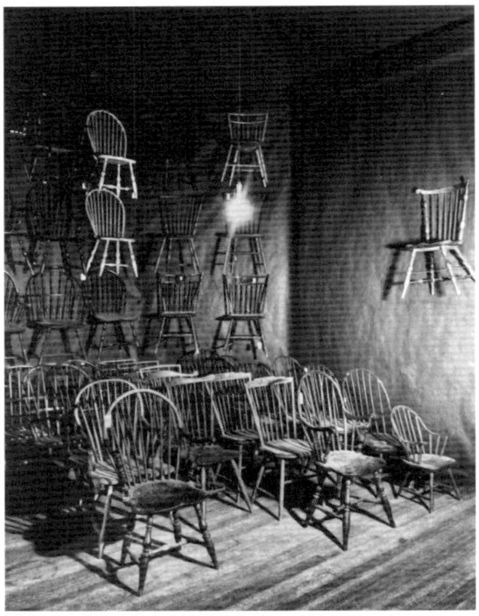

Fig. 4
Andy Warhol,
Raid the Icebox, 1969–70.
© 2008 Andy Warhol Foundation for the Visual Arts / ARS, New York.

fig. 4 Warhol is also right up there in this history. His 1969–70 *Raid the Icebox*, drawn from the storerooms of the museum at the Rhode Island School of Design, was an early instance of the increasingly common concept of inviting an artist to peruse not only what is considered by the curators suitable for display but also what is in the vault, out of sight. The plan, according to the RISD museum director, was to share

7. Swizzle sticks and souvenir buildings are two of the collection examples in Mitch Tuchman, *Magnificent Obsessions: Twenty Remarkable Collectors in Pursuit of Their Dreams* (San Francisco: Chronicle Books, 1994), pp. 33–35 and 69–71.

8. See Marilynn Gelfman Karp, *In Flagrante Collecto: Caught in the Act of Collecting* (New York: Abrams, 2006), pp. 35–36, 46–47, 144–45, and 314–21.

the riches of the storeroom with institutions in Texas and Louisiana that didn't have the same sort of reserves, with the added twist of asking an important contemporary artist to do the picking. Warhol's selection was decidedly different from the museum's standard—and was notable for both what he did and what he didn't choose. There were plenty of paintings, though generally earlier rather than recent; Native American blankets, ceramics, and baskets were extensively represented, but he ignored the Asian textiles; parasols, hat boxes, and shoes abounded, but no hats or dresses; and he scooped up a group of Windsor chairs that had been saved mainly to serve as spare parts. For many of the categories, Warhol avoided making specific choices by simply taking everything, including, most famously, over two hundred pairs of women's shoes—with the requirement that each have its own catalogue entry, forcing the museum to give these objects a level of individual attention they otherwise would never have had.[9] The ostensibly unmediated relationship to the storeroom continued in the exhibition itself, as Warhol called for duplicating its mix of happenstance and utilitarian order by displaying the shoes in their original storage cabinet, presenting other objects in stacks, and simply leaning paintings up against the wall with sandbags to keep them from sliding. The apparent lack of intervention, as was typical of Warhol's production, was precisely what gave the exhibition its specific character.

By the time he was invited to browse the RISD storerooms, Warhol himself had significantly built his own collections, which held a number of analogous categories, such as Americana from folk art to furniture, and Native American textiles, ceramics, masks, and metalwork—plus plenty of other groups of objects, running the gamut from decorative art to kitsch, and, of course, those many, many cookie jars. A level of excess, in danger of crossing the divide between collection and hoard, is suggested by stories about purchases that jammed his cupboards without ever being removed from their shopping bags (somewhat akin to William Randolph Hearst's warehouses full of objects never removed from crates) or descriptions of the artist living in only a portion of his house once the piles of goods made many rooms impassible. Then there are the Time Capsules, Warhol's apparatus for handing off to others the problem of sorting out his stuff, which presciently acknowledged how one decade's refuse could, if properly frozen in place, become another's valued evidence. Immediately after his death, the distinction between Warhol's work and his collection was sharply drawn by his executors, despite the ambiguities implied by his practice. The blurs in this distinction were reasserted in 2002 by the Andy Warhol

9. Warhol's process of selection is described in Daniel Robbins, "Confessions of a Museum Director," and David Bourdon, "Andy's Dish," in *Raid the Icebox 1 with Andy Warhol* (Providence: Museum of Art, Rhode Island School of Design, 1969), pp. 8–24.

Museum's exhibition of his former possessions in conjunction with his own artworks, a show that required the museum to track down and borrow back many of the same items that had been so dramatically dispersed.[10]

A prospective benefit of inviting artists to sort through and rearrange a collection is the implementation of forms of presentation that curators may not think of or would not feel at liberty to undertake. For example, Scott Burton displayed only the bases from Constantin Brancusi's sculptures as his contribution to the first of the Museum of Modern Art's series of Artist's Choice exhibitions in 1989; Louise Lawler emphasized a group of ceramic thimbles described by curator Trevor Fairbrother as "minor" for her 1991 *Connections* installation at Boston's Museum of Fine Arts.[11] The thimbles—which were a collection in themselves, donated to the museum by Louise D. Alden in 1962 along with the cabinet she had used for their display—illustrate a problem posed to the museum by this particular kind of donated collection: the logic of an individual's private interest, whether in a range of works or a single object type, must give way to a paradigm based on noteworthy examples, as judged against a larger canon not centered upon the holdings of any single institution.

It is striking how strategies of institutional critique associated with Conceptual art have focused attention on material objects and their history. Fred Wilson, in particular, is well known for his use of Conceptual strategies to engage with material culture. In 1992, for a project titled *Mining the Museum*, he incisively rearranged the Maryland Historical Society's collection, in the process uncovering previously hidden evidence relating to the region's African American and Native American populations, and creating unexpected tensions by playing with museum conventions in grouping artifacts by object type and period. Although this counternarrative relied entirely upon an already formed institutional assembly, the rearrangement unquestionably constituted an example of Wilson's work—in contrast to Warhol's *Raid the Icebox*. The project also emphasized the role of the artist as researcher, focusing upon objects that already had a recorded history, prior to the artist's attention, in the con-

10. Sotheby's helped the museum retrieve the very objects they had so successfully sent back out into the world not many years earlier. One aspect of the task was simplified by the fact that a single collector, Gedalio Grinberg, bought the majority of the 175 jars for sale, paying $198,605 of the $247,830 they commanded. He in turn loaned a large selection to the museum. See Rita Reif, "At the Warhol Sale, A Hunt for Collectibles," *New York Times*, April 28, 1988. On connections between *Raid the Icebox* and Warhol's collection, see *Possession Obsession: Andy Warhol and Collecting*, ed. John W. Smith (Pittsburgh: Andy Warhol Museum, 2002), particularly Pamela Allara, "Please Touch, Warhol's Collection as Alternative Museum," pp. 40–48, and Michael Lobel, "Warhol's Closet," pp. 65–74.

11. Trevor Fairbrother, "Museum / Sleuthing Storage: The 'Connections' Series at the Museum of Fine Arts Boston," in *Deep Storage: Collecting, Storing, and Archiving in Art*, ed. Ingrid Schaffner and Matthias Winzen (Munich: Prestel, 1998), p. 211.

text of a historical society, where paintings that might not be valued for their artistry were intermixed with objects just as likely to derive their significance from their provenance.

Another aspect of the artist-as-researcher is apparent when the artist extends the relationship with the artifact to the collecting process itself—and there are clear distinctions, as well as parallels, between the creation of a work based on the temporary rearrangement of an already existing collection of artifacts and the artist's own act of assembly. While Wilson set up evocative juxtapositions, Susan Hiller, in her early work with such culturally specific artifacts as potsherds and postcards, tended to emphasize her subjects' status as suspended fragments in grid-based arrangements. Her collection of postcards, tracked down from 1972 to 1976, show images of waves crashing in upon jetties and other built structures over captions incorporating the phrase "rough seas." Their presentation, titled *Dedicated to the Unknown Artist*, confronts the viewer with the phenomenon of multiplication, rather than with that of isolated points of comparison. While the anonymous postcard creators are unlikely to have been amateur, these proliferating images nonetheless call to mind the Fabiolas. Artists, by assembling and presenting a collection, pass along to the viewer, with little additional comment, their own fascination with a particular form of cultural production.

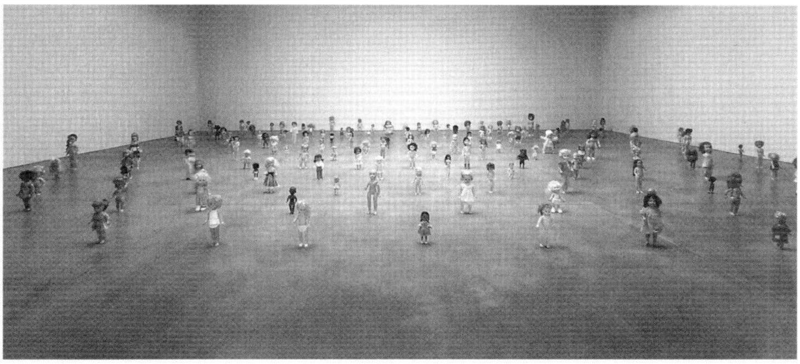

Fig. 5
Zoe Leonard,
Mouth Open, Teeth Showing, 2000.
© Z. Leonard. Courtesy of the artist and the Paula Cooper Gallery, New York.
Photo: Tom Powel.

By contrast, the used dolls that Zoe Leonard presented in a gridlike array for a 2000 installation titled *Mouth Open, Teeth Showing* (the title taken from a categorical description used by doll collectors) might hardly have seemed worthy of attention were it not for the unexpected nature of their assembly. Leonard, like others, interweaves a collection of objects with a photographic archive, her records of the quirky markets and other independent operations that are quickly disappearing in the face of the ubiquitous chain stores and their attendant commercial uniformity. The dolls reek of the outmoded or discarded, an association emphasized by their initial presentation in conjunction with stacks of tattered suitcases Leonard acquired to *fig. 5* transport her flea-market finds. Yet, it was the specific play between the gendered character of the all-female dolls and the minimalist activation of space, through objects arranged directly on the floor, that gave the arrangement as a whole a significance obviously greater than its unprepossessing components.

If the items in Warhol's collection gained value through the association with their former owner, Leonard has made the process far more official by presenting the collection as a work, and selling it as such to Bill and Ruth True, who have subsequently exhibited it at Western Bridge, their private-public exhibition space in Seattle. With their connection to the artist secure, the dolls are in no danger of being dismissed as a minor collection. Not only is Leonard's act of collecting transformed by its outcome as a work destined for public display, but the exhibition site established by their new owner bears little connection to that assumed by Benjamin, where the collector possessed a far more exclusive relationship to the object. There are indeed many potential ambiguities associated with the growing tendency among private collectors to establish galleries in which to display collections that happen to include work once thought of as suitable only for public institutions.

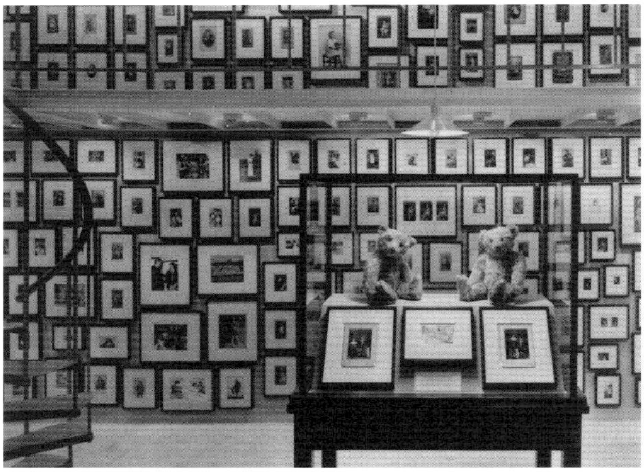

Fig. 6
Ydessa Hendeles,
Partners (The Teddy Bear Project), 2001.
Installation at the Haus der Kunst, Munich, 2003.
Courtesy the Ydessa Hendeles Art Foundation. Photo: Robert Keziere.

The ongoing collecting and exhibition activity of Ydessa Hendeles posits an overlapping of the activities of artists who function like curators and the ostensible *fig. 6* inverse, a creatively inclined curator-collector. For her 2003 *Partners* exhibition organized for Munich's Haus der Kunst, Hendeles combined objects with various kinds of authorship, juxtaposing those by a roster of contemporary artists with groupings of images by photojournalists, family snapshots, and found photographs. Two galleries, dubbed *The Teddy Bear Project*, contained more than three thousand found photographs unified only by the appearance of a stuffed bear in some part of the image. The exhibition also included teddy bears themselves, plus a rare metal windup toy of Minnie Mouse with Felix the Cat, and an apparently sleeping but actually taxidermied dog by Maurizio Cattelan. These objects joined a variety of groupings, some created through repetition or by related thematics; others, such as works by Hanne Darboven and On Kawara, were inherently serial in their structure. Many of the juxtapositions were held together by a subtext of twentieth-century violence, documented photographically, that then circled back, via a kneeling figure of Hitler by Cattelan, to the role of the Haus der Kunst, which hosted the Great German Art Exhibitions during the Nazi era. The accompanying exhibition catalogue also bears the imprint of the curator-collector, who explicates her take on an assembly of material notable for the diversity in its authorship.[12]

In calling her own photo collections "projects," Hendeles has adopted an intrinsically ambiguous term already favored by artists for activities that may or may not be readily defined as artworks. Her carefully choreographed ensembles point to the tensions embedded in works that play with the conventions of collecting or archiving found materials, particularly when that work is in turn assimilated into yet another collection with an active interpretive agenda operating along similar lines. During an earlier era of large-scale private collection building, paintings belonging to royalty were likely to be cut down or enlarged to suit the agenda of the assembly as a whole. While the physical object is hardly likely to be tampered with in a similar fashion today, there remains the issue of the interpretive context within which the artist's own declarations about the work shares discursive space with other strong readings. It seems important to ask whether there is a difference in kind, or just degree, between the understanding a collector might convey through the act of arrangement and the staging of alternative narratives, such as, for example, David Wilson's Borges-esque mix of plausible and fantastic in the Museum of Jurassic Technology, or Walid Raad's extrapolations from Lebanon's recent history in the Atlas Group files.

And finally, in the midst of all these considerations of the varied approaches to material culture to which artists have turned their attention, there is the matter of painting, which Alÿs's Fabiola project inevitably forces to the surface. Many commentators have compared the process of exploration underpinning Alÿs's often open-ended activities to the deliberate aimlessness of the Situationist *dérive*, yet less attention has been paid to the connections that might be drawn between his pursuit of vernacular image production and Asger Jorn's realization of the Situationist concept of *détournement*, carried out via crudely rendered insertions into secondhand paintings. Conceptually driven forms of engagement with popular practice or taste include John Baldessari's *Commissioned Paintings*, made by Sunday painters asked to

12. See Ydessa Hendeles, *Partners* (Cologne: Verlag der Buchhandlung Walther König, 2003).

copy photographs of fingers pointing at everyday objects that Baldessari provided, and Vitaly Komar and Aleksandr Melamid's paintings resulting from the analysis of surveys of collective taste in different countries. These projects tacitly acknowledge the ongoing status of painting in the popular imagination, long after its critical and institutional dethronement in the contemporary art world.

Writing in the first half of the twentieth century, Clement Greenberg didn't hesitate to attack the very qualities that have helped to ensure the ongoing popularity of such work below the art-historical radar. "Self-evidently, all kitsch is academic; and conversely, all that's academic is kitsch," was his unequivocal condemnation.[13] Not coincidentally, the multitude of copies Alÿs has harvested are all based on a canvas that an academic painter, Jean-Jacques Henner, showed in Paris at the Salon in 1885—anyone who knows his or her art history will recognize this moment, judged in retrospect, as exactly when academic success stopped counting for much of anything, now that posterity has awarded victory to the unofficial artists of the avant-garde. According to the canonical account of modernism with which Greenberg is so indelibly associated, history painting lost pride of place to the lower genres of landscape, portraiture, and still life, as narrative gave way to paintings inspired by direct observation, and that, in turn, established the basis for an abstract engagement with the medium as such. Thomas Crow has further turned the argument with his suggestion that the Abstract Expressionist painting that emerged from the lower genres also absorbed the scale and formal ambitions of history painting, in a double move that left popular forms of representational painting "with virtually no claim to the status of art at all."[14] But genre painting never really went away, if one doesn't limit one's field of vision to the norm constituted by the self-defined cutting edge. You will find no shortage of painters out there if you want your child, dog, or racehorse immortalized in homage to the great tradition—and those who rise to the top of a given niche market may even be able to make a decent living in the process.[15]

Amateurs have also retained an indefatigable interest in this medium, and their varied results are well represented in the collection that Jim Shaw assembled and exhibited under the title *Thrift Store Paintings*. This project arguably offers one of the closest parallels, with respect to object type as well as source, to Alÿs's Fabiola assembly; however, the vernacular painting that piqued Shaw's interest, in contrast

13. Clement Greenberg, "Avant-Garde and Kitsch" (1939), reprinted in *Clement Greenberg: The Collected Essays and Criticism*, vol. 1, ed. John O'Brian (Chicago: University of Chicago Press, 1986), p. 12.

14. Thomas Crow, "The Simple Life: Pastoralism and the Persistence of Genre in Recent Art," in *Modern Art in the Common Culture* (New Haven: Yale University Press, 1996), p. 176.

15. For example, a profile of golf-course artist Linda Hartough reported prices for her paintings as ranging from $50,000 to $225,000, and a substantial additional business in prints. See Ginia Bellafante, "On the Green with the Rembrandt of the Back 9," *New York Times*, June 11, 2006.

to Alÿs's, was not the obvious copy but, rather, earnestly undertaken portraits, animals, and multifigure scenes, as well as what might best be described as the amateur surreal. Shaw set himself a maximum price of twenty-five dollars, which did not seem to curtail his collecting activities, perhaps because he was generally uninterested in anything that seemed too skillfully executed. Subsets can be identified, and there is clearly a certain aesthetic at work, which Shaw himself described as an initial pursuit of "ugly portraits or paintings that were unintentionally fucked up," as well as a general engagement with "slightly lurid" content.[16] Just over a hundred examples were shown in Los Angeles in 1990, and almost two hundred at the New York gallery Metro Pictures in 1991, his own sizable collection supplemented by ones borrowed from other like-minded collectors. Notwithstanding the obvious connections to Shaw's other forms of artistic expression, the collection was not clearly defined as a work nor was the exhibition for sale, despite its display in a commercial gallery in New York.

What's significant in these latter cases, as well as in the Fabiola collection, is the dominance not only of painting but painting as image making. Fabiola's reappearance en masse provides evidence of an ongoing attraction both for her from the faithful of many countries and for the representational practices that have charted their own course without directly contesting the modernist framing of the twentieth century, just ignoring it. Equally noteworthy is the ongoing practice of copying paintings, long after its apparent banishment as a mainstream artistic exercise by the latter part of the nineteenth century. And it seems somehow fitting that Henner's original has disappeared, leaving us with only the procession of simulacra, but proffering the intriguing possibility that the prototype might not be found precisely because it has been swept up in the sea of proliferation. What links these hand-painted copies, and accounts for their remarkably consistent iconography—despite a reach that extends across multiple countries and even continents—is the underlying role played by mechanical reproduction. Even though the paintings depend on a reproduced image as vehicle, the decision to paint evidently represents an opposing desire, in the midst of the mass-produced, for all that the traditional, handmade art form evokes.

Ultimately, the paintings themselves are fascinating in their own right as objects, not simply as an idea. In the diverse hands of his interpreters, Henner's academic prototype has been reinvented in ways that suggest the screen of stereotypes or prior expectations brought to the task by each copyist. In a number, Henner's rather

---

16. Ralph Rugoff, "Jim Shaw: Recycling the Subcultural Straitjacket" (interview), *Flash Art* 163 (March–April 1992), p. 93.

sweetly insipid model has acquired the exaggerated features of a greeting-card cutie, and others become more alarming than saintly due to the presumably unintentional crudeness of their rendering. There are also shifts that hint at discrepancies in the reproductions used as source material, as Fabiola faces the opposite direction or appears in a different-colored veil. Particularly striking are the variations in the fold in her head covering, which at times resembles a sudden extrusion, a hook, a loop, even a spiral, and it is this fold, rather than facial features, that Alÿs has pointed to as her most significant identifying trait. A postcard that Dia conservator Francesca Esmay found tucked into the back of one canvas purchased by Alÿs in Antwerp provides a hint about the image's dissemination, as well as a telling demonstration of the amateur's interpretation of Henner's prototype. This picture postcard presents a color reproduction of the painting that has been overdrawn with a grid clearly intended as an aid to transferring the image. Yet the work that apparently resulted from this diligence is a crude approximation. The slight squaring off of Fabiola's head covering became a decided rectangle, interrupted by a hornlike interpretation of the fold; the face has lost almost all traces of modeling; and the slightly weak chin suddenly juts out at the bottom, under lips that have also acquired a unique shape of their own. If, indeed, as the presence of the postcard seems to indicate, this painting was directly created from the reproduction, it was done by an artist who did not have the necessary skills to translate academic conventions, or who perhaps did not even perceive the differences.

An obvious irony is that these objects would never have made it into the museum on their own merits. One might therefore be tempted to describe Alÿs's role in the process as somehow akin to the fabled Trojan Horse, smuggling in paintings that should by all rights have been stopped at the door, except that there was no deception here; the Hispanic Society and subsequent venues have known from the start exactly what they were going to be getting. The attraction was therefore not subterfuge, being offered one artist and getting some other goods entirely. Rather, if Alÿs is in some sense the vessel by which these works enter the institution, it is a transparent container, wheeled into the museum with its contents in plain view. It took the interest of an artist whose peripatetic practice can far more readily be understood as an offshoot of Conceptual and performance strategies to direct renewed attention, at the turn of the twenty-first century, to the history of *Fabiola* and her subsequent representations. Now these paintings, which might not be thought of as art on their own, have gained renewed attention from a project that itself might or might not have the status of an artwork.

Who gets to claim the status of artist, and which of the artist's activities are defined as art? Artists and nonartists alike seem to be busy collecting mass-produced objects; talented and untalented individuals also continue to apply paint to canvas. It's not typical to refer to used paintings, in the way one speaks of other secondhand merchandise, but it may be appropriate here, given how, in the almost century-long interval since Duchamp's provocative claim regarding the mass-produced, we have somehow come full circle, to handmade paintings as readymades. Whereas Duchamp's engagement with industrial production appeared in the context of a trajectory that initially seemed aligned with modernist painting, Alÿs's not only started with the quotidian but also came to painting through isolated popular forms that would in all likelihood have remained outside the contemporary art world's span of attention were it not for his consideration. The shift from artist *and* collector to artist *as* collector may seem slight, yet the space between those descriptions opens on to many other points of overlap or slippage, like such related composites as artist-curator, or collector-author. Alÿs's project directs attention not just backward, to the previous history of the objects he has assembled, but also forward, to an ongoing exchange between consumption and production taking place both within and beyond the evolving definition of the work of art.

FRANCIS ALŸS: INSTIGATOR/INVESTIGATOR

Lynne Cooke

I

At first glance, all the works look remarkably alike, for they share a single subject depicted in accordance with its canonical iconography: a fourth-century Christian saint known as Fabiola, portrayed as a young woman in profile, facing left, wearing a crimson veil. Since the original is long lost, the model or prototype on which all were based must have been sourced in the form of a reproduction, perhaps an illustration in a book or a magazine, perhaps a picture postcard or an engraved print. Yet no mechanically reproduced images are included here; each object has been made by hand. *fig. 4*

Closer study reveals that within the collection's unusually narrow compass there is an enormous range; and, once that initial impression of homogeneity is dispelled, the three hundred or so objects quickly distinguish themselves from one another. The spectrum of media is immediately striking: oil paint, gouache, embroidery, enamel, plaster, ceramic, and, in one particularly memorable instance, seeds and beans. There is also a surprising breadth in the makers' technical skills. Only a few demonstrate the proficiency expected of a professional artist; most must have been made by amateurs. Yet, it's often precisely those technical limitations, or handicaps, that make a particular rendering compelling; see, for example, no. 119. Further differences may be attributed to the fact that, whether consciously or not, some of these painters supplemented the standardized schema by interjecting features belonging to another model, sometimes living, more often probably ideal or imaginary.[1] The original, the single prototype from which virtually all these works derive, is a lost painting by a late-nineteenth-century French academician.[2] In its iconography, style, and

The author thanks the Clark/Getty workshop "Art History and the Present," 2007–2008, for providing a stimulating forum in which to develop some of the ideas in this essay.

1. Francis Alÿs, the owner of the collection, argues: "I personally see them as all different: each seems to project some kind of personal ideal of womanhood or to disguise, consciously or not, a familiar face with the features of Fabiola." (Alÿs, e-mail message to the author, July 17, 2007.)
2. Evidence suggesting the paintings were copied from reproductions of the lost original is found, for example, in the variations in size, the reversal of the motif so that Fabiola faces right (in several instances), and the substitution of the tonally similar green for the customary red in the cloak. Evidence that suggests no color photograph had ever been taken of the original may be deduced from the date of the work's disappearance (1889) but also from the wide range of reds employed for the

composition, Jean-Jacques Henner's portrait is unexceptional, even quite conventional; by contrast, the delicate rendering of her physiognomy is deceptively subtle and, as evidenced by these examples, not easily replicated.[3]

Little noted in the ecclesiastical pantheon for centuries after her canonization in AD 537, Fabiola finally escaped from obscurity on the wave of the Catholic Revival that swept late-nineteenth-century Europe. According to her first advocate, the early Church Father Saint Jerome, this noble Roman matron left her abusive husband and remarried, only to be widowed some years later. After converting to Christianity and making public penance for the sin of divorce, she then devoted the remainder of her life (and fortune) to charitable work, reputedly founding the first hospital for the poor and needy on the outskirts of Rome in the late fourth century. Fabiola's rise to cult status began in the 1850s when a racier version of her story was published in the guise of a romantic historical novel of the kind popularized by Sir Walter Scott. Limned by a British prelate and leading pillar of the Catholic Revival, Cardinal *fig. 1* Nicholas Wiseman, *Fabiola, or the Church of the Catacombs* became a best seller and was read by generations of impressionable young minds.

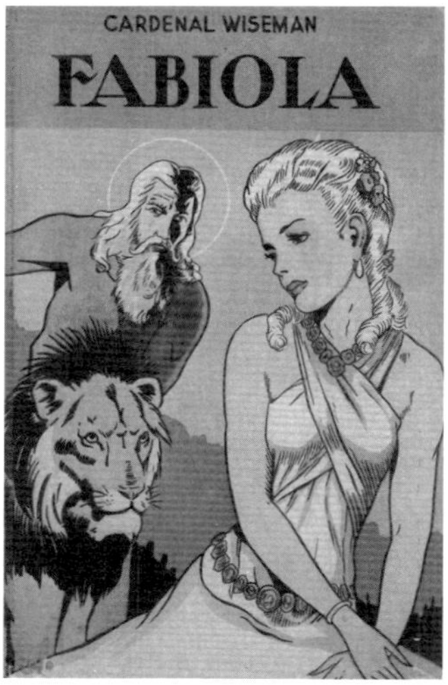

Fig. 1
Cover of Cardinal Wiseman's novel, *Fabiola*, published by Editorial Diana, Mexico City, 1953.

veil (following Jean-Jacques Henner's known taste, Venetian red being most favored), and in the red-green reversals. Some of the Fabiola paintings may also have come from second-generation images, that is, from postcards made of a copy by another artist rather than from a reproduction of Henner's original.

3. Henner's depiction had its visual sources in the portraiture of secular subjects that the Bellinis and other Venetian artists introduced in the sixteenth century. Given that profile portraiture was linked to Classical as distinct from Christian traditions of representation, his iconography could be said to meld intimations of her patrician background with the Christian virtues she acquired through her penance, charitable deeds, and piety.

Revered as the protector of abused women, Fabiola is also extolled as the patron of nurses; her popular veneration may therefore owe much to the concurrent growth of the modern nursing profession through the efforts and example of Florence Nightingale. Prior to Henner's portrayal in the mid-1880s there seem to have been very few visual representations of this worthy Roman paragon.[4] Standardized depictions of *fig. 2*

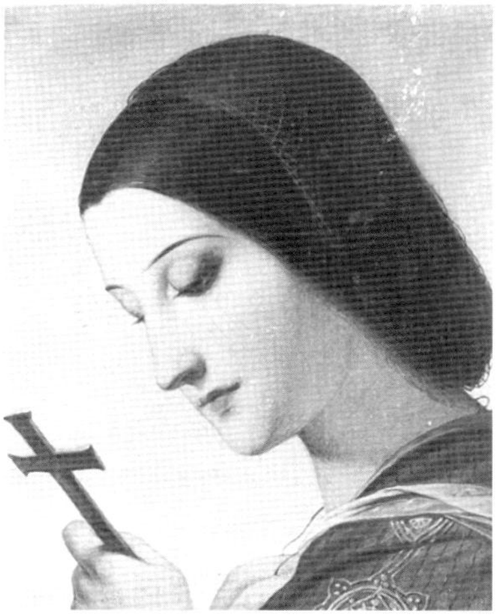

Fig. 2
Edward Jakob von Steinle,
Fabiola, 1855.
Städelsches Kunstinstitut,
Frankfurt am Main.

saints in the Catholic liturgy usually distinguish one from another by means of personal attributes; Saint Jerome, for example, is identifiable by his red cardinal's hat, skull, and faithful lion. When widespread devotion to an individual saint led to the dedication of altars, private chapels, and even churches in his or her name, the canonical iconography expanded from the representation of an iconic figure, with attributes, to genre scenes, in which key episodes in the hagiography are elaborated.

Although unquestionably esteemed, especially among women, Fabiola does not seem to have become the object of an official or public worship expressed in the form of dedicated sites and shrines; though widespread, devotion to her has remained at the level of the private, as personal supplication. Henner's economic head shot was consequently never supplemented by narrative variants, such as scenes of this pious

4. The only other iconographic rendering of Fabiola known to this author is by Edward Jakob von Steinle, whose version, an oil painting dating from 1855 (the year after the publication of Wiseman's book), is now in the collection of the Städelsches Kunstinstitut, Frankfurt aM. Until recently, the Louvre sold reproductions of this work, a perennial favorite. For current discussions relating to works depicting Fabiola, see *Antiques and the Arts Online*, http://antiquesandhearts.com/forumresponse.asp (accessed February 7, 2008).

matron nursing the infirm.[5] His thus-definitive rendering, while undoubtedly a religious icon, is infused with a degree of naturalism and animation that makes her seem unexpectedly available, and somehow contemporary. Since her signature features—a simple red cloak and a limpid profile—are, however, so basic, artists have stuck closely to Henner's canonical portrayal to ensure that those seeking her sanctity could instantly recognize her. Because this faithful adherence to the icon's fundamental lineaments is therefore prerequisite, any trace of subjective or expressive distortion is likely more inadvertent than intentional.

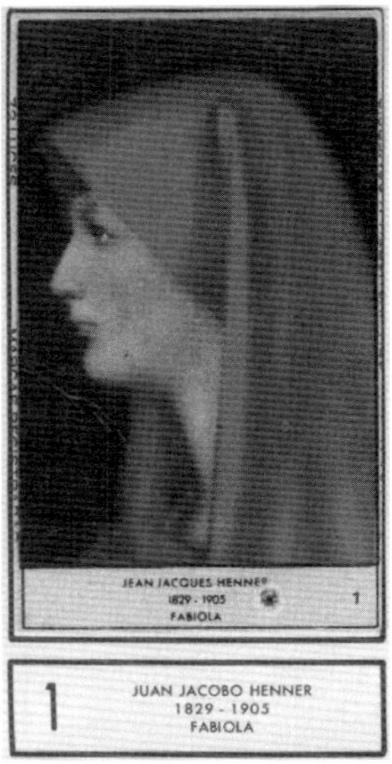

Fig. 3
Clasicos de Lujo matchbook cover featuring Jean-Jacques Henner's *Fabiola*, 1885.

fig. 3 Copies of Henner's image rapidly proliferated in printed media, as well as in painting. Far into the second half of the twentieth century, popular interest continued to generate a considerable mass market for photographic reproductions.[6] In addition, as attested by this ever-growing collection amassed from cities throughout western Europe and Latin America, hand-painted versions by both professional and amateur artists still find a ready audience. Although some of the works in this collection have

5. Namesake to many women in Mexico and Belgium, including the dowager queen, Fabiola was also the subject of a film directed by Alessandro Blasetti, released in 1949, based on Cardinal Wiseman's novel. See, also, Fabiola Santiago, "St. Fabiola: An Art Exhibit Reminds a Cuban Exile How She Learned to Appreciate Her Name," *Miami Herald* (February 2, 2008), p. 1E.
6. A series of some 254 Clasicos de Lujo matchbook covers, sold throughout Mexico in the mid-twentieth century, featured renowned old master paintings. The first in the series (preceding works by Velázquez, Titian et al.), is devoted to Henner's *Fabiola*.

a venerable patina, close inspection reveals that most were made in the later part of the last century. On occasion, artificial aging has been reinforced by the accidents of history. Shorn of the frames that once would have enhanced and protected them, many bear abraded edges or are otherwise damaged. None, however, reveal the type of restoration customarily accorded to artworks that are highly valued, whether for financial or sentimental reasons. And, tellingly, no attempt has been made by their current owner to redeem their fall from grace by disguising the signs that almost all were sourced from flea markets and similar haunts: their lowly status is incontestable.[7] The kinds of unconventional media employed, plus the unusually broad range of supports, which includes, inter alia, glass and velvet, effectually blur those conventional distinctions and boundaries between artisanal or handcrafted practices and traditional fine-art techniques. While most could literally be described as copies after an old master painting, it is unlikely that they were undertaken for the usual—that is, pedagogical—reasons: both the rudimentary levels of technical proficiency and the obscurity into which Henner's reputation has fallen argues against that hypothesis.[8] If the striking homogeneity of the collection depends on a single subject, the collection's identity and character resolutely rely on not simply the handwrought but the utilitarian—for these works were produced for functional, rather than purely aesthetic, ends.

---

7. Given these parameters, both printed reproductions and "fakes" (those made specifically to pique this now-well-known artist's interest) are rigorously excluded from the collection. In 1997 Francis Alÿs sent some sixty Fabiolas to be shown in the second biennial of Saaremaa, Estonia. When these works were shipped back to him, he discovered that almost thirty had been replaced with substitutes, crude versions made to simulate his originals, which had mysteriously disappeared. Wishing to conceal the fact that they had lost or otherwise appropriated his works, the Estonian organizers seemingly hoped to fool him into believing that the substitutes—the copies they commissioned of his copies—were actually works that he had collected. This subgroup of twenty-six examples, identified in the collection catalogue as A through Z, are notable for an acidulous orange-red in the palette and a cursory, loose handling. More recently, Alÿs discovered that an acquaintance with a certain technical proficiency had been making versions that he presented to Alÿs not as examples of his own devising but as chance discoveries made when visiting flea markets and junk stores. Alÿs immediately removed them from the collection. Among objets d'art, such as jewelery and dishes, he distinguishes those commercially manufactured from those that require the intervention of an individual hand, such as enameled objects.
8. Copies were traditionally made by professional artists or apprentices who took on the servile task of making a version of an old master painting to attain or refine their manual skills or to demonstrate their prowess in a particular artistic style or idiom. Alternatively, copies might be commissioned by collectors who wished to have their own version or replica of an acclaimed masterpiece, or even by newly founded institutions seeking to educate their untutored general audiences; as vehicles that could form the tastes of novice viewers according to standards and values established by the academic canon, such copies served pedagogical ends.

From the first tentative discussions concerning the exhibition of this exceptional collection, the owner placed restrictions on its presentation. Neither conventional white-cube galleries, normative to the display of modernist and contemporary artworks, nor raw warehouse spaces of the kind generally preferred for post-sixties installation art were deemed suitable. In their stead, he stipulated a historicizing context like that reserved for old master paintings, where the works should be hung Salon style. To date, two venues have met these requirements: the Hispanic Society of America in New York City (where the collection was on view from September 2007 through early April 2008) and the Los Angeles County Museum of Art (where it will be exhibited from September 2008 through January 2009). The former was founded in the early twentieth century by a single wealthy patron, Archer Huntington. Over decades, Huntington amassed an unparalleled collection devoted to many facets of Hispanic culture, from its Neolithic beginnings onward. In 1908, a facility comprising a library and museum, which he had in large part designed himself, was opened to the public on the Upper West Side of Manhattan. In addition to a vast number of visual-art objects and an unrivaled research library, the Hispanic Society houses an impressive cartography collection and an ethnographic archive of more than a hundred thousand photographs that document the modes and mores of rural Spanish peoples in the late nineteenth and early twentieth centuries. Within its miscellaneous corpus of visual objects are collections of ceramic tiles, ironwork (locks and door hinges), ecclesiastical textiles, ceremonial platters, abbesses' amulets, and much else. In many respects, its installation departs from current museological standards; for example, it eschews any privileging of its masterpieces in any particular art form through less hierarchical taxonomic groupings: quantity seems as important as selectivity, and typological uniformity as instructive as variation. While not a former domestic residence, as are the sites of the Frick Collection and the Isabella Stewart Gardner Museum, the Hispanic Society has nonetheless a distinctly individual, if not personal, character.

Founded by the county, and hence a civic institution, LACMA is an encyclopedic museum whose holdings have principally been amassed over the past forty years from purchase and bequest. True to type, its collections range from contemporary to antiquity, from Western to non-Western, from the fine to the decorative arts and newer technologies. A location adjacent to the suite of galleries housing the European old masters collection within LACMA's sprawling campus was selected for the presentation of the Fabiola collection. Sequestered in a room whose decor, while tailored to the needs of this display, still resembles that of its neighbors, the collection will once again be hung according to conventions established by the Salon; that is, the paintings will be closely aligned in serried rows on walls that are painted in a dark tone, with the objects displayed nearby in period-style vitrines. Each presentation is accompanied by copies of the collection's catalogue raisonné, in which the usual scholarly apparatus has been brought to bear on each item in the checklist, even though these mostly anonymous exhibits have scant pedigrees and slim provenances. Memorable more for its miscellaneous details than for its ability to confer a legitimating authority, this reference tool does not escape a hint of parody.[9]

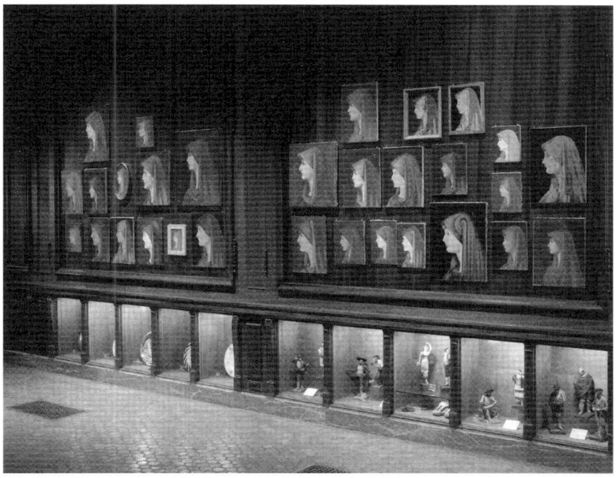

Fig. 4
"Francis Alÿs: Fabiola." Installation at the Hispanic Society of America, New York City, September 2007–April 2008.
Photo: Cathy Carver.

Cued by public and press announcements, visitors seeking "Fabiola" at the Hispanic Society expected to find a contemporary art project commissioned by Dia Art Foundation from the much-admired Belgian-born Mexico-based artist, Francis Alÿs. Alÿs's conceptually driven practice has meant, however, that he has neither a signature style nor a studio-based production: he tends to work on a project-by-project basis, with each site-related undertaking assuming a distinct content and formal idiom. Thus few among the audience could have anticipated the form and the scope of his in situ intervention, let alone its context, for many had never previously visited this cherished, if little-known, organization.[10] No signage was introduced on the plaza to direct visitors to the northern pavilion where the Fabiola collection was installed, since it was hoped that they would explore the rich collections of the host institution, whose highlights include paintings by Velázquez, El Greco, and Goya, before discovering Alÿs's contribution. On leaving the main building and crossing *fig. 4*

9. "Flea markets are black holes of the signified," Cuauhtémoc Medina argues eloquently, "places where objects lose their inherited meanings that gave them a sense of belonging, where they acquire new meanings as they pass to other hands." (Medina, "Fabiola: Who [doesn't] know[s] her?" in *Fabiola* [Mexico City: Curare, 1994], p. 11.)
10. Information based on informal study of visitors and press response.

the plaza to the northern annex where the Society's collection of nineteenth-century paintings usually hang, viewers entered the first of a pair of rooms containing the Fabiolas. Hung in groups on mahogany-paneled walls and framed by moldings, the collection was juxtaposed with a display, in small vitrines inset into the lower part of the gallery walls, of nineteenth- and early twentieth-century vernacular pottery, gathered from regions throughout Spain and the New World. As confounding as it was revealing, the conjunction of the Fabiolas with these functional, artisanal objects generated myriad questions regarding their role and function in vernacular and populist traditions; the longevity and transmission of widely dispersed images, forms, and modes; and the stability and porousness of the communities in which they were generated. In addition, the premises, protocols, and parameters that underpin Alÿs's collection of paintings contrast dramatically with those shaping the Hispanic Society's collection of admittedly largely forgotten nineteenth-century Salon painters that they have supplanted for the duration of this show; from this substitution yet another set of reflections, regarding the precarious status of masterpieces and the ephemerality of fame, emerges. Nonetheless, over and above such speculation based in difference, there is nonetheless a compelling sense of kinship between the two ventures, which makes the peerless older institution an ideal venue for Alÿs's more modest enterprise. In their maverick independence, both collections evidence a strong indifference to norms that in the past—and still today—have shaped the formation of art collections in the public and private spheres alike.

At LACMA, by contrast, the encounter will be somewhat differently staged in that the majority of visitors to this encyclopedic museum are not necessarily aficionados of contemporary art and, hence, are probably unfamiliar with the name Alÿs. Strolling through the old master wing of the museum they will suddenly come upon a gallery devoted exclusively to the Fabiolas. Recourse to the accompanying brochure may alert them to the fact that, contrary to first impressions, this ensemble of works does not belong to the institution but is an intervention, a contemporary art project in the guise of a collaboration between the owner of a specialized private collection and the museum's department of European art. Questions relating to the procedures and protocols of art history's disciplinary apparatus may surface at LACMA more urgently than at the Hispanic Society, where in response to the tenor of that singular collection, issues of a broader cultural dimension prevail. By contrast, questions relating to the role of the donor or patron have less pertinence here than at the Hispanic Society, where the identity and motivations of each instigator immediately piqued curiosity. Nevertheless, at both venues, the historicizing context serves to deflect the question of whether this intervention in itself constitutes a work authored by Alÿs—that is, whether it is a work in his oeuvre. Equally crucial at LACMA is the way that, once again Alÿs deflects the mantle of guest curator in order to foreground ethnographic issues and that he does so without condescending to his material, that is, without becoming the interpreter of the cultural alterity of artifacts outside the canonical corpus.[11]

Over the past four decades, interventions by contemporary artists in the hallowed precincts of museums of all types and from all eras have become a familiar aesthetic strategy; indeed, so routine has institutional critique become that it is now codified as a historical category. Such practices typically probe power relations as well as ideological and disciplinary structures, proper to the museological field. Originating in the late sixties in the radical site-specific and site-related works of Michael Asher, Hans Haacke, and Marcel Broodthaers, this genealogy provides a readymade filter for viewing Alÿs's project, given that the vehicle through which his collection has been brought into the public arena is as an art project initiated and curated by a contemporary art institution, namely Dia. With his celebrated, if confounding, "museum fictions," the Belgian-born Broodthaers sought, as Douglas Crimp argues, to "reveal the true historical conditions of collecting as they now exist."[12] In his brilliant analysis of the greatest of these, the *Musée d'art moderne, Département des Aigles* (1968–72), Crimp explores the various ways in which Broodthaers focused on institutional framing conditions and their ideological determinations by parsing his project through several quite distinct types of context.[13] His multifaceted entity took the form of an enormous collection of heterogeneous artifacts, artworks, and reproductions

11. See Hal Foster, "The Artist as Ethnographer," in *The Traffic in Culture: Refiguring Art and Anthropology*, ed. George E. Marcus and Fred R. Myers (Berkeley: University of California Press, 1995), pp. 302–9. Foster identifies five characteristics that, he believes, have contributed to the discipline of anthropology becoming prized by the vanguard edge of contemporary art practice: it is "the science of alterity"; it "takes culture as its object"; it is "considered contextual; it is thought to arbitrate the interdisciplinary; and it is premised on reflexivity, self-critique lies at its core" (p. 305). In an important article teasing out Foster's initial characterization of the so-called ethnographic turn, Miwon Kwon addresses the problematic question of authorship in terms highly relevant here. "To speak authoritatively now . . . is considered an oppressive act," she writes. That is, conjectures on cultural phenomena, "on their social, political, and historical meaning and significance are held in suspicion because there is a tendency to automatically align assertions of interpretive authorship with the exercise of authoritarian power." As a result, she contends "while there remains critical energy around the deconstruction of interpretative processes, there persists a secret interdiction on interpretation itself." (Kwon, "Experience vs. Interpretation: Traces of Ethnography in the Works of Lan Tuazon and Nikki S. Lee," in *Site-Specificity: The Ethnographic Turn* [London: Black Dog Publishing, 2000], p. 77.)

12. Douglas Crimp, "This Is Not a Museum of Art,"in *Marcel Broodthaers* (New York: Rizzoli, in association with Walker Art Center, Minneapolis, 1989), p. 72.

13. Not incidentally, as Crimp notes, the "institutional 'overvaluation' of art produced a secondary effect, which Benjamin called 'the disintegration of culture into commodities,' and Broodthaers referred to as 'the transformation of art into merchandise'" (p. 80).

unified solely by the fact that they shared a single motif—the eagle. First exhibited at the artist's own studio in Brussels in 1968 as an assembly of packing crates and postcards, these labile presentations culminated in 1972 in Kassel at Documenta 5. At its most expansive, *Musée d'art moderne* comprised loans, which Broodthaers duly classified and labeled according to museum protocols, from some forty-three august institutions, as well as numerous private individuals. While individually fascinating, the items in this absurdly cacophonous ensemble were vested with the power and authority that such institutions bestow on their holdings, even while on loan. They were nonetheless but the pretext for the artist's larger impulse to deconstruct and reflexively destabilize, dismantle, and pick apart embedded structures and practices.

While the placement of Alÿs's collection in these institutions prompts interpretation by reference to the policies, programs, and politics of each host organization, it is additionally freighted by what in recent critical literature is deemed an ethnographic turn.[14] The lineaments of his enterprise might, for example, become more sharply etched when seen in the context of Huntington's grandiose ambitions and the almost limitless resources the nineteenth-century philanthropist deployed in pursuit of fantasies of completeness and closure. For, the lightness of Alÿs's touch in salvaging the lowly and neglected is highlighted when contrasted with the quasi-colonialist predations of his predecessor. Were, conversely, the Fabiolas to be placed in a contemporary venue, a white-walled gallery, they would likely be viewed as kitsch, while simultaneously if perversely savored for their weirdness and ineptitude. That was the fate of Jim Shaw's collection of thrift-store paintings when it was recently exhibited in a contemporary gallery. The resulting transvaluation is completely at odds with Alÿs's modus operandi.

The shards of a resilient, but nonetheless threatened, cultural practice, Alÿs's flea-market finds exemplify resistance to the substantial losses spawned by a rapidly changing world; hence, a trace of melancholy permeates viewers' initial impressions of wonder. In requiring a historicizing venue, he makes an interpretative maneuver designed, above all, to center attention back on the *image* of Fabiola, that is, on the elusive prototype somehow ever present among the myriad searching approximations. Alÿs mirrors Broodthaers in his penchant for the confounding gesture. However, in contrast to the older artist's fictive museums devised for deconstructive ideological ends, Alÿs's Fabiola collection focuses on the objects—on their roles and identities, both individual and collective—as cultural artifacts: in short, it represents an ethnographic scrutiny. As the artist-collector has asked himself repeatedly over the past fifteen years: "Why that image in particular? What gives it that power to resist . . . first, mechanical reproduction and, now, digital reproduction? Is the ritual/act

14. See note 11.

of painting a requisite for conferring on the image its aura? What is it that made it become an icon, an object beyond any consideration of taste? How has it served as a reminder of the existence of a completely parallel and separate art scene from, say, 'ours,' one with its own references and obsessions?"[15]

II

Several years after he relocated to Mexico City and abandoned his vocation as an architect, Francis Alÿs decided to make an art collection for himself. A young artist with limited resources, he had developed a fascination with various forms of artisanal production and an interest in the structure and role of the (art) market as it impacts economies of production.[16] He therefore resolved to build a collection from "hand-painted" copies of masterpieces of Western art, which he hoped to find in the flea markets and antique and junk stores he loved to frequent. However, he soon discovered that in lieu of the journeyman renderings of Raphael's *Sistine Madonna*, Leonardo's *Last Supper*, Jean-François Millet's *Angelus*, and like works that he assumed copyists would favor, he confronted pictures of a young female saint whom he quickly learned was Fabiola. Most of his early acquisitions were made serendipitously, on his wanderings through places as far-flung as Maastricht and Mexico City; more recently colleagues and acquaintances have supplemented his finds with theirs. Beginning as a modest, almost casual quest, Alÿs's deliberately low-key venture has evolved in unanticipated ways. Far from terminating when it reached the bounds of a domestically scaled collection, it is ongoing and open-ended: there is no inevitable, even conceivable, closure.

With the copy as its founding precept, Alÿs's collection ostensibly privileges the replica over the original, the anonymous over the renowned, the artisan or amateur over the professional, and the lowly or kitsch over the precious. This veneration of unknown artisans is fully in keeping with his practice, for he has long worked with craftsmen of various kinds, sometimes collaboratively, pooling and exchanging skills as needed. Similarly, his redirection of the putative collection into an investigatory venture dovetails with his willingness to allow the conception of any project, its governing logic and axioms, to move in directions he could not have fully foreseen at its start. Struck first by how little this subject was known to art-world professionals schooled, as he is, in traditional fine-art histories as well as in vanguard practices, and second by the breadth of the motif's geographical dispersion and its evident

15. Alÿs, e-mail message to the author, July 17, 2007.

16. See Olivier Debroise, "Entry and Exit: A New Internalization of Mexican Art 1987–1992," in *La Era de la Discrepancia: Arte y cultura visual en México/The Age of Discrepancies: Art and Visual Culture in Mexico, 1968–1997*, ed. Debroise (Mexico City: Universidad Nacional Autónoma de México, 2006), pp. 338–47.

abundance, Alÿs realized that he was faced not only with an alternative economy but with distinct if unfamiliar circuits of aesthetic appreciation (as well as spiritual faith).

The transformation of his highly personal approach to making a private collection into an investigation of issues grounded in cultural history crystallized with the first public presentation of the Fabiolas.[17] Within the short period of two years, Alÿs

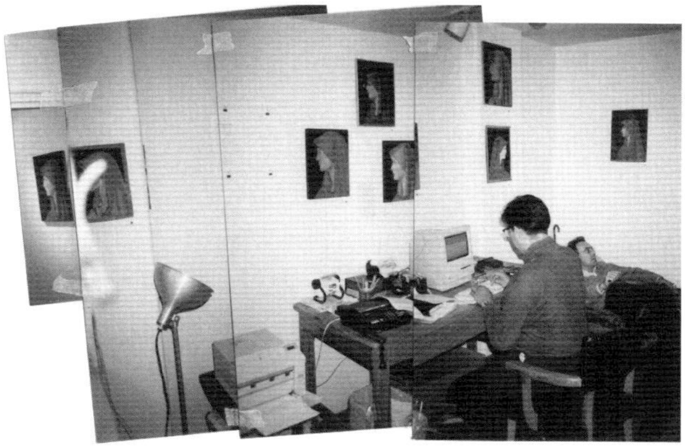

Fig. 5
"Fabiola: Una investigación de Francis Alÿs, en colaboración con Curare, Espacio Crítico para las Artes." Installation at Curare, Mexico City, September–October 1994.
Photo courtesy Cuauhtémoc Medina.

fig. 5 had acquired some twenty-eight examples. In September 1994, they were installed throughout Mexico City's vanguard venue Curare, in the stairwell and office, as well as the gallery proper. Founded in the late 1980s by a close-knit group of artists, art historians, critics, and theorists, Curare melded discursive investigation with exhibition programming, archiving, lecture series, and research. This event was presented under the rubric "Una investigación de Francis Alÿs, en colaboración con Curare, Espacio Crítico para las Artes." Jointly organized by three of the founders, Flavio Gonzalez Rossetti, Pascale Rossignol, and Olivier Debroise, it was deemed a "project" (as distinct from an exhibition) and was accompanied by a modest publication whose cover was made from shelving paper with a faux wood veneer pattern. Above

17. The formative influence of a research project that Alÿs undertook in Venice in the mid-1980s for his thesis as a student in architecture and urban planning should not be underestimated in any consideration of his reconceptualization of the Fabiola project as an "investigation." The object of that study was the symbolic, as well as practical, exclusion of animals and dogs from the public arena in the Veneto during the Renaissance, as La Serenissima sought to regulate its largely still-medieval urban entities. The city of Palmanova was thus projected ex-nihilo as the prominent model for the ideal city. Alÿs garnered much of the evidence with which he traced this exclusionary process from visual imagery, particularly from the paintings of the period. (The impact of these works on the formation of his painterly idiom has frequently been noted.)

a handwritten "signature" printed in silver ink was a small reproduction of Henner's portrait of the demure saint; Alÿs had purchased these images in considerable quantity from the vestry of a local church and then attached them one by one to each cover. If the design and production values made the publication appear more like an *fig. 6*

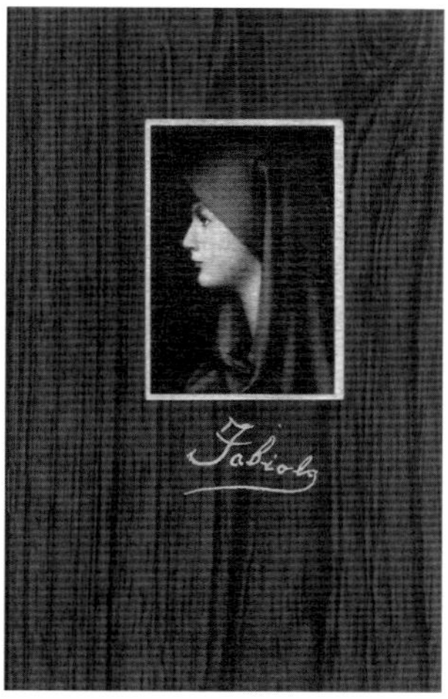

Fig. 6
Cover of *Fabiola*,
published by Curare,
Mexico City, 1994.

artist's book than a catalogue per se, the contents belied this impression. Both of its texts were printed in Spanish and English. The first, written by Alÿs and titled "Fabiola, or the Silent Multiplication," described the artist's plan to make a collection of copies of famous masterpieces for himself, and his surprise at the outcome: "Fabiola indicated a different criterion of what a masterwork could be."[18] Given this realization, the final sentence of his brief preface seems laced with irony: "It is an honor for me to show my collection to this educated audience."[19] The second, by art critic and historian Cuauhtémoc Medina, traces the shift away from the originating impulse in greater detail: motivated by an interest "in the process of the copy, and by the circulation of images that go beyond established art circles, Alÿs set out to find the painting(s) that average people have most frequently taken as models for reproduction."[20] Matching not the irony but the sentiment of Alÿs's concluding statement, Medina, too, was forced to concede: "There is no doubt that this hypothesis entailed a prejudice, namely that 'public taste' would appropriate the same referents that intellectuals believed capable of arousing tremendous popularity." His analysis of the image and its origins ends with the following series of questions:

18. Alÿs, "Fabiola, or the Silent Multiplication," in *Fabiola* (Mexico City: Curare, 1994), p. 4.

19. Ibid.

20. Medina, p. 11.

"How have we not before recognized this taste? How can we adapt this to our preconceived hierarchy of values?"[21]

The somewhat separate issue of what is the status, indeed the definition, of a copy in this particular instance proved of equal concern to both artist and critic alike. "Every time it is repainted the source is erased as a referent," Medina asserts. "The original is reproduced as an original."[22] There is no contradiction in this seeming contradiction: for, as paintings, these handmade artifacts have the aura and stature of originals, while as devotional objects or icons, they strictly replicate a prototype. To much of its intended or primary audience, the claim that these objects are copies is therefore meaningless.[23]

The final component in this revealing publication was a checklist of the twenty-eight items on display. For each entry, the name of the artist (where known), the place and date of acquisition, and the price paid were provided. The most expensive purchase was probably number twenty, signed "Dora 82," bought in Mexico City in 1994 for 180 Mexican pesos (see no. 075). By contrast, number thirteen, an anonymous example acquired in London in September 1993 cost five British pounds (see no. 103), and number seventeen, signed with the initials "R. B." was received as a gift in Maastricht, the Netherlands, in November 1993 (see no. 066). Eschewing such forms of data as dimensions, media, and materials, honored by the art historian and museum curator, this list favors information of prime interest not only to the collector but also to the social historian and ethnographer.

While Alÿs readily acknowledges that the totality of these objects constitutes a collection, he shies away from using the term "collector" to describe his relationship to this material, preferring in its stead "instigator."[24] Implicit in the latter is the notion of goading or urging forward, provoking and inciting; of open-ended agency; of a

21. Ibid.
22. Ibid., p. 12.
23. The notion that copying might (re)gain a generative potential within a contemporary art practice is something that Alÿs had already explored: This was precisely what he was attempting in a concurrent project undertaken with a group of *rotulistas*, or professional sign painters, whose activities are endemic to Mexico City.
24. Several years previously, Alÿs had made a work titled *The Collector* that comprised a small magnetized "dog," which he took on walks through the streets of the inner city. Each walk ended when the animal was completely covered with stray bits of metal that had fortuitously attached themselves to its body over the course of their wanderings. Three years later, he himself assumed that title when he wore a pair of magnetized shoes through the streets of Havana. The notion that informs both projects is of an accumulator of valueless material, whose identity and coherence are defined by a single simple characteristic, in this case, by being magnetic, rather than by any larger purpose or design. Structurally, this model is isomorphic to the initial conception underpinning his making of a collection: whatever he encountered that fit the single simple rubric of a handmade copy of an old master.

venture begun without any anticipation of closure; and of an act of initiation rather than of resolution. In this respect, the instigator is the very antithesis of the personal collector, that rare specimen so eloquently defined by Walter Benjamin, whose "true" collector is a singular type who "represents his fulfillment, insofar as he realizes the liberation of things from the bondage of utility."[25] That is, in seeking the completeness and integrity essential to forming a personal, as distinct from a merely private, collection, Benjamin's collector renders useless those objects he covets. By this criterion, Alÿs is the antipode of the collector. For through the Curare project, he began to speculate more on the former use value—the role and function—of these and similar unmoored artifacts. The presentation at Curare thus became the first in what is now conceived as an open-ended series of investigations based on its exhibition in sites that can act as discursive frameworks and, moreover, sites that can stimulate investigation in poetic as distinct from scientific or political terms.[26] Some years later, Alÿs mused on the evolution of his practice: "The intention is to generate situations, stories, events that can provoke a sudden, unexpected distancing from the immediate situation and, how can I put it, . . . shake up your assumptions about the way things are. . . . they . . . destabilize . . . that is, they open up, for just an instant—in a flash—a different vision of the situation, from the inside."[27]

Concurrent with the presentation of his Fabiola collection to that small if "educated" audience, Alÿs's practice centered on a number of ongoing bodies of work that responded to his immediate context. Several engaged his adopted milieu by making, taking, or finding images during his daily walks through the bustling historic inner city, the site of civic and regional government, as well as of a thriving gray-market economy that had grown in the aftermath of the devastation wrought by the 1985

25. Benjamin, quoted in Crimp, p. 72.

26. There have been several false starts in this investigation: The next time Alÿs presented the Fabiolas was in "Antechamber," a thematic group exhibition held at the Whitechapel Art Gallery, London, in 1997. Each artist in the show was asked to present a work of his or her own together with a second work that was particularly meaningful to him or her. Alÿs presented a sampling of works from an ongoing project with the *rotulistas*; he fulfilled the requirement of a work that was inspiring to him by presenting a selection of fifty Fabiolas. He found, however, that the juxtaposition of copies of two quite different orders brought more confusion than enlightenment to the role played by notions of authorship, copy, and original in what were for him quite distinct projects. The third venue for the Fabiola project was also planned for 1997, the second biennial of Saaremaa, Estonia. (See note 7.) After his experience at the Whitechapel, Alÿs began to refine his exhibition strategies; thereafter, he tended to favor showing one project at a time, whether new or not. For more comprehensive shows, he devised a thematic, such as works relating to the locus of his studio in Mexico City or to the subject of the rehearsal.

27. Alÿs, "Fragments of a Conversation in Buenos Aires," in *A Story of Deception: Patagonia 2003–2006* (Buenos Aires: Fundación Eduardo F. Constantini, 2006), p. 82.

earthquake. One particularly rich series, the photographically based *Ambulantes* (1992–2006), comprises images of pedestrians pushing and heaving the tools of their trade or carting and hauling prized goods and essential supplies. Walks also served to record the hordes of street dogs and people slumbering in the downtown milieu (*Sleepers*, 1999–2006). Wandering through run-down but lively neighborhoods, where he once lived and still has a studio, provided the artist with occasions for scru-

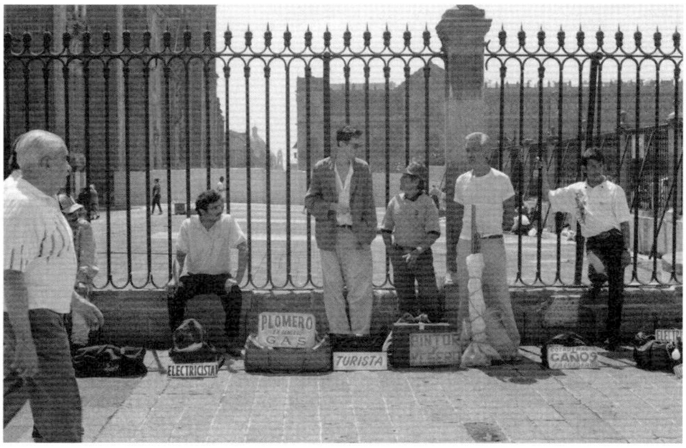

Fig. 7
Francis Alÿs, *Turista*, 1994. Photographic documentation of an action, Mexico City.
Courtesy of the artist and David Zwirner Gallery.

fig. 7 tinizing not merely the street life but his own place within it. In another piece, which again takes the form of documentary photography, he appears among a line of workers seeking employment who advertise their skills by placing a small sign with the name of their trade at their feets, while they wait outside the cathedral for prospective employers. Alÿs's sign identifies his calling as that of a "tourist." What he (as a returning immigrant) has to offer derives from the fact that he is an outsider who special-

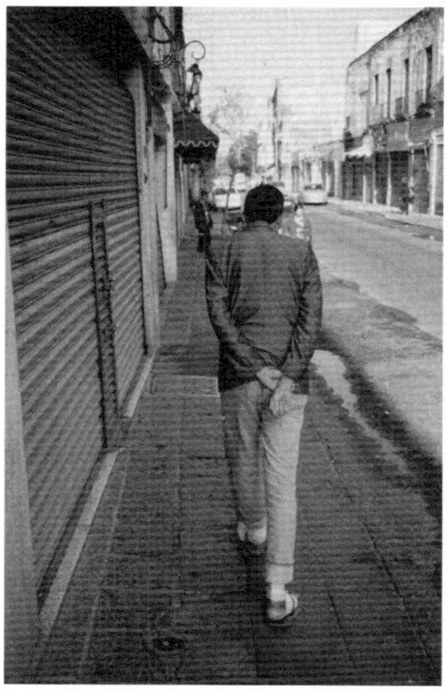

Fig. 8
Francis Alÿs, *Doppelgänger*, 1999–present. One of eighty 35 mm slides.
Courtesy of the artist and David Zwirner Gallery.

izes in sites/sights, a peripatetic observer who is drawn by what, to him, must appear novel and unfamiliar.[28]

This abiding preoccupation with his personal and professional identity in his chosen habitat similarly fuels *Doppelgänger* (1999–present), a series of photographs of pedestrians who seemed momentarily to Alÿs to resemble himself, when glimpsed either from behind or at a distance; alter egos, they presumably belonged in this environment in ways he felt he did not. And, in yet another, related work, *The Swap* (1995), again recorded photographically, he mimics the behavior of people who stand outside subway entrances trading goods over the course of a day. Contrasting with these more conceptual and ephemeral engagements, Alÿs also took up the practice *fig. 8*

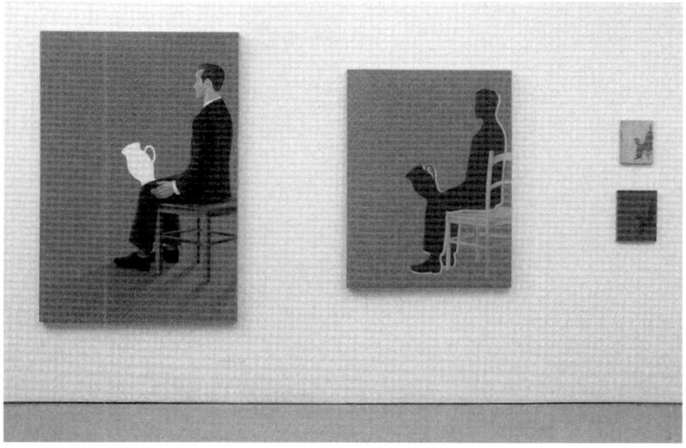

Fig. 9
Francis Alÿs, in collaboration with Juan Garcia and Emilio Rivera, *Untitled (Sign Painting Project)*, 1993–97.
Courtesy of the artist and David Zwirner Gallery.

of painting, basing his style and iconography in part on the work of *rotulistas*, or sign painters, whose ability to communicate succinct but vivid messages is locally in high demand by the largely illiterate population who engage in a mostly preindustrial economy. His burgeoning interest in painting quickly spawned an interactive collaboration, in which—far from simply making copies of Alÿs's "originals"—the sign painters created their own variants, to which Alÿs, in turn, responded in a multistage dialogue. Assembled into a catalogue of wares that could be commissioned by prospective buyers, these works were marketed according to the size of the painting and amount of labor involved, rather than by reference to the identity of its author. By forsaking conventional hierarchies that privilege the touch of the fine artist over that of the craftsman, Alÿs sought to create an alternative economy in which every contributor could make a living. *fig. 9*

28. In 1993 and 1994, Alÿs relocated to Brussels for part of the year to teach in a university architectural department. This job provided him with the means to live in Mexico City for the rest of the year. Thereafter, he resided full-time in his preferred city, supported by his art practice.

At the core of all of these early works is Alÿs's ambiguous role as participant/ observer of a cultural scene he inhabited and engaged but did not yet feel fully part of. As such, it conjures the quintessential trope of the ethnographer who, while doing fieldwork, reflexively observes the outcome, recognizing the role that his/her own subjectivity plays in the interpretative process. For Alÿs, the stakes are high in this embrace of ethnography's methodological paradigm—as the traces of self-mocking irony in certain of these works attest. A certain pathos ensues when the subject of one's study is the site not simply of projected fantasies of belonging but of self-displacement.

Even as he began to work elsewhere for specific exhibitions abroad or on site-related commissions, Alÿs continued to base his practice on taking walks. Paseos now became the vehicle through which he could fluidly and anonymously insert himself into unfamiliar milieus and, so, begin to learn something of the contexts in which *fig. 10* he was about to work and in which the work would be received. *Sometimes doing something poetic can become political and sometimes doing something political can become poetic* (2004), the most recent instance of this genre, involved retracing a

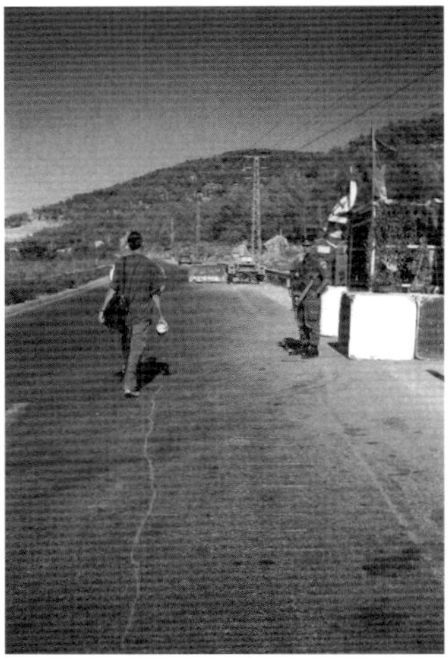

Fig. 10
Sometimes doing something poetic can become political and sometimes doing something political can become poetic, 2004. Photographic documentation of an action, Jerusalem.
Courtesy of the artist and David Zwirner Gallery.

historic boundary, once drawn with a green pencil on a map of Jerusalem, with green paint spilled from a can that the artist carried along that hypothetical border in a walk across present-day Jerusalem. Although typologically this piece has affinities with earlier pieces made in Mexico City and São Paulo, the social and political dimension of each is very different. In commentaries on Alÿs's walks, affinities are often persuasively drawn with the Situationists' concept of *dérive*, while Baudelaire's *flâneur* is posed as their antimony. But it is Michel de Certeau's characterization of the place of walking in the modern urban environment that ultimately seems most pertinent, and that best frames this aspect of Alÿs's practice, as Cuauhtémoc Medina, among others, has recognized. "Alÿs's walks were conceived on the assumption," he writes, "that they would be read, thought, seen, imagined and retold by others, and that their agency would depend on their dissemination as stories. . . . This is similar to what Certeau had envisioned when suggesting that 'Physical moving about has the itinerant function of yesterday's or today's "superstitions." Travel (like walking) is a substitute for the legends that used to open up space to something different.'"[29]

The primary distinction between this Fabiola project and most of Alÿs's more recent projects is that, normally, the latter evolve in relation to a specific context or venue and are then dispersed to museums and galleries as "nonsites," to borrow Robert Smithson's term: comprising documentary composites of textual and visual material, research tools, videos, photographs, notes, letters, sketches, and the like, those works are also usually supplemented by publications that add additional layers of critique from various disciplinary positions. The (non)site that allows such juxtapositions of miscellaneous and heterogeneous materials is, as Michel Foucault has shown, the site of discourse; and, hence, for Alÿs the place where stories, fables, rumors, and the like may be both generated and confirmed. Originating outside his art practice, this Fabiola endeavor only subsequently acquired a site-related reference: a historicizing context. But, once again, the principal role of that frame or filter was to provide a discursive ground cognate with that established by the documentary compendia in a work such as *Sometimes doing something.* Whether or not the Fabiola project is formally acknowledged as a work within Alÿs's oeuvre is thus of far less moment than recognition of the remarkable degree to which it prefigures the ethics, politics, and poetics of his maturing practice.[30] In short, it signals the adoption of a more proactive role, that of "instigator/investigator," alongside that of participant/observer, so memorably enshrined in the wryly freighted moniker "tourist."[31]

What has not, however, been analyzed to date is the extent to which more broadly and fully, in its ethic as much as its aesthetic, Alÿs's practice is aligned with that of Certeau. In his introduction to *The Practice of Everyday Life*, the French sociologist outlines the scope of his study in the following terms: "The purpose of this work is to make explicit the systems of operational combination . . . which also compose a 'culture,' and to bring to light the models of action characteristic of users whose

29. Medina, "Fable Power," in *Francis Alÿs* (London: Phaidon, 2007), p. 78.

30. Alÿs is, of course, aware that, as a collection made by a well-recognized artist rather than by, say, a dentist or an antiquarian, it has a certain cache and, presumably, an enhanced market value.

31. In a number of subsequent works, based in walks taken while traveling abroad, Alÿs occasionally again exploited the role of the tourist. See, for example, *The Loop* (1997), with documentation of his related e-mail correspondence with Olivier Debroise, and *Narcotourism* (1996).

status as the dominated element in society (a status that does not mean they are either passive or docile) is concealed by the euphemistic term 'consumers.'"[32] Assessing what had to that date been undertaken, this highly influential cultural historian noted, "Many, often remarkable, works have sought to study the *representations of a society*, on the one hand, and its *modes of behavior* on the other. Building on our knowledge of these social phenomena," he concluded, "it seems both possible and necessary to determine the *use* to which they are put by groups or individuals."[33] Alÿs's practice vis-à-vis Mexico where he personally and professionally grounds and identifies himself, similarly engages these dual modalities: the representations of a society and the behavior expressed in the most public of arenas, everyday urban life. Those projects he makes in Mexico City are based on intimate knowledge mined from extensive observation and study; those conceived elsewhere, however, are the products of different tactics: sometimes he requires an intense if necessarily short-lived immersion in endemic situations, as was the case with *Bridge/Puente* (2006), which depended on a collaboration between communities of fishermen in Cuba and Florida. Sometimes they involve more opportunistic interventions in response to unique sets of circumstances. Such, for example, was the case with *The Modern Procession* (2002), conceived to mark the enforced exodus of the Museum of Modern Art's collection from its permanent home on West Fifty-third Street in Manhattan to temporary exile in Queens.

The focus of Certeau's book is on neither behaviors nor images per se but on their implication—the way that, together, these ruses, tactics, and various kinds of poaching and appropriation, when pushed to their ideal limits, "compose the network of an antidiscipline."[34] Wresting and negotiating agency under the radar of dominant and official forms, or even within their very matrix, they become the means by which people everywhere surreptitiously empower themselves, enriching and enhancing their lives. Other, related modes evolve more serendipitously, by default as much as design. "Although they are composed with the vocabularies of established languages," Certeau writes, "and although they remain subordinated to the prescribed syntactical forms . . . the[ir] trajectories trace out the ruses of other interests and desires that are neither determined nor captured by the systems in which they develop."[35] The Fabiolas, too, are clearly "composed in the vocabularies of established languages" (namely, the well-recognized academic idiom of late-nineteenth-century painting); and they, too, "remain subordinated to the prescribed syntactical forms" (since this saint was never the subject of a major devotion). In their singular melding of the

32. Michel de Certeau, introduction to *The Practice of Everyday Life* (Berkeley: University of California Press, 1984), pp. XI–XII.

33. Ibid., p. XII. My italics.

34. Ibid., p. XV.

35. Ibid., pp. XVIII.

handwrought and the copied, as in their low-key but extensive infiltration into the lives of the faithful worldwide, these devotional images may be seen as readymade exemplars of Certeau's thesis. It is therefore not surprising that for institutionalized, that is, academic and art-world, audiences Fabiola's roles and functions have almost completely eluded identification and analysis. In Alÿs's more recent projects, the pivotal event—and generative core—of the project is organized in ways that, symbolically and structurally, conform again to Certeau's model of an antidiscipline.

Encountered in the context of the Hispanic Society where they fit almost seamlessly—as if they had long been housed there—the Fabiolas startle the unsuspecting viewer. Hesitation (Is this some Duchampian prank?) and puzzlement (Who is responsible for this? Who is the curator? Who is the collector? Are they one and the same?) perhaps follow. Yet the danger of ideological condescension, ever present in ethnographic inquiry, is avoided. The "normality and inevitability" in the installation, reinforced by the tactical absence of any author, allows wonder and fascination to prevail. "Through the gratuity or absurd quality of the poetic act," Alÿs argues, "art provokes a moment of suspension of meaning, a brief sensation of senselessness that reveals the absurd of the situation, and, through this act of transgression, that makes you step back or step out and resume/revise your *a prioris* regarding this reality. . . . In the best of all cases, it can open up—even if just for a few seconds—a new, other, perspective on the situation."[36]

36. Alÿs, "Fragments of a Conversation in Buenos Aires," p. 82.

LETTER 77

To Oceanus on the Death of Fabiola

Saint Jerome

Many years have passed since I consoled the venerated Paula, while her wound was still fresh, for the falling asleep of Blesilla. Four summers have rolled by since I wrote to Bishop Heliodorus a funeral panegyric on Nepotian, spending all the strength that I possessed in giving expression to my grief. About two years have elapsed since I sent a brief letter to my dear Pammachius on the sudden passing of his Paulina, for I blushed to say more to so learned a man or to repeat to him his own thoughts, lest I should seem, not so much to be comforting a friend, as in foolish ostentation to be instructing one already perfect. To-day, my son Oceanus, the task of duty you impose upon me is one that I gladly accept and would even seek unasked; for dealing with new virtues I shall make an old subject fresh. In those other cases I had to assuage a mother's love, an uncle's grief, and a husband's yearning; and as the persons differed I had to apply from the Scriptures a different remedy.

On this occasion you give me as my subject Fabiola, the glory of the Christians, the wonder of the Gentiles, the sorrow of the poor, and the consolation of the monks. Whatever point I take first pales in comparison with what is to come. Shall I tell of her fastings? Her alms are greater still. Shall I praise her humility? It is outstripped by the ardor of her faith. Shall I mention her studied squalor, her plebeian dress, and the slave's garb she choose in condemnation of silken robes? It is a greater thing to change one's disposition than to change one's dress. We part with arrogance less easily than with gold and jewels. Even when these are thrown away, we sometimes pride ourselves on our ostentatious shabbiness and make a bid for popular favor by offering poverty as its price. A virtue that is concealed and cherished in the inner consciousness looks to God alone as judge. So the eulogy I bestow upon her must be altogether new: I must neglect all the rules of rhetoric and begin my story at the cradle of her conversion and penitence. Others perhaps might remember their school-days and bring forward Quintus Maximus:

"The man who by delaying
saved the state,"

and with him the whole Fabian family. They might tell of their conflicts and describe their battles, and boast that Fabiola had come of so noble a line, showing in the root a glory which they could not find in the branch. I for my part, who am a lover of the inn at Bethlehem, and the Lord's stable where the Virgin in childbirth brought forth an infant God, I will bring forward a handmaid of Christ who shall rely not on the fame of ancient history but on the humility of the Church.

As at the very outset there is a rock in the path, and I am faced by the storm of censure that was directed against her for having taken a second husband and abandoned her first, I shall not praise her for her conversion until I have cleared her from this charge. We are told that her first husband was a man of such heinous vices that even a prostitute or a common slave could not have put up with them. If I describe them, I shall mar the heroism of the woman, who preferred to bear the blame of separation rather than to expose to shame the man who was one body with her, and thus reveal the stains upon his character. This only I will say, and it is a plea sufficient to excuse a chaste matron and a Christian wife. The Lord ordained that a wife must not be put away except for fornication, and that, if she was put away, she must remain unmarried. A command that is given to men applies logically also to women. It cannot be that an adulterous wife should be put away and an unfaithful husband retained. If "he which is joined to a harlot is one body," she who is joined to a filthy whoremonger is one body with him also. The laws of Caesar are different from the laws of Christ: Papinian commands one thing, our Paul another. Among the Romans men's unchastity goes unchecked; seduction and adultery are condemned, but free permission is given to lust to range the brothels and to have slave girls, as though it were a person's rank and not the sensual pleasure that constituted the offense. With us what is unlawful for women is equally unlawful for men, and as both sexes serve God they are bound by the same conditions. Fabiola, as men say, put away a vicious husband; she put away a man who was guilty of this and that crime; she put him away because—I almost mentioned the scandal which the whole neighborhood proclaimed but which his wife alone refused to reveal. If she is blamed because after repudiating her husband she did not remain unmarried, I will readily admit her fault, provided that I may put in the plea of necessity. "It is better," says the apostle, "to marry than to burn." She was a very young woman and she could not remain a widow. She saw another law in her members warring against the law of her mind, and she felt herself dragged like a chained captive into carnal intercourse. She thought it better to confess her weakness openly and to accept the dark stain that such a lamentable marriage would bring, rather than to claim to be the wife of one husband and under that disguise to ply the harlot's trade. The same apostle expresses his wish that "young widows should marry, bear children, and give no handle to calumny." And then at once he gives his reason: "For some are already turned aside after Satan." Fabiola therefore had convinced herself, and thought that she was justified in putting away her husband. She did not know the Gospel's strict ordinance, which precludes Christian women from marrying again in their first husband's lifetime, whatever their case may be. Thus she evaded the other assaults of the devil, but this one wound from him she unwittingly received.

But why do I linger over the forgotten past, seeking to excuse a fault for which she herself confessed her penitence? Who would believe that after the death of her second husband, at a time when widows, having shaken off the yoke of slavery, are wont to grow careless and indulge in license, frequenting the public baths, flitting to and fro in the squares, showing their harlot faces everywhere—who, I say, would believe that it was then that she came to herself, put on sackcloth and made public confession of error. On the eve of passover, in the presence of all Rome, she took her stand among the other penitents in the church of that Lateranus who perished formerly by Caesar's sword. There before bishop, presbyters, and weeping populace she exposed to view her disheveled hair, wan face, soiled hands, and dust-stained neck. What sins would not such lamentation purge away? What stains so deep that these tears would not wash them out? By a threefold confession Peter annulled his threefold denial. Aaron did a sacrilegious act by fashioning a calf's head in gold; but his brother's prayers made amends. David, that saintly and most merciful man, committed both murder and adultery; but he atoned for it by fasting for seven days. He lay on the ground, he groveled in the ashes, he forgot his royal power, he sought for light in the darkness. He turned his eyes only to Him whom he had offended and cried with a lamentable voice: "Against thee, thee only have I sinned, and done this evil in thy sight," and, "Restore unto me the joy of thy salvation and uphold me with thy free spirit." So it came about that he who by his virtues taught me first how I might stand and not fall, by his penitence taught me how if I fell I might rise again. Do we read of any among the kings so wicked as Ahab, of whom the Scripture says: "There was none like unto Ahab which did sell himself to work wickedness in the sight of the Lord?" But when he was rebuked by Elijah for shedding Naboth's blood and heard the prophet threaten him with God's wrath: "Thou hast killed and taken possession: behold I will bring evil upon thee and will take away thy posterity," and so on, then: "he rent his clothes, and put sackcloth upon his flesh and fasted in sackcloth and went softly. Then came the word of the Lord to Elijah the Tishbite, saying: "Seest thou how Ahab humbleth himself before me? Because he humbleth himself before me, I will not bring the evil in his days." O happy penitence, which drew God's eyes to itself, and by a confession of error changed the sentence of the Lord's wrath! The same conduct is attributed to Manasseh in the Chronicles, to Nineveh in the book of the prophet Jonah, and to the publican in the Gospel. The first not only earned God's pardon but regained his kingdom; the second broke the force of God's impending anger; the third smiting his breast with his fists would not lift his eyes to heaven, and yet by the humble confession of his faults he went away more justified than the Pharisee with his arrogant boasting of his virtues. This, however, is not the place to preach penitence, or to say of it, as though I were writing against Montanus and Novatus, that it is a victim well pleasing to the Lord and that a broken spirit is God's sacrifice. Nor will I quote the words: "I prefer the repentance of a sinner rather than his death," or "Arise, arise, O Jerusalem," or any other of the many sayings which are noised abroad by the trumpets of the prophets.

This one thing I will say, for it is both useful to my readers and pertinent to the present case. Fabiola was not ashamed of the Lord on earth, and He will not be ashamed of her in heaven. She laid bare her wound to all, and Rome beheld with tears the scar upon her livid body. She uncovered her limbs, bared her head, and closed her mouth. She did not enter God's church but like Miriam, the sister of Moses, sat apart outside the camp, until the priest who had cast her out should call her back again. She came down from her throne of luxury, she took up the millstone and ground meal, with unshod feet she passed through rivers of tears. She sat upon coals of fire, and these became her aid. She beat the face by which she had won her second husband's love, she abhorred all jewelry, she could not bear even to look upon fine linen, she shrank from all adornment. If she had committed adultery her grief could not have been greater, and she went to the expense of many remedies in her eagerness to cure one wound.

I have lingered long in describing Fabiola's penitence, and my barque has grounded in shallow waters; but I wished to open up a wider and unimpeded field for her praises. When she was restored to communion before the eyes of the whole church, what did she do? Did she forget her sorrows in the midst of happiness, and determine after being shipwrecked to face once more the dangers of the main? Nay, she preferred to break up and sell all that she could lay hands on of her property—it was a large one and suitable to her rank—and when she had turned it into money she disposed of everything for the benefit of the poor. First of all she founded an infirmary and gathered into it sufferers from the streets, giving their poor bodies worn with sickness and hunger all a nurse's care. Need I describe here the diverse troubles from which human beings suffer, the maimed noses, the lost eyes, the scorched feet, the leprous arms, the swollen bellies, the shrunken thighs, the dropsical legs, and the diseased flesh alive with hungry worms? How often did she carry on her own shoulders poor filthy wretches tortured by epilepsy! How often did she wash away the purulent matter from wounds which others could not even endure to look upon! She gave food with her own hand, and even when a man was but a breathing corpse, she would moisten his lips with drops of water. I know that many wealthy and devout persons by reason of their weak stomachs carry on this work of mercy by the agency of others, and show mercy with the purse, not with the hand. I do not blame nor do I by any means construe their lack of fortitude as lack of faith. But while I excuse their weakness, I extol to the skies the ardent zeal that perfect courage possesses. A great faith makes light of discomfort: it knows the retribution that fell upon the rich man clothed in purple, who in his pride refused Lazarus's aid. The sufferer whom we despise and cannot bear to behold, whose very aspect turns our stomachs, is a man like ourselves, formed of the same clay, made out of the same elements. Whatever he suffers we may possibly suffer also. Let us regard his wounds as our own, and then all our lack of sympathy for others will be overcome by our pity for ourselves.

"Had I a hundred tongues, a hundred mouths
With voice of brass, I could not tell the names"

of all the maladies which Fabiola treated. She was, indeed, such a comforter that many poor people who were well fell to envying the sick. Not but what she showed the same generosity to the clergy, monks, and virgins. What monastery was there which her purse did not aid? What naked or bedridden sufferer did she not supply with clothes? On what indigent person did she not pour out her swift and lavish donations? Rome was not large enough for her compassionate kindness. She went from island to island, and traveled round the Etruscan Sea, and through the Volscian province, with its lonely curving bays, where bands of monks have taken up their home, bestowing her bounty either in person or by the agency of holy men of the faith.

Then suddenly, and to every one's surprise, she sailed to Jerusalem, where she was welcomed by a great concourse of people, and for a short time was my guest. When I remember that meeting, I seem to see her still as I saw her then. Blessed Jesus, with what fervor and zeal did she study the sacred volumes! In her eagerness to satisfy her hunger, she ran through the prophets, the gospels, and the psalms; she suggested questions and stored up my answers in her heart's repository. Nor did her eagerness to hear ever bring with it satiety; increasing her knowledge she also increased her sorrow, and as though oil were cast upon fire she supplied fuel ever for a more burning zeal. One day we were occupied with Moses's Numbers, and she modestly questioned me as to the meaning of its mass of names. Why was it, she asked, that individual tribes were grouped in so many different ways in different places, and how did it happen that the soothsayer Balaam in prophesying the future mysteries of Christ foretold His coming more plainly than almost any of the prophets.

I replied as best I could, and I think I satisfied her inquiries. So she unrolled the book further, and came to the passage where the list is given of all the halting places by which the people on leaving Egypt made their way to the river Jordan. She asked me the meaning and the origin of each name, and in some cases I hesitated, in others I hurried through without stumbling, in very many I had frankly to confess ignorance. Thereupon she began to press me harder, expostulating with me as though it were not allowed me to be in ignorance of what I do not know, and declaring that she herself was unworthy of understanding such mysteries. Why say more? I was ashamed to refuse her, and she compelled me to promise a special work on this subject for her use. Up till this moment I have deferred writing it; but my delay, I now see, was God's will, and it is now consecrated to her memory. As a previous treatise addressed to her clothed her in priestly vestments, so now she may rejoice that she has passed through the wilderness of this world and come at last to the land of promise.

But let me continue the task I have begun. While I was seeking a dwelling suitable for so great a lady, whose desire for solitude included an unwillingness not to visit the place where Mary once lodged, suddenly messengers flew this way and that and the whole Eastern world trembled. We were told that swarms of Huns had poured forth from the distant Sea of Azov, midway between the icy river Tanais and the savage tribes of the Massagetae, where the gates of Alexander keep back the barbarians behind the rocky Caucasus. Flying hither and thither on their swift steeds, said our informants, these invaders were filling the whole world with bloodshed and panic. At that time the Roman army was absent, being kept in Italy by reason of civil war. Of this race Herodotus tells us that under Darius, king of the Medes, they held the East captive for twenty years, and exacted a yearly tribute from the Egyptians and the Ethiopians. May Jesus save the Roman world from such wild beasts in the future! Everywhere their approach was unexpected, they outstripped rumor by their speed, and they spared neither religion nor rank nor age; nay, even for wailing infants they had no pity. Children were forced to die, who had only just begun to live, and in ignorance of their fate smiled amid the brandished weapons of the foe. The general report was that they were making for Jerusalem, and that it was their excessive greed for gold that urged them to flock to that city. The walls of Antioch, neglected in the careless days of peace, were hastily repaired. Tyre, desirous of cutting herself off from the land, sought again her ancient island. We too were compelled to prepare ships, and to wait on the seashore as a precaution against the enemy's arrival; to fear the barbarians more than shipwreck, however fierce the winds might be; for we had to think not so much of our own lives as of the chastity of our virgins. At that time also there was a certain dissension amongst us, and our domestic quarrels seemed more important than any fighting with barbarians. I myself clung to my fixed abode in the East; and could not give up my inveterate longing for the Holy Land. Fabiola, however, who only had her traveling baggage and was a stranger in every land, returned to her native city to live in poverty where she had been rich, to lodge in the house of another, she who had once entertained many guests, and—not to prolong my story unduly—to pay over to the poor before the eyes of Rome all that she had sold with Rome for witness.

This only do I grieve for, that we in the Holy Land lost in her a most precious jewel. Rome recovered what she had lost, and the shameless tongue of slander was confuted by the testimony of the heathens' own eyes. Let others praise her pity, her humility, her faith: I will rather extol the ardor of her soul. The treatise in which as a young man I urged Heliodorus to be a hermit she knew by heart, and when she looked upon the walls of Rome she complained that she was their prisoner. Forgetful of her sex, unmindful of her frailty, she craved only for solitude and was in truth where her soul lingered. Her friends' advice could not restrain her, so anxious was she to escape from the fetters of Rome. She said that to weigh out money and distribute it carefully showed a lack of faith. She desired not to hand over the task of almsgiving to others, but to spend all that she possessed, and then herself to receive a dole in Christ's name. In such haste was she, and so impatient of delay, that you might have thought her always on the brink of departure. So, as she was ever making ready, death could not find her unprepared.

As I sing her praises, my dear Pammachius suddenly rises before me. Paulina sleeps that he may keep vigil; she has gone before her husband, that may leave him behind to serve Christ. He was his wife's heir, but others now possess that inheritance. A man and a woman contended for the privilege of setting up Abraham's tent in the harbor of Rome; and this was the struggle between the two, who should be first in that contest of kindness. Each won and each lost. Both confess themselves victors and vanquished, for what each desired they carried out together. They join purses and combine their plans, harmony might increase what rivalry would have wasted. Hardly said, the thing was done; a hostel was purchased and a crowd flocked to it for hospitality; for "There is no more travail in Jacob nor distress in Israel." The seas brought in travelers for the land to welcome. Rome sent others, who hastened to enjoy the comforts of the mild shore before they set sail. What Publius did once in the island of Malta for a single apostle and—not to leave room for contradiction—for a single ship, they did many times for many men. Not only did they relieve the wants of the destitute; their generosity was at every one's service and provided even for those who possessed something themselves. The whole world heard that a Home for Strangers had been founded in the port of Rome, and Britain knew in the summer what Egypt and the Parthians had learned in the spring.

It is written: "All things work together for good to them that fear God," and in the death of the noble lady the words have been proved true. She had a presentiment of what was to happen, and had written to several monks, that they might come and relieve her from the heavy burden under which she groaned, and that she might make to herself friends of the mammon of unrighteousness, to receive her into everlasting habitations. They came, and were welcomed as friends; she fell asleep, as she had wished, and having at length rid herself of her burden, soared more lightly to heaven. How great had been the wonder of Fabiola's life Rome showed when she was dead. She had scarcely drawn her last breath and paid the debt of her soul to Christ, when

"Flying rumor heralding
such woe"

brought the peoples of the whole city to attend her funeral. Psalms re-echoed loudly and cries of "Alleluia" shook the gilded roofs of the temples.

"Young men and old unite in
song to praise
A woman and her fame to
heaven raise."

Not so gloriously did Furius triumph over the Gauls, Papirius over the Samnites, Scipio over Numantia, or Pompey over the

peoples of the Black Sea. They conquered physical strength, she overcame spiritual iniquities.
I hear it still: the crowds that went before the bier, the swaying multitude that attended her obsequies in throngs, no streets, no colonnades could contain, no overhanging roofs could hold the eager onlookers. On that day Rome saw all her peoples gathered together. Every one flattered himself that he had a share in the glory of her penitence. No wonder that men exulted in her salvation, seeing that the angels in heaven rejoiced over her conversion.

This, the best gift of my aged powers, I present to you, Fabiola, as a funeral offering of respect. I have praised virgins, widows, and married women who have kept their vestments always white, "who follow the Lamb whithersoever He goeth." Blessed indeed is the praise of her whose life has been stained by no foulness. Let envy hold aloof, let jealousy be silent. If the father of the house be good, why should our eye be evil? She who fell among thieves has been carried home upon Christ's shoulders. "In our father's house there are many mansions." "Where sin hath abounded, grace hath much more abounded." "To whom more is forgiven, the same loveth more."

Translated by F. A. Wright

Catalogue of Works

The following catalogue was compiled by Francesca Esmay, conservator, Dia Art Foundation. Indistinct inscriptions and signatures are indicated in red type.

DIMENSIONS: 13 ¾ x 8 ⅞ x ⅛ inches (34.9 x 22.5 x 0.32 cm)
DATE: Unknown
MEDIA: Paint on canvas mounted on paperboard
CONDITION: Good
PROVENANCE: Flea market, Brussels, Belgium, 1995, 50 Belgian francs
NOTES: Painting support is an advertising remnant; the verso depicts a woman's profile in the position typical of Fabiola portraits. Signed "A. Thues."

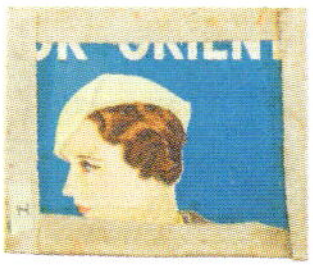

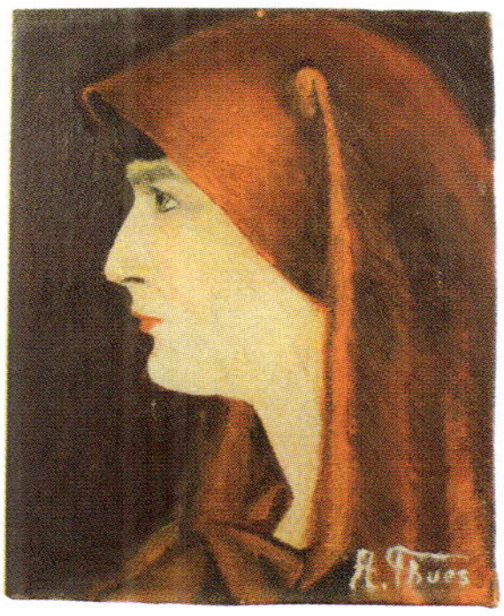

001

DIMENSIONS: 10 ¾ x 7 ¾ x ¾ inches (27.3 x 19.7 x 1.91 cm)
DATE: Unknown
MEDIA: Paint on canvas
CONDITION: Good
PROVENANCE: Rotterdam, Netherlands, 2002
NOTES: Subject's hood and cloak exhibit extensive and complex draping.

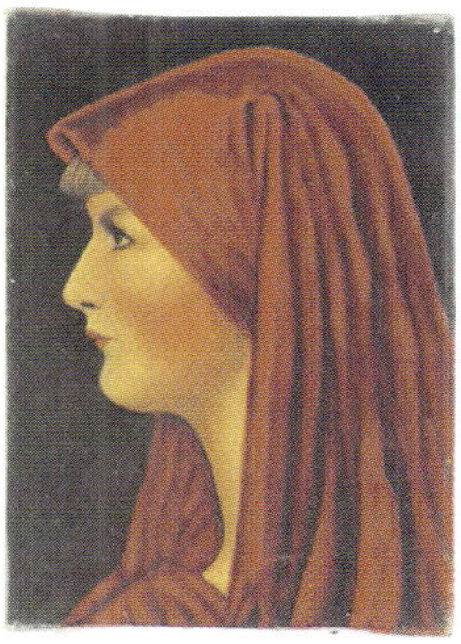

002

DIMENSIONS: 10 ¼ x 9 ⅛ x ¼ inches (26 x 23.2 x 0.64 cm)
DATE: Unknown
MEDIA: Probably pastel on paperboard with a coating or fixative, mounted on wood composite panel
CONDITION: Fair—Surface has unknown accretion, possibly biological and appears to be a "bloom." There are also small losses along a prior frame edge.
PROVENANCE: Braderie de Lille, France, 1995, 20 French francs
NOTES: Subject exhibits a common Fabiola feature, in that there are two distinct segments of the bangs, one hanging naturally down, the other extending up beyond the edge of the hood.

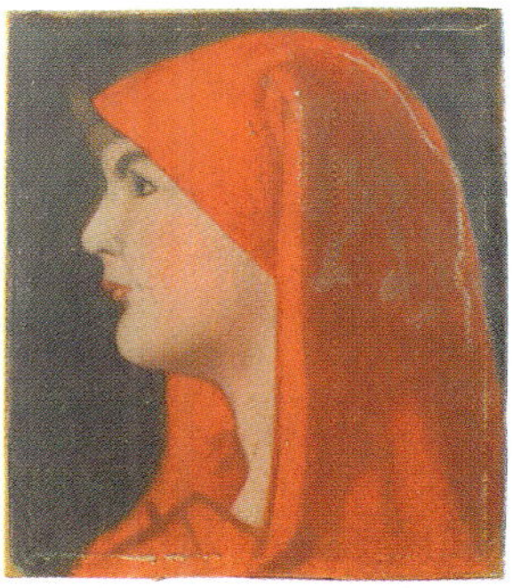

003

DIMENSIONS: 12 ½ x 9 ⅜ x ¼ inches (31.8 x 23.8 x 0.64 cm)
DATE: Unknown
MEDIA: Paint on panel or composite board
CONDITION: Good/Fair—There are several surface scuffs and abrasions throughout.
PROVENANCE: Kemmel, Belgium, September 7, 2003, 2 euros
NOTES: Signed "Vanachter."

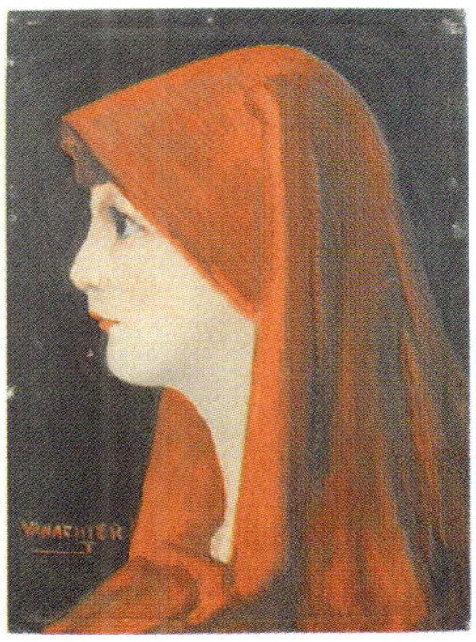

004

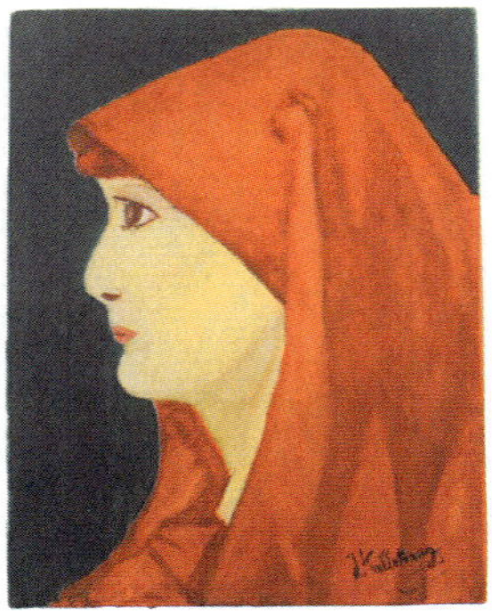

005

DIMENSIONS:	11 ¾ x 9 ½ x ½ inches (29.8 x 24.1 x 1.27 cm)
DATE:	Unknown
MEDIA:	Paint on canvas
CONDITION:	Good
PROVENANCE:	Mechelen, Belgium, November 1, 1999, 50 euros
NOTES:	The subject's eye has an odd scale in relation to nose, mouth, and jaw. Signed "J. Kollebaug."

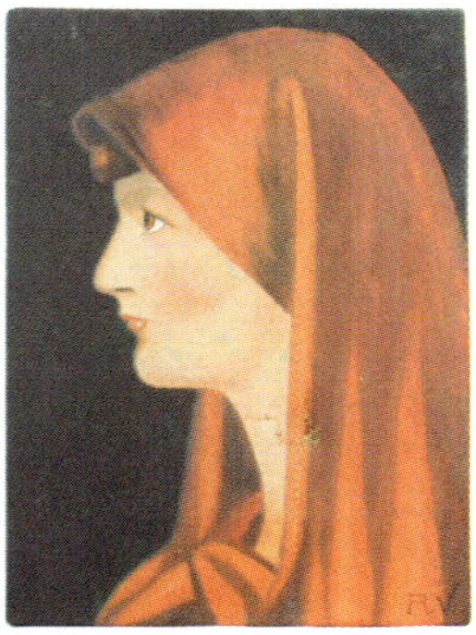

006

DIMENSIONS:	11 x 8 ¼ x ⅝ inches (27.9 x 21 x 1.59 cm)
DATE:	Unknown
MEDIA:	Paint on canvas
CONDITION:	Fair/Poor—There is a major tear in the canvas support in the area of the subject's neck—approx. 3" square.
PROVENANCE:	Douai, France, September 21, 2003, 1.5 euros
NOTES:	Signed "R. V."

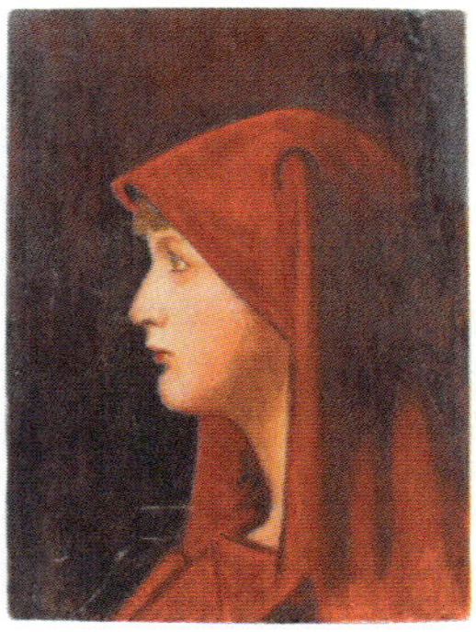

008

DIMENSIONS:	12 ⅝ x 9 ½ x ½ inches (32.1 x 24.1 x 1.27 cm)
DATE:	Unknown
MEDIA:	Paint on canvas
CONDITION:	Good/Fair—There are several surface scuffs along the bottom proper right area.
PROVENANCE:	Paris (Porte de Vichy), France, January 2, 2001
NOTES:	This work loosely resembles the depiction of Fabiola in reproductions of the Jean-Jacques Henner original.

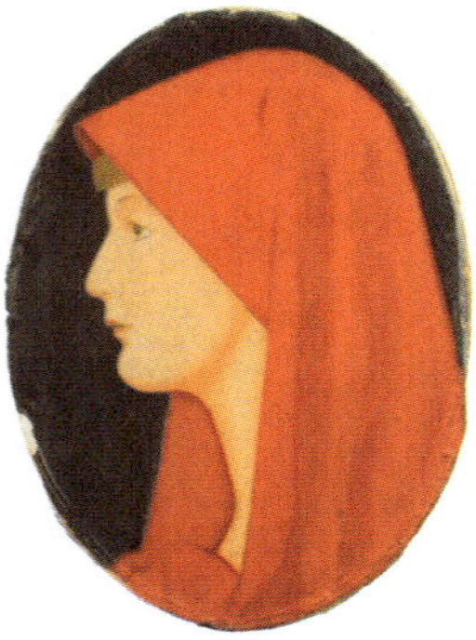

009

DIMENSIONS:	9 ⅝ x 7 ¼ x ¾ inches (24.4 x 18.4 x 1.91 cm)
DATE:	Unknown
MEDIA:	Paint on oval-shaped panel or board
CONDITION:	Good—There is a loss (approx. ¾" long) on the proper right side.
PROVENANCE:	Guadalajara, Mexico, September, 1996, 80 Mexican pesos
NOTES:	The subject is sparingly depicted.

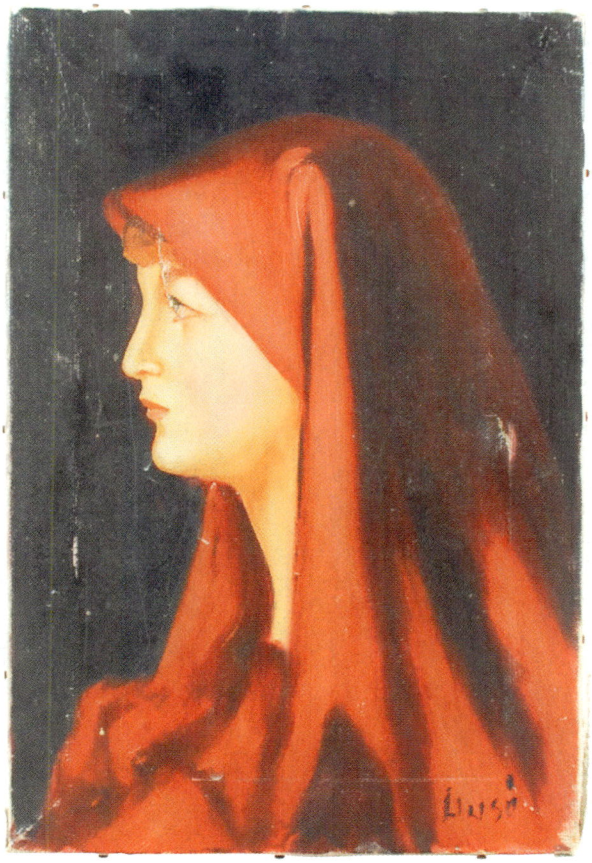

007

DIMENSIONS:	11 ¾ x 8 x ½ inches (29.8 x 20.3 x 1.27 cm)
DATE:	Unknown
MEDIA:	Paint on canvas
CONDITION:	Poor—There are two severe tears in the canvas support, one beginning at subject's eye level and extending up 2", and the other is in the back of the subject's neck area. The stretcher has created a pattern of creases in the painting that are visible from the front.
PROVENANCE:	Vienna, Austria, December 2000
NOTES:	Signed "Linsi."

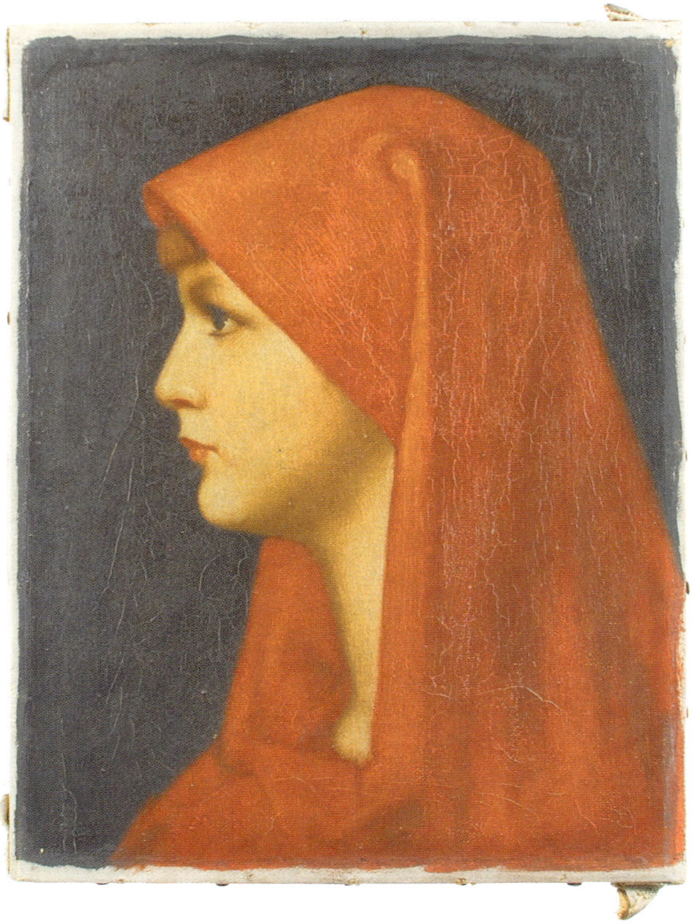

010

DIMENSIONS:	12 ⅝ x 9 ⅞ x ½ inches (32.1 x 25.1 x 1.27 cm)
DATE:	Unknown
MEDIA:	Paint on canvas
CONDITION:	Good/Fair—There are extensive cracks throughout paint layer.
PROVENANCE:	Paris, France, 1997, 200 French francs
NOTES:	Receipt from Musée National Jean-Jacques Henner, Paris, dated July 26, 2002, for a catalogue purchase for 53 euros, inserted into stretcher on verso. This work has a close resemblance to reproductions of the Jean-Jacques Henner original.

DIMENSIONS: 12 ¾ x 7 ¾ x ⅝ inches (32.4 x 19.7 x 1.59 cm)
DATE: 1971
MEDIA: Oil on panel or board, framed
CONDITION: Fair—Slight cracking in paint layer and abrasion or loss in upper region of hood.
PROVENANCE: Unknown
NOTES: As in several examples, this Fabiola has greenish shading along and below the jawline and eyebrow, possibly suggesting bruises or injury. "VMS 1971" inscribed on proper left lower corner. Piece is framed in an oval-shaped, gilded wood frame.

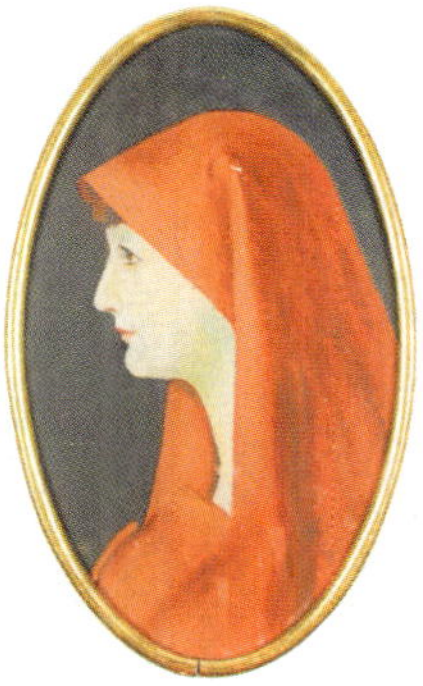

011

DIMENSIONS: 13 ¾ x 9 ⅞ x ⅛ inches (34.9 x 25.1 x 0.32 cm)
DATE: Unknown
MEDIA: Paint on paperboard or Masonite panel
CONDITION: Fair/Poor—Numerous accretions throughout surface, especially whitish drips that occur along the upper proper right corner and side. There is also an area of abraded paint near the subject's neck.
PROVENANCE: Tournai, Belgium, May 25, 2003, 0.5 euros
NOTES: There is a strong suggestion of gathered hands beneath the cloak in the lower center region of this painting. Subject's gaze is distinctly upward, and subject also has a slight smile. Signed "Desmet."

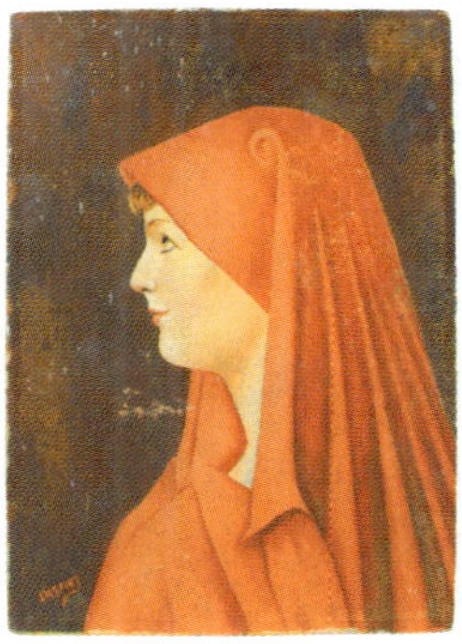

012

DIMENSIONS: 10 x 8 x ⅝ inches (25.4 x 20.3 x 1.59 cm)
DATE: Unknown
MEDIA: Oil on canvas
CONDITION: Fair—Surface has areas of abrasion.
PROVENANCE: Mexico City, Mexico, May 2, 2003, 1000 Mexican pesos
NOTES: There is an area of overpaint—possibly not original—in the area of the subject's forehead that is clearly obscuring bangs. This overpaint extends below the eyebrow line and reaches the beginning of the subject's nose bridge.

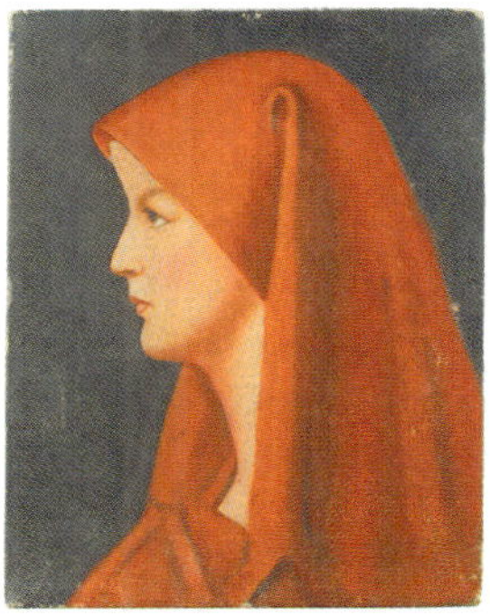

013

DIMENSIONS: 14 ¾ x 10 ½ x ½ inches (37.5 x 26.7 x 1.27 cm)
DATE: Unknown
MEDIA: Paint on canvas (very tightly woven textile)
CONDITION: Good/Fair
PROVENANCE: Netherlands, September 3, 2003, 30 euros
NOTES: The subject is sparingly depicted.

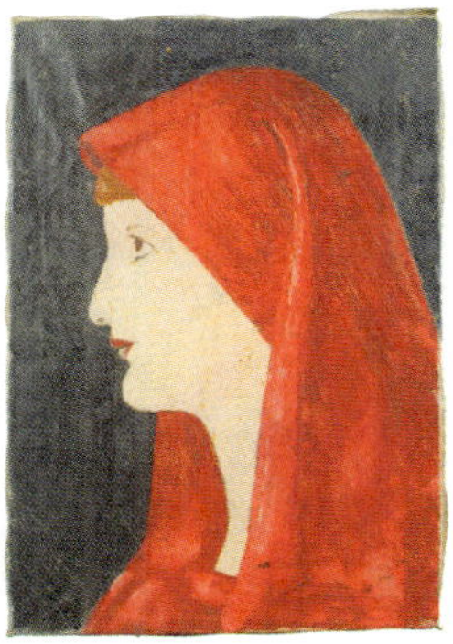

014

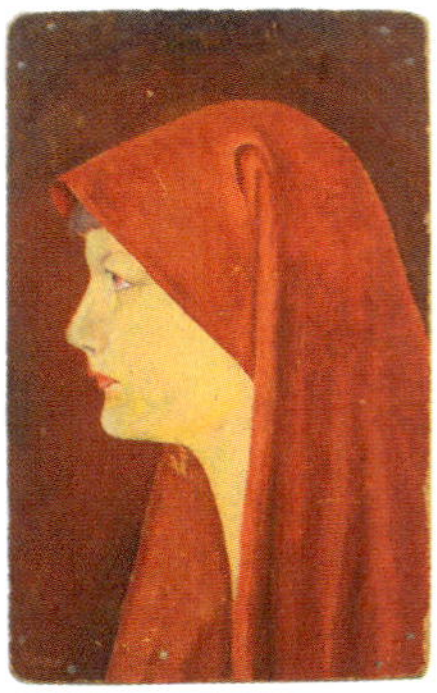

015

DIMENSIONS:	9 ⅞ x 6 ¼ x ⅞ inches (25.1 x 15.9 x 2.22 cm)
DATE:	1937
MEDIA:	Oil on paperboard or Masonite panel
CONDITION:	Fair—Slight surface scratches and accretions visible throughout painting.
PROVENANCE:	Mexico City, Mexico, gift of Veronica Macias
NOTES:	Signed "Perez 37."

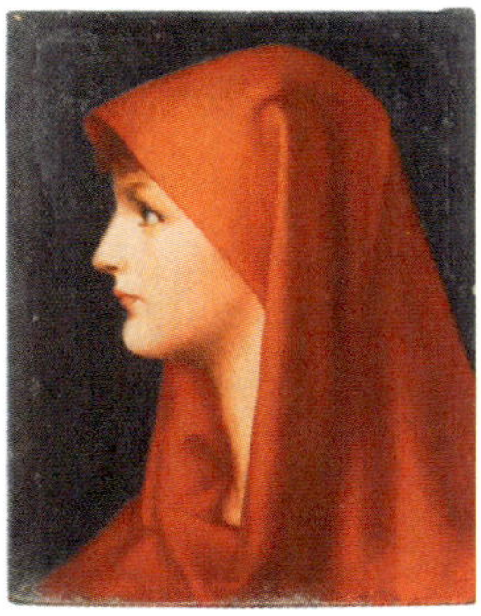

016

DIMENSIONS:	7 ¼ x 5 ¾ x ¼ inches (18.4 x 14.6 x 0.64 cm)
DATE:	Unknown
MEDIA:	Oil on paperboard or Masonite panel
CONDITION:	Good
PROVENANCE:	Amsterdam, Netherlands, 1996, 25 florins
NOTES:	This work bears a close resemblance to reproductions of the Jean-Jacques Henner original.

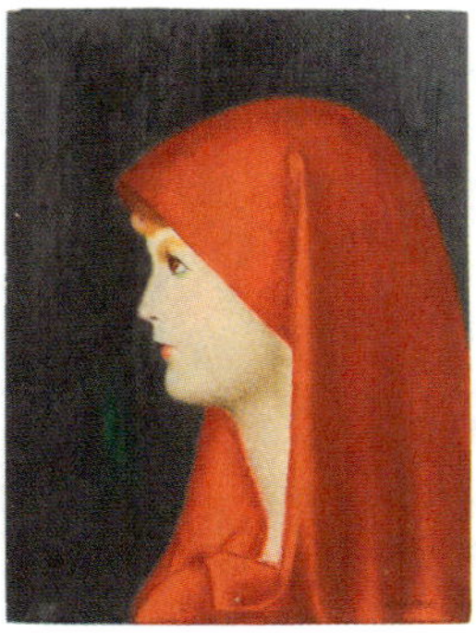

017

DIMENSIONS:	9 ½ x 7 ⅛ x ¼ inches (24.1 x 18.1 x 0.64 cm)
DATE:	Unknown
MEDIA:	Oil on wood composite panel
CONDITION:	Good
PROVENANCE:	Thiery Nord, France, 1997, 30 French francs
NOTES:	Subject exhibits a childlike appearance. "Fabiola Musée du Louvre" on blue bordered label on verso. This work is virtually identical to no. 253. Signed "F. Heyden."

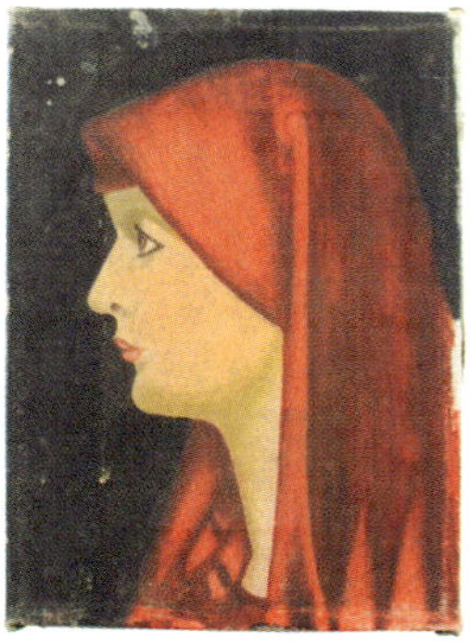

019

DIMENSIONS:	9 ½ x 7 ⅛ x ½ inches (24.1 x 18.1 x 1.27 cm)
DATE:	1943
MEDIA:	Paint on canvas
CONDITION:	Fair/Poor—Surface overall has unknown soiling and accretions. Stretcher has created cracking and creases in the front of the canvas.
PROVENANCE:	Unknown
NOTES:	Signed "O. V. 1943."

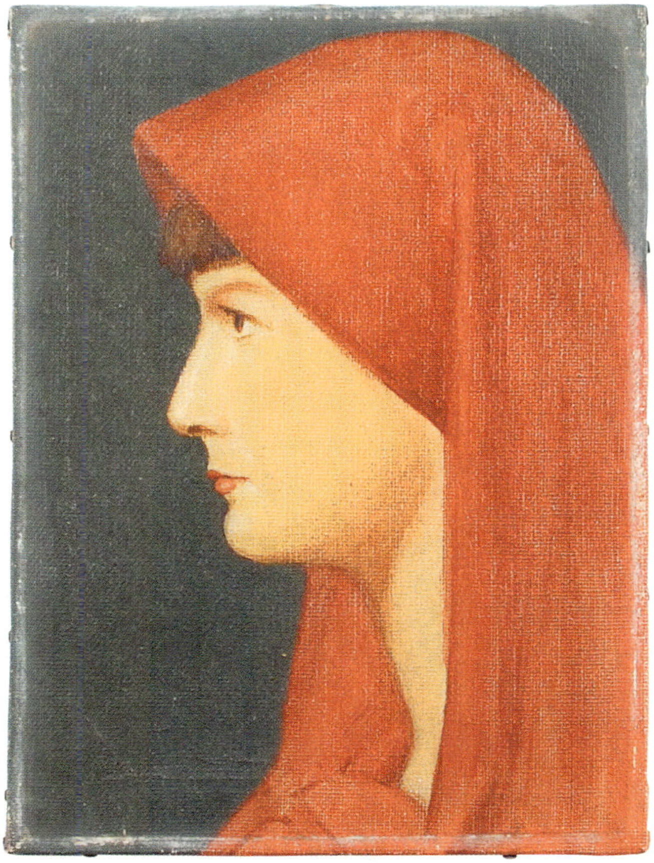

018

DIMENSIONS:	9 ¼ x 7 x ½ inches (23.5 x 17.8 x 1.27 cm)
DATE:	Unknown
MEDIA:	Paint on canvas
CONDITION:	Good
PROVENANCE:	Vienna, 2000

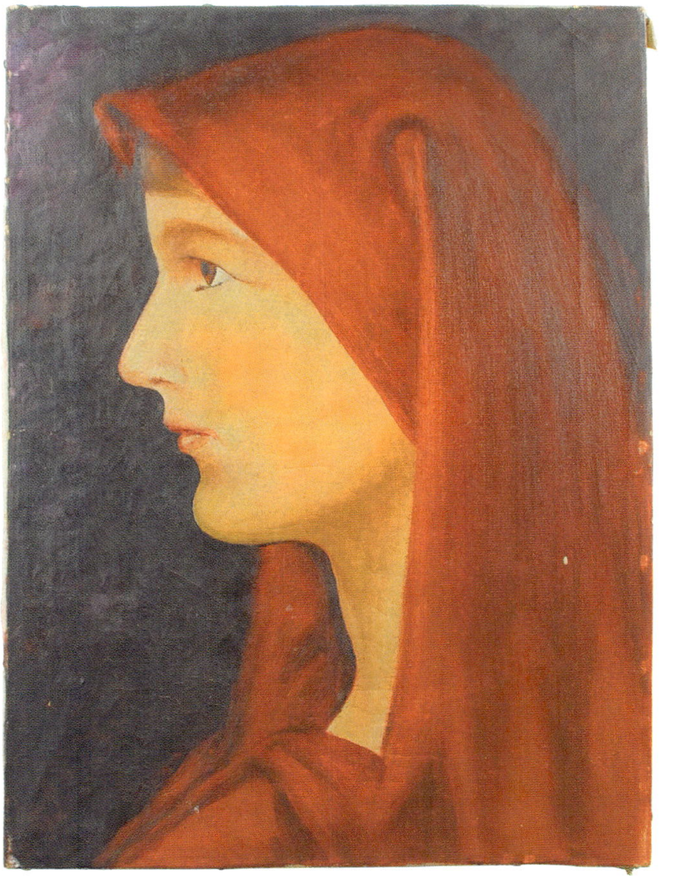

022

DIMENSIONS:	15 ¾ x 11 ¾ x ⅝ inches (40 x 29.8 x 1.59 cm)
DATE:	Unknown
MEDIA:	Paint on canvas
CONDITION:	Good/Fair—Cracking appears in the paint layer throughout the surface.
PROVENANCE:	Lille, France, December 2001, 58 French francs
NOTES:	Subject's bangs have no volume.

DIMENSIONS:	15 ¾ x 11 ¾ x ⅝ inches (40 x 29.8 x 1.59 cm)
DATE:	Unknown
MEDIA:	Paint on canvas
CONDITION:	Good
PROVENANCE:	Munich, Germany, October 2001
NOTES:	Signed "J. Hofmann."

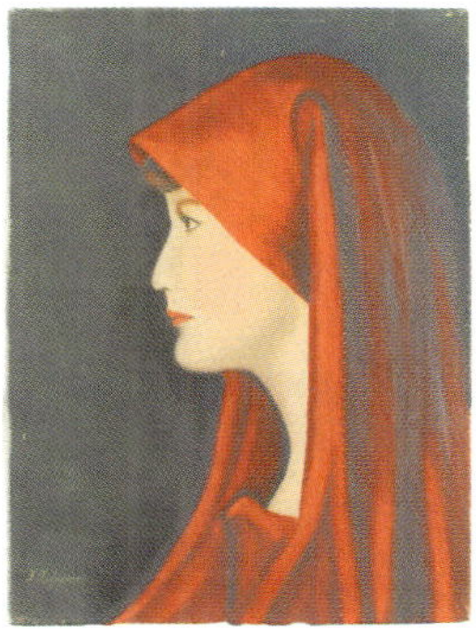

020

DIMENSIONS:	11 ¾ x 7 ¾ x ⅞ inches (29.8 x 19.7 x 2.22 cm)
DATE:	Unknown
MEDIA:	Paint on canvas
CONDITION:	Fair—Prior restoration clearly visible on subject's cheek (patch to canvas support visible from verso). There are also large losses in the paint layer at upper corners and lower proper right corner.
PROVENANCE:	Antwerp, Belgium, August 1996, 200 Belgian francs, gift of Beatrice Diercxsens
NOTES:	Signed "[?].M."

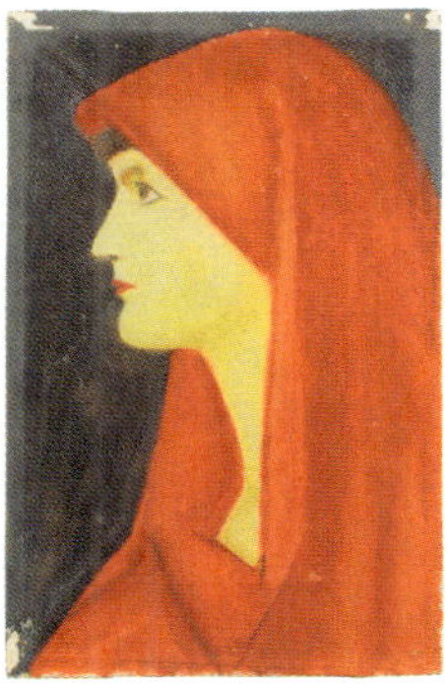

021

DIMENSIONS:	9 ½ x 7 ⅛ x ⅝ inches (24.1 x 18.1 x 1.59 cm)
DATE:	Unknown
MEDIA:	Paint on canvas
CONDITION:	Fair—Numerous losses in the paint layer, especially in the center of the proper left side. Also there are several areas of abraded surfaces.
PROVENANCE:	Unknown
NOTES:	Signed "Baetens P."

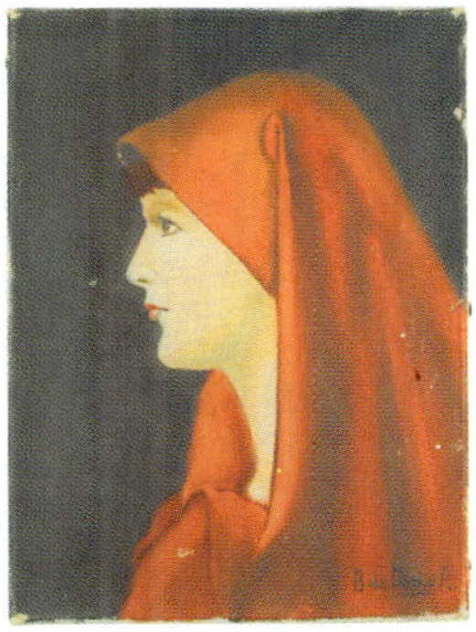

023

DIMENSIONS:	11 ⅝ x 7 ¾ x ¾ inches (29.5 x 19.7 x 1.91 cm)
DATE:	Unknown
MEDIA:	Paint on panel or board
CONDITION:	Poor/Fair—Very soiled surface and numerous losses throughout paint layer.
PROVENANCE:	Brussels, Belgium, May 1993, 100 Belgian francs
NOTES:	Signed "Meertens" on proper right lower corner.

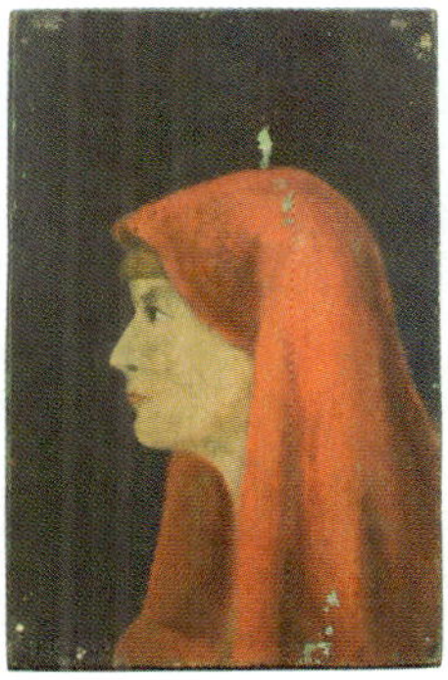

024

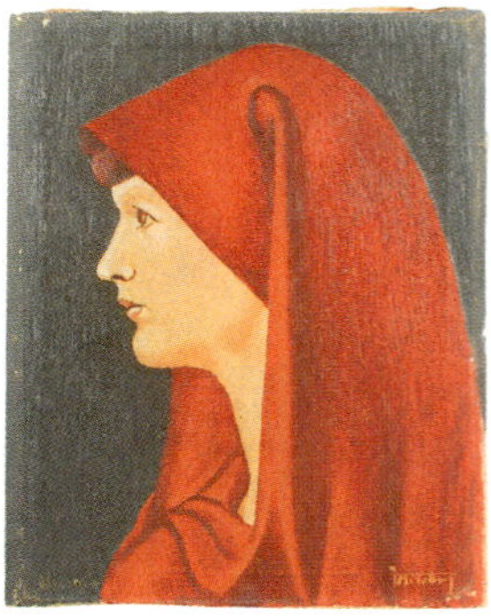

025

DIMENSIONS: 11 ⅝ x 9 ½ x ½ inches (29.5 x 24.1 x 1.27 cm)
DATE: Unknown
MEDIA: Paint on canvas
CONDITION: Fair—Numerous surface cracks throughout painting and small areas of losses and abrasions in the paint layer along top and sides.
PROVENANCE: Eeklo, Belgium, October 5, 1997, 100 Belgian francs
NOTES: Signed “Henner” on lower proper right corner and illegible signature on lower proper left.

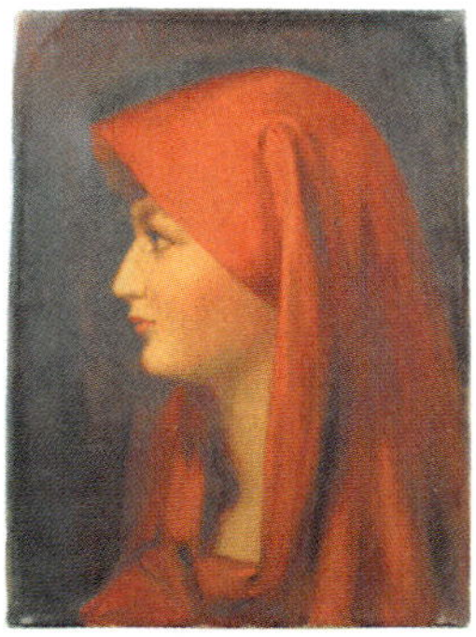

026

DIMENSIONS: 15 ¾ x 11 ⅞ x ½ inches (40 x 30.2 x 1.27 cm)
DATE: Unknown
MEDIA: Paint on canvas
CONDITION: Good/Fair
PROVENANCE: Copenhagen, Denmark, 1996
NOTES: Signed “d’après J. J. Henner” on proper right side.

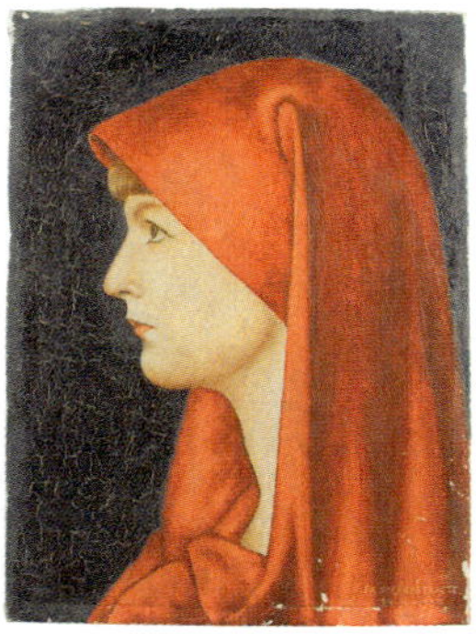

027

DIMENSIONS: 12 ¾ x 9 ½ x ⅝ inches (32.4 x 24.1 x 1.59 cm)
DATE: 1939
MEDIA: Oil on canvas
CONDITION: Poor/Fair—Extensive cracking in background, while the paint layer in the face area is stable overall. There are numerous losses in the paint layer at the lower proper left corner.
PROVENANCE: Belgium, 1997, 600 Belgian francs
NOTES: Signed “Fr. Verhoestraete. 24–10–1939.”

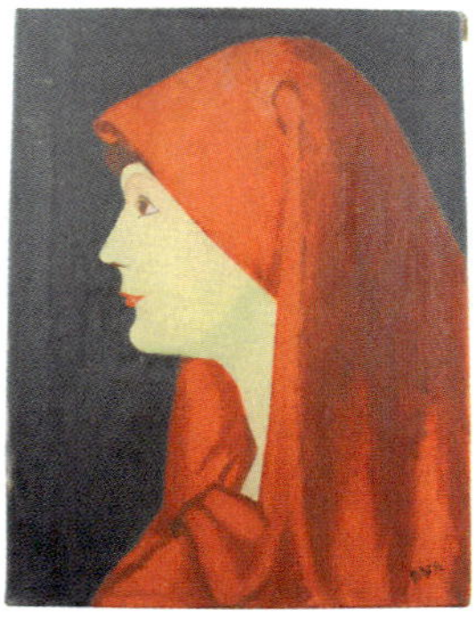

028

DIMENSIONS: 17 ⅞ x 13 ¾ x ¾ inches (45.4 x 34.9 x 1.91 cm)
DATE: Unknown
MEDIA: Paint on canvas
CONDITION: Good
PROVENANCE: Rohan, France, August 8, 1999, 180 French francs
NOTES: Subject displays signs of heavy makeup application throughout entire exposed skin surface. There are particularly significant amounts of makeup in the eye area. Signed “DVA.”

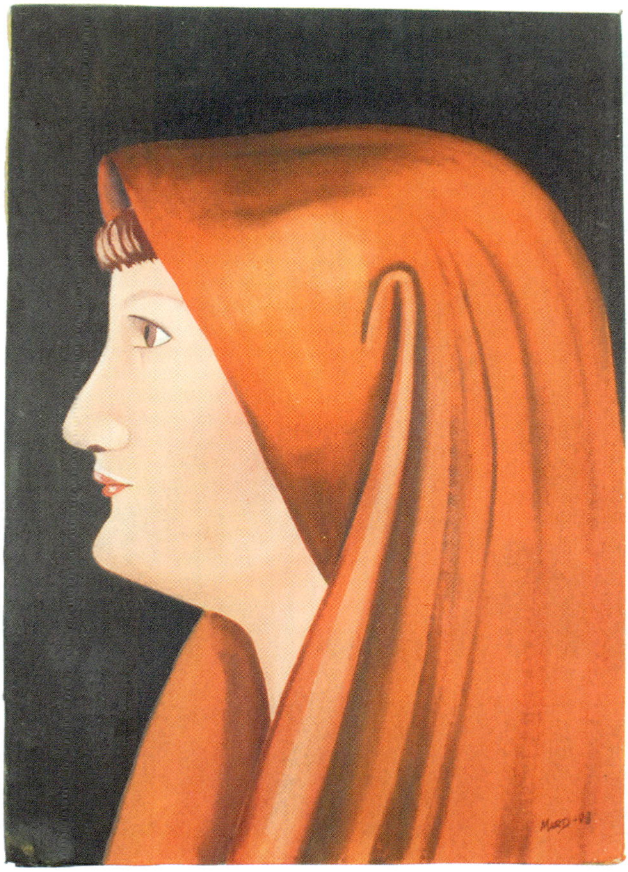

029

DIMENSIONS:	12 ¾ x 9 ¼ x ¾ inches (32.4 x 23.5 x 1.91 cm)
DATE:	1998
MEDIA:	Acrylic on canvas mounted on panel or board
CONDITION:	Good
PROVENANCE:	Mexico, March 1998, 300 Mexican pesos
NOTES:	Subject has noticeably masculine features and appearance. Signed "Marty–98."

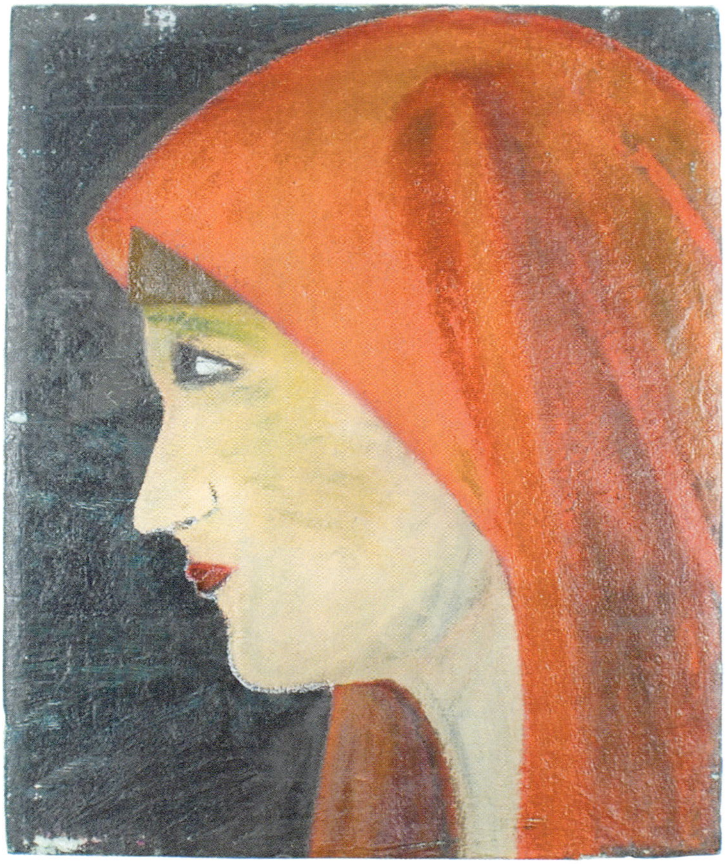

031

DIMENSIONS:	11 ¾ x 9 ⅞ x ⅞ inches (29.8 x 25.1 x 2.22 cm)
DATE:	Unknown
MEDIA:	Paint on canvas
CONDITION:	Good
PROVENANCE:	Unknown
NOTES:	This painting shows a closer view of the subject than is typical. The composition places the top of the subject's head at the uppermost point of the image plane, and there is a limited view of the neck and hood.

DIMENSIONS: 15 ½ x 11 ¾ x 1 ⅛ inches (39.4 x 29.8 x 2.86 cm)
DATE: Unknown
MEDIA: Pastel on paper, glazed and framed
CONDITION: Fair—There are significant stains in subject's face and throughout the surface overall.
PROVENANCE: Verviers, Belgium, April 24, 2000, 400 Belgian francs
NOTES: Signed "M. M."

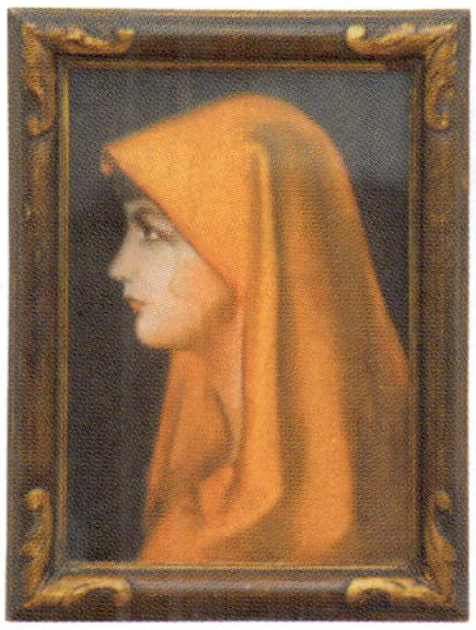

030

DIMENSIONS: 12 x 10 x 2 ⅜ inches (30.5 x 25.4 x 6.03 cm)
DATE: 1941
MEDIA: Pastel on paper, framed
CONDITION: Good
PROVENANCE: Unknown
NOTES: Subject's demeanor appears unusually dour and stern. Signed "O. Seha 1941."

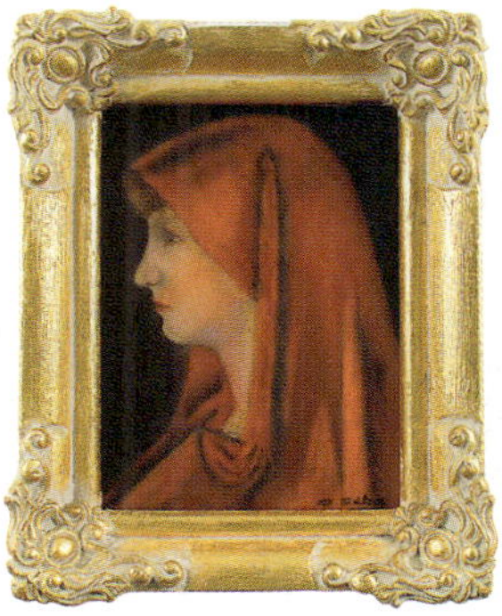

032

DIMENSIONS: 14 ¼ x 9 ⅞ x ¾ inches (36.2 x 25.1 x 1.91 cm)
DATE: Unknown
MEDIA: Paint on paperboard mounted on wood support
CONDITION: Fair—Several small losses and an abraded area on subject's cheek. Greenish accretion at top proper right corner. There are losses and small tears or folds in the paperboard support at all four corners.
PROVENANCE: Unknown
NOTES: Subject has an extremely pale complexion. Signed "Karitoa R. S."

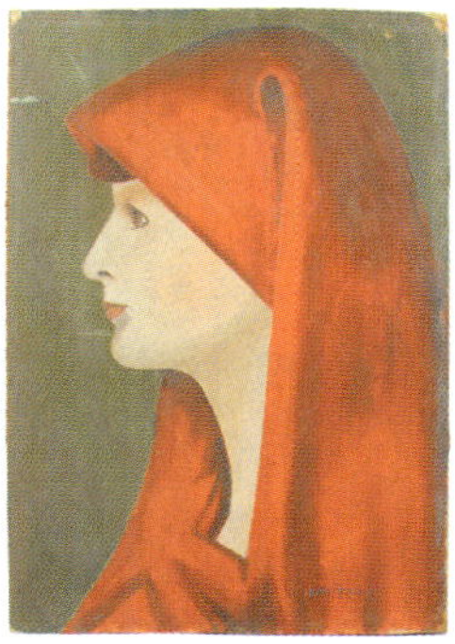

033

DIMENSIONS: 8 ⅞ x 7 ¾ x ¾ inches (22.5 x 19.7 x 1.91 cm)
DATE: Unknown
MEDIA: Paint and pencil on paper, glazed and framed
CONDITION: Good—Slight staining along proper right edge of window mat.
PROVENANCE: Metz, France, June 7, 2003, 15 euros
NOTES: Signed "M. Quack."

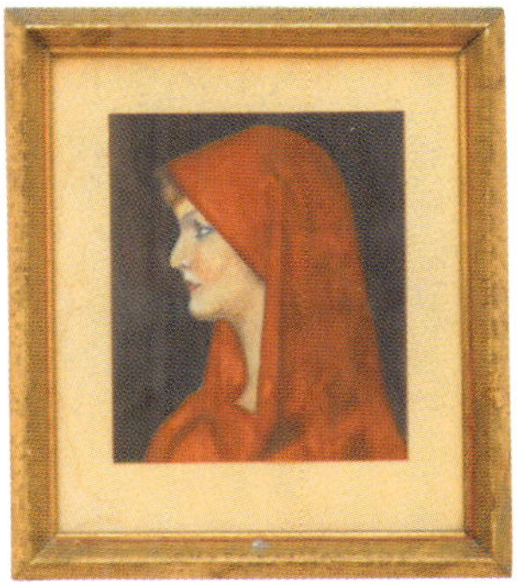

034

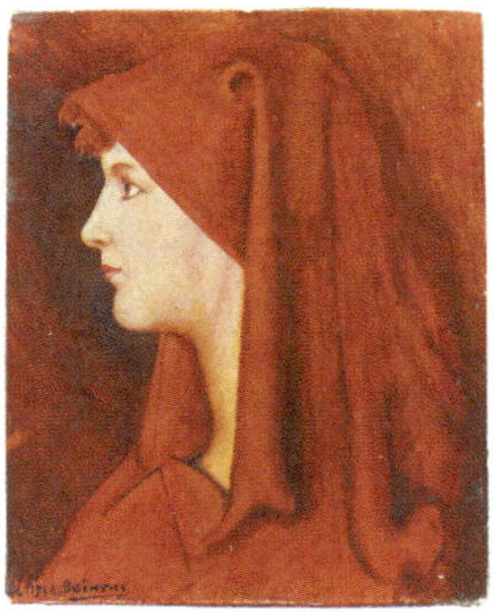

035

DIMENSIONS:	13 ¼ x 10 ⅞ x ⅝ inches (33.7 x 27.6 x 1.59 cm)
DATE:	1954
MEDIA:	Paint on canvas mounted on wood composite panel or board
CONDITION:	Good
PROVENANCE:	Lille, France, November 1995, exchange
NOTES:	Subject exhibits a common Fabiola feature, in that there are two distinct segments of the bangs, one hanging naturally down, and the other extending up beyond the edge of the hood. Signed "K. 1954 Beinrus."

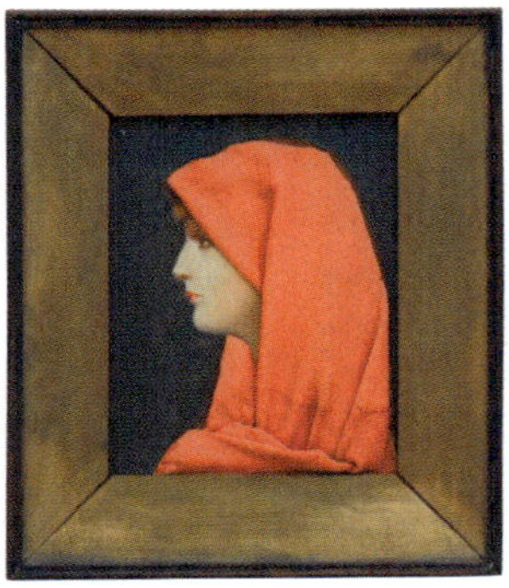

036

DIMENSIONS:	11 ¾ x 10 ⅜ x 1 ⅛ inches (29.8 x 26.4 x 2.86 cm)
DATE:	Unknown
MEDIA:	Paint on panel or board with textile, glazed and framed
CONDITION:	Good/Fair—There is a stain that runs horizontally across the textile at the height of the subject's neck.
PROVENANCE:	Unknown
NOTES:	"Fabiola" on verso.

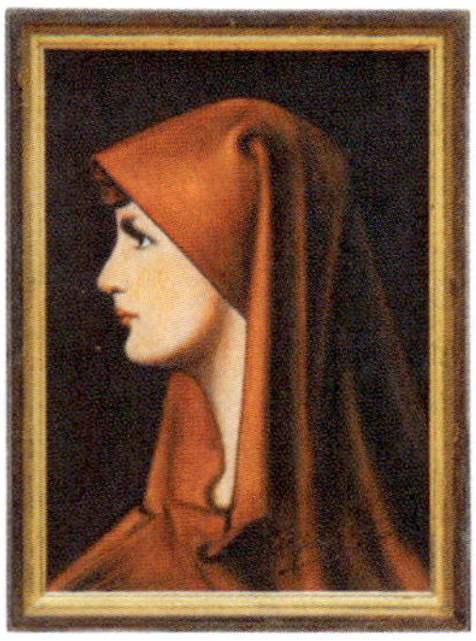

038

DIMENSIONS:	15 ½ x 11 ½ x 1 inches (39.4 x 29.2 x 2.54 cm)
DATE:	1949
MEDIA:	Pastel on paper, glazed and framed
CONDITION:	Good
PROVENANCE:	Etterbeek, Belgium, May 30, 2003, 8 euros
NOTES:	Signed "M. Chimpont 1949."

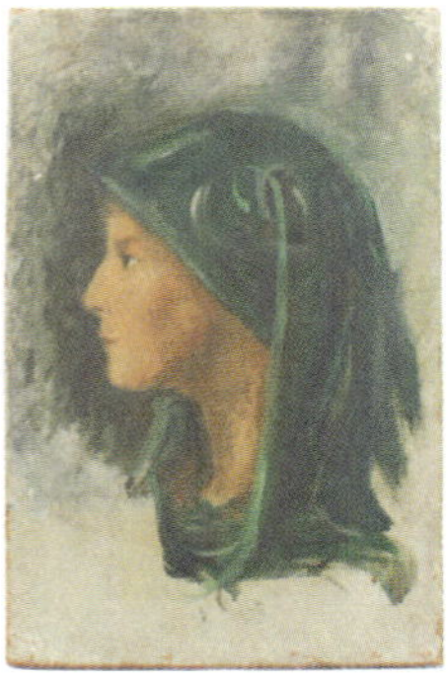

039

DIMENSIONS:	16 ⅛ x 10 ¾ x ⅝ inches (41 x 27.3 x 1.59 cm)
DATE:	Unknown
MEDIA:	Paint on canvas
CONDITION:	Fair/Poor—There are two tears in the canvas support in the subject's upper neck and ear area. There is also a prior restoration that includes a patch to the canvas from the verso at subject's nose level.
PROVENANCE:	Graz, Austria, August 1996, 160 shillings
NOTES:	Subject is wearing a green veil, as opposed to red, which is typical in other Fabiola portraits.

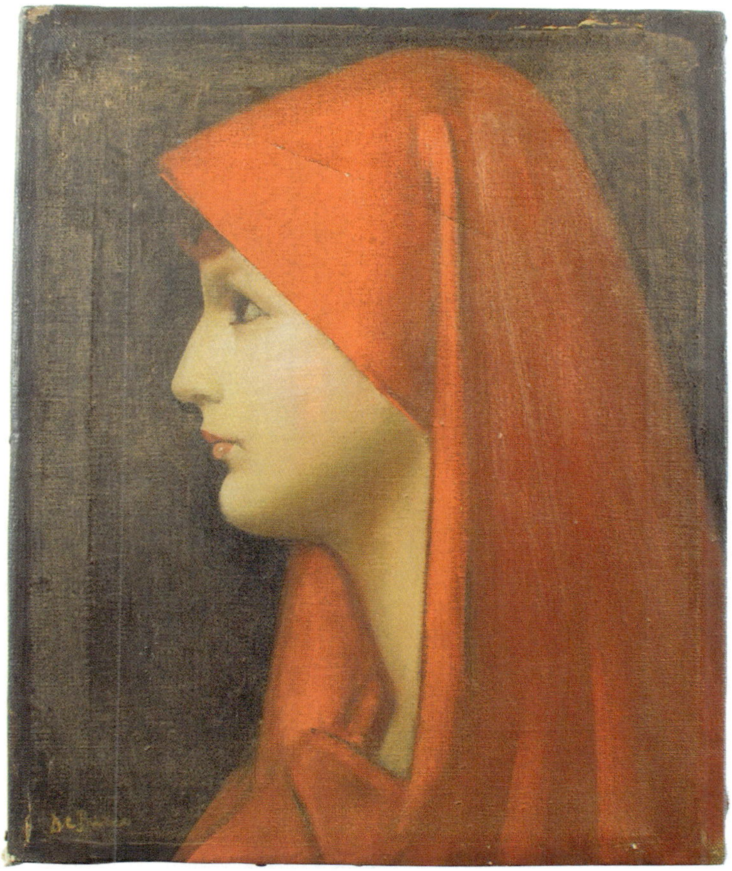

037

DIMENSIONS:	14 ¼ x 11 ¾ x ⅝ inches (36.2 x 29.8 x 1.59 cm)
DATE:	Unknown
MEDIA:	Paint on canvas
CONDITION:	Fair/Poor—There is a large—approx. 6" long—diagonal tear in the painting that appears to have been caused by a blade. There is an unknown coating on the surface of the painting that is yellow in tone (except at the edges, which were previously covered by a frame).
PROVENANCE:	Lille, France, June 1993, 180 French francs
NOTES:	This portrait might be considered among the closest in this collecction in resembling the Jean-Jacques Henner original. Signed "De Burrs."

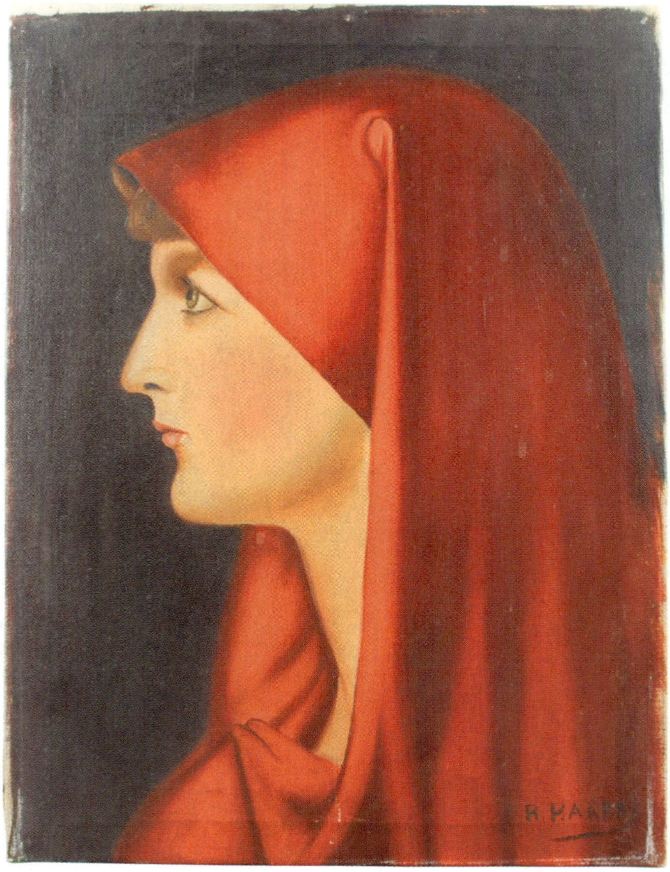

041

DIMENSIONS:	15 5/8 x 11 7/8 x 1/2 inches (39.7 x 30.2 x 1.27 cm)
DATE:	Unknown
MEDIA:	Paint on canvas
CONDITION:	Good
PROVENANCE:	Tournai, Belgium, December 1996, gift of Edith De Kindt
NOTES:	Signed "R. P. Arre."

DIMENSIONS: 19 ¾ x 15 ⅞ x ⅞ inches (50.2 x 40.3 x 2.22 cm)
DATE: Unknown
MEDIA: Paint on canvas
CONDITION: Good/Fair
PROVENANCE: Sweden, 1998, 140 kronur
NOTES: This is a particularly close view of Fabiola. The uppermost portion of the hood extends out of the picture plane. Two triangular abstract forms at the closer proper left corner indicate folds in the subject's hood. The subject's sharp, heavily delineated features lend a cartoonish appearance, especially in the eye area. Signed "Walga do."

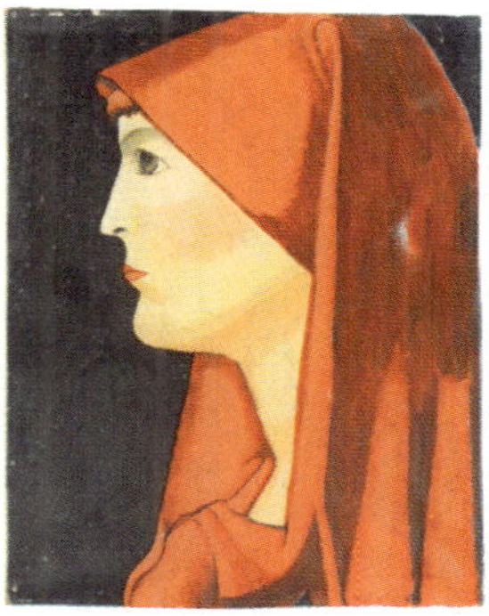

040

DIMENSIONS: 19 ¾ x 15 ¾ x ½ inches (50.2 x 40 x 1.27 cm)
DATE: Unknown
MEDIA: Paint on canvas
CONDITION: Good/Fair
PROVENANCE: Verona, Italy, 1998, 15,000 lire
NOTES: Subject sits on a green background, as opposed to a black or other color typical of other Fabiola paintings. Signed "Dumoná."

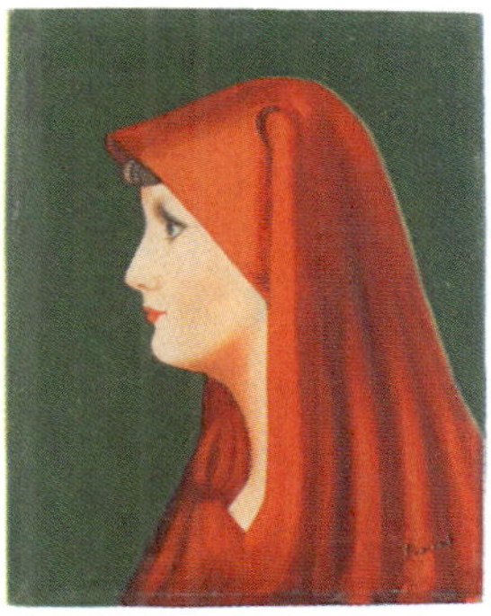

042

DIMENSIONS: 15 x 12 ¾ x ½ inches (38.1 x 32.4 x 1.27 cm)
DATE: Unknown
MEDIA: Acrylic on canvas
CONDITION: Good—Slight accretions or losses along edges.
PROVENANCE: Brussels, Belgium, 1998, 600 Belgian francs
NOTES: Subject's cast and complexion are unnaturally grayish. Signed "J. Hillevaert."

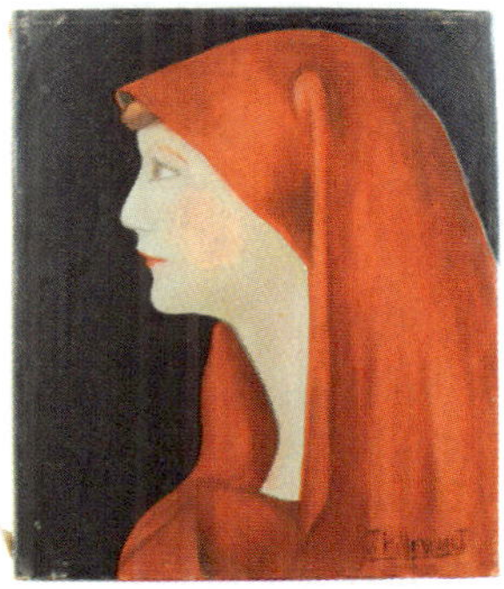

043

DIMENSIONS: 11 ½ x 9 ⅝ x ¼ inches (29.2 x 24.4 x 0.64 cm)
DATE: Unknown
MEDIA: Needlepoint on mesh support mounted on a panel or composite board
CONDITION: Good
PROVENANCE: Unknown
NOTES: "FABIOLA" printed on mesh support on verso. This is clearly a commercially available pattern for needlepoint crafts, which explains the consistent composition, color palette, shading, and toning evident with nearly every needlepoint representation of Fabiola. Painting of two cranes in flight on verso.

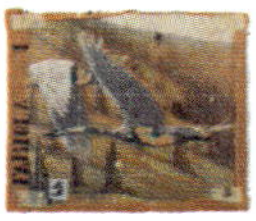

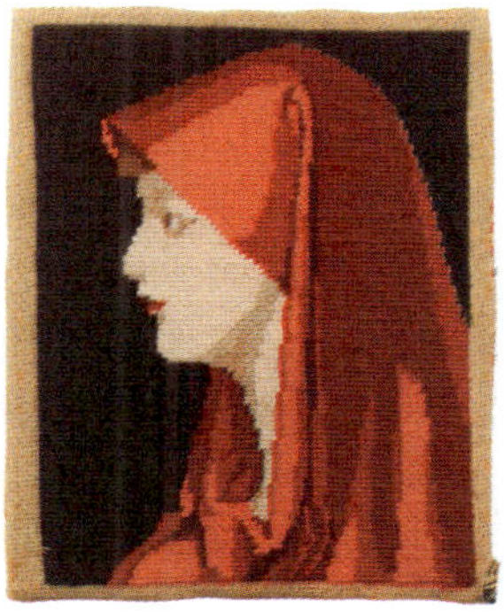

044

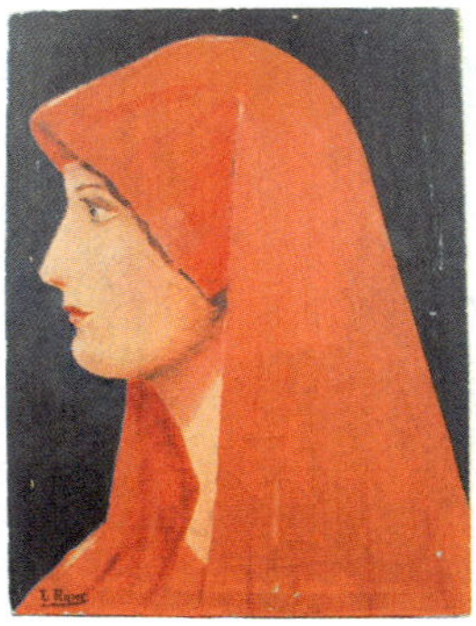

045

DIMENSIONS:	15 ¾ x 11 ⅞ x ⅝ inches (40 x 30.2 x 1.59 cm)
DATE:	Unknown
MEDIA:	Paint on canvas
CONDITION:	Fair/Poor—Extensive cracking throughout surface and numerous losses in paint layer especially along the edges.
PROVENANCE:	Mexico, May 1999
NOTES:	In this instance, the prime vertical fold of the hood is depicted as a single straight line. Illegible writing in pencil on verso of stretcher. Signed "G. Rome."

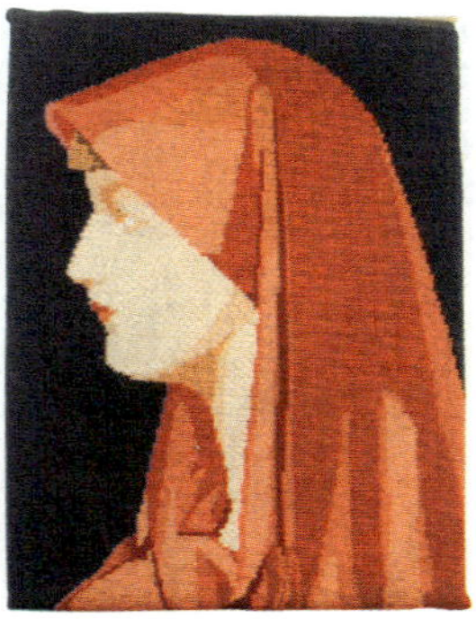

046

DIMENSIONS:	15 ¾ x 11 ¾ x ¾ inches (40 x 29.8 x 1.91 cm)
DATE:	Unknown
MEDIA:	Needlepoint on mesh support mounted on frame
CONDITION:	Good
PROVENANCE:	Unknown
NOTES:	Considering the medium, a stunning achievement in portraiture.

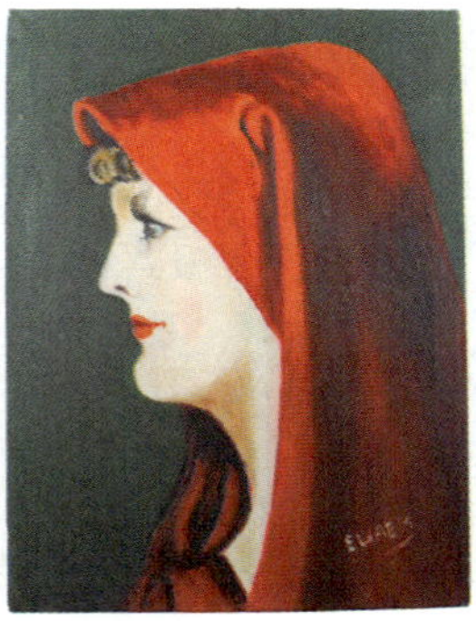

047

DIMENSIONS:	15 ¾ x 11 ⅞ x ½ inches (40 x 30.2 x 1.27 cm)
DATE:	Unknown
MEDIA:	Oil on canvas
CONDITION:	Good
PROVENANCE:	Brussels, Belgium, spring 1995
NOTES:	Subject displays signs of heavy makeup application throughout entire exposed skin surface; in this case, the coloration approaches the theatrical. Signed "E. Waem."

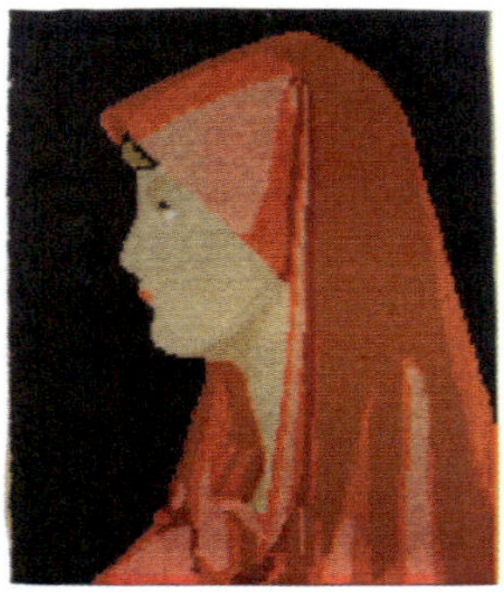

048

DIMENSIONS:	16 ¾ x 14 ⅛ x ½ inches (42.5 x 35.9 x 1.27 cm)
DATE:	Unknown
MEDIA:	Needlepoint on mesh support mounted on wood frame
CONDITION:	Good
PROVENANCE:	Unknown
NOTES:	The drapery suggests medieval fashion.

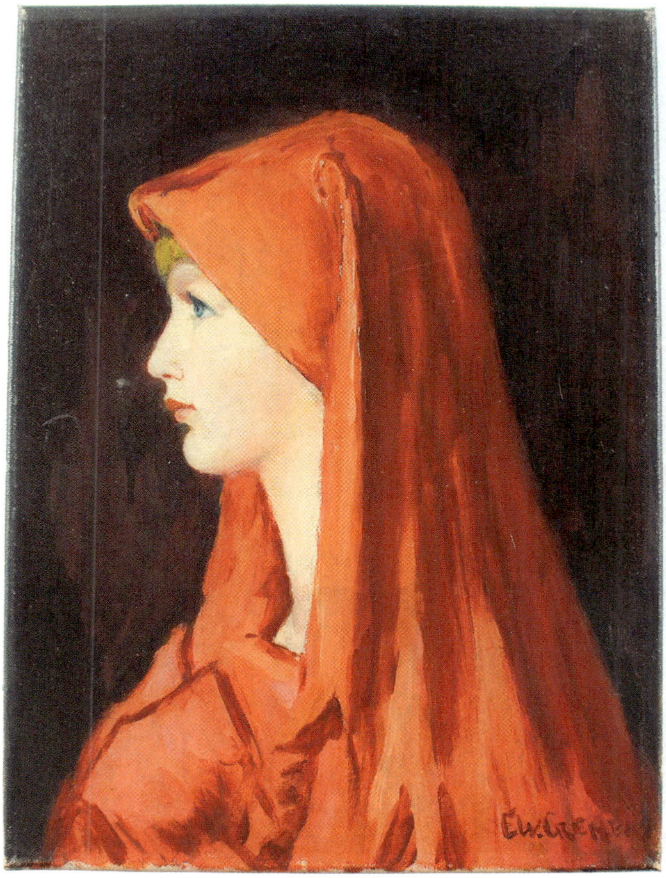

049

DIMENSIONS:	15 ¾ x 11 ⅞ x ¾ inches (40 x 30.2 x 1.91 cm)
DATE:	Unknown
MEDIA:	Paint on canvas
CONDITION:	Good
PROVENANCE:	Düsseldorf, Germany, 1995
NOTES:	Figure has noticeably fair coloring and complexion (i.e., blond hair and blue eyes) as compared with other Fabiolas, whose coloring is typically darker. Signed "E. W. Creners." This is one of two paintings in the collection by Creners, which are very similar. See no. 130.

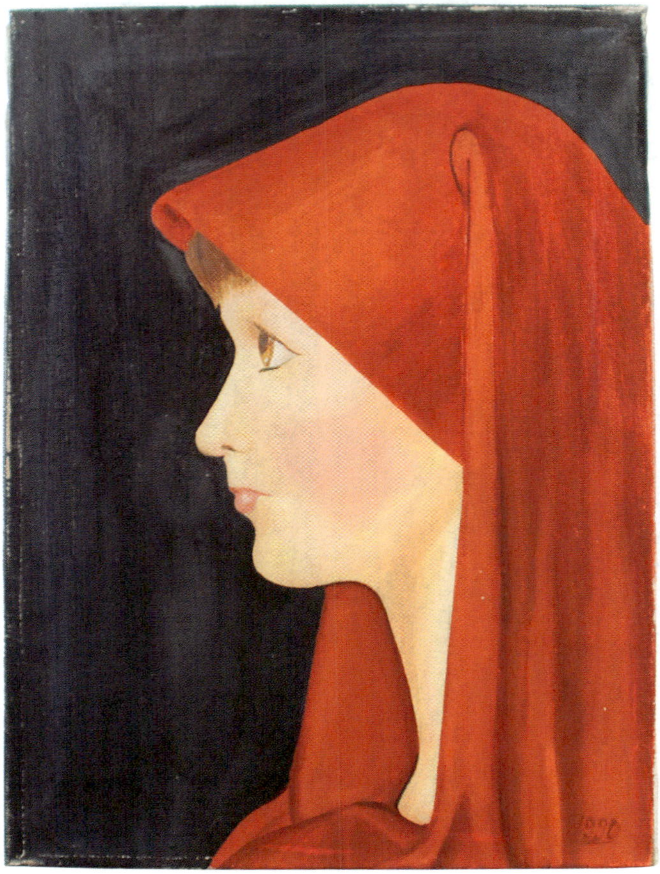

051

DIMENSIONS:	15 ¾ x 11 ¾ x ¾ inches (40 x 29.8 x 1.91 cm)
DATE:	1990
MEDIA:	Acrylic on canvas
CONDITION:	Good
PROVENANCE:	Eeklo, Belgium, October 4, 1998
NOTES:	Subject has youthful and innocent appearance, a quality accentuated by rosy cheeks and a disproportionately large eye. Date inscribed on recto in proper left lower corner.

DIMENSIONS:	16 ½ x 11 ⅝ x ¾ inches (41.9 x 29.5 x 1.91 cm)
DATE:	Unknown
MEDIA:	Paint on canvas
CONDITION:	Good
PROVENANCE:	Netherlands, 1997, 400 Belgian francs
NOTES:	"Kemmel (6/9/99)" in pencil on verso. Signed "Bonnvy T. P."

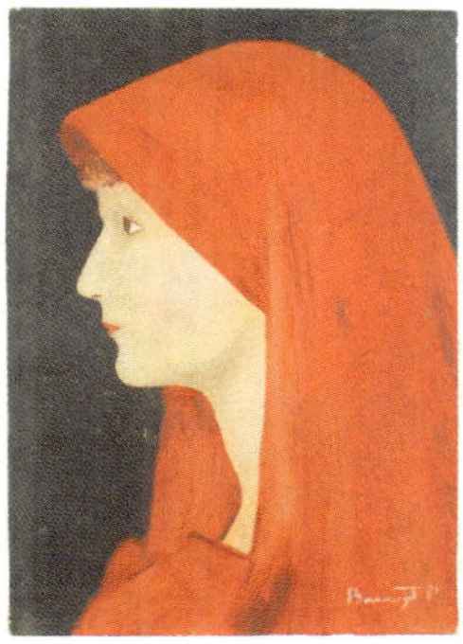

050

DIMENSIONS:	15 ⅞ x 11 ¾ x ⅝ inches (40.3 x 29.8 x 1.59 cm)
DATE:	Unknown
MEDIA:	Paint on canvas
CONDITION:	Fair—Several areas of cracking in paint layer are evident, and the canvas support also has several areas of indentations. There are abraded sections with minor paint losses along the edges.
PROVENANCE:	Unknown
NOTES:	Signed "Darolo."

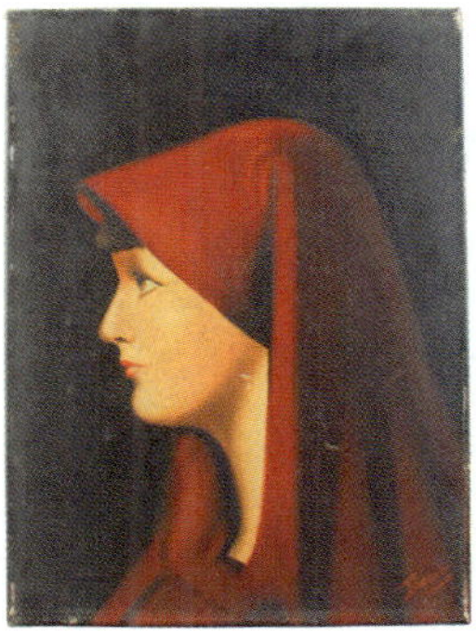

052

DIMENSIONS:	15 ¾ x 11 ⅞ x ⅝ inches (40 x 30.2 x 1.59 cm)
DATE:	Unknown
MEDIA:	Paint on canvas
CONDITION:	Fair—There is a large and severe tear in the canvas support near the subject's ear area.
PROVENANCE:	Unknown
NOTES:	Signed "J. Vérulpens."

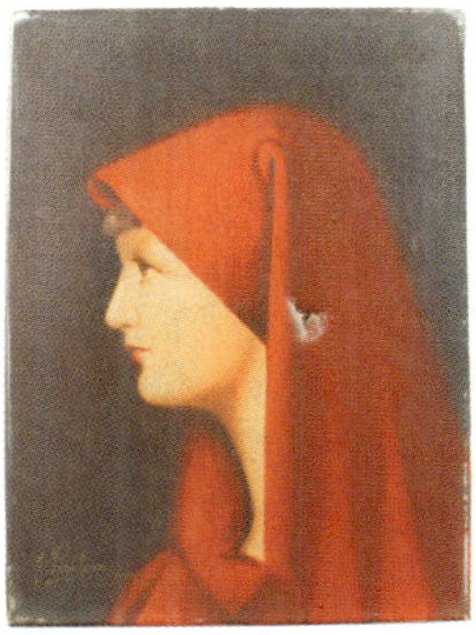

053

DIMENSIONS:	15 ⅞ x 11 ¾ x ⅞ inches (40.3 x 29.8 x 2.22 cm)
DATE:	Unknown
MEDIA:	Acrylic on canvas
CONDITION:	Good
PROVENANCE:	Mexico City, Mexico, January 2001, 400 Mexican pesos
NOTES:	Subject has a severe dental overbite. Signed "Medich."

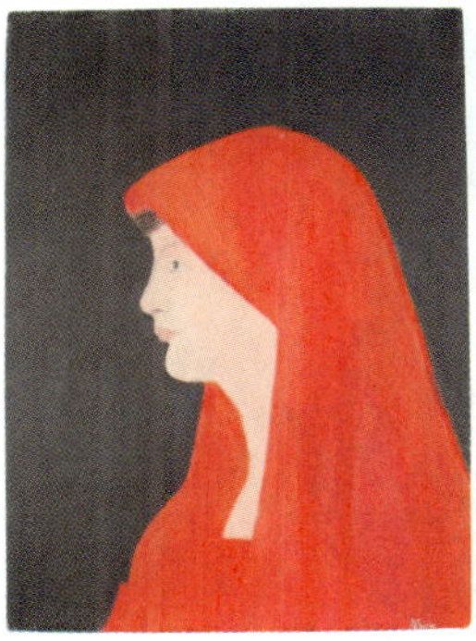

054

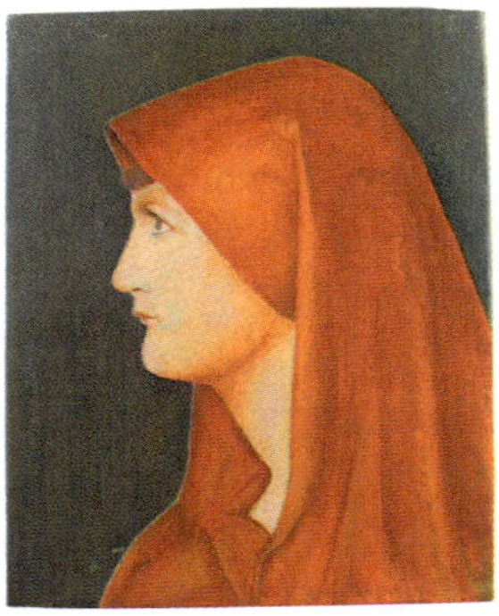

055

DIMENSIONS:	16 ¼ x 13 ⅛ x ⅝ inches (41.3 x 33.3 x 1.59 cm)
DATE:	Unknown
MEDIA:	Paint on canvas
CONDITION:	Good—Although there is a small tear or puncture at the lower proper right corner.
PROVENANCE:	Barcelona, Spain, June 2000, 90 pesetas
NOTES:	Subject's gaze is distinctly upward.

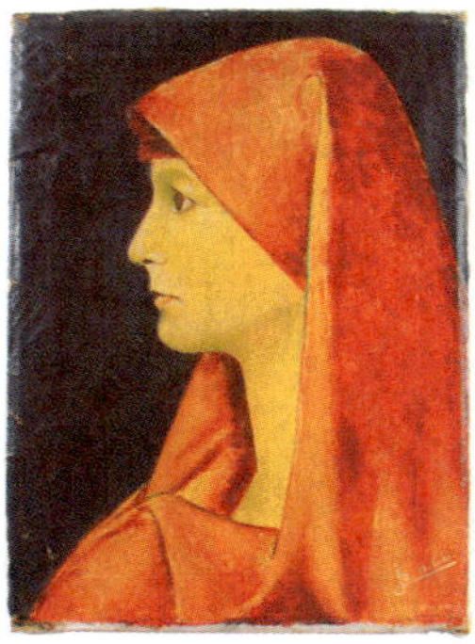

056

DIMENSIONS:	15 ⅞ x 11 ⅝ x ½ inches (40.3 x 29.5 x 1.27 cm)
DATE:	1941
MEDIA:	Oil on canvas
CONDITION:	Fair—The painting has a very yellowed varnish layer and extensive cracks throughout surface. There are a few minor losses along the edges of the painting.
PROVENANCE:	Unknown
NOTES:	Subject is depicted with an unhealthy pallor. Signed "jo—15–8–41."

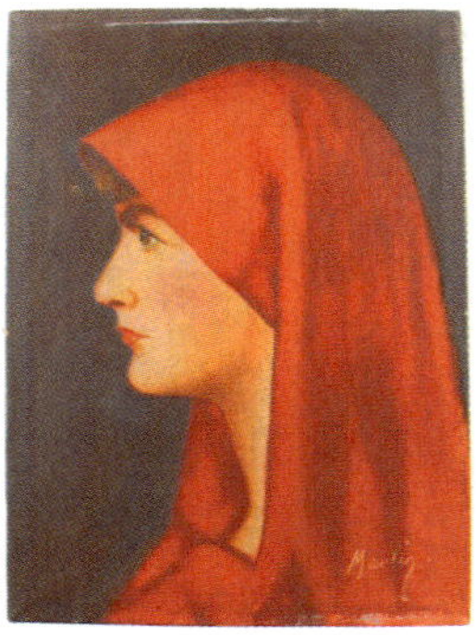

057

DIMENSIONS:	15 ¾ x 11 ¾ x ⅜ inches (40 x 29.8 x 0.95 cm)
DATE:	Unknown
MEDIA:	Paint on canvas
CONDITION:	Good/Fair—There is a puncture and tear in the painting at the subject's forehead level. There are also small losses along sides and edges.
PROVENANCE:	Eeklo, Belgium, October 4, 1999, 200 Belgian francs
NOTES:	Signed "Martin."

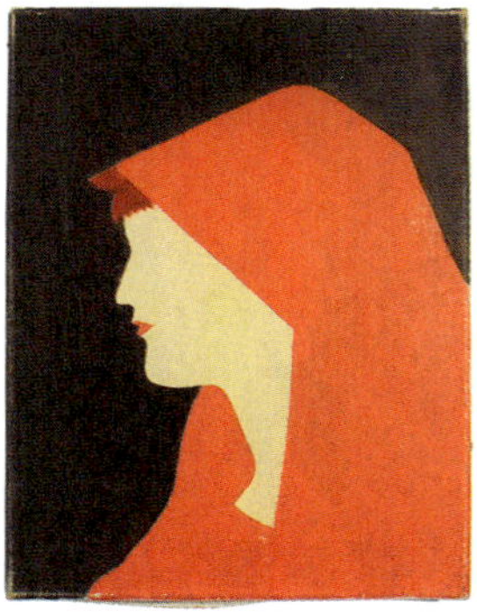

058

DIMENSIONS:	11 ¾ x 9 ¼ x ⅝ inches (29.8 x 23.5 x 1.59 cm)
DATE:	Unknown
MEDIA:	Paint on canvas
CONDITION:	Fair—Approx. 1"-wide surface accretion on cheek of figure. A few areas of surface abrasion.
PROVENANCE:	Paris, France, 1997, 70 French francs
NOTES:	Subject exhibits a common Fabiola feature, in that there are two distinct segments of the bangs, one hanging naturally down, and the other extending up beyond the edge of the hood. In addition, the hood is depicted with three angles, as opposed to one curved line. Most noteworthy is the work's flat two-dimensional composition, devoid of any indication of depth.

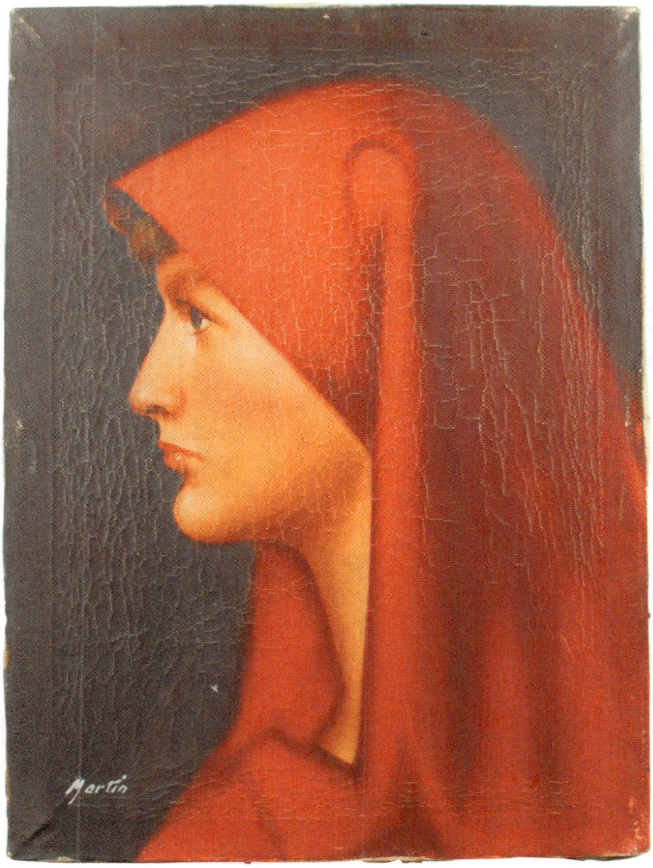

059

DIMENSIONS:	15 ¾ x 11 ¾ x ⅜ inches (40 x 29.8 x 0.95 cm)
DATE:	Unknown
MEDIA:	Paint on canvas
CONDITION:	Fair/Poor—Significant cracking throughout surface; much of it makes the paint layer extremely unstable and susceptible to major losses.
PROVENANCE:	Maldegem, Brugge, Belgium, July 23, 2002
NOTES:	Signed "Martin."

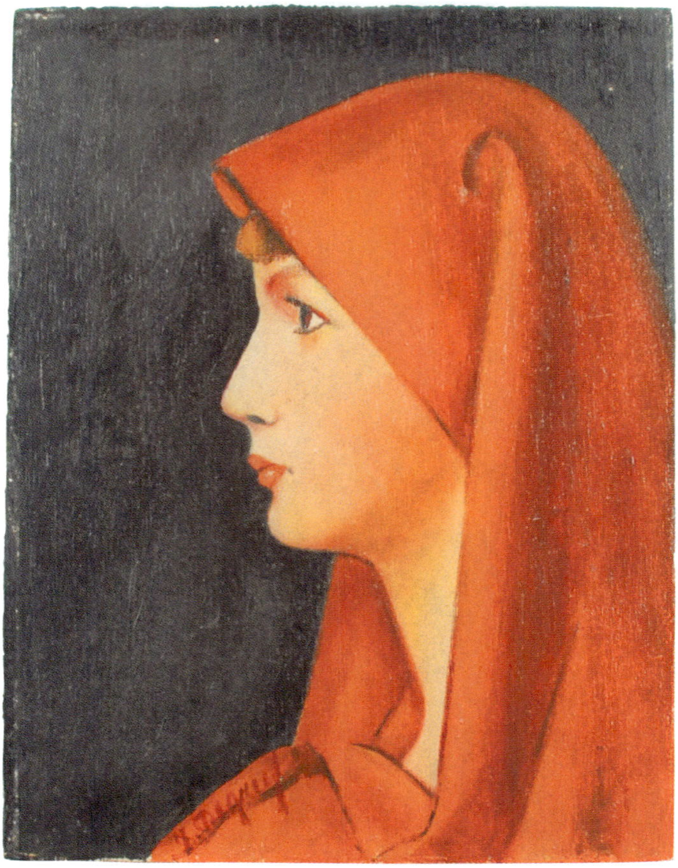

060

DIMENSIONS:	11 ⅝ x 9 x ¼ inches (29.5 x 22.9 x 0.64 cm)
DATE:	Unknown
MEDIA:	Paint on wood composite panel or board
CONDITION:	Good
PROVENANCE:	Unknown
NOTES:	Signed "X. Degeuy."

DIMENSIONS: 15 ¾ x 11 ¾ x ⅝ inches (40 x 29.8 x 1.59 cm)
DATE: Unknown
MEDIA: Paint on canvas
CONDITION: Good
PROVENANCE: Belgium, 1997, gift of Edith De Kindt
NOTES: Fabiola exhibits a down-turned mouth.
Signed "A. Vankaster."

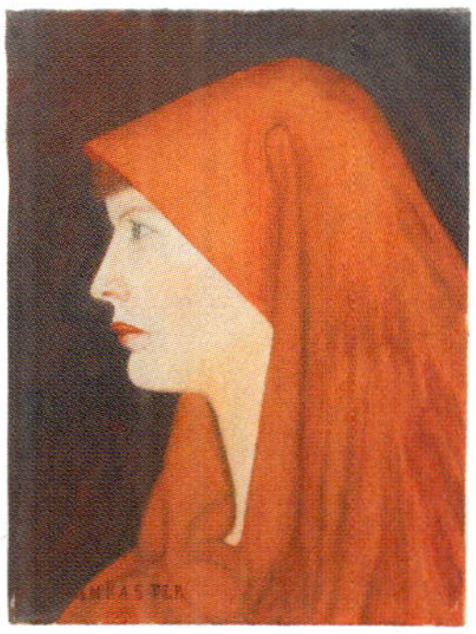

061

DIMENSIONS: 11 ⅝ x 8 x ¾ inches (29.5 x 20.3 x 1.91 cm)
DATE: Unknown
MEDIA: Paint on canvas
CONDITION: Fair—Surface abrasions and slight losses in black ground
PROVENANCE: Antwerp (Bouwcentrum), Belgium, March 1, 1998, 200 Belgian francs
NOTES: Subject is depicted with an unhealthy pallor. Antique postcard tucked into verso of stretcher. Written on the verso of the postcard is: "LA FABIOLA, J. J. Henner 1829–1905/ Louvre." The front of the postcard has been overlaid with a grid as a study indicating it could have been used as a guide for copying.

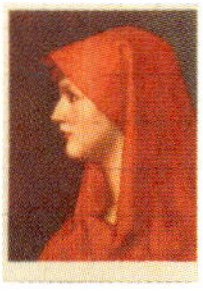

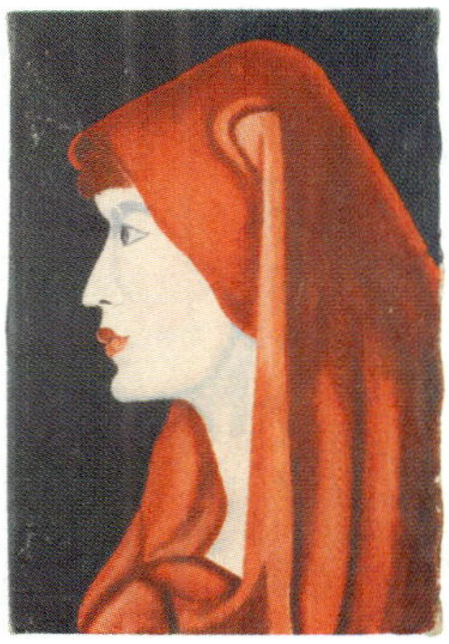

062

DIMENSIONS: 15 ⅞ x 11 ⅞ x ¾ inches (40.3 x 30.2 x 1.91 cm)
DATE: Unknown
MEDIA: Paint on canvas
CONDITION: Fair—Extensive surface cracking throughout paint layer.
PROVENANCE: Putte, Belgium, October 27, 1999, 400 Belgian francs
NOTES: Signed "J. Torck."

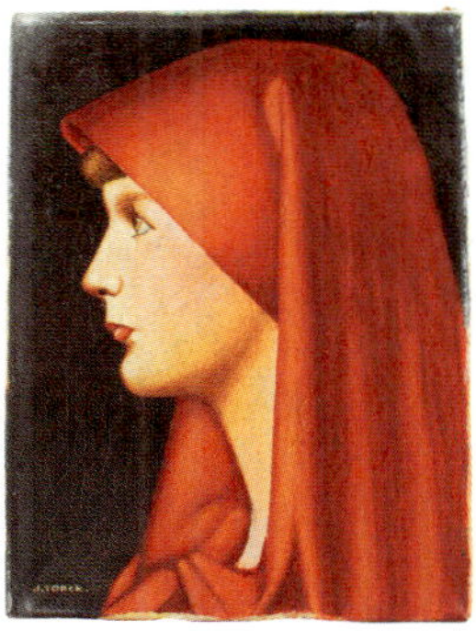

063

DIMENSIONS: 14 ⅛ x 11 x ⅝ inches (35.9 x 27.9 x 1.59 cm)
DATE: Unknown
MEDIA: Paint on canvas
CONDITION: Good
PROVENANCE: Mexico, 1995, 350 Mexican pesos
NOTES: Signed "Martinez."

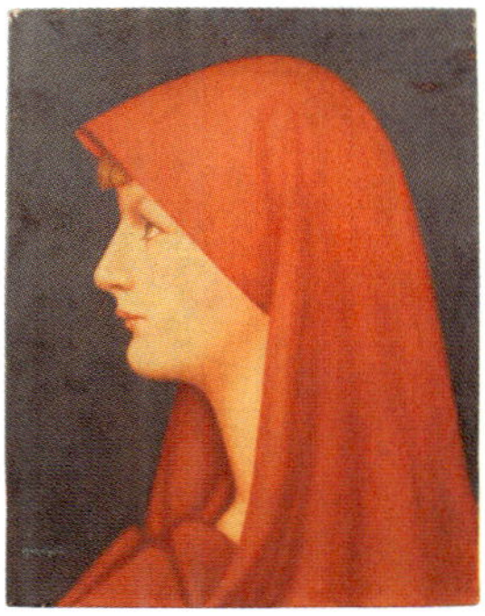

064

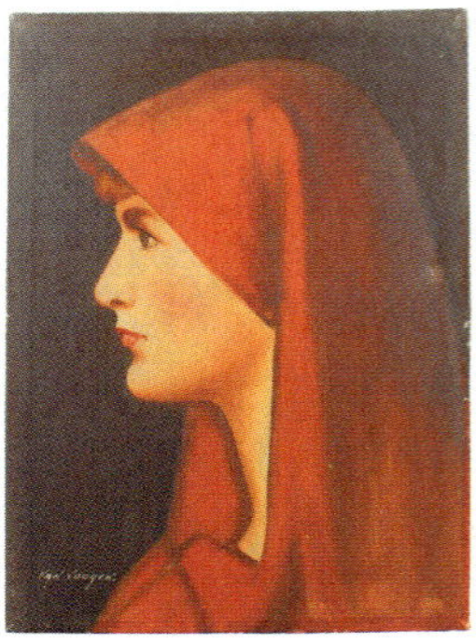

065

DIMENSIONS:	15 ¾ x 11 ¾ x ½ inches (40 x 29.8 x 1.27 cm)
DATE:	Unknown
MEDIA:	Paint on canvas
CONDITION:	Good
PROVENANCE:	Ciney, Belgium, April 16, 2001, 400 Belgian francs
NOTES:	Signed "Van Vooren."

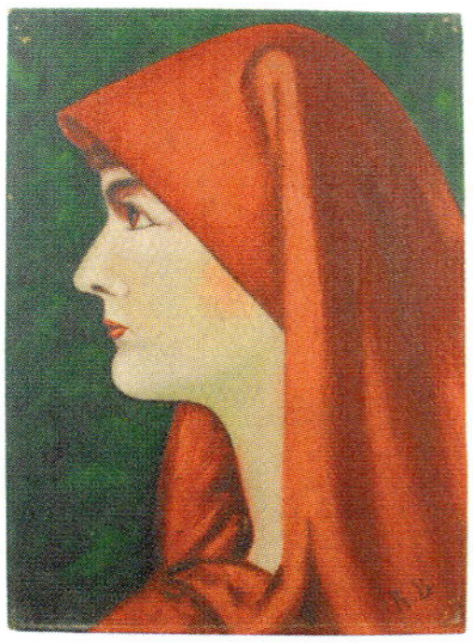

066

DIMENSIONS:	16 ¼ x 11 ⅞ x ⅞ inches (41.3 x 30.2 x 2.22 cm)
DATE:	Unknown
MEDIA:	Paint on paperboard or Masonite panel
CONDITION:	Good—There are a few losses or abrasions.
PROVENANCE:	Maastricht, Netherlands, November 1993, gift
NOTES:	Background is green, as opposed to dark or black, as is typical of other paintings. Possibly in an attempt to achieve the look of canvas, the artist used the textured side of the Masonite panel or paperboard. Signed "R. B."

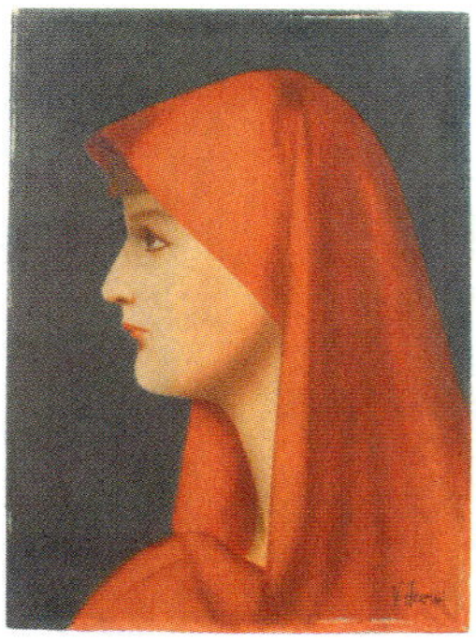

067

DIMENSIONS:	15 ¾ x 11 ⅝ x ⅜ inches (40 x 29.5 x 0.95 cm)
DATE:	Unknown
MEDIA:	Paint on canvas
CONDITION:	Good—There are slight abrasions and losses along edges and sides.
PROVENANCE:	Maastricht, Netherlands, 2000, gift
NOTES:	Signed "V. Herman."

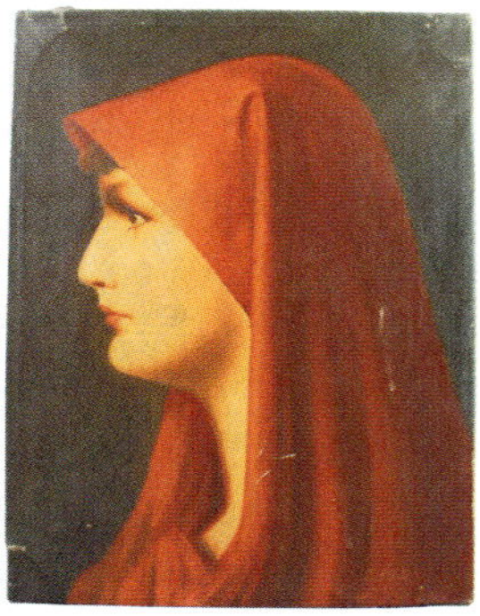

069

DIMENSIONS:	17 ¾ x 13 ¾ x ⅝ inches (45.1 x 34.9 x 1.59 cm)
DATE:	Unknown
MEDIA:	Paint on canvas
CONDITION:	Fair—Several losses, especially in hood area.
PROVENANCE:	Antwerp, Belgium, March 10, 2001, 650 Belgian francs
NOTES:	Signed "Seys."

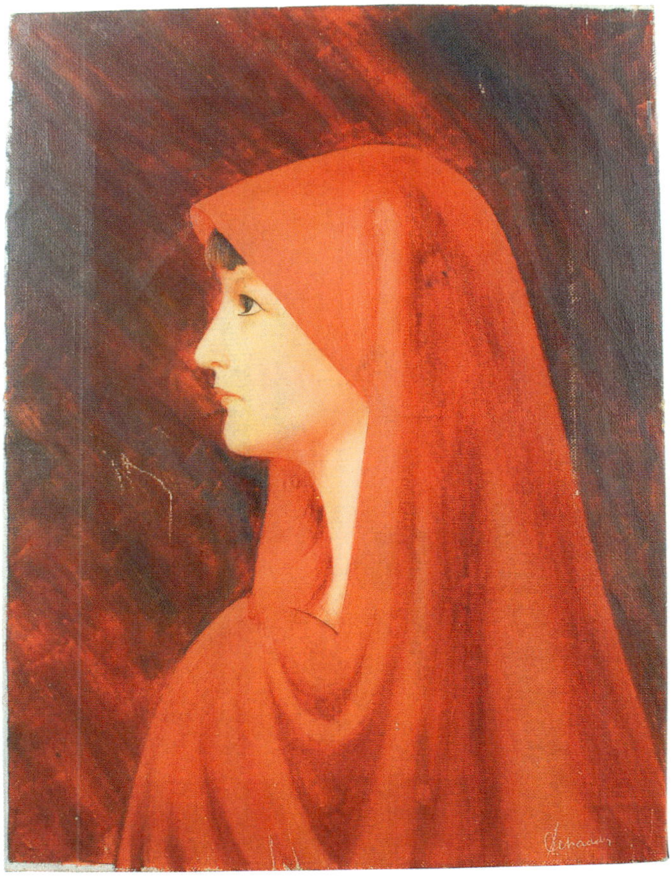

068

DIMENSIONS:	16 ⅛ x 12 ⅜ x ¾ inches (41 x 31.4 x 1.91 cm)
DATE:	Unknown
MEDIA:	Paint on canvas
CONDITION:	Fair—Stretcher has created creases and indentations that are visible from the front, and there are a few areas of abraded paint.
PROVENANCE:	Brussels, Belgium, September 1992, 100 Belgian francs
NOTES:	The view of the subject includes a larger portion of the upper torso than is typical in other Fabiola portraits. Signed "Schaddy."

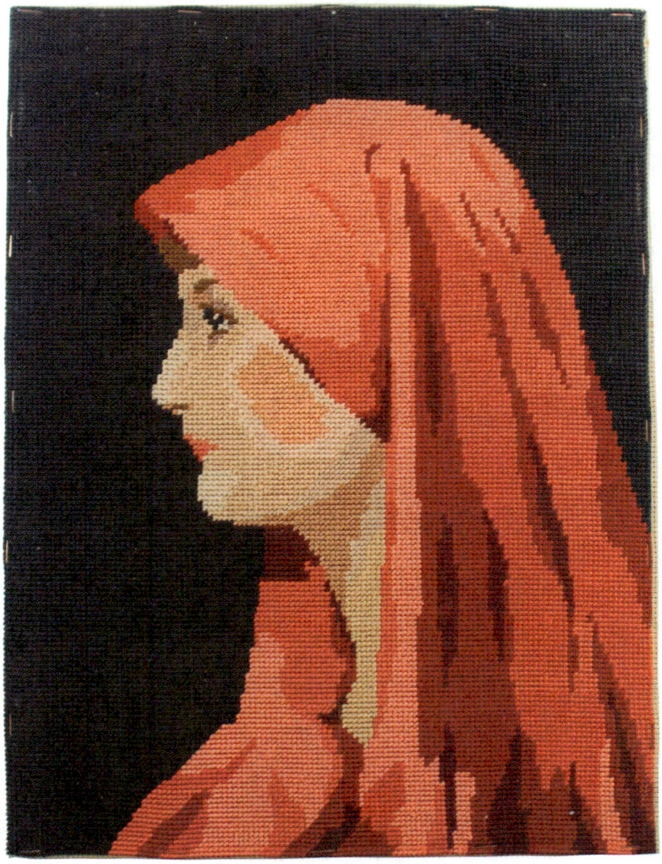

072

DIMENSIONS:	17 5/8 x 13 3/8 x 3/8 inches (44.8 x 34 x 0.95 cm)
DATE:	Unknown
MEDIA:	Needlepoint on mesh mounted on wood composite panel or board
CONDITION:	Good
PROVENANCE:	Unknown
NOTES:	This is clearly a commercially available pattern for needlepoint crafts, which explains the consistent composition, color palette, shading, and toning with nearly every needlepoint representation of Fabiola.

DIMENSIONS: 15 ¾ x 11 ¾ x ¾ inches (40 x 29.8 x 1.91 cm)
DATE: 1984
MEDIA: Paint on canvas
CONDITION: Good/Fair—Unknown layer of surface accretion throughout surface. Substantial losses along edges that reveal a blue paint layer below—these losses are a result of a prior framing.
PROVENANCE: Mexico City, Mexico, May 1994, 65 Mexican pesos
NOTES: Subject has dour and stern demeanor. Inscribed, dated, and signed "Fabiola 1984/Humberto Pavia/Alunso Mexico."

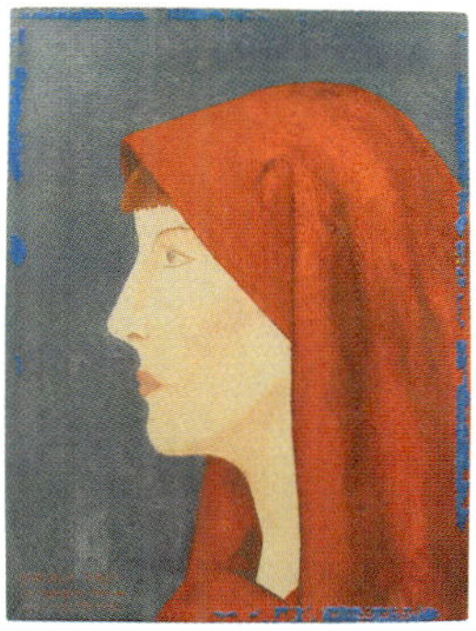

070

DIMENSIONS: 11 ½ x 9 ½ x ¼ inches (29.2 x 24.1 x 0.64 cm)
DATE: Unknown
MEDIA: Needlepoint on mesh support mounted on paperboard
CONDITION: Good
PROVENANCE: Unknown
NOTES: "FABIOLA" printed on mesh support on verso. This is clearly a commercially available pattern for needlepoint crafts. It explains the consistent composition, color palette, shading, and toning evident in nearly every needlepoint representation of Fabiola.

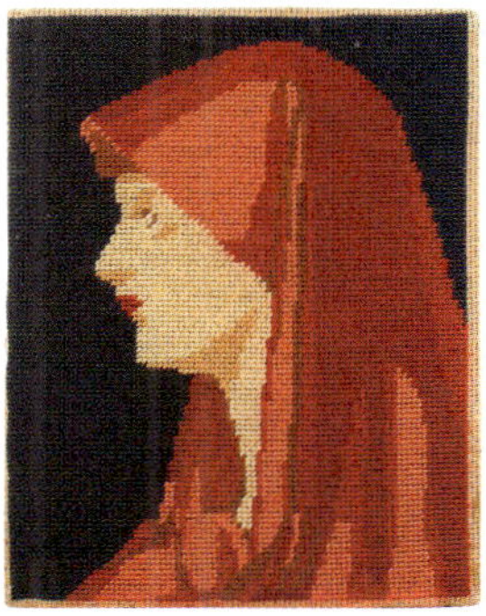

071

DIMENSIONS: 15 ⅝ x 11 ¾ x ⅝ inches (39.7 x 29.8 x 1.59 cm)
DATE: Unknown
MEDIA: Oil on canvas
CONDITION: Fair—Overall surface condition good, although there is a half circle–shaped tear (approx. 1" in length) at the top of subject's head.
PROVENANCE: Unknown
NOTES: Signed "Grassi."

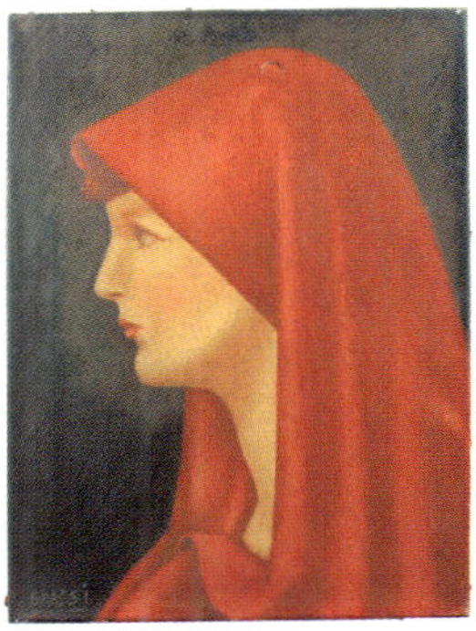

073

DIMENSIONS: 17 ¼ x 14 ⅛ x ⅛ inches (43.8 x 35.9 x 0.32 cm)
DATE: Unknown
MEDIA: Paint on canvas mounted on paperboard
CONDITION: Fair—There are holes in each of the four corners that were likely caused as a result of a prior mounting or hanging system.
PROVENANCE: Avignon, France, 2003, 40 French francs
NOTES: Fabiola's jawline and features impart a masculine appearance. Signed "Richard R."

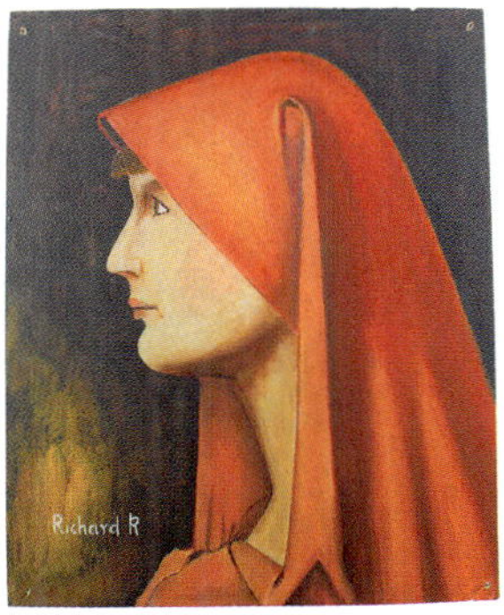

074

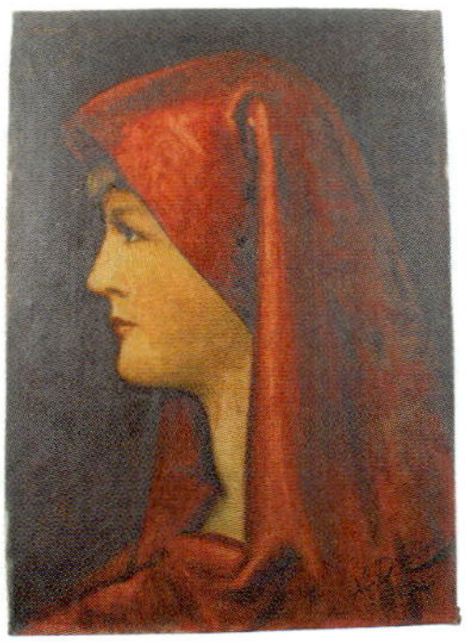

076

DIMENSIONS: 18 ½ x 13 x ½ inches (47 x 33 x 1.27 cm)
DATE: 1939 or 1959
MEDIA: Oil on canvas
CONDITION: Good
PROVENANCE: Unknown
NOTES: Inscribed on top proper right corner with an illegible phrase and "Jeanne," dated "29–6–1939" (or "29–6–1959"). Signed in the lower proper left corner "Al D. Clerck. LIER."

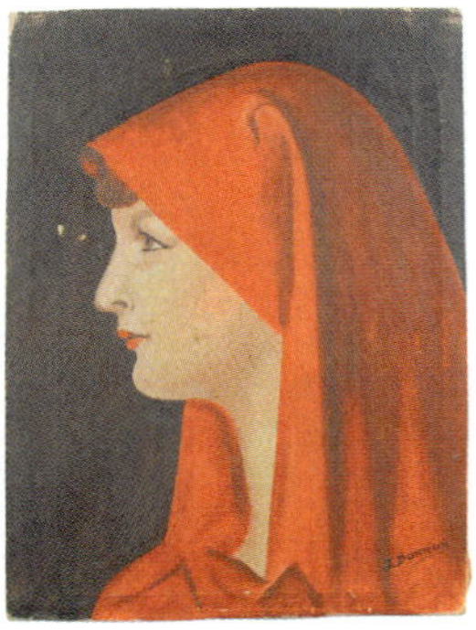

077

DIMENSIONS: 15 ¾ x 11 ¾ x ⅝ inches (40 x 29.8 x 1.59 cm)
DATE: Unknown
MEDIA: Oil on canvas
CONDITION: Fair—There are two tears in the canvas at the subject's eye level, and the painting has a network of cracks throughout. The stretcher has created creases and indentations that are visible from the front of the painting.
PROVENANCE: Lille, France, 1998, 110 French francs
NOTES: Signed "J. Durieux."

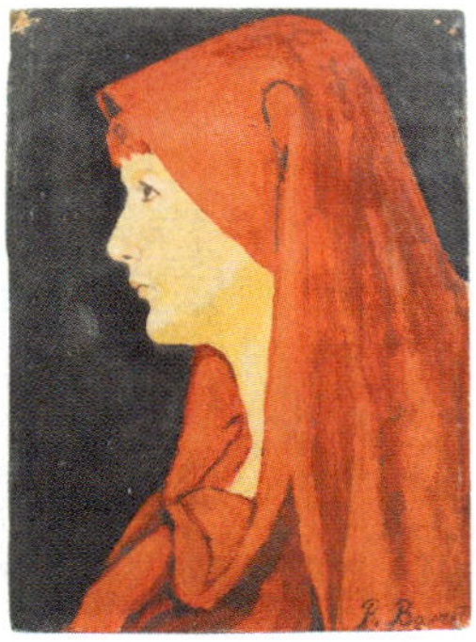

078

DIMENSIONS: 13 ⅜ x 9 ⅞ x ⅝ inches (34 x 25.1 x 1.59 cm)
DATE: Unknown
MEDIA: Paint on canvas on board
CONDITION: Fair—Top proper right corner of canvas is detached from panel support below.
PROVENANCE: Brussels, Belgium, July 1994
NOTES: Signed "B. Baert."

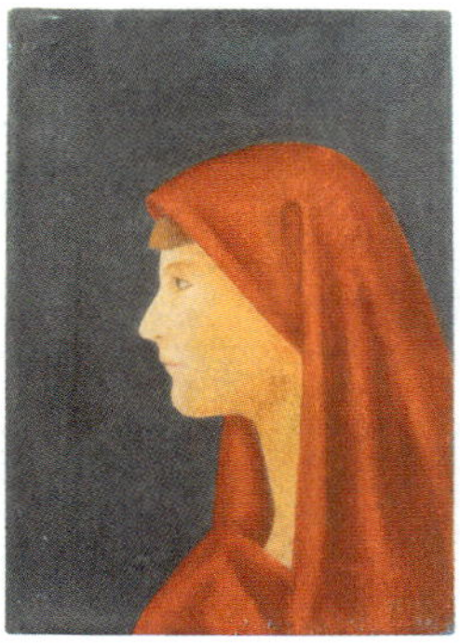

079

DIMENSIONS: 13 ¾ x 9 ⅞ x ¾ inches (34.9 x 25.1 x 1.91 cm)
DATE: Unknown
MEDIA: Paint on canvas
CONDITION: Fair/Good
PROVENANCE: Mexico City, Mexico, August 1994, 60 Mexican pesos
NOTES: Signed "Peter." It appears that the figure has a varnish layer or coating that is separate or different from the background.

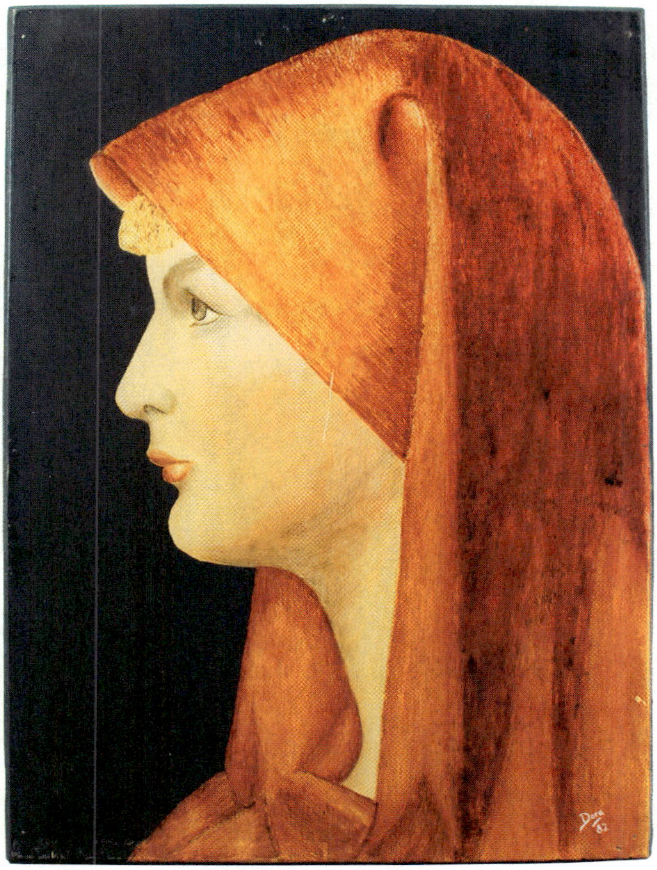

075

DIMENSIONS:	15 ⅝ x 11 ¾ x ⅞ inches (39.7 x 29.8 x 2.22 cm)
DATE:	1982
MEDIA:	Paint on panel or board
CONDITION:	Good—Subject has a 1 ½" scratch in cheek area.
PROVENANCE:	Mexico City, Mexico, February 1994, 180 Mexican pesos
NOTES:	Signed "Dora 82."

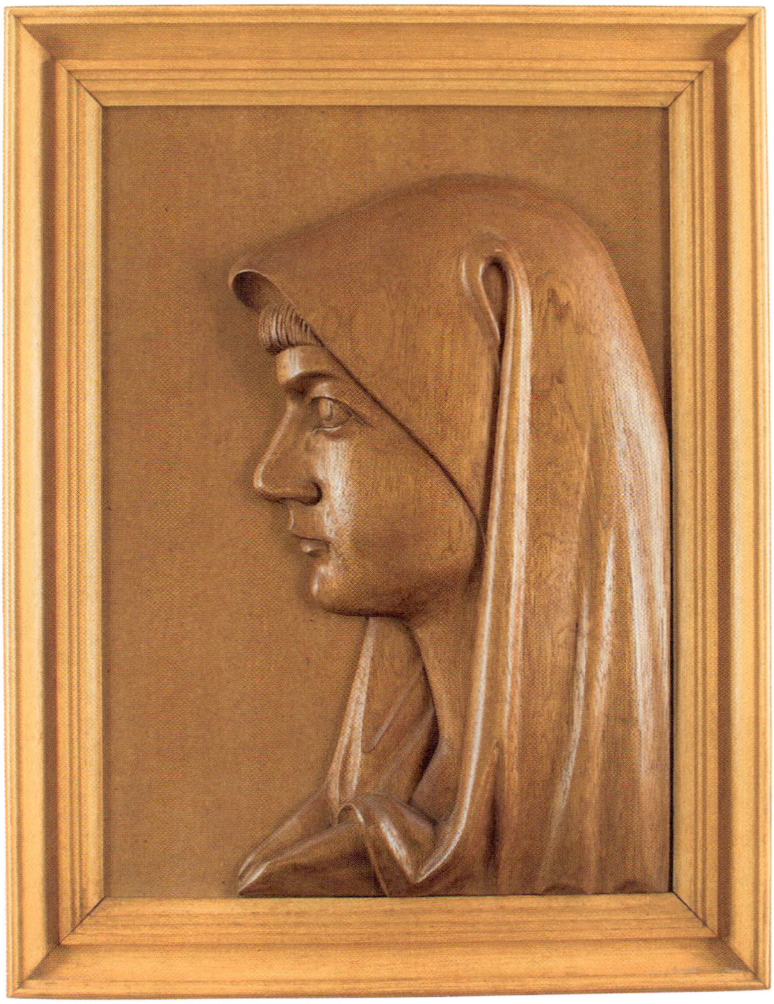

080

DIMENSIONS:	18 ½ x 14 ¼ x 1 ⅛ inches (47 x 36.2 x 2.86 cm)
DATE:	Unknown
MEDIA:	Carved wood relief
CONDITION:	Good
PROVENANCE:	Belgium
NOTES:	Carved facial features do not conform to classical Western standards.

DIMENSIONS:	13 ⅞ x 9 ⅞ x ½ inches (35.2 x 25.1 x 1.27 cm)
DATE:	Unknown
MEDIA:	Oil on canvas
CONDITION:	Fair—Unknown surface accretion approx. 4 ½" long, running from eye level of subject to upper edge of painting. Minor creases or wrinkles in the canvas are visible throughout the painting. There are a few minor losses along the edges.
PROVENANCE:	Unknown
NOTES:	Signed "D'après Henner, L. Suys."

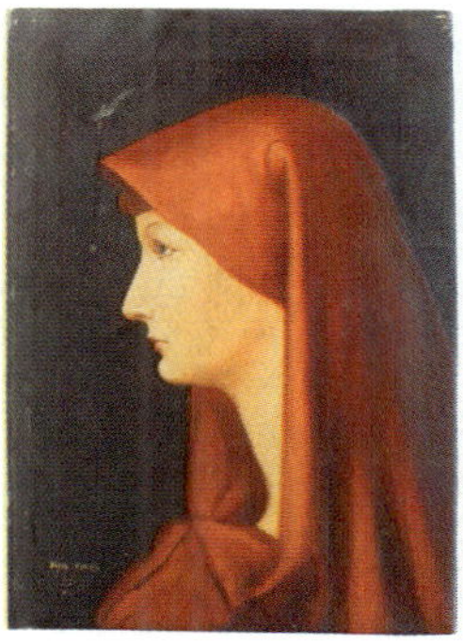

081

DIMENSIONS:	9 x 6 ⅝ x ¼ inches (22.9 x 16.8 x 0.64 cm)
DATE:	Unknown
MEDIA:	Paint on wood composite panel or board
CONDITION:	Poor—There is a severe loss in the paint layer at the area of the subject's head. This appears to have been caused by significant scraping or abrasion. There are also losses along the edges and sides.
PROVENANCE:	Verviers, Belgium, April 24, 2000, 500 Belgian francs
NOTES:	Subject exhibits a childlike appearance. Signed "F. Heyden."

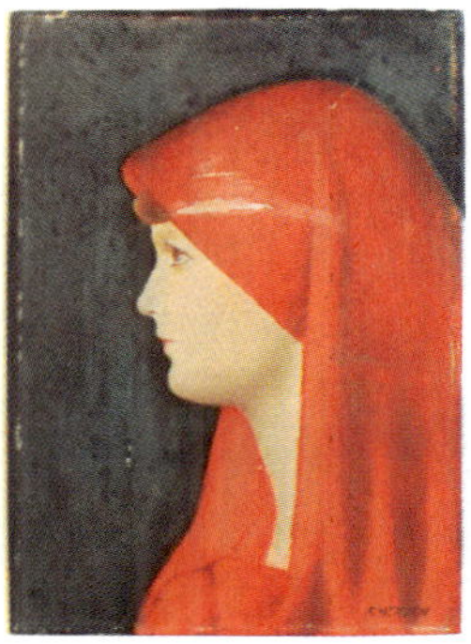

082

DIMENSIONS:	13 ¾ x 9 ⅞ x ⅝ inches (34.9 x 25.1 x 1.59 cm)
DATE:	Unknown
MEDIA:	Paint on canvas
CONDITION:	Good/Fair—There is a puncture and tear in the painting at the lower proper left corner.
PROVENANCE:	Unknown
NOTES:	This work has a close resemblance to reproductions of the Jean-Jacques Henner original. Signed "Sermanto."

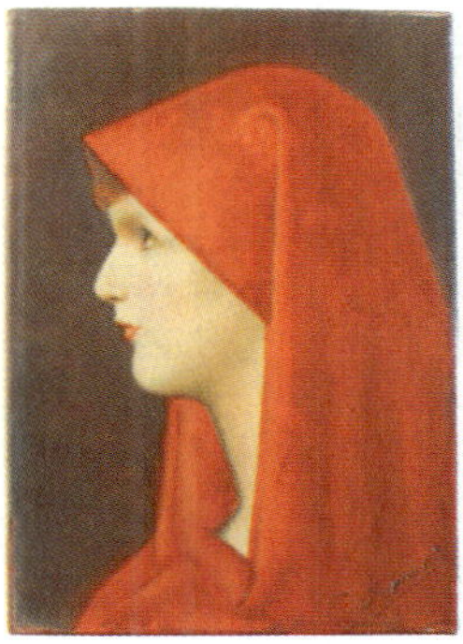

083

DIMENSIONS:	15 ¾ x 11 ⅞ x ⅜ inches (40 x 30.2 x 0.95 cm)
DATE:	Unknown
MEDIA:	Paint on canvas
CONDITION:	Good—There is a white accretion at the top center edge of the painting.
PROVENANCE:	Villers-la-Ville, Belgium, June 19, 1999, 100 Belgian francs
NOTES:	Signed "Frans Huys."

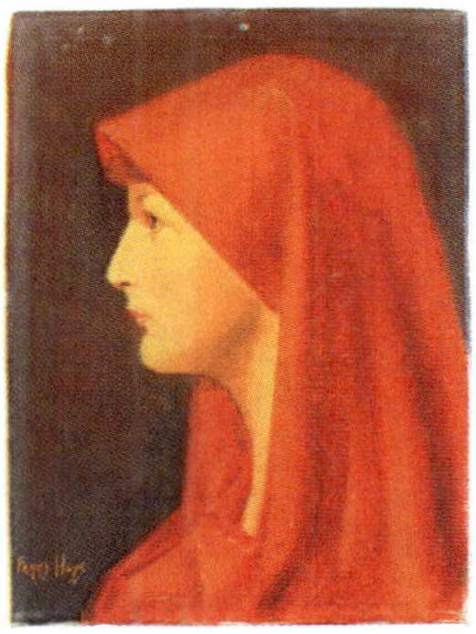

084

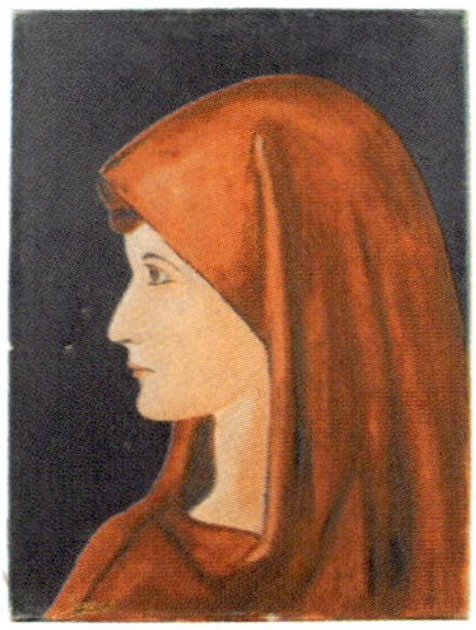

085

DIMENSIONS:	15 ¾ x 11 ¾ x ⅝ inches (40 x 29.8 x 1.59 cm)
DATE:	Unknown
MEDIA:	Paint on canvas
CONDITION:	Fair—There are two punctures in the canvas support at subject's nose level.
PROVENANCE:	Mons, Belgium, April 1998, 400 Belgian francs
NOTES:	Subject's demeanor appears particularly devout. Signed "Segers."

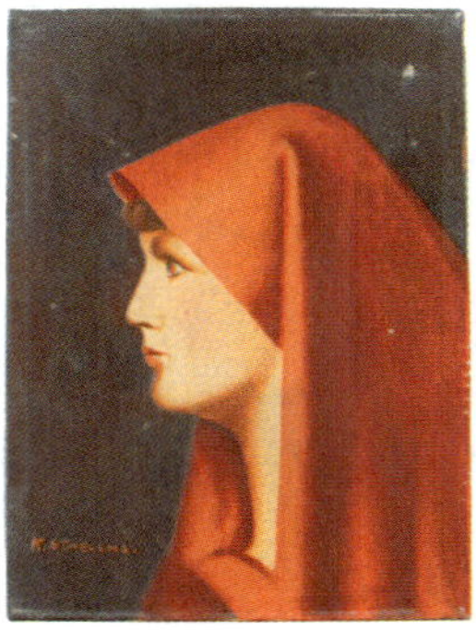

086

DIMENSIONS:	15 ¾ x 11 ¾ x ⅜ inches (40 x 29.8 x 0.95 cm)
DATE:	Unknown
MEDIA:	Paint on canvas
CONDITION:	Fair—There are small losses and tears in the canvas support and paint layer throughout.
PROVENANCE:	Brugge, Belgium, September 27, 1998
NOTES:	Signed "K. Staelens."

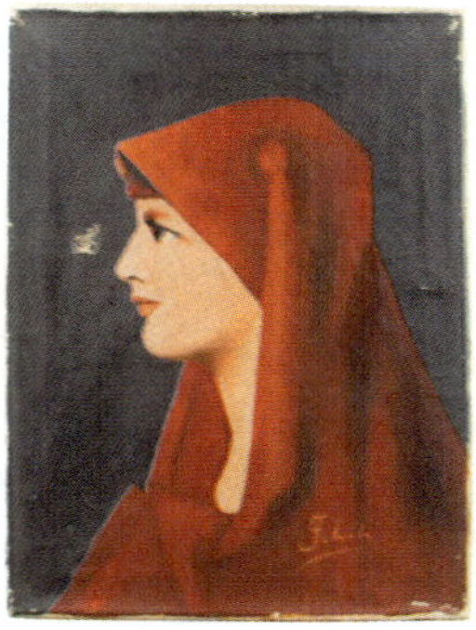

087

DIMENSIONS:	15 ¾ x 11 ¾ x ¾ inches (40 x 29.8 x 1.91 cm)
DATE:	Unknown
MEDIA:	Paint on canvas
CONDITION:	Fair/Poor—Stretcher has created creases and indentations in the canvas that are visible from the front, and there are losses along the edges and sides. There is also a large area of loss and significant stress to the canvas support at the subject's eye level. This area has been marginally repaired and addressed with a patch on the verso.
PROVENANCE:	Brussels, Belgium, January 1993, 100 Belgian francs
NOTES:	Inscribed "Fabiola."

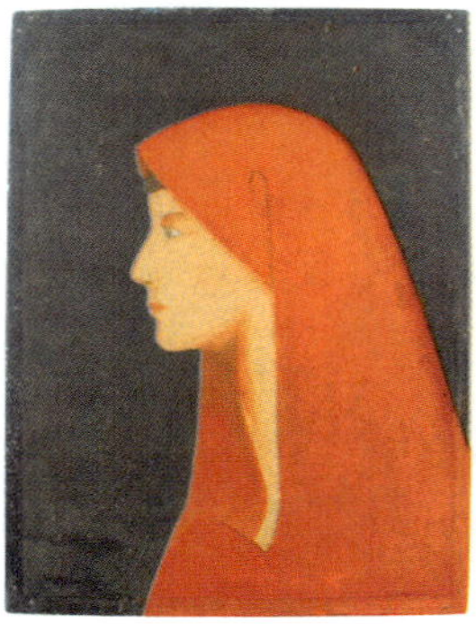

089

DIMENSIONS:	15 x 11 ⅜ x ⅝ inches (38.1 x 28.9 x 1.59 cm)
DATE:	Unknown
MEDIA:	Paint on wood composite panel or board
CONDITION:	Good/Fair
PROVENANCE:	Brussels, Belgium, March 1994, gift
NOTES:	Surface of the painting appears to have been burnished or treated in some way, perhaps in an effort to artificially age the painting.

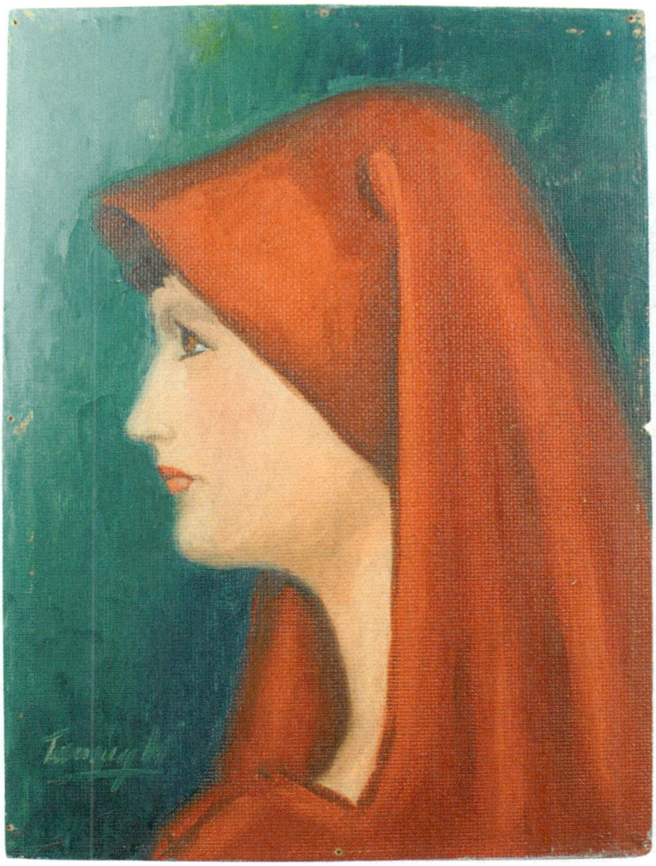

088

DIMENSIONS:	15 ⅞ x 12 x ⅛ inches (40.3 x 30.5 x 0.32 cm)
DATE:	Unknown
MEDIA:	Paint on panel or board
CONDITION:	Good
PROVENANCE:	Grammene (Deinze), Belgium, August 16, 2003, 1 euro
NOTES:	Painting has green background, as opposed to black as is typical of other Fabiola depictions. Signed "Tenguy M."

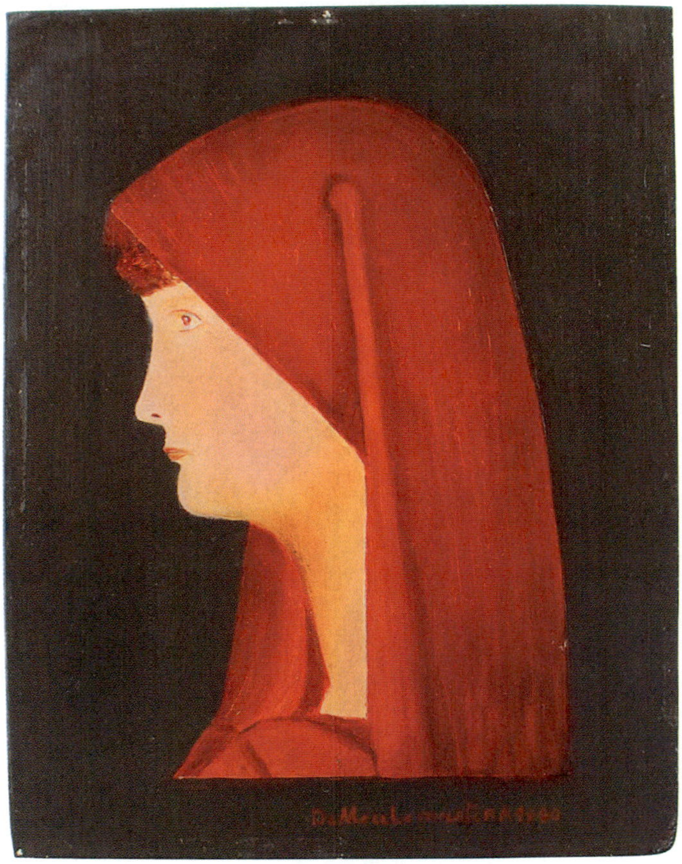

090

DIMENSIONS:	10 ¾ x 8 ½ x ⅛ inches (27.3 x 21.6 x 0.32 cm)
DATE:	1980
MEDIA:	Paint on paperboard or panel
CONDITION:	Good
PROVENANCE:	Ghent, Belgium, 1999, 150 Belgian francs
NOTES:	Signed “De Meulemeester A 1980.”

DIMENSIONS: 19 ¾ x 15 x ¾ inches (50.2 x 38.1 x 1.91 cm)
DATE: 1949
MEDIA: Paint on paperboard or Masonite panel
CONDITION: Good
PROVENANCE: Unknown
NOTES: Subject exhibits a common Fabiola feature, in that there are two distinct segments of the bangs, one hanging naturally down, and the other extending up beyond the edge of the hood. In addition, the hood is depicted with three angles, as opposed to one curved line. This portrait also has a prominent chin, as seen in the reproduction of the original Henner portrait. Signed "R. Pelfrêne 6–49."

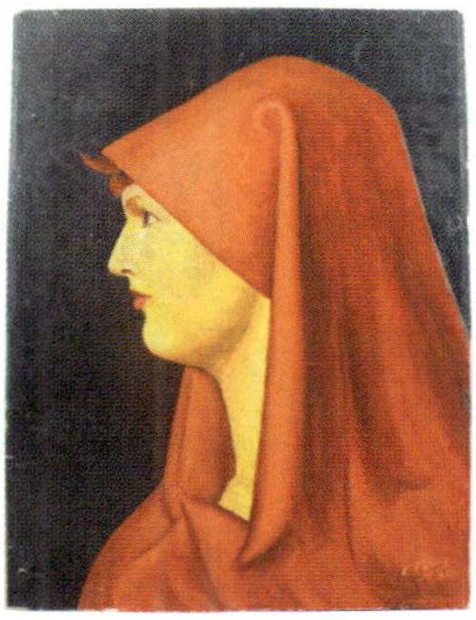

091

DIMENSIONS: 15 ⅞ x 11 ¾ x ⅝ inches (40.3 x 29.8 x 1.59 cm)
DATE: Unknown
MEDIA: Paint on canvas
CONDITION: Good
PROVENANCE: Unknown
NOTES: Signed "Tiesnjans—naar Henner."

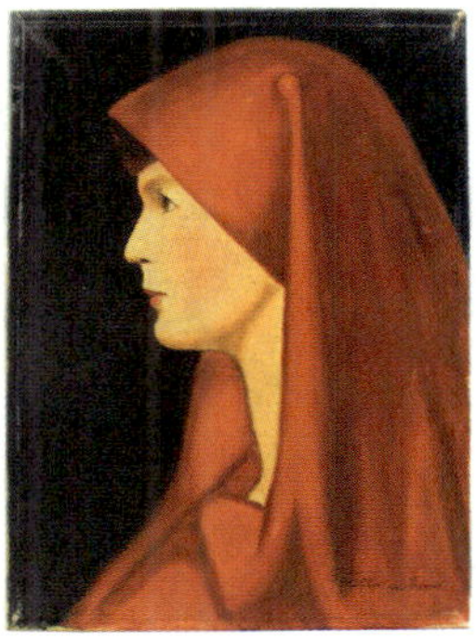

092

DIMENSIONS: 15 ¾ x 11 ¾ x ⅝ inches (40 x 29.8 x 1.59 cm)
DATE: Unknown
MEDIA: Paint on canvas
CONDITION: Fair/Good—Small puncture in canvas support and loss in paint layer at center height of proper right side. Minor surface abrasions throughout.
PROVENANCE: Brussels, Belgium, 1994, 250 Belgian francs
NOTES: Signed "G. Debaets."

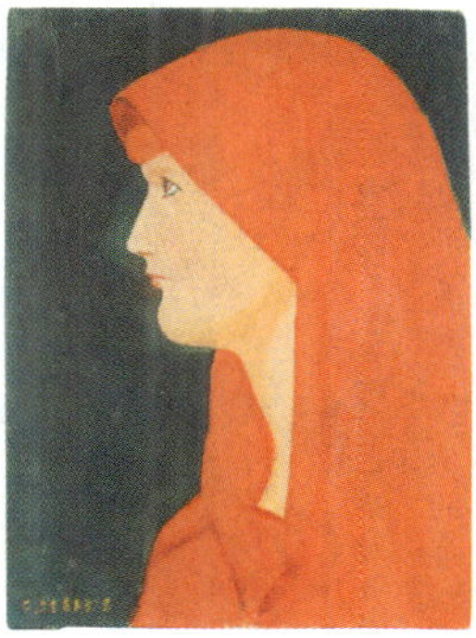

093

DIMENSIONS: 19 ¾ x 16 x ⅝ inches (50.2 x 40.6 x 1.59 cm)
DATE: Unknown
MEDIA: Paint on canvas
CONDITION: Poor—Extensive cracking throughout surface and numerous losses in the paint layer in area of most severe cracking. Abraded surfaces and losses are visible, especially along edges.
PROVENANCE: Unknown
NOTES: Signed "Adhaine."

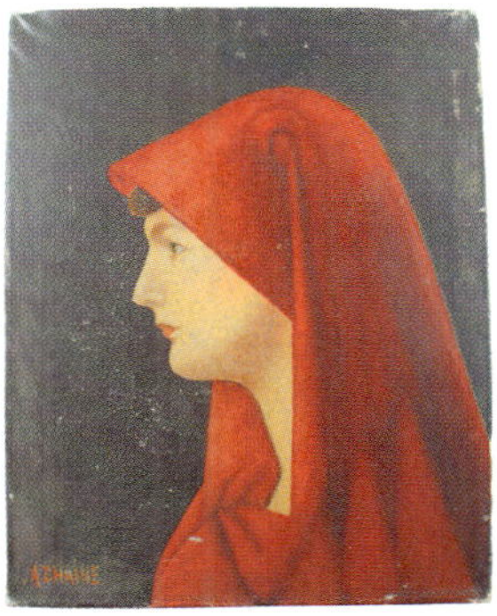

094

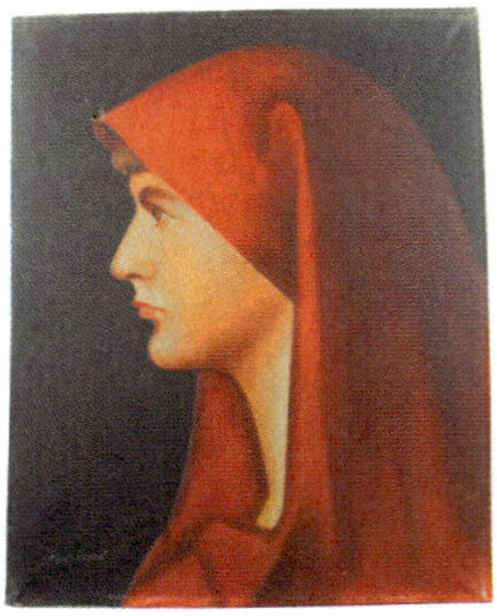

095

DIMENSIONS: 19 ¾ x 15 ⅞ x ½ inches (50.2 x 40.3 x 1.27 cm)
DATE: Unknown
MEDIA: Paint on canvas
CONDITION: Fair—Surface is in good condition except for two large punctures in the paint layer and canvas support located at the top of the subject's hood.
PROVENANCE: Unknown
NOTES: Signed "Van Vooren."

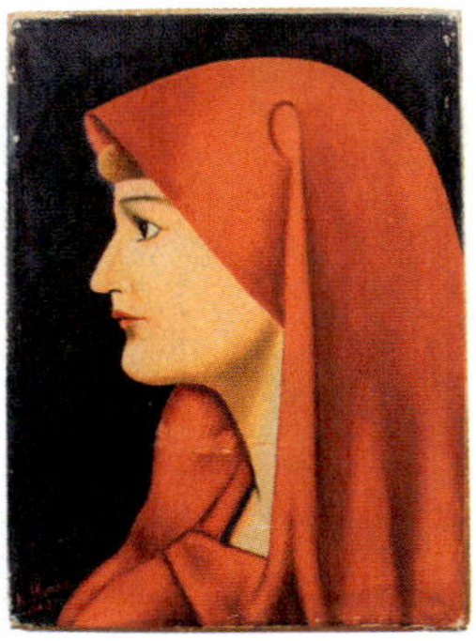

097

DIMENSIONS: 16 x 11 ¾ x ¾ inches (40.6 x 29.8 x 1.91 cm)
DATE: 1953
MEDIA: Oil on canvas
CONDITION: Fair—Superficial loss approx. 1 x ¾" (perhaps only in the varnish layer) at neck height in hood. Several other losses in the paint layer occur along edges.
PROVENANCE: Brussels, Belgium, December 1993, 300 Belgian francs
NOTES: Signed "K. Steurs.1953"

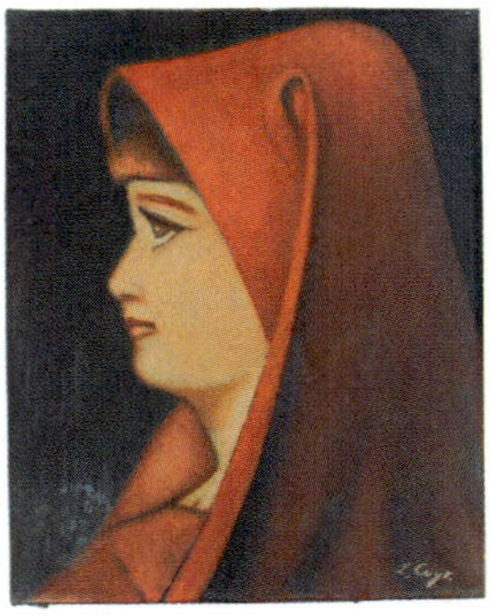

098

DIMENSIONS: 19 ⅝ x 15 ¾ x ⅝ inches (49.8 x 40 x 1.59 cm)
DATE: Unknown
MEDIA: Paint on canvas
CONDITION: Fair
PROVENANCE: Unknown
NOTES: The scale of subject's features, especially the eye and the perceived depth of her head, create a confusing composition. Signed "L. Coyt."

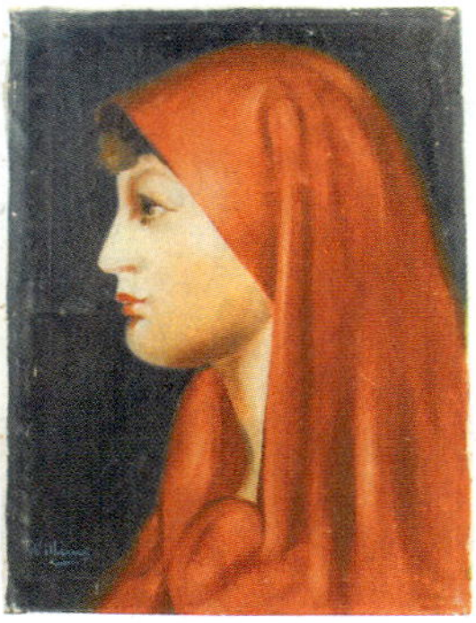

099

DIMENSIONS: 15 ½ x 11 ⅞ x ⅝ inches (39.4 x 30.2 x 1.59 cm)
DATE: Unknown
MEDIA: Paint on canvas
CONDITION: Fair—Numerous cracks in the paint layer throughout and possible biological growth or accretion at top proper left corner. Stretcher structure has created creases and marks in the canvas, which are visible from the front. There is a small indentation from the verso around the area of the top "ear."
PROVENANCE: Brussels, Belgium, September 23, 1994, 300 Belgian francs
NOTES: Signed "Willims."

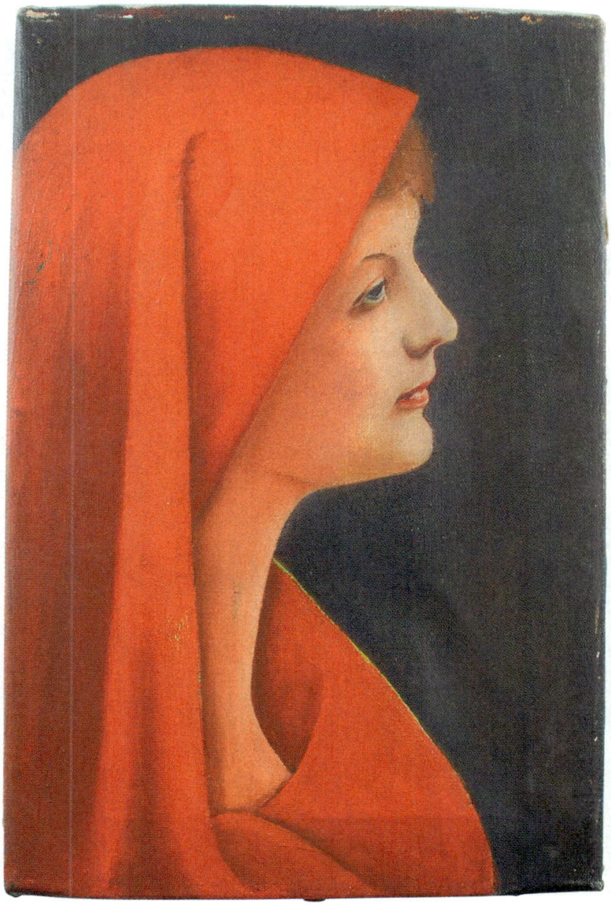

096

DIMENSIONS:	16 ¼ x 10 ⅞ x ¾ inches (41.3 x 27.6 x 1.91 cm)
DATE:	Unknown
MEDIA:	Paint on canvas
CONDITION:	Good/Fair—There are three prior restorations that involved patches to the canvas support from the verso.
PROVENANCE:	Lille, France, 1995, 80 French francs
NOTES:	Subject is facing the proper left side of the painting, as compared with the right, as is typical of nearly all other paintings. The subject's gaze is also different, as if the figure's posture is softened and is glancing upward.

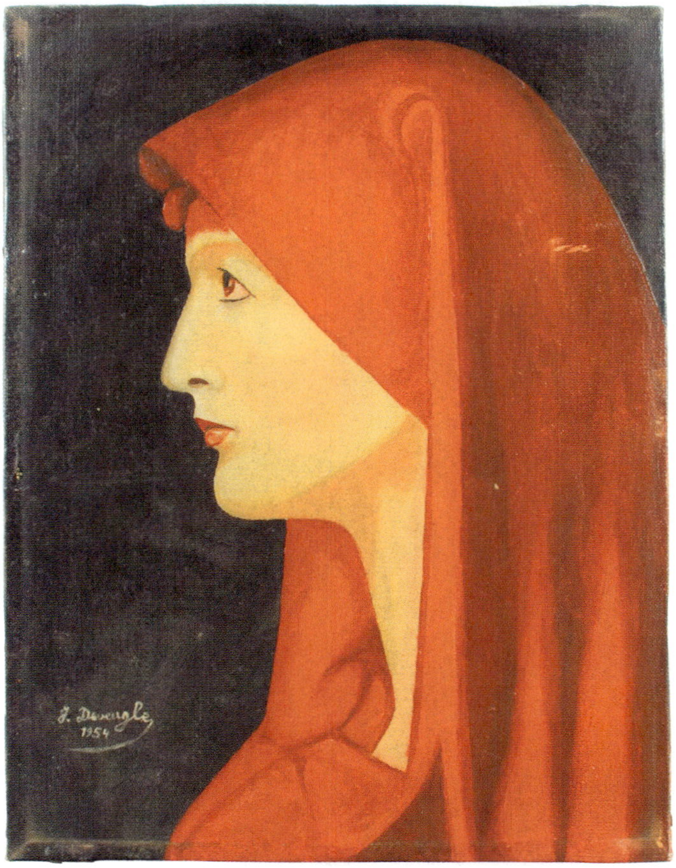

100

DIMENSIONS:	13 ¾ x 10 ½ x ½ inches (34.9 x 26.7 x 1.27 cm)
DATE:	1954
MEDIA:	Paint on canvas
CONDITION:	Good—There is a small area of abrasion in the paint layer at the back of the subject's hood.
PROVENANCE:	Unknown
NOTES:	Subject's gaze is distinctly upward. Signed "J. Deveugle."

DIMENSIONS: 19 ⅝ x 15 ¾ x ⅝ inches (49.8 x 40 x 1.59 cm)
DATE: Unknown
MEDIA: Paint on canvas
CONDITION: Good
PROVENANCE: Unknown
NOTES: Signed "H. Geenens."

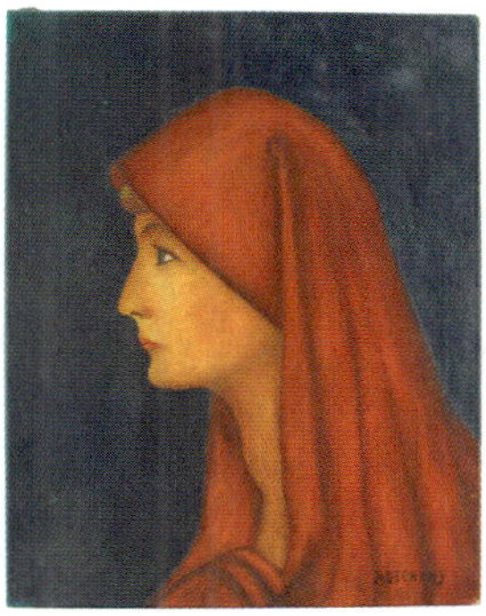

101

DIMENSIONS: 15 ¾ x 11 ¾ x ¾ inches (40 x 29.8 x 1.91 cm)
DATE: Unknown
MEDIA: Paint on canvas
CONDITION: Good
PROVENANCE: June 1998, gift of Thierry Le Clerco
NOTES: Signed "De Vadder Fr."

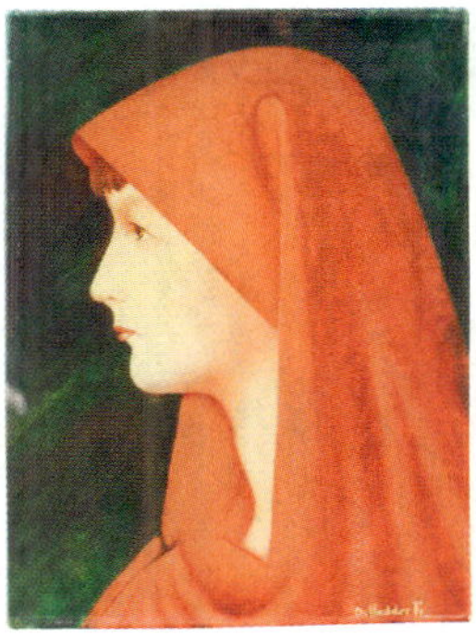

102

DIMENSIONS: 15 ¾ x 11 ¾ x ¾ inches (40 x 29.8 x 1.91 cm)
DATE: Unknown
MEDIA: Paint on panel or board
CONDITION: Good/Fair—There are numerous small losses and abrasions in the paint layer throughout.
PROVENANCE: London, England, September 1993, 5 British pounds
NOTES: Like several examples in this collection, this Fabiola has dark coloration throughout face, which could possibly suggest bruises or injury.

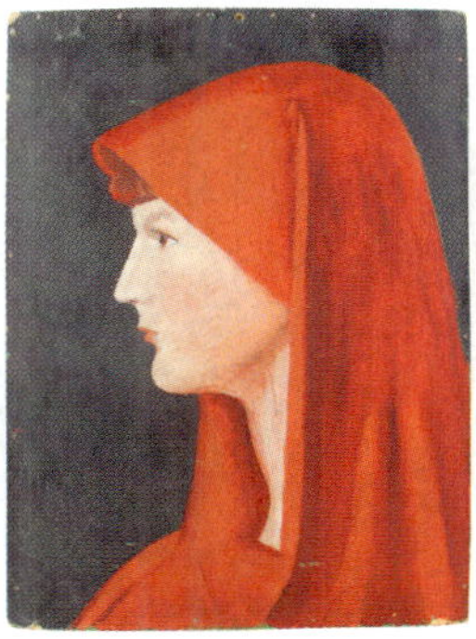

103

DIMENSIONS: 19 ⅝ x 15 ⅞ x ½ inches (49.8 x 40.3 x 1.27 cm)
DATE: Unknown
MEDIA: Paint on canvas
CONDITION: Fair/Poor—The canvas is extremely loose from the stretcher. There is a prior repair to a severe tear in the canvas support.
PROVENANCE: Unknown
NOTES: Signed "Van Vooren."

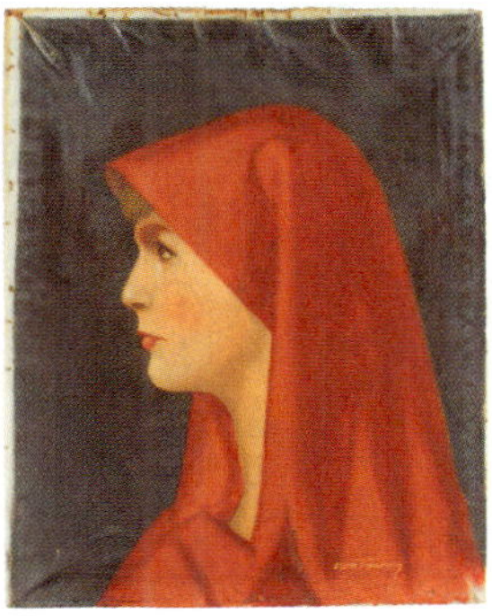

104

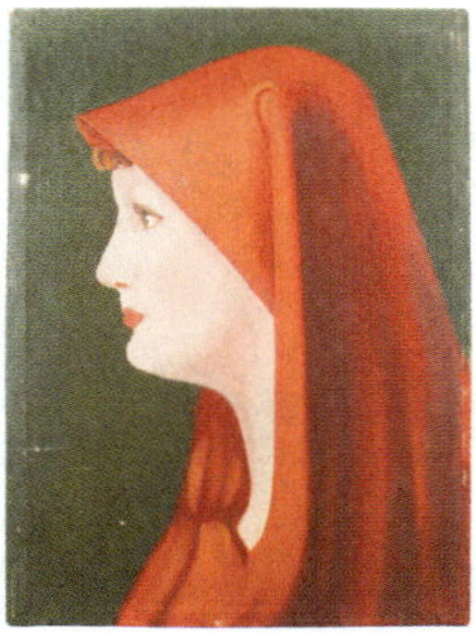

105

DIMENSIONS:	15 ¾ x 11 ¾ x ½ inches (40 x 29.8 x 1.27 cm)
DATE:	Unknown
MEDIA:	Paint on canvas
CONDITION:	Fair—Several areas of loss, most significant of which is located at subject's forehead level along the proper right side. The painting has a splatterlike accretion pattern throughout.
PROVENANCE:	Flea market, Brussels, Belgium, October 1995, 100 Belgian francs
NOTES:	Subject's chin is particularly thick and protruding.

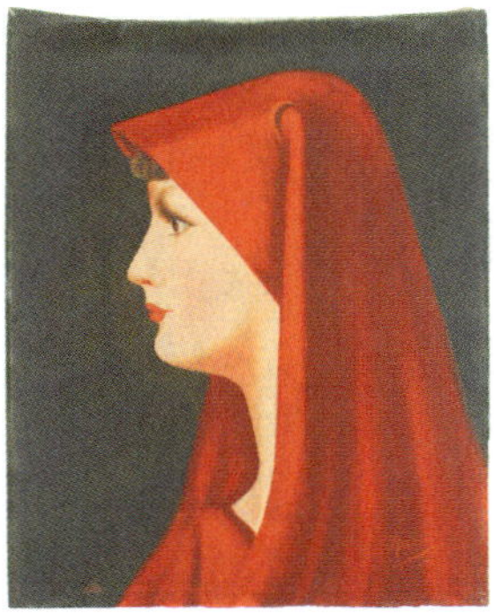

106

DIMENSIONS:	19 ¾ x 15 ⅞ x ½ inches (50.2 x 40.3 x 1.27 cm)
DATE:	Unknown
MEDIA:	Paint on canvas
CONDITION:	Poor—There is significant deformation of the stretcher.
PROVENANCE:	Hannut, Belgium, January 12, 2002, 1500 Belgian francs
NOTES:	Signed "Marco."

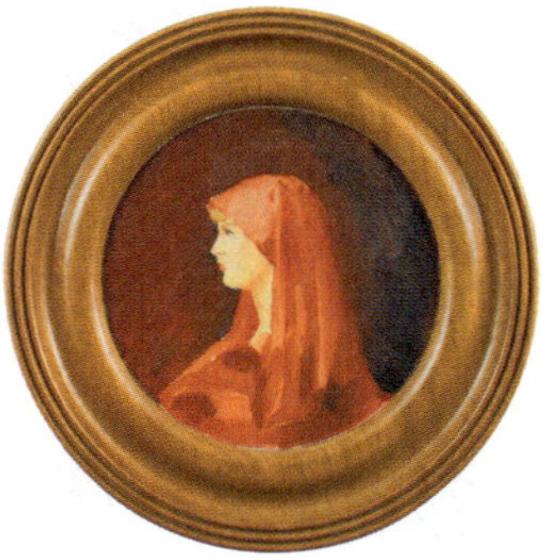

108

DIMENSIONS:	12 inches diameter x 1 inch (30.5 cm diameter x 2.54 cm)
DATE:	Unknown
MEDIA:	Paint on canvas mounted on solid wood circular frame
CONDITION:	Good
PROVENANCE:	Rotterdam, Netherlands, 2002
NOTES:	The subject is depicted with fair coloring (blond hair, blue eyes, etc.), as opposed to the darker complexions common to most other Fabiola portraits.

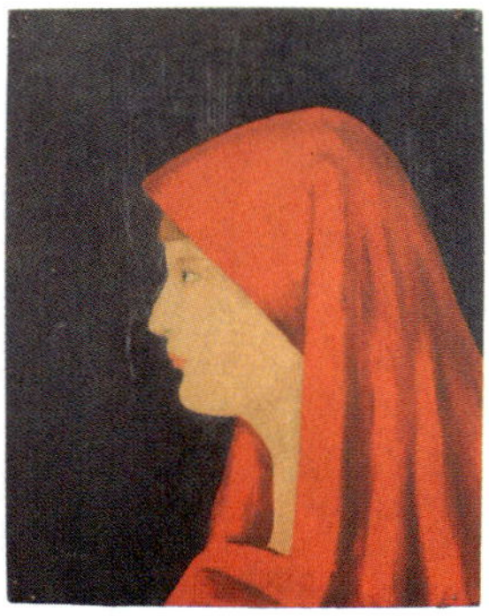

109

DIMENSIONS:	16 x 12 ⅞ x ½ (40.6 x 32.7 x 1.27 cm)
DATE:	Unknown
MEDIA:	Painting on preprimed canvas board nailed to wood support
CONDITION:	Fair—Minor surface scuffs and abrasions throughout.
PROVENANCE:	Lille, France, October 1993, 50 French francs
NOTES:	Signed "Dubois."

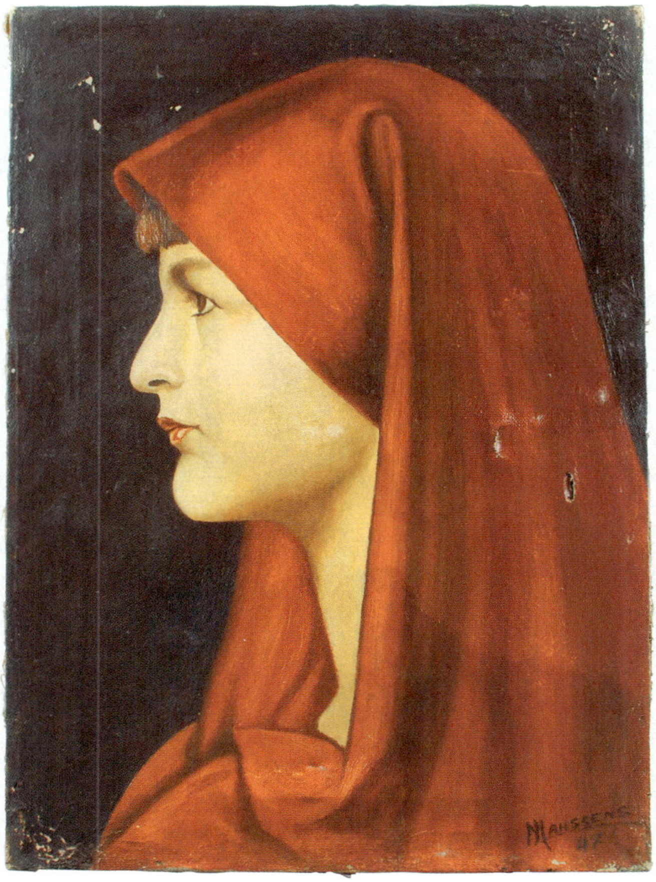

107

DIMENSIONS:	15 ⅞ x 11 ¾ x ⅜ inches (40.3 x 29.8 x 0.95 cm)
DATE:	1947
MEDIA:	Oil on canvas
CONDITION:	Fair/Poor—Stretcher has created creases and indentations in the canvas that are visible from the front, and there are losses along the edges and sides. There are also two significant tears in the canvas support in the midregion of the hood.
PROVENANCE:	Unknown
NOTES:	Signed "Mahssen G 47."

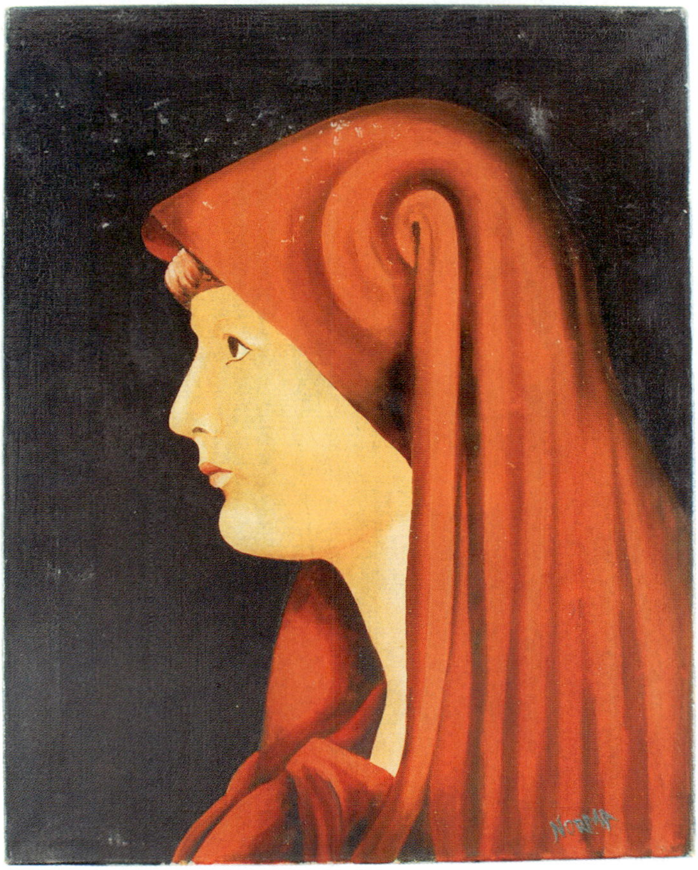

112

DIMENSIONS:	19 ¾ x 15 ⅞ x ⅝ inches (50.2 x 40.3 x 1.59 cm)
DATE:	Unknown
MEDIA:	Paint on canvas
CONDITION:	Good
PROVENANCE:	Unknown
NOTES:	Prime vertical fold in subject's hood is accompanied by reverberating curves and straight lines to indicate additional folds. Signed "Norma."

DIMENSIONS: 19 ⅞ inches diameter x 1 ¼ inches (50.5 cm diameter x 3.15 cm)
DATE: Unknown
MEDIA: Paint on solid wood circular support and frame
CONDITION: Good/Fair—There are numerous small losses and accretions throughout surface.
PROVENANCE: Flea market, Brussels, Belgium, 1998, 200 Belgian francs
NOTES: Signed, but illegible.

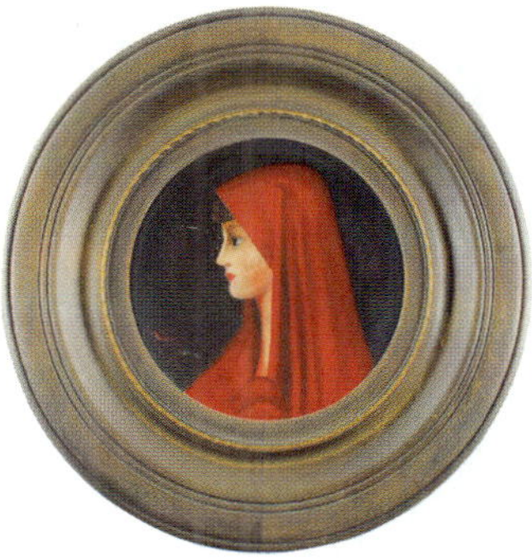

110

DIMENSIONS: 15 ¾ x 11 ¾ x ½ inches (40 x 29.8 x 1.27 cm)
DATE: Unknown
MEDIA: Paint on canvas
CONDITION: Good
PROVENANCE: Unknown
NOTES: There is confusing shading along the jawline of this Fabiola, which, to some, might suggest hair growth. Signed "Fred."

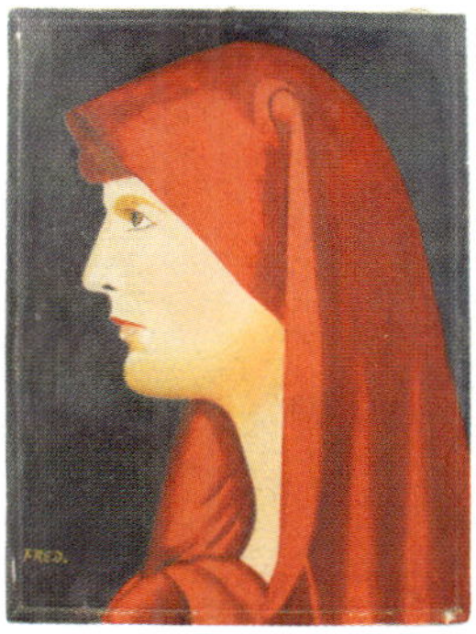

111

DIMENSIONS: 15 ¾ x 11 ¾ x ⅝ inches (40 x 29.8 x 1.59 cm)
DATE: Unknown
MEDIA: Paint on canvas
CONDITION: Good—Slight accretion on top of hood.
PROVENANCE: Mexico, 1996, 280 Mexican pesos
NOTES: Subject displays signs of heavy makeup application throughout entire exposed skin surface. This is particularly evident in the eyelashes and lip area.

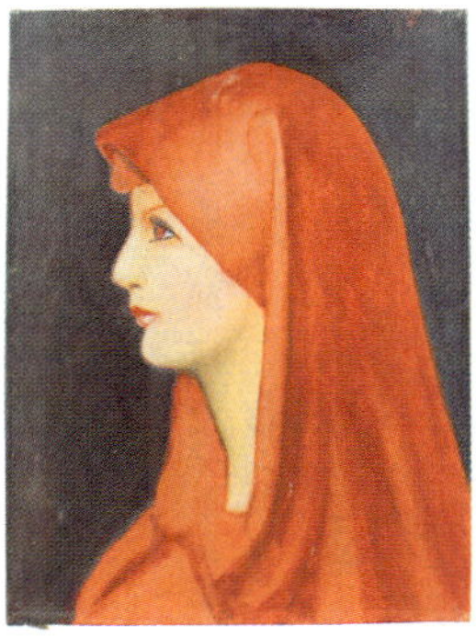

113

DIMENSIONS: 19 ¾ x 15 ⅝ x ⅝ inches (50.2 x 39.7 x 1.59 cm)
DATE: Unknown
MEDIA: Paint on canvas
CONDITION: Fair—There are several losses and tears in the paint layer and canvas support.
PROVENANCE: Unknown
NOTES: Signed "Trudy d'après Henner."

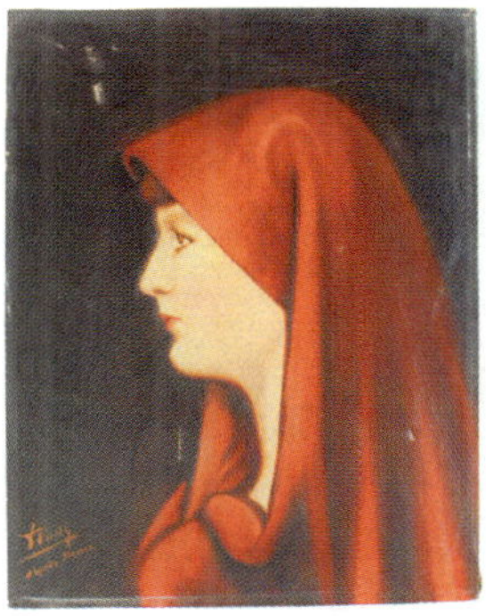

114

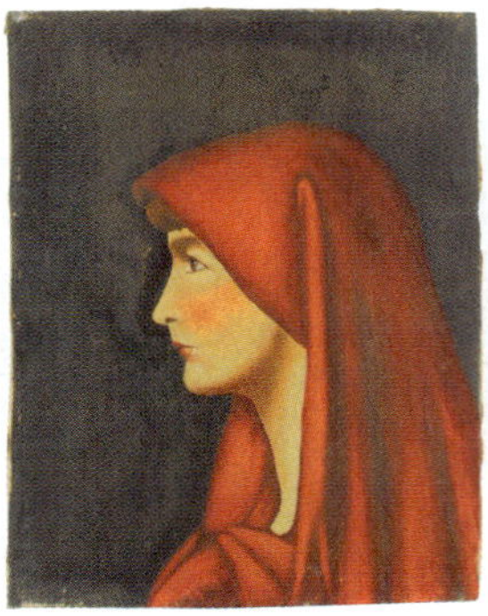

115

DIMENSIONS:	19 ¾ x 15 ⅝ x ⅝ inches (50.2 x 39.7 x 1.59 cm)
DATE:	Unknown
MEDIA:	Paint on canvas
CONDITION:	Fair—Extensive cracking throughout surface.
PROVENANCE:	Unknown
NOTES:	Subject is depicted with a dour and stern demeanor.

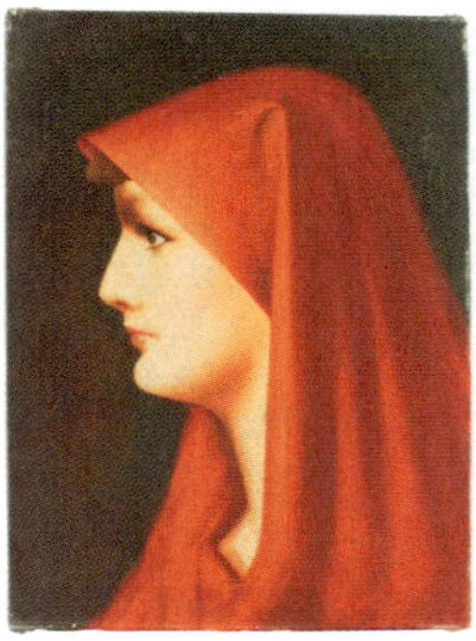

116

DIMENSIONS:	15 ¾ x 11 ¾ x ⅝ inches (40 x 29.8 x 1.59 cm)
DATE:	Unknown
MEDIA:	Paint on canvas
CONDITION:	Good
PROVENANCE:	Flea market, Brussels, Belgium, October 1998, 800 Belgian francs
NOTES:	Signed "Seys."

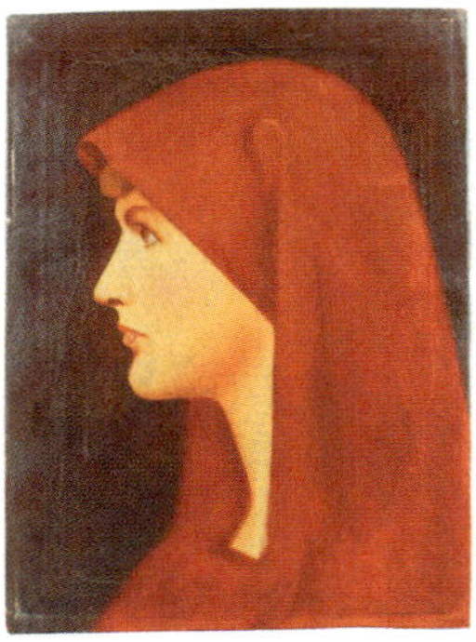

117

DIMENSIONS:	15 ¾ x 11 ¾ x ⅜ inches (40 x 29.8 x 0.95 cm)
DATE:	Unknown
MEDIA:	Paint on canvas
CONDITION:	Good/Fair—Surface cracks are present throughout painting.
PROVENANCE:	Mechelen, Belgium, February 1997, 5000 Belgian francs

---

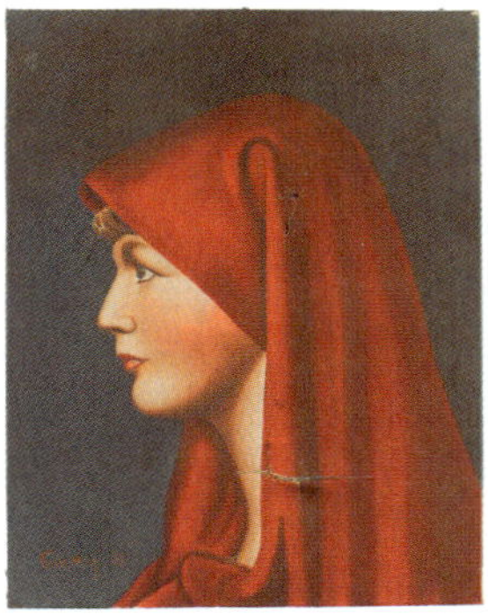

118

DIMENSIONS:	19 ⅝ x 15 ¾ x ⅝ inches (49.8 x 40 x 1.59 cm)
DATE:	1983
MEDIA:	Paint on canvas
CONDITION:	Poor—There are several severe tears and losses in the paint layer and canvas support. Prior restorations and repairs are visible from the verso.
PROVENANCE:	London, England, 1997, 20 British pounds
NOTES:	Purchased when Fabiola collection was shown at the Whitechapel Art Gallery. Signed "Eamy 83."

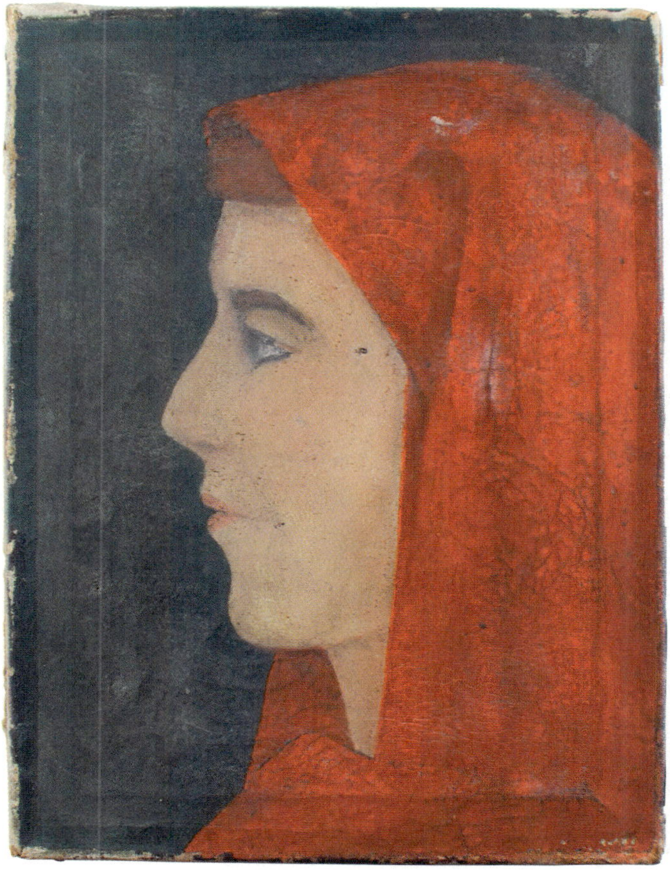

119

DIMENSIONS: 15 ¾ x 11 ¾ x ⅝ inches (40 x 29.8 x 1.59 cm)
DATE: Unknown
MEDIA: Paint on canvas
CONDITION: Poor—Surface cracks throughout entire painting, and small losses correspond to some areas of cracking. There is a whitish haze or cast to the surface—perhaps attributable to a prior coating such as wax. There is possible biological growth on the surface.
PROVENANCE: Tournai, Belgium, March 1993, 150 Belgian francs
NOTES: The painting depicts a closer view of the subject as compared with the typical composition seen in other paintings. Furthermore, the characteristics in the depiction resemble an adolescent male.

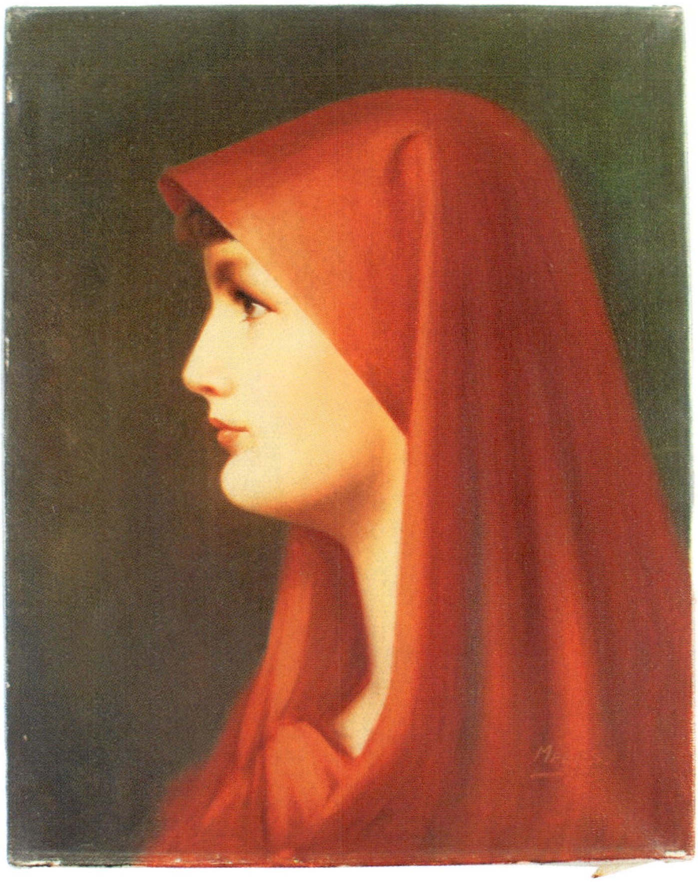

120

DIMENSIONS:	19 ¾ x 15 ⅞ x ⅝ inches (50.2 x 40.3 x 1.59 cm)
DATE:	Unknown
MEDIA:	Paint on canvas
CONDITION:	Good
PROVENANCE:	Mechelen (Nekkerhal), Belgium, February 1998, 1500 Belgian francs
NOTES:	Signed “Meers.”

DIMENSIONS: 11 ¾ x 15 ⅞ x ⅞ inches (29.8 x 40.3 x 2.22 cm)
DATE: Unknown
MEDIA: Paint on panel or board
CONDITION Fair—Overall surface condition good, although there is an area of loss and accretions at the lower proper right corner.
PROVENANCE: Brussels, Belgium, July 1994, 200 Belgian francs
NOTES: As opposed to the canonical appearance of the Henner original, subject has what appears to be a severe dental underbite. In addition, subject's eye is oddly scaled, when compared to nose, mouth, and jaw. Signed "R. Nieuwborg."

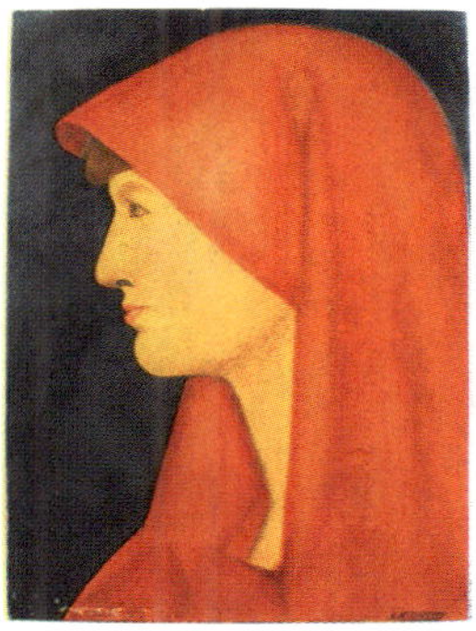

121

DIMENSIONS: 19 ¾ x 15 ⅞ x ½ inches (50.2 x 40.3 x 1.27 cm)
DATE: Unknown
MEDIA: Paint on canvas
CONDITION: Fair
PROVENANCE: Brussels, Belgium, March 16, 2001, 300 Belgian francs
NOTES: Signed "J. Vérulpens."

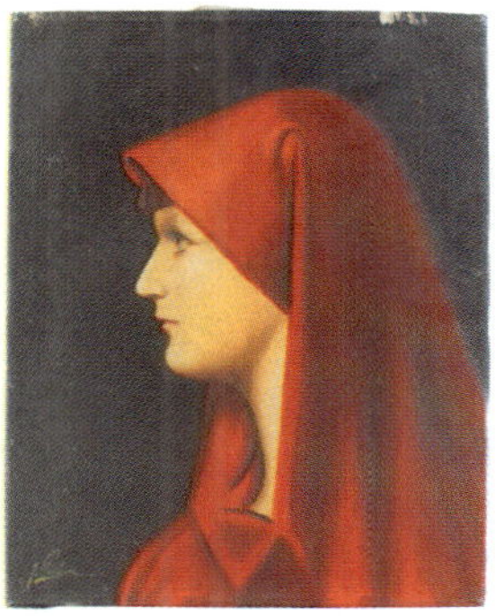

122

DIMENSIONS: 15 ¾ x 11 ¾ x ¼ inches (40 x 29.8 x 0.64 cm)
DATE: Unknown
MEDIA: Oil on canvas
CONDITION: Fair—Whitish surface accretions occur along sides and top and bottom edges, likely a result of a prior framing method.
PROVENANCE: Skärholmen, Stockholm, Sweden, May 1998, 230 kronur
NOTES: Signed "J[?]"

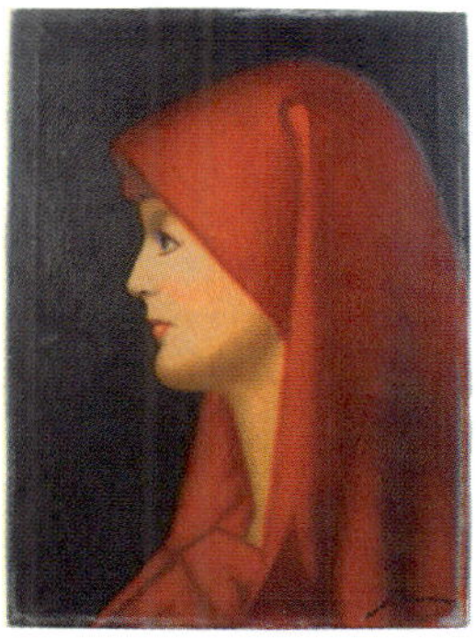

123

DIMENSIONS: 19 ¾ x 16 x ½ inches (50.2 x 40.6 x 1.27 cm)
DATE: Unknown
MEDIA: Paint on canvas
CONDITION: Poor—There are many major losses and tears. Paint surface and canvas support are severely compromised. Canvas has lost appropriate tension.
PROVENANCE: Flea market, Brussels, Belgium, 1997, 20 Belgian francs
NOTES: Signed "J. Vérulpens."

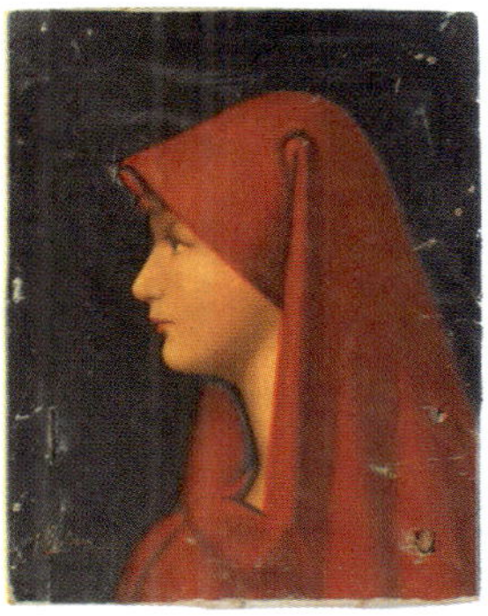

124

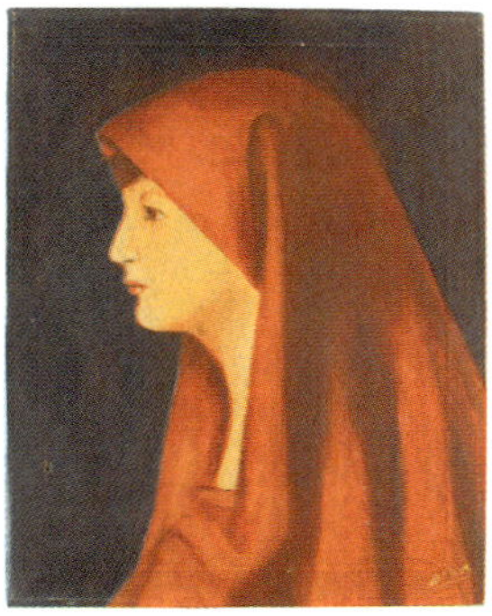

126

DIMENSIONS:	19 ⅝ x 15 ¾ x ½ inches (49.8 x 40 x 1.27 cm)
DATE:	Unknown
MEDIA:	Paint on canvas
CONDITION:	Fair—There are a few small losses and tears.
PROVENANCE:	Rome, Italy, 2003, 40 euros
NOTES:	Signed "Diva."

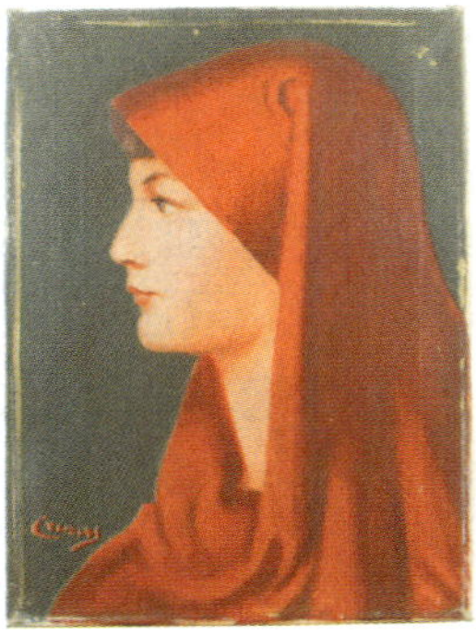

127

DIMENSIONS:	15 ¾ x 11 ¾ x ⅝ inches (40 x 29.8 x 1.59 cm)
DATE:	Unknown
MEDIA:	Paint on canvas
CONDITION:	Fair—Stretcher has caused creases and indentations that are visible from the front, and there are losses and abrasions along the sides and edges. There is also some gold-colored overpaint along the sides and edges that is likely related to a prior frame.
PROVENANCE:	Unknown
NOTES:	Signed "Cremers."

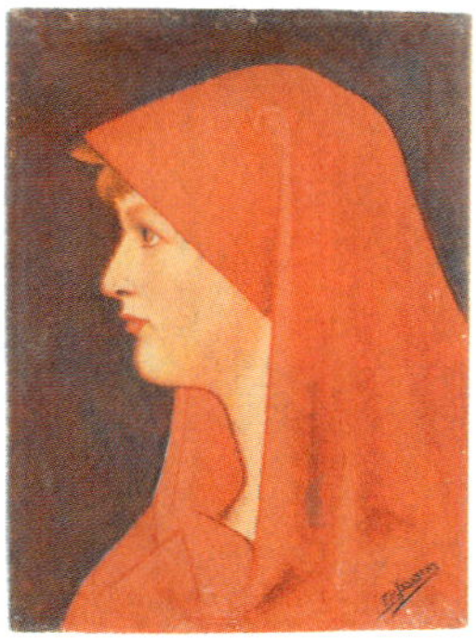

128

DIMENSIONS:	15 ¾ x 11 ¾ x ½ inches (40 x 29.8 x 1.27 cm)
DATE:	Unknown
MEDIA:	Paint on canvas
CONDITION:	Good
PROVENANCE:	Unknown
NOTES:	This work has a close resemblance to postcard reproductions of a Fabiola portrait misattributed to Jean-Jacques Henner. Subject exhibits a common Fabiola feature, in that there are two distinct segments of the bangs, one hanging naturally down, the other extending up beyond the edge of the hood. Signed "Em Janssens."

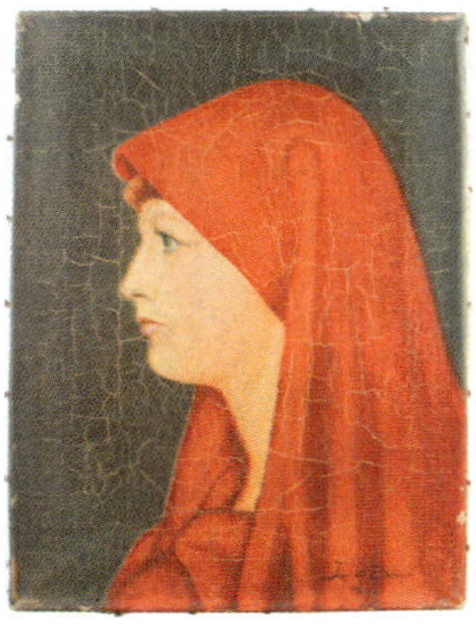

129

DIMENSIONS:	15 ⅞ x 12 x ⅝ inches (40.3 x 30.5 x 1.59 cm)
DATE:	1945
MEDIA:	Paint on canvas
CONDITION:	Poor—Extensive cracking throughout surface. Abraded surfaces and losses are visible especially along edges.
PROVENANCE:	Antwerp, Belgium, 1997, 1200 Belgian francs
NOTES:	Signed "Jacq. De Bruyn. 20/10.1945."

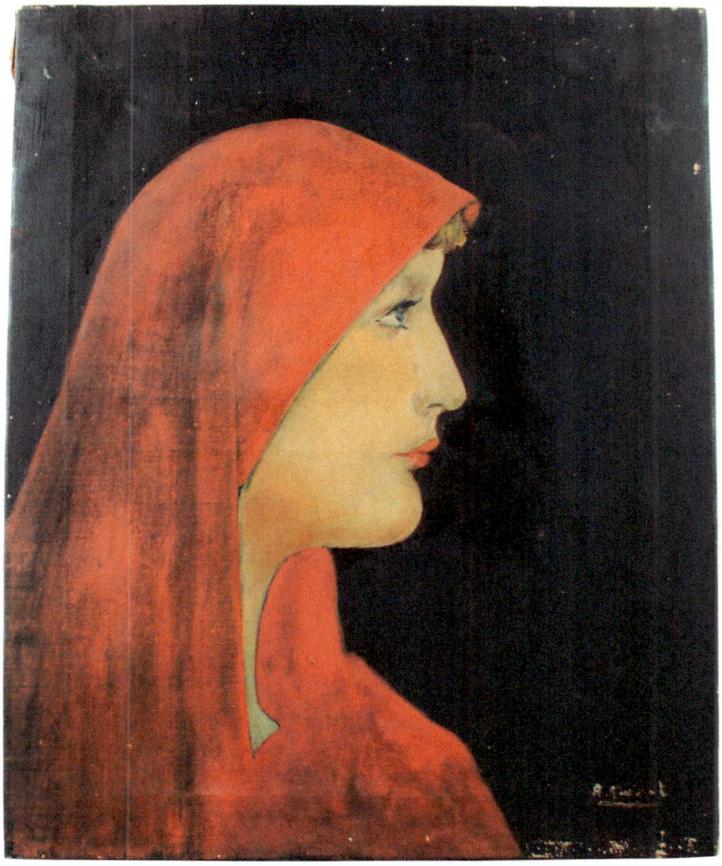

125

DIMENSIONS: 18 x 15 x ½ inches (45.7 x 38.1 x 1.27 cm)
DATE: Unknown
MEDIA: Oil on canvas
CONDITION: Fair—Stretcher has created creases and indentations in the canvas that are visible from the front.
PROVENANCE: Paris, France, October 1993, 30 French francs
NOTES: Note that subject is facing toward the proper left, rather than the proper right, which is typical. Signed "R. Saint."

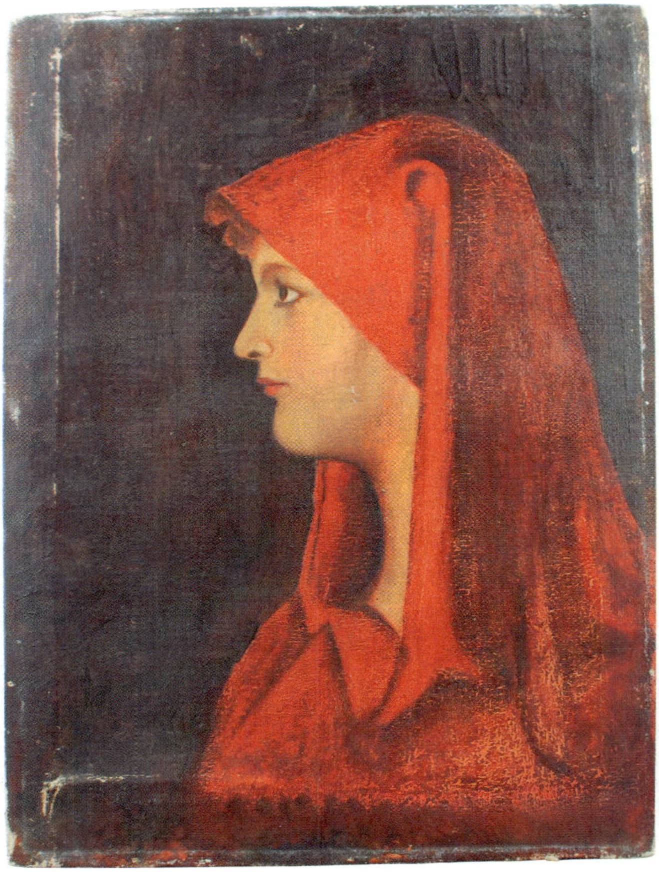

133

DIMENSIONS:	17 x 12 ¾ x ⅝ inches (43.2 x 32.4 x 1.59 cm)
DATE:	Unknown
MEDIA:	Paint on canvas
CONDITION:	Poor—Stretcher has created severe creases and losses in the front of the painting. Red paint layer is cracking and appears to be moving separately in relation to paint layers and ground below.
PROVENANCE:	Lille, France, November 1995, exchange
NOTES:	Subject exhibits a common Fabiola feature, in that there are two distinct segments of the bangs, one hanging naturally down, and the other extending up beyond the edge of the hood. Possible inscription along bottom edge of painting—illegible.

DIMENSIONS: 15 ¾ x 11 ¾ x ¾ inches (40 x 29.8 x 1.91 cm)
DATE: Unknown
MEDIA: Paint on canvas
CONDITION: Fair—There are significant losses and tears in the canvas support just above the subject's forehead. There are also losses along the sides and edges.
PROVENANCE: Unknown
NOTES: Signed "E. W. Creners." This is one of two paintings in the collection by Creners that are virtually identical. See no. 049.

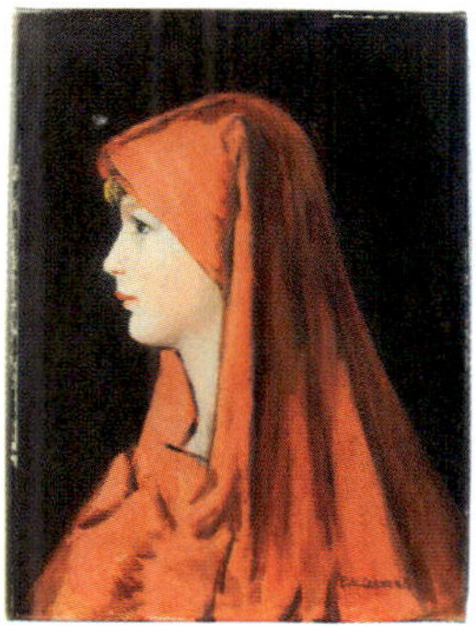

130

DIMENSIONS: 15 ⅝ x 11 ¾ x ¾ inches (39.7 x 29.8 x 1.91 cm)
DATE: 1973
MEDIA: Acrylic on canvas
CONDITION: Good
PROVENANCE: Belgium, 1998, 600 Belgian francs
NOTES: Signed "J. Magermans 1973 d'après HENNER."

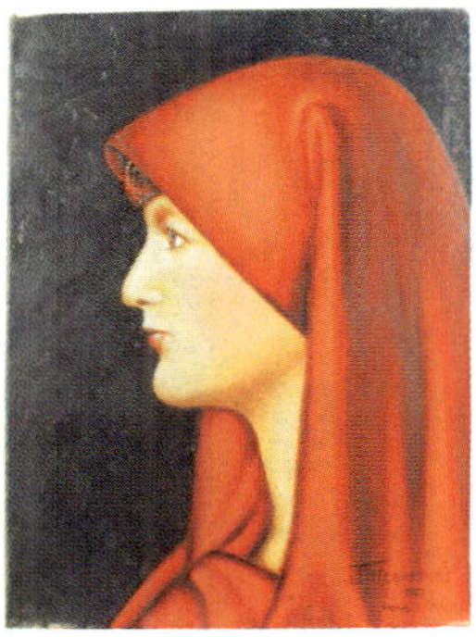

131

DIMENSIONS: 15 ¾ x 11 ¾ x ⅛ inches (40 x 29.8 x 0.32 cm)
DATE: Unknown
MEDIA: Needlepoint on mesh support mounted on paperboard
CONDITION: Good
PROVENANCE: Paris, France, 1995, 10 French francs
NOTES: This needlepoint depiction is noteworthy in its color palette, particularly in the vibrancy of the oranges and reds. Also there is dramatic articulation of folds in the hood and cloak areas, which is in stark contrast to the flatness of the subject's neck and face.

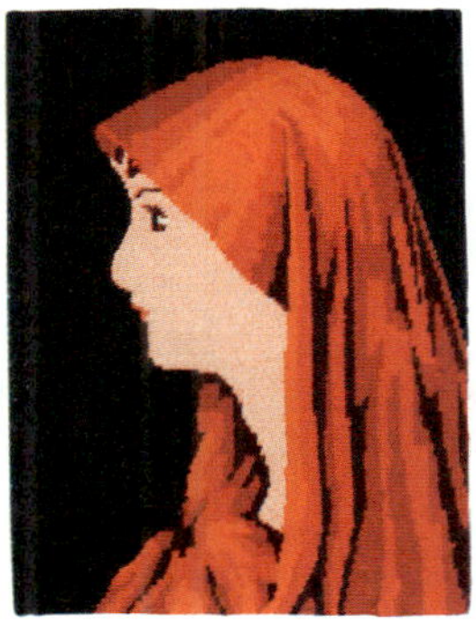

132

DIMENSIONS: 23 ⅝ x 19 ¾ x ⅝ inches (60 x 50.2 x 1.59 cm)
DATE: Unknown
MEDIA: Paint on canvas
CONDITION: Good/Fair
PROVENANCE: Antwerp, Belgium, March 10, 2001, 500 Belgian francs
NOTES: Signed "J. B. Seminck."

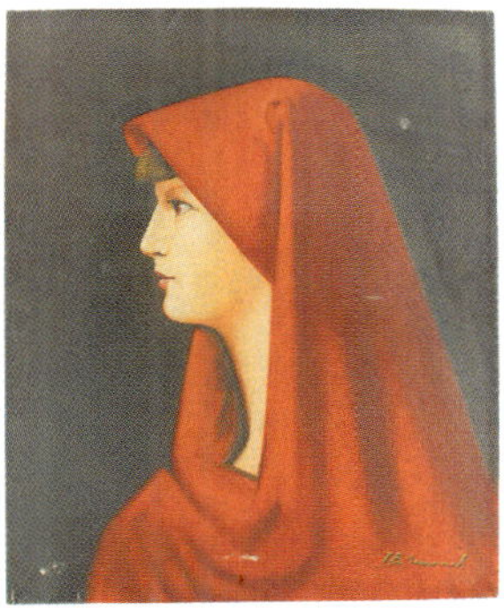

134

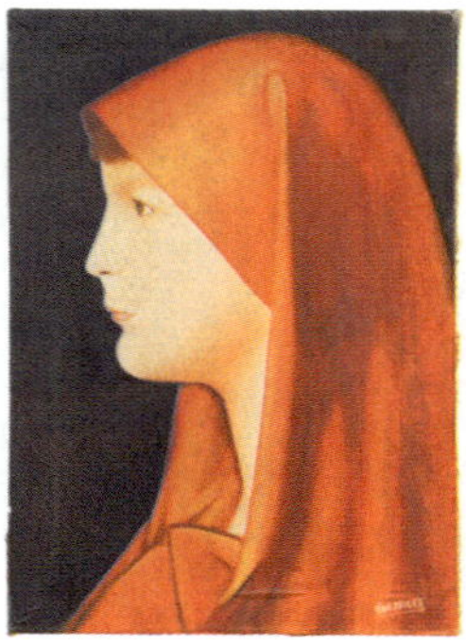

135

DIMENSIONS:	26 3/8 x 19 x 5/8 inches (67 x 48.3 x 1.59 cm)
DATE:	Unknown
MEDIA:	Paint on canvas
CONDITION:	Good
PROVENANCE:	Flea market, Brussels, Belgium, 2004, 80 euros
NOTES:	Signed "Van Snick R."

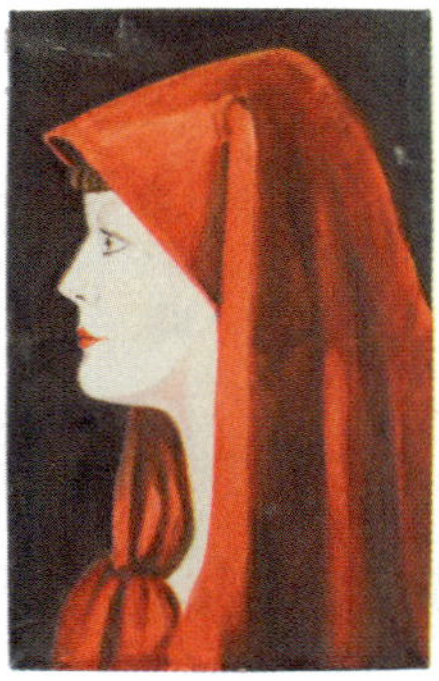

136

DIMENSIONS:	20 3/8 x 12 7/8 x 1 1/8 inches (51.8 x 32.7 x 2.86 cm)
DATE:	Unknown
MEDIA:	Paint on canvas
CONDITION:	Good/Fair—There are numerous minor surface scuffs and abrasions.
PROVENANCE:	Unknown
NOTES:	Intricate drapery is visible in subject's hood and cloak on subject's right. Fabiola displays signs of heavy makeup application throughout entire exposed skin surface; in this case, the coloration approaches the theatrical.

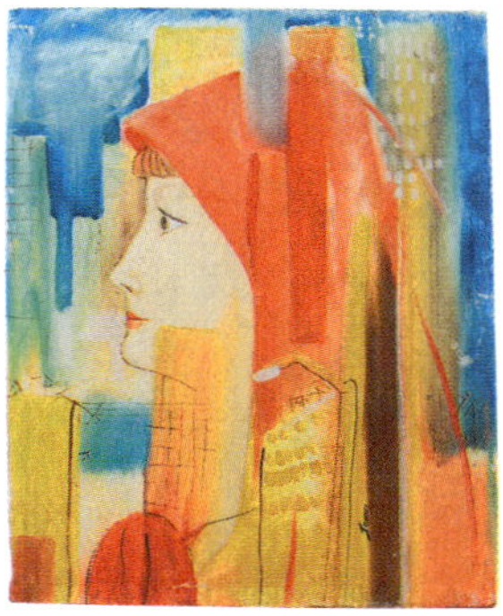

137

DIMENSIONS:	17 3/4 x 14 1/4 x 1 3/4 inches (45.1 x 36.2 x 4.45 cm)
DATE:	Unknown
MEDIA:	Paint on canvas
CONDITION:	Good—Black accretion across subject's face and general head area approx. 5" long.
PROVENANCE:	Mexico City, Mexico, 2002
NOTES:	Subject is immersed and surrounded by a modern, urban, architectural cityscape and is depicted at a significantly larger scale than that of the buildings. She is both obscured and framed by her surroundings. Signed "Jemus."

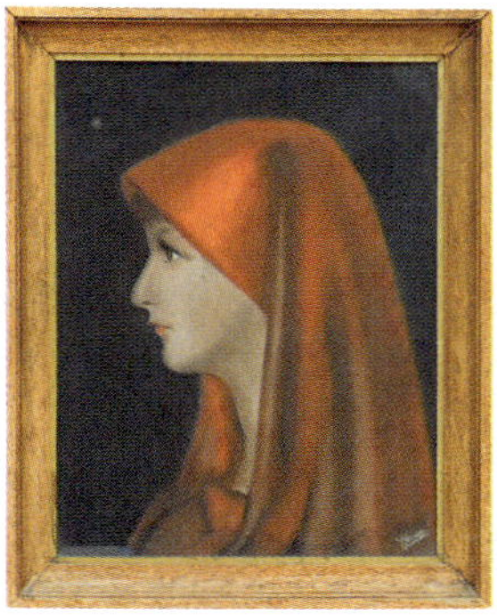

138

DIMENSIONS:	23 x 19 x 1 1/2 inches (58.4 x 48.3 x 3.81 cm)
DATE:	Unknown
MEDIA:	Pastel on paper, glazed and framed
CONDITION:	Fair—There is staining along the bottom edge.
PROVENANCE:	Brussels, Belgium, June 14, 2003, 25 euros
NOTES:	Signed "Hausen."

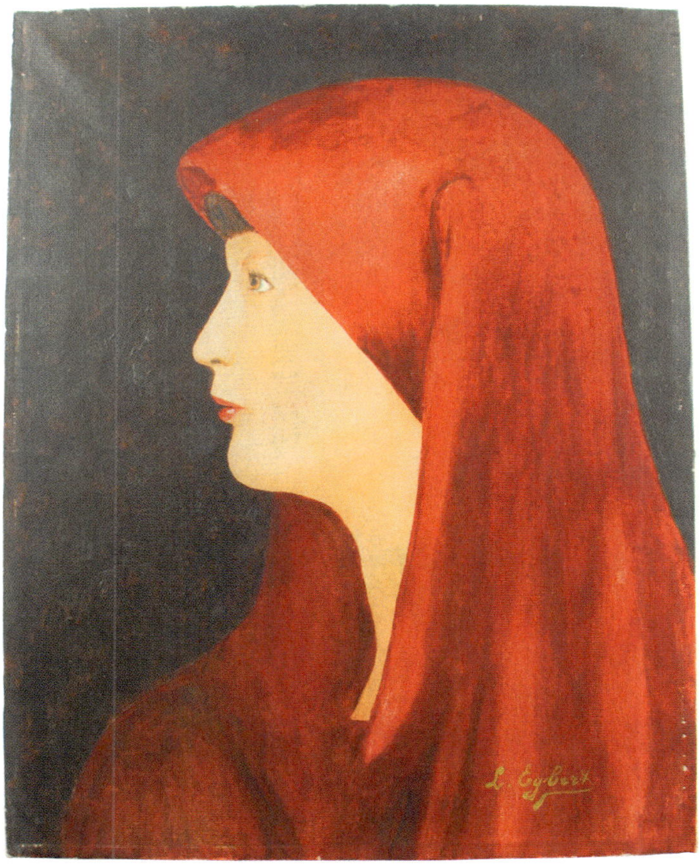

139

DIMENSIONS:	19 7/8 x 15 7/8 x 5/8 inches (50.5 x 40.3 x 1.59 cm)
DATE:	Unknown
MEDIA:	Paint on canvas
CONDITION:	Good
PROVENANCE:	Maastricht, Netherlands, January 1995, 40 gulden
NOTES:	Signed "L. Egbert."

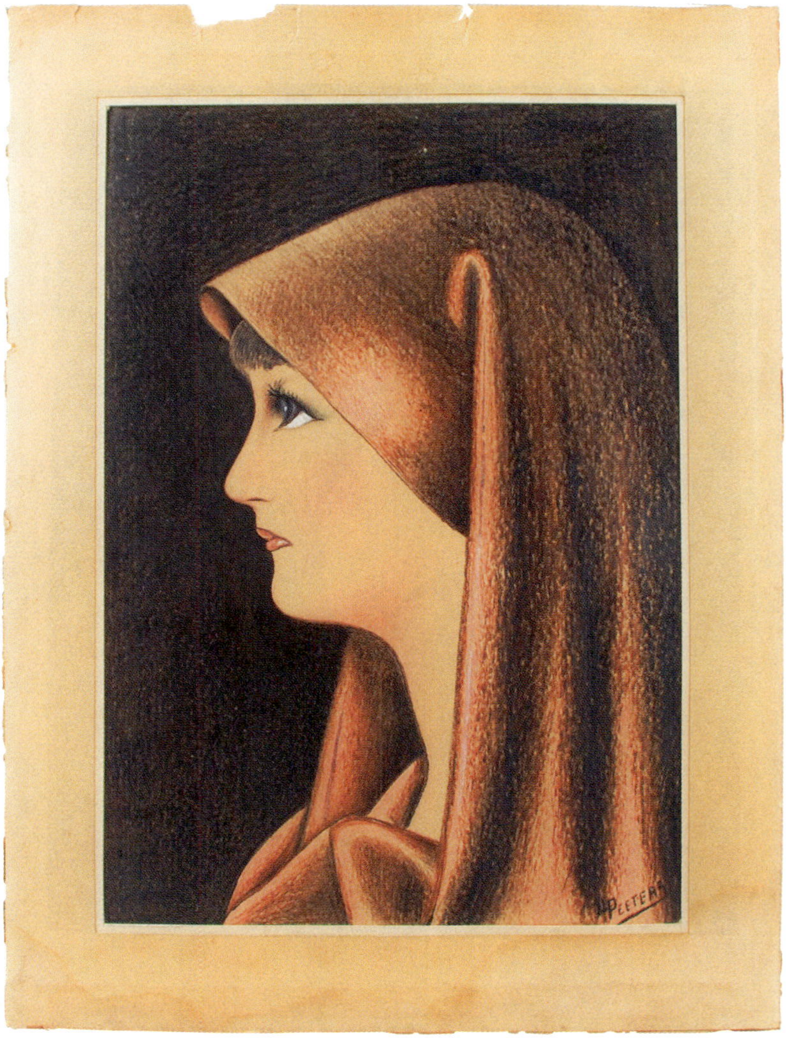

142

DIMENSIONS:	14 ¾ x 11 x 1/16 inches (37.5 x 27.9 x 0.16 cm)
DATE:	Unknown
MEDIA:	Pencil on paper, glazed and framed
CONDITION:	Good
PROVENANCE	Namur, Belgium, January 5, 2003, 75 euros
NOTES:	Subject's gaze is distinctly upward. Signed "H. Peeters."

DIMENSIONS: 14 ⅝ x 10 ⅝ x ⅜ inches (37.1 x 27 x 0.95 cm)
DATE: Unknown
MEDIA: Pastel on paper, glazed and framed
CONDITION: Good
PROVENANCE: Unknown
NOTES: Signed "R. B."

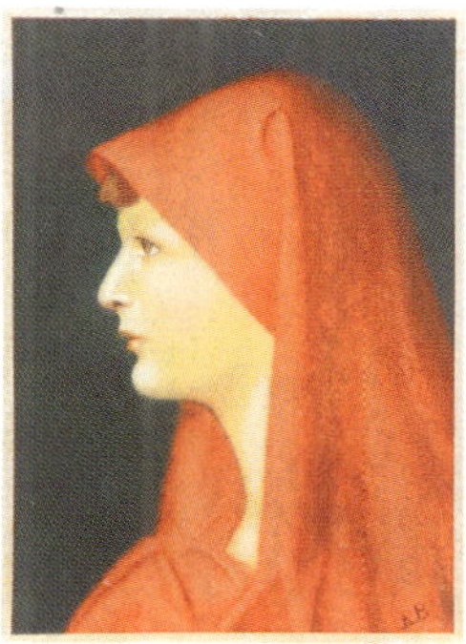

140

DIMENSIONS: 19 ⅝ x 15 ¾ x ½ inches (49.8 x 40 x 1.27 cm)
DATE: Unknown
MEDIA: Paint on canvas
CONDITION: Good—Small accretions.
PROVENANCE: Kortrijk, Belgium, March 1997, 400 Belgian francs
NOTES: Signed "Van Vooren."

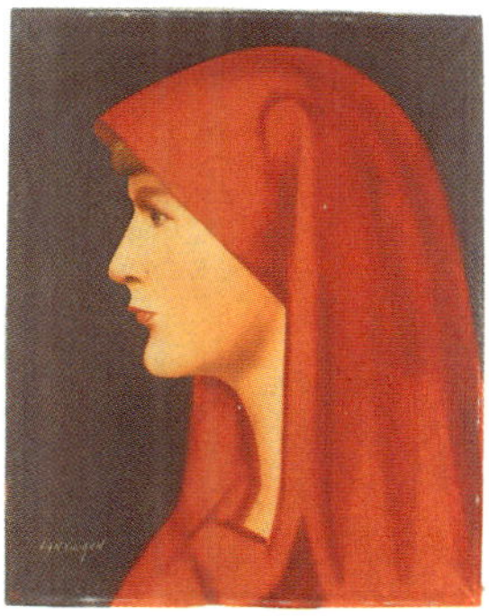

141

DIMENSIONS: 15 ¾ x 11 ⅞ x ⅛ inches (40 x 30.2 x 0.32 cm)
DATE: Unknown
MEDIA: Paint on paperboard or panel
CONDITION: Good/Fair
PROVENANCE: Portobello Road, London, England, July, 7, 2002, 20 British pounds
NOTES: Signed "P. Barr."

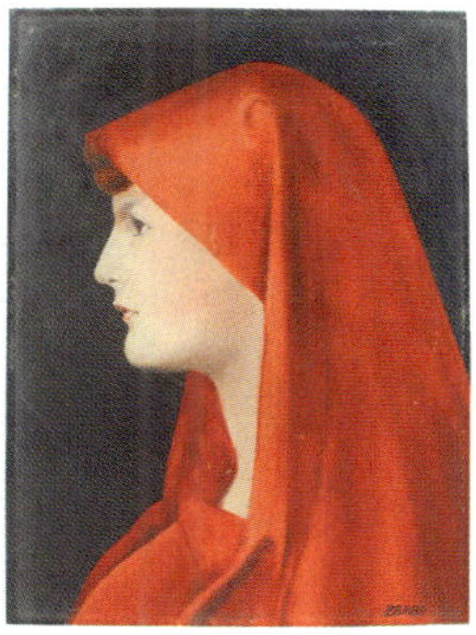

143

DIMENSIONS: 19 ¾ x 15 ¾ x ½ inches (50.2 x 40 x 1.27 cm)
DATE: Unknown
MEDIA: Paint on canvas
CONDITION: Good—There are slight abrasions and losses along sides and edges.
PROVENANCE: Mons, Belgium, December 1992, 120 Belgian francs
NOTES: Signed "Marco."

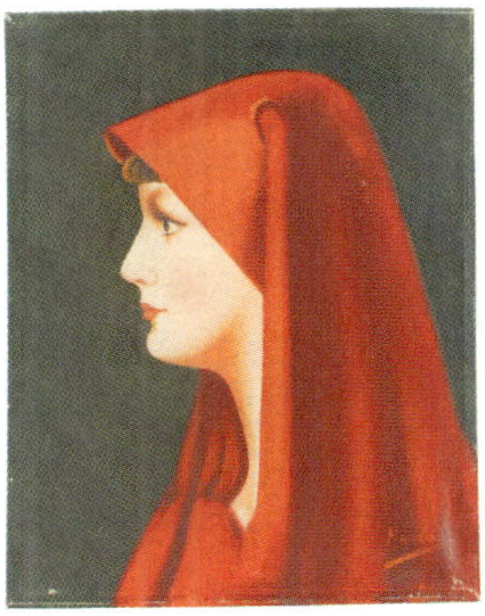

144

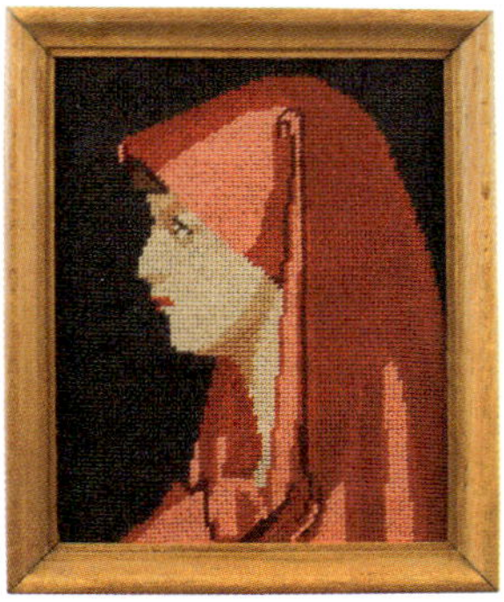

145

DIMENSIONS: 13 ⅛ x 11 x 1 ¼ inches (33.3 x 27.9 x 3.18 cm)
DATE: Unknown
MEDIA: Needlepoint on mesh support, framed
CONDITION: Good
PROVENANCE: Unknown
NOTES: The depiction features a distinctive black outline of the prime vertical fold in the subject's hood.

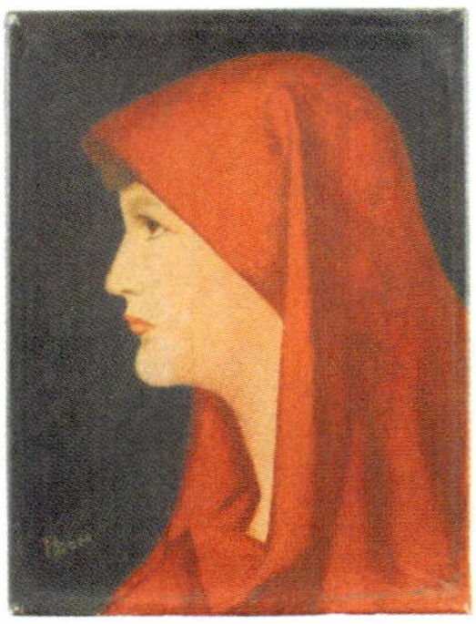

147

DIMENSIONS: 10 ⅜ x 8 x ¾ inches (26.4 x 20.3 x 1.91 cm)
DATE: Unknown
MEDIA: Paint on canvas
CONDITION: Good
PROVENANCE: Unknown
NOTES: Signed "P. Dom."

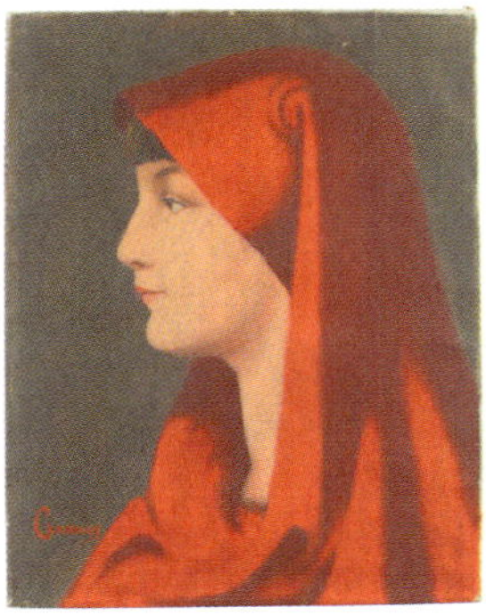

148

DIMENSIONS: 19 ⅞ x 15 ¾ x ⅝ inches (50.5 x 40 x 1.59 cm)
DATE: Unknown
MEDIA: Paint on canvas
CONDITION: Good
PROVENANCE: Sint-Niklaas, Belgium, March 1997, 450 Belgian francs
NOTES: Subject's gaze gives the impression of a distant (perhaps distracted) Fabiola. Signed "Cremers."

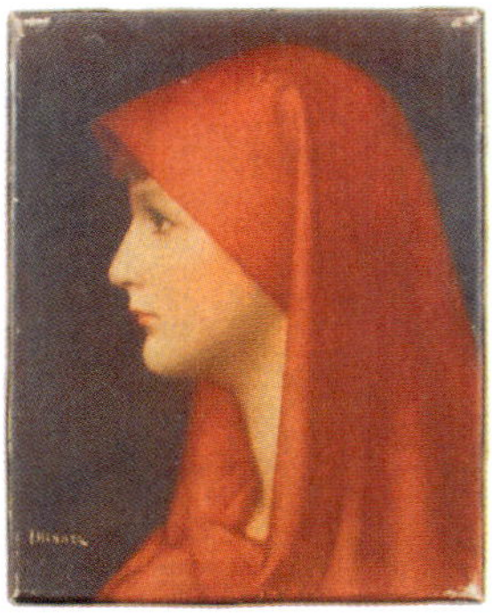

149

DIMENSIONS: 13 ⅜ x 8 ⅜ x ¾ inches (34 x 21.3 x 1.91 cm)
DATE: Unknown
MEDIA: Photograph mounted on canvas
CONDITION: Good—Small losses at corners.
PROVENANCE: 1998, gift of Fred de Vos
NOTES: This portrait might be considered as among the closest in resembling the Jean-Jacques Henner original. Signed "J. Henner."

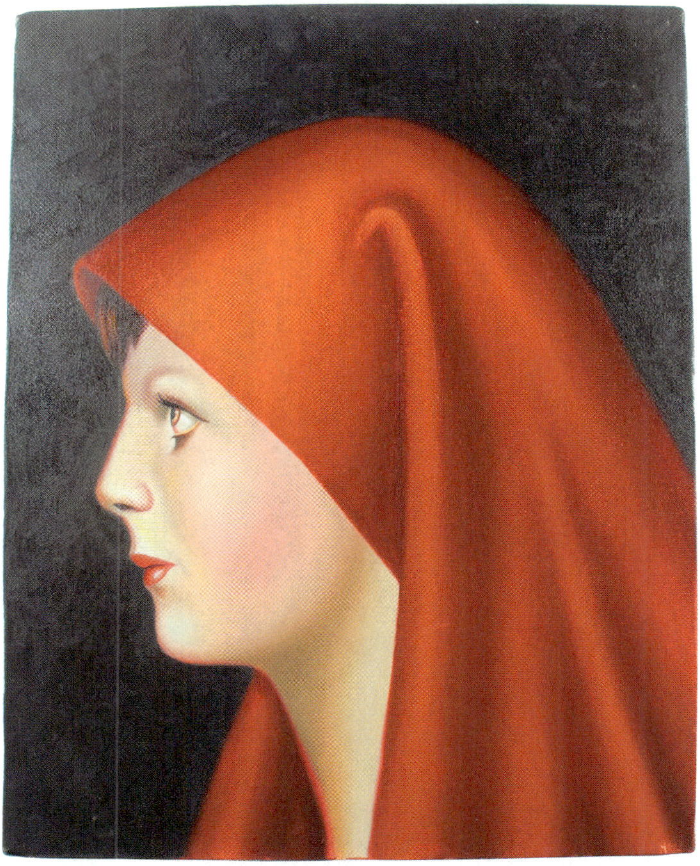

146

DIMENSIONS:	20 ¼ x 15 ⅞ x ⅝ inches (51.4 x 40.3 x 1.59 cm)
DATE:	Unknown
MEDIA:	Acrylic on canvas
CONDITION:	Good
PROVENANCE:	Mexico, January 1997, 80 Mexican pesos
NOTES:	Subject is depicted in a closer view than is typical. Subject displays signs of heavy makeup application throughout entire exposed skin surface and has an airbrushed aesthetic, perhaps drawn from magazines. Subject's gaze is distinctly upward. Signed "Suzana—776–0539"

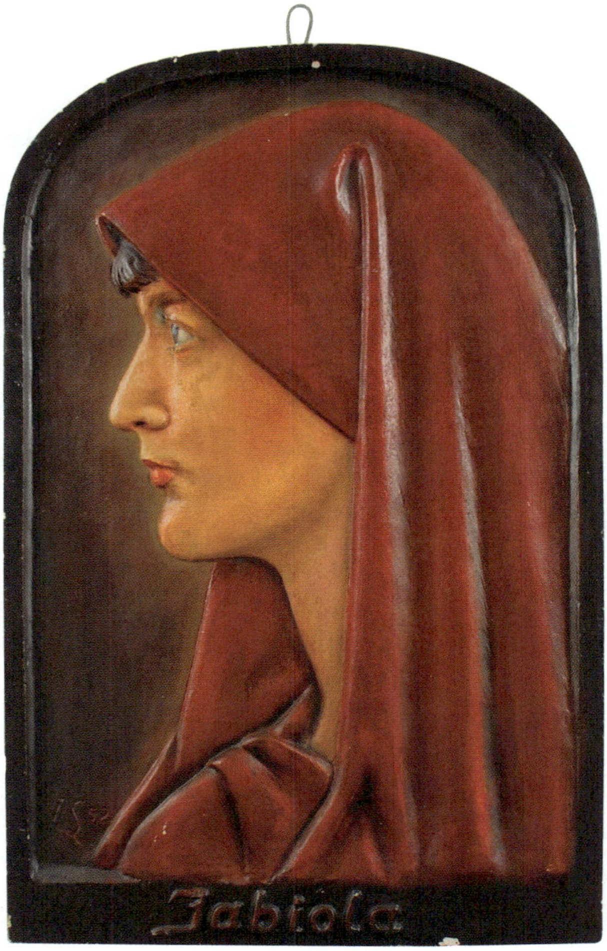

154

DIMENSIONS:	15 ¾ x 10 ½ x ⅝ inches (40 x 26.7 x 1.59 cm)
DATE:	1952
MEDIA:	Painted plaster relief
CONDITION:	Good/Fair—Small losses along outer edges.
PROVENANCE:	Unknown
NOTES:	"Fabiola" inscribed in relief along the bottom. Signed "R S 52."

DIMENSIONS:	9 ½ x 7 ⅛ x ½ inches (24.1 x 18.1 x 1.27 cm)
DATE:	1955
MEDIA:	Oil on canvas
CONDITION:	Good/Fair—Minor losses and abrasion throughout surface.
PROVENANCE:	Unknown
NOTES:	Signed "G. Froment 1955."

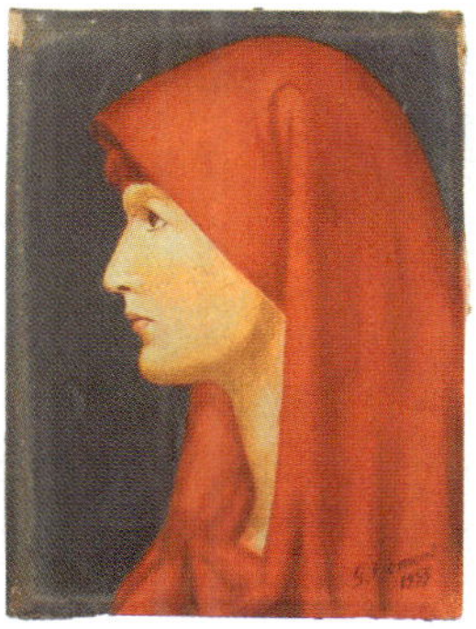

150

DIMENSIONS:	19 ⅝ x 15 ⅝ x ½ inches (49.8 x 39.7 x 1.27 cm)
DATE:	Unknown
MEDIA:	Paint on canvas
CONDITION:	Fair
PROVENANCE:	Mexico, February 1997, 300 Mexican pesos
NOTES:	The olive-green background of this portrait is atypical.

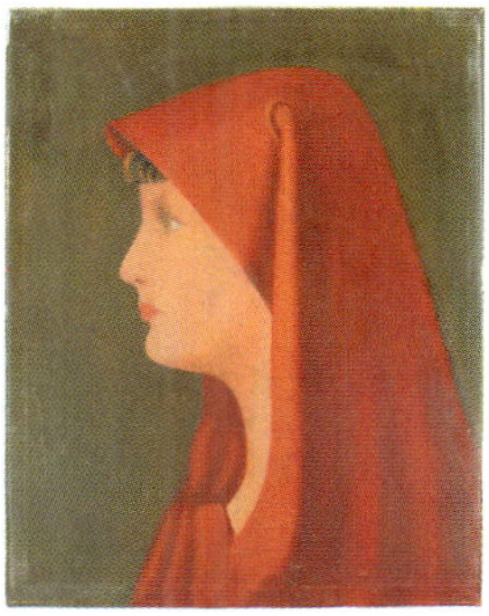

151

DIMENSIONS:	15 ½ x 11 ½ x 1 ¾ inches (39.4 x 29.2 x 4.45 cm)
DATE:	Unknown
MEDIA:	Paint on wood composite panel or board, framed
CONDITION:	Poor—Support for the paint layer (top veneer of wood composite panel) is severely cracking and checking. Extensive vertical separations in the support panel extend through the paint layer. There are three large losses from the faux-gilt frame that surrounds the piece.
PROVENANCE:	Unknown
NOTES:	Signed "E. Lerville [partially visible] d'après Henner."

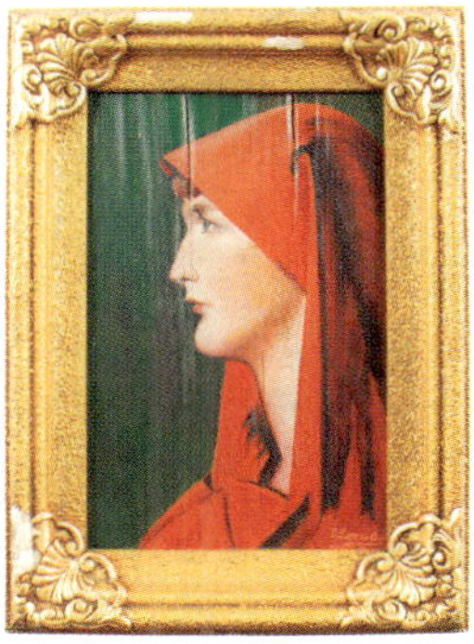

152

DIMENSIONS:	19 ⅝ x 15 ⅝ x ¾ inches (49.8 x 39.7 x 1.91 cm)
DATE:	Unknown
MEDIA:	Paint on canvas
CONDITION:	Good
PROVENANCE:	Flea market, Belgium, 1996, 400 Belgian francs
NOTES:	Signed "J. Plasqui."

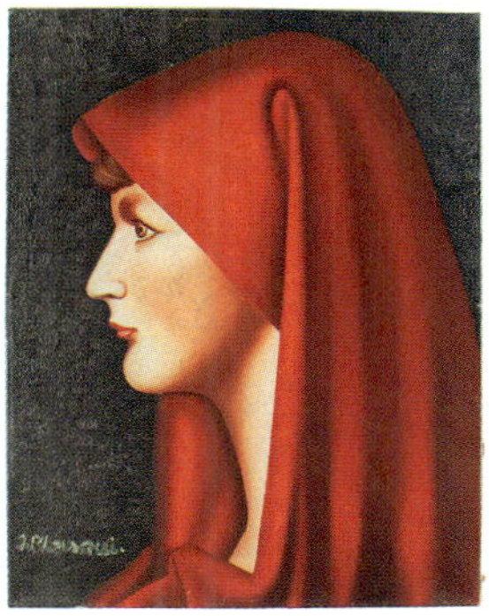

153

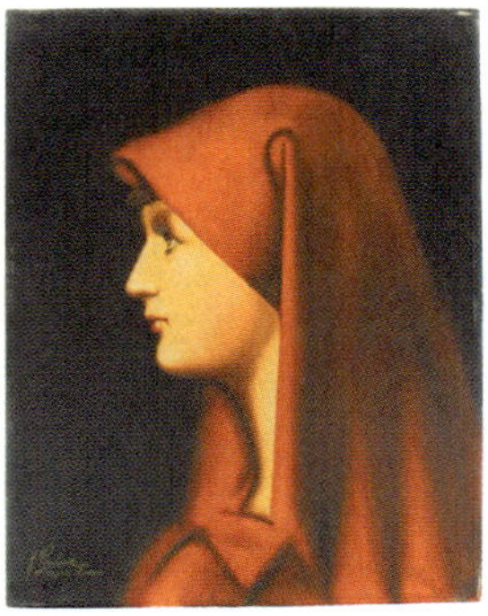

155

DIMENSIONS:	19 ⅝ x 15 ⅝ x ½ inches (49.8 x 39.7 x 1.27 cm)
DATE:	1949
MEDIA:	Paint on canvas
CONDITION:	Good
PROVENANCE:	Flea market, Brussels, Belgium, September 28, 1997, 500 Belgian francs
NOTES:	"Fabiola 28–9–97 Marche aux Puces Jeu du Balle 500 BeF." on Francis Alÿs postcard for *Untitled*, 1991/92, which is tucked into lower corner of the frame on the verso. "10/8/49" in pencil on verso of stretcher. Signed "J. Vérulpens d'après Henner."

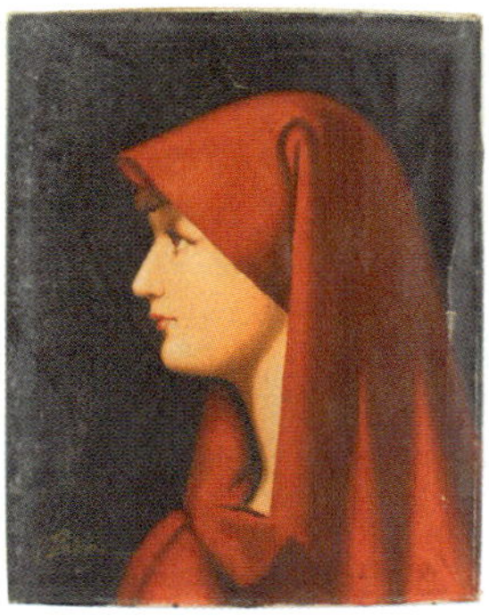

156

DIMENSIONS:	19 ⅝ x 15 ¾ x ⅝ inches (49.8 x 40 x 1.59 cm)
DATE:	Unknown
MEDIA:	Paint on canvas
CONDITION:	Fair
PROVENANCE:	Belgium, 1995, gift of Frederic de Smedt
NOTES:	Signed "J. Vérulpens."

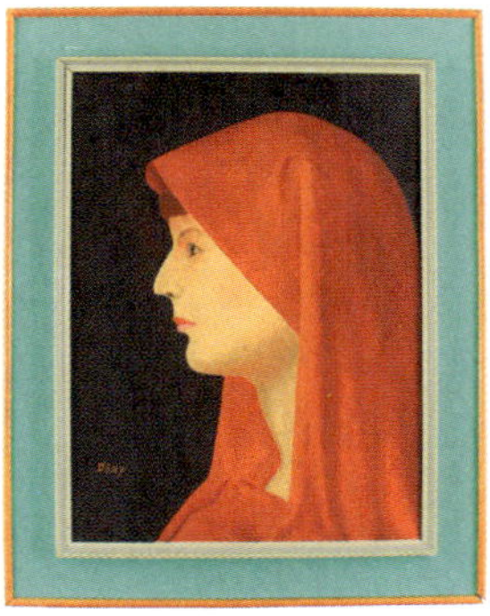

158

DIMENSIONS:	20 ⅛ x 16 ¼ x 1 inches (51.1 x 41.3 x 2.54 cm)
DATE:	Unknown
MEDIA:	Paint on canvas, framed
CONDITION:	Good
PROVENANCE:	Aachen, Germany, 1998, 35 German marks
NOTES:	Signed "Deny."

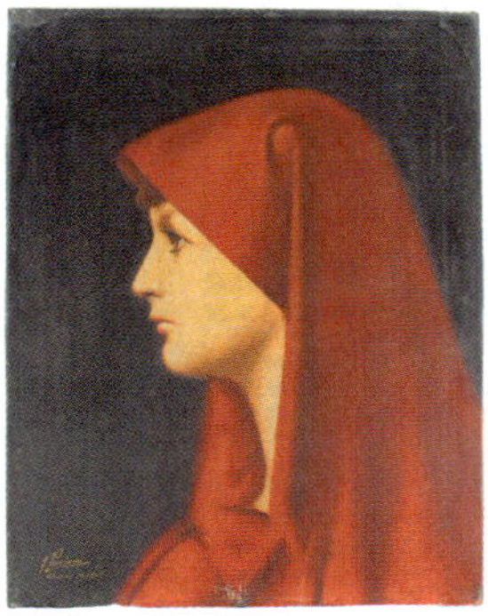

159

DIMENSIONS:	19 ¾ x 15 ⅞ x ½ inches (50.2 x 40.3 x 1.27 cm)
DATE:	Unknown
MEDIA:	Paint on canvas
CONDITION:	Good/Fair
PROVENANCE:	December 1998, gift of Frederic de Smedt
NOTES:	Signed "J. Vérulpens d'après Henner."

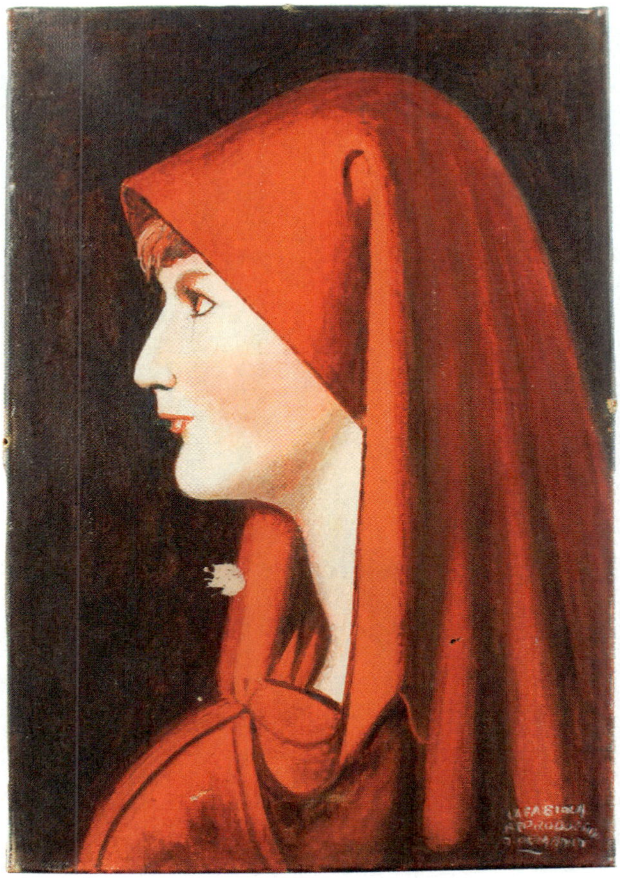

157

DIMENSIONS:	15 ¾ x 11 x ¾ inches (40 x 27.9 x 1.91 cm)
DATE:	Unknown
MEDIA:	Paint on canvas
CONDITION:	Fair—There is a large accretion below subject's chin, and there are also several tears and losses in the canvas support.
PROVENANCE:	Unknown
NOTES:	Inscribed "La Fabiola Reproduction J. Henner."

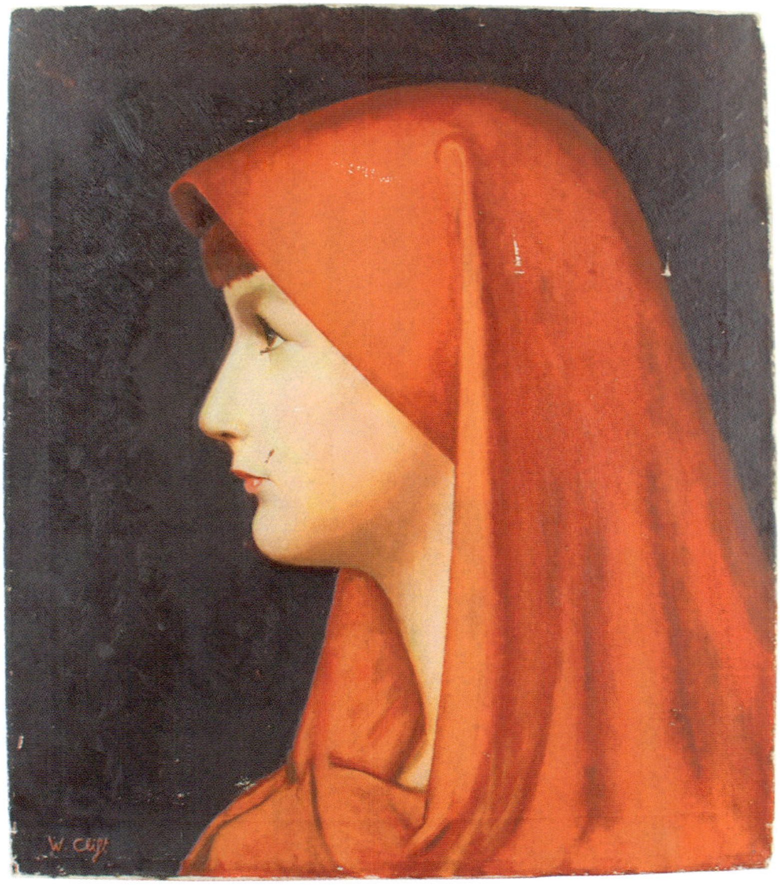

162

DIMENSIONS:	24 ¾ x 21 ⅞ x ⅞ inches (62.9 x 55.6 x 2.22 cm)
DATE:	Unknown
MEDIA:	Paint on canvas
CONDITION:	Fair—There are numerous accretions and surface scuffs throughout surface and paint layer.
PROVENANCE:	New York City, United States, October 1996, 60 U.S. dollars
NOTES:	Signed "W. Clift."

DIMENSIONS:	17 ⅜ x 14 ⅛ x ⅛ inches (44.1 x 35.9 x 0.32 cm)
DATE:	Unknown
MEDIA:	Paint on canvas mounted on paperboard or panel
CONDITION:	Good
PROVENANCE:	Unknown
NOTES:	Signed "A. De Schepere."

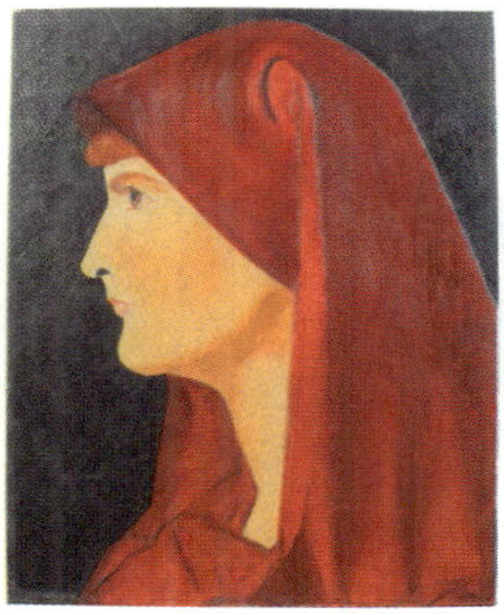

160

DIMENSIONS:	19 ¾ x 13 x ½ inches (50.2 x 33 x 1.27 cm)
DATE:	Unknown
MEDIA:	Paint on canvas
CONDITION:	Fair—There are extensive cracks throughout the surface and bluish gray accretions toward the bottom center edge of the painting.
PROVENANCE:	Copenhagen, Denmark, May 1998, 8 kroner
NOTES:	The greenish background in this portrait is atypical.

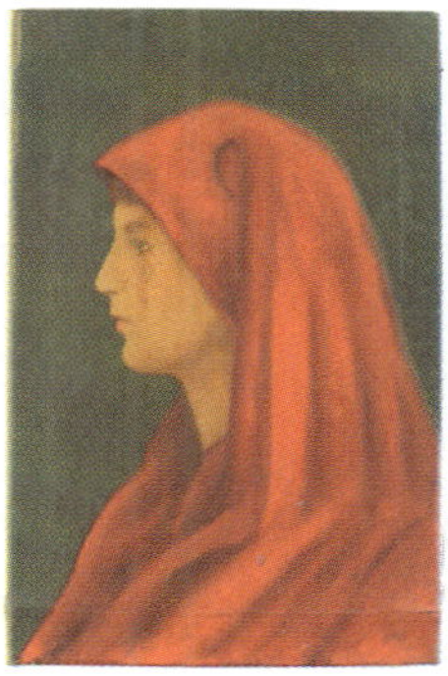

161

DIMENSIONS:	25 ¾ x 19 ¾ x ⅝ inches (65.4 x 50.2 x 1.59 cm)
DATE:	1963
MEDIA:	Paint on canvas
CONDITION:	Good
PROVENANCE:	Belgium
NOTES:	"Dejaeger A J wawter Str. 29 St. Michiels 1963" in pencil on verso. Signed "De. Jaeger.Aug."

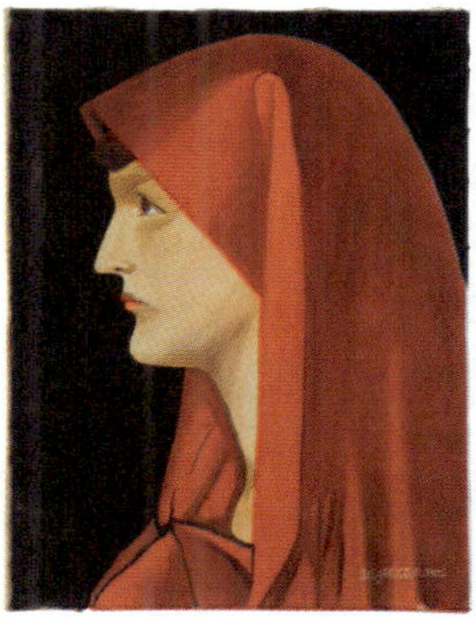

163

DIMENSIONS:	19 ½ x 15 ½ x ⅝ inches (49.5 x 39.4 x 1.59 cm)
DATE:	Unknown
MEDIA:	Paint on canvas
CONDITION:	Good/Fair—Minor losses and abrasion throughout surface.
PROVENANCE:	Unknown
NOTES:	Signed "Francis Huys."

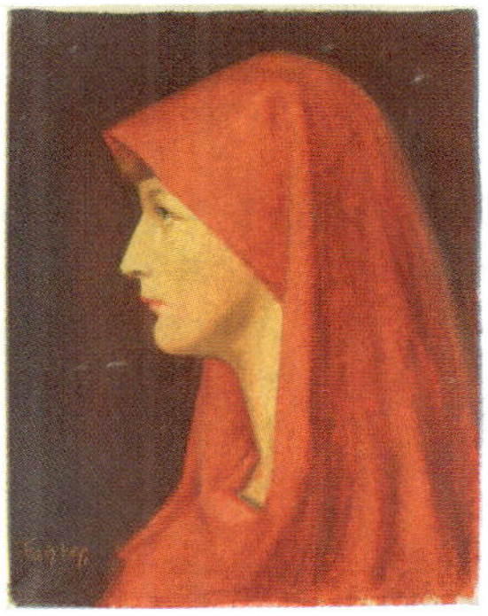

164

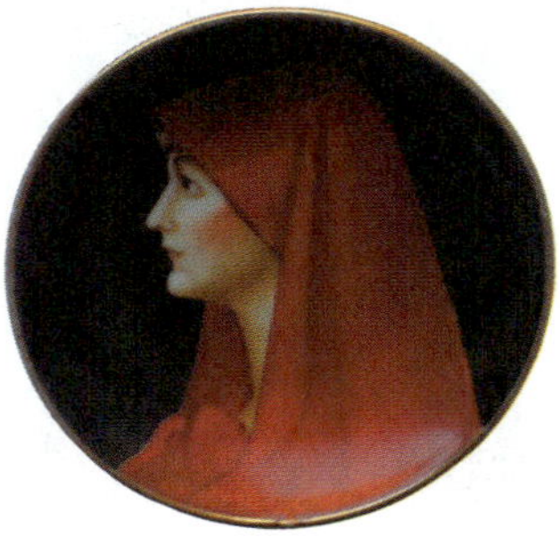

165

DIMENSIONS: 4 inches diameter x ⅝ inches (10.3 cm diameter x 2.1 cm)
DATE: Unknown
MEDIA: Painted ceramic dish
CONDITION: Good—Paint layer is stable and has only minor abrasions. There are small losses in the gold rim on the edge. There are unknown accretions on the bottom of the dish—likely wax.
PROVENANCE: Collection Laura Fields
NOTES: "Italy Fabiola" in brown on verso and manufacture stamping in green—C and O with diagonal lines and a crown.

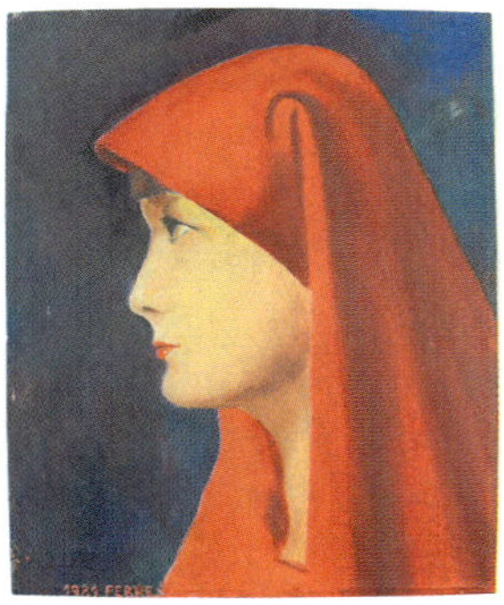

166

DIMENSIONS: 23 ⅝ x 19 ⅝ x 1 ⅛ inches (60 x 49.8 x 2.86 cm)
DATE: 1981
MEDIA: Paint on canvas
CONDITION: Good/Fair—There are a few areas of abrasion in the paint layer.
PROVENANCE: Brussels, Belgium, September 1995, 500 Belgian francs
NOTES: Signed "1981 Perre."

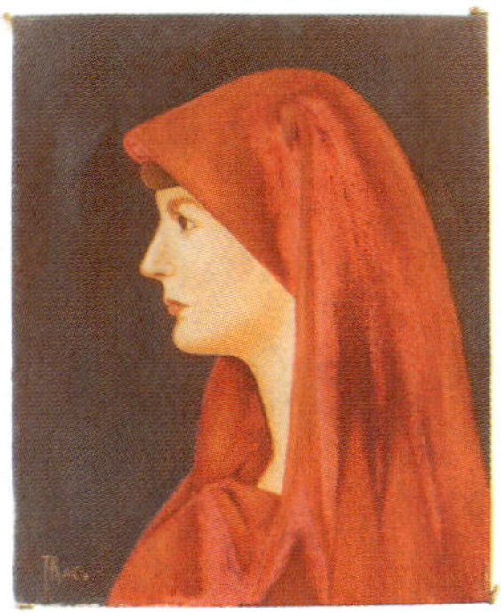

167

DIMENSIONS: 19 ¾ x 15 ⅞ x ½ inches (50.2 x 40.3 x 1.27 cm)
DATE: Unknown
MEDIA: Paint on canvas
CONDITION: Good
PROVENANCE: Unknown
NOTES: Signed "Raes."

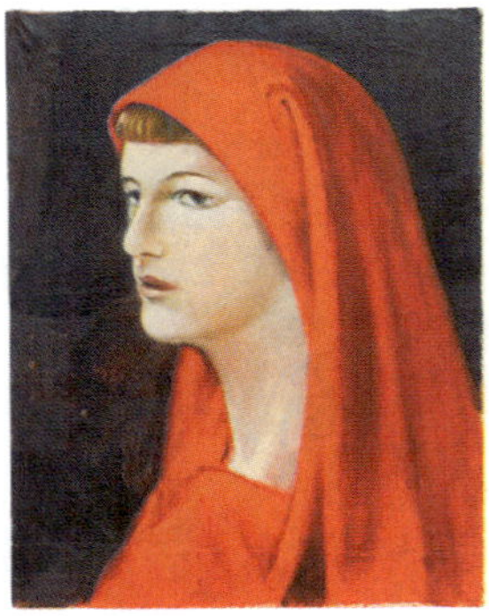

168

DIMENSIONS: 29 ½ x 23 ¾ x ⅞ inches (74.9 x 60.3 x 2.22 cm)
DATE: Unknown
MEDIA: Paint on canvas
CONDITION: Good/Fair—There are numerous cracks throughout surface. There is a crease that runs horizontally along the bottom edge of the painting.
PROVENANCE: Mexico
NOTES: "Ma. Christina Ansa del Real del Monte" in pencil on verso. Subject's gaze is looking slightly outward and toward the viewer. As opposed to the straight, conventional profile position typical of other Fabiolas, this position exposes both eyes. Also subject's lips are slightly parted.

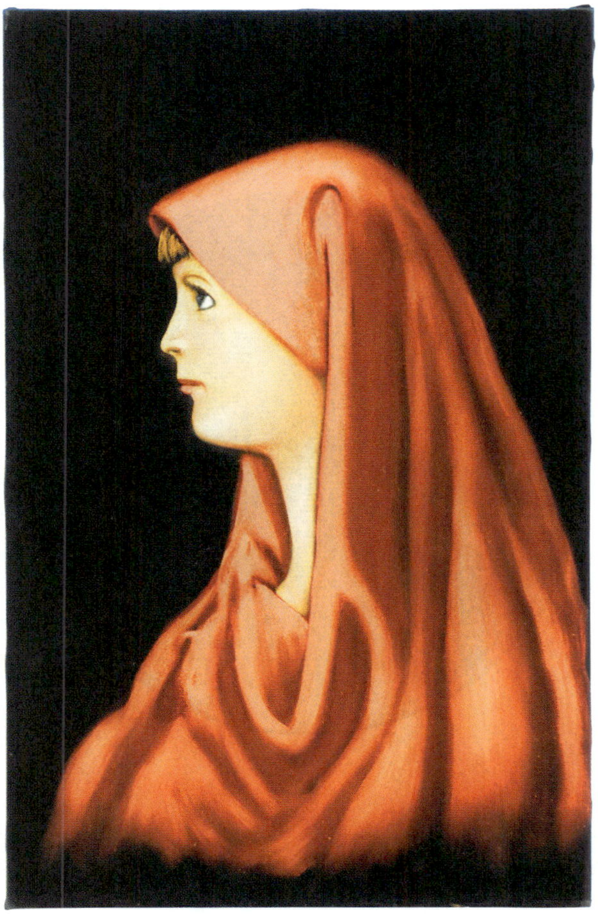

169

DIMENSIONS:	35 ¼ x 23 x ⅞ inches (89.5 x 58.4 x 2.22 cm)
DATE:	Unknown
MEDIA:	Paint on velvet textile support mounted on wood composite panel or board
CONDITION:	Good
PROVENANCE:	Mexico
NOTES:	Subject does not engage the bottom of the picture plane and therefore appears to float.

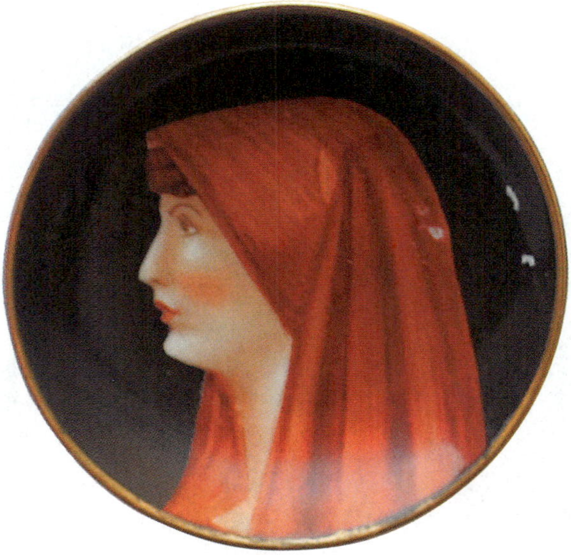

173

DIMENSIONS:	4 inches diameter x ⅝ inches (10.3 cm diameter x 2.1 cm)
DATE:	Unknown
MEDIA:	Painted ceramic dish
CONDITION:	Fair—Paint layer is in stable condition, although there are losses at back of subject's head and hood area. There are areas of discoloration in the ceramic glaze on the bottom of the dish.
PROVENANCE:	Collection Bettina Funcke
NOTES:	"Fabiola Italy Nell' Genova" in red on verso. Small decal on verso of a flag and a large ship "L.DA VINCI" on verso.

DIMENSIONS: 16 5/8 x 13 7/8 x 1 inches (42.2 x 35.2 x 2.54 cm)
DATE: Unknown
MEDIA: Needlepoint on mesh support mounted on panel or board
CONDITION: Good
PROVENANCE: Maastricht, Netherlands, November 1994, 40 gulden
NOTES: The prime vertical fold of the hood has a distinctive outline.

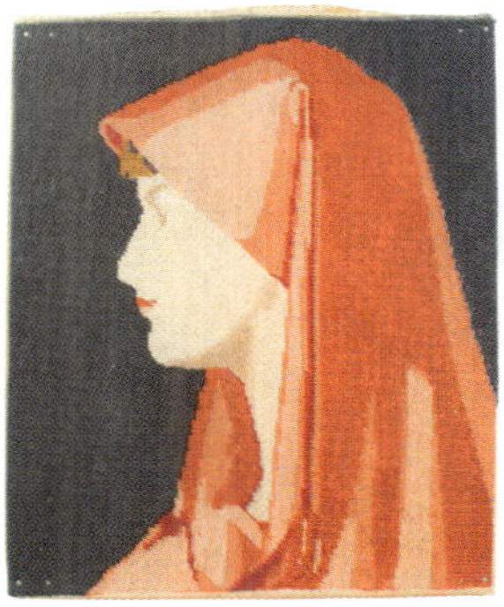

170

DIMENSIONS: 19 5/8 x 15 3/4 x 5/8 inches (49.8 x 40 x 1.59 cm)
DATE: Unknown
MEDIA: Paint on paperboard or Masonite panel
CONDITION: Good—There are small losses at the edges.
PROVENANCE: Tournai, Belgium, October 1995, 1000 Belgian francs
NOTES: Subject exhibits a common Fabiola feature, in that there are two distinct segments of the bangs, one hanging naturally down, and the other extending up beyond the edge of the hood. Subject's gaze is distinctly upward. Signed "Desmet. A."

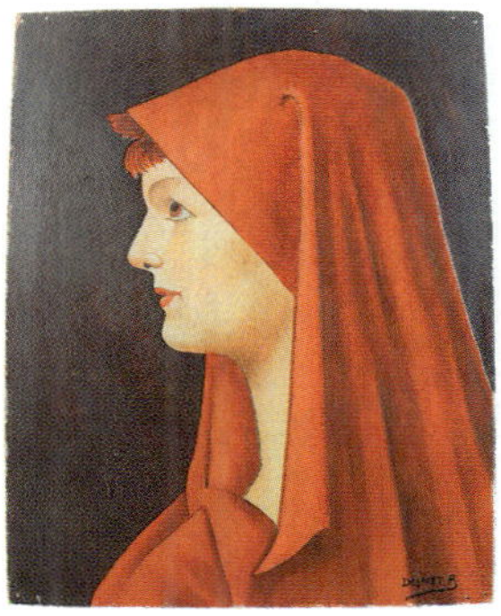

171

DIMENSIONS: 17 3/4 x 15 x 5/8 inches (45.1 x 38.1 x 1.59 cm)
DATE: Unknown
MEDIA: Paint on paperboard or Masonite panel
CONDITION: Good—There are small losses and accretions, possibly biological, along the edges.
PROVENANCE: Lille, France, September 1995, 70 French francs
NOTES: Signed "Alexander."

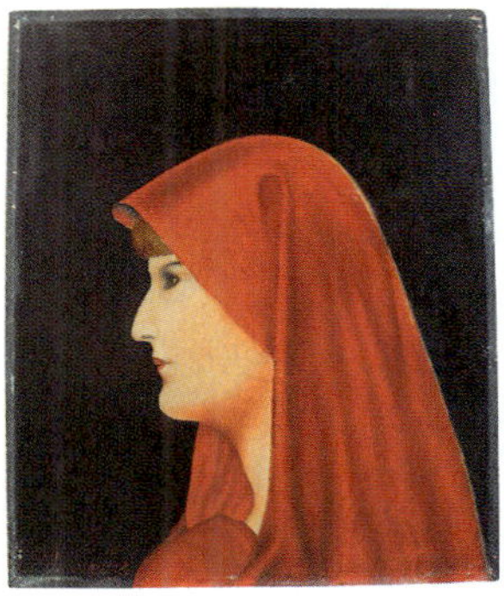

172

DIMENSIONS: 15 5/8 x 11 7/8 x 5/8 inches (39.7 x 30.2 x 1.59 cm)
DATE: Unknown
MEDIA: Paint on canvas
CONDITION: Good—Slight staining or unknown accretion below eye area of subject.
PROVENANCE: Madrid, Spain, 2001, 60 pesetas
NOTES: Signed "J. Henner."

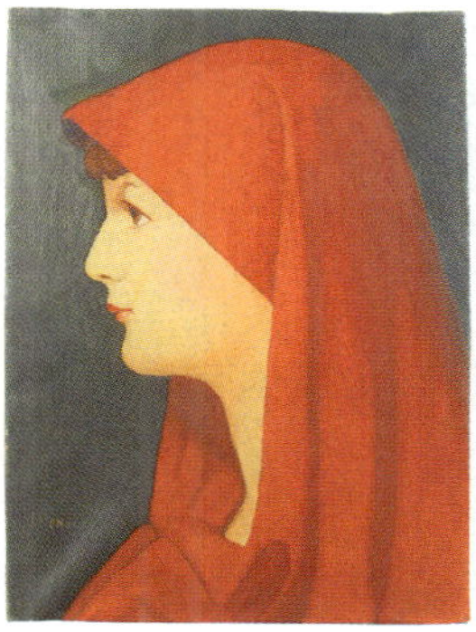

174

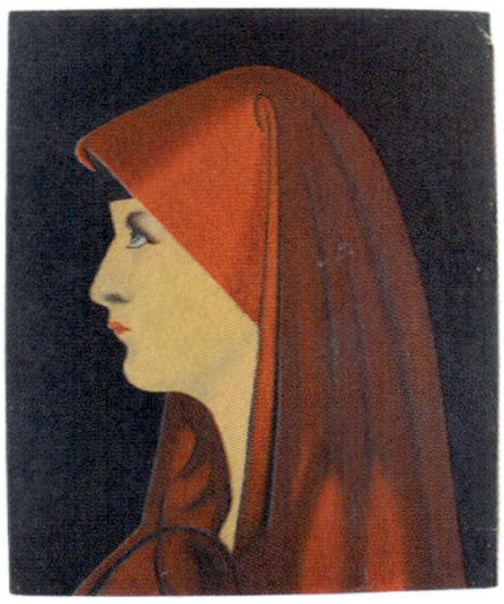

175

DIMENSIONS:	23 ⅝ x 19 ¾ x 1 inches (60 x 50.2 x 2.54 cm)
DATE:	Unknown
MEDIA:	Paint on wood composite panel or board
CONDITION:	Good—Slight accretion near subject's ear level.
PROVENANCE:	Brussels, Belgium, September 1993, 150 Belgian francs
NOTES:	Subject's gaze is distinctly upward.

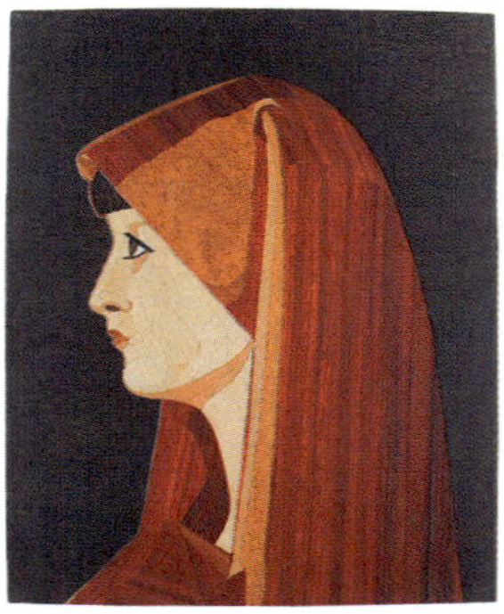

176

DIMENSIONS:	24 x 19 ⅝ x 1 inches (61 x 49.8 x 2.54 cm)
DATE:	Unknown
MEDIA:	Fabiola is depicted in wood veneer marquetry of a variety of wood species.
CONDITION:	Good
PROVENANCE:	Unknown

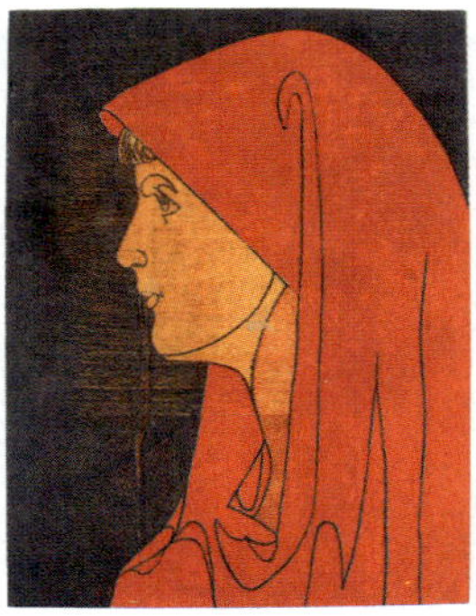

177

DIMENSIONS:	21 ¾ x 16 ¾ x ¼ inches (55.2 x 42.5 x 0.64 cm)
DATE:	Unknown
MEDIA:	Drawing and painting on wood composite panel or board
CONDITION:	Good
PROVENANCE:	Unknown
NOTES:	Fabiola is depicted in a simple line drawing. Wood grain is a prominent element of the composition.

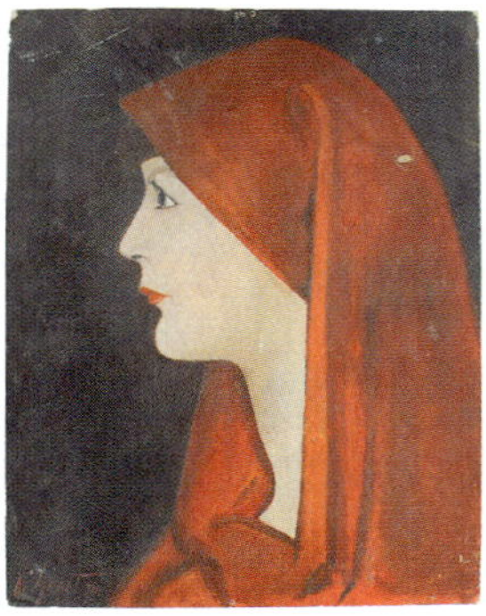

178

DIMENSIONS:	19 ⅝ x 15 ⅝ x ⅛ inches (49.8 x 39.7 x 0.32 cm)
DATE:	1970
MEDIA:	Paint on canvas mounted on paperboard
CONDITION:	Fair/Poor—There are numerous areas of stains and surface soiling on the piece.
PROVENANCE:	Belgium, 200 Belgian francs, gift of Louise
NOTES:	"Fabiola Naar J. Henner" in pen on separate area on verso. Signed "De Groot 70."

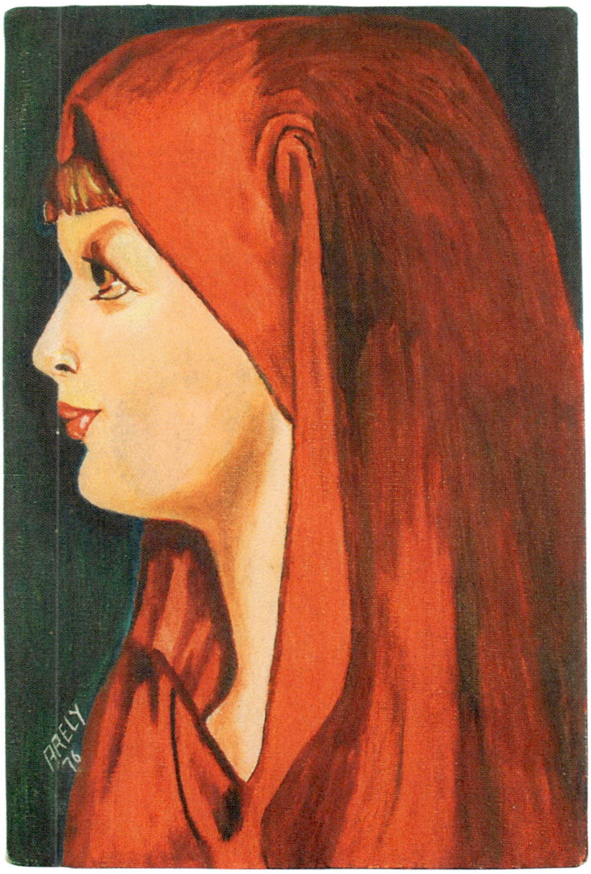

179

DIMENSIONS:	11 ¾ x 8 x ¾ inches (29.8 x 20.3 x 1.91 cm)
DATE:	1976
MEDIA:	Acrylic on canvas
CONDITION:	Good
PROVENANCE:	Mexico, circa 2005
NOTES:	"Nuevas" on small white scrap of paper, taped to verso of painting. Signed "ARELY '76."

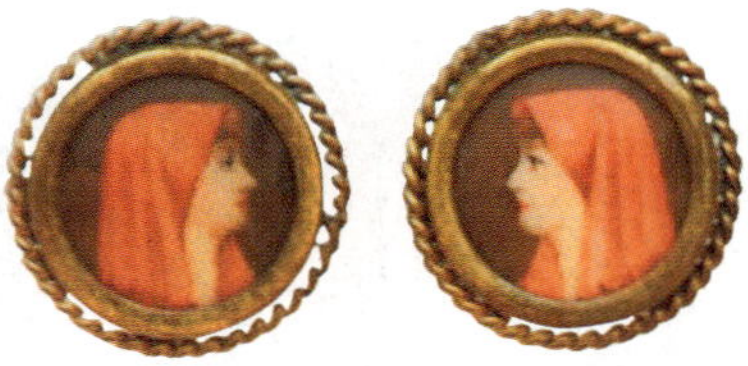

183

DIMENSIONS:	⅞ inch diameter (2.22 cm diameter)
DATE:	Unknown
MEDIA:	Pair of clip-on earrings with image of Fabiola. Paint on unknown support within two brass settings.
CONDITION:	Good—Paint and settings are in good and stable condition.
PROVENANCE:	France, 2005
NOTES:	Paintings are signed "L. Lachenal." Stolen during the exhibition at the Hispanic Society of America, September 2007.

DIMENSIONS:	21 ¾ x 16 ½ x 1 inches (55.2 x 41.9 x 2.54 cm)
DATE:	1928
MEDIA:	Pastel on paper mounted on wood composite panel or board
CONDITION:	Good
PROVENANCE:	Unknown
NOTES:	Signed "F. Espejo S 24/12/28."

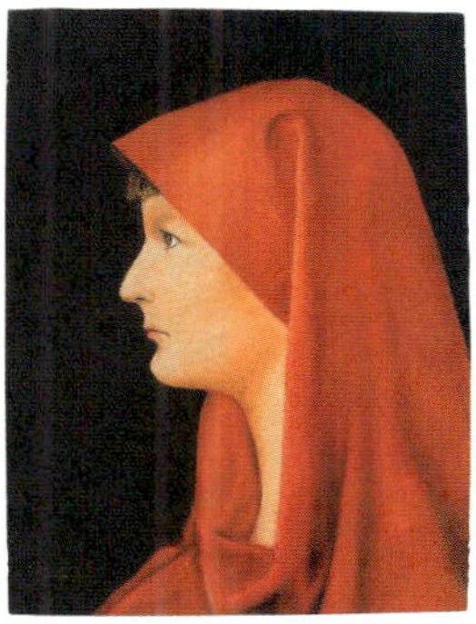

180

DIMENSIONS:	13 ¾ x 11 ¾ x ½ inches (34.9 x 29.8 x 1.27 cm)
DATE:	1983
MEDIA:	Paint on canvas, framed
CONDITION:	Fair/Good—There are several areas of paint loss throughout the entire surface.
PROVENANCE:	Unknown
NOTES:	Signed "Cristina 83."

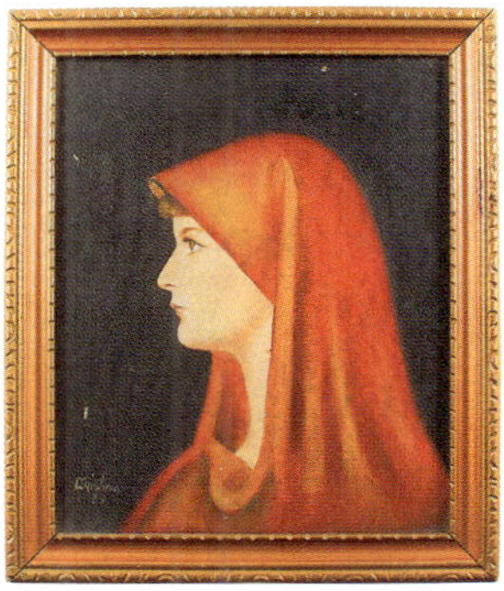

181

DIMENSIONS:	19 ½ x 15 ½ x 2 inches (49.5 x 39.4 x 5.08 cm)
DATE:	Unknown
MEDIA:	Paint on canvas, framed
CONDITION:	Good—Small white accretions in lower proper left corner and small losses from frame.
PROVENANCE:	Mexico, circa 2005
NOTES:	"Primavera 1936/Invierno 1981" in paint on verso. Signed "Gracie." There is a taped note to the verso that says "Nuevas."

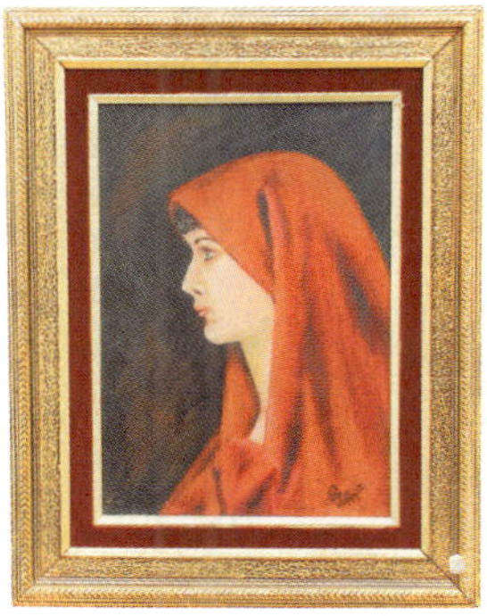

182

DIMENSIONS:	20 ¼ x 15 ⅝ x ½ inches (51.4 x 39.7 x 1.27 cm)
DATE:	Unknown
MEDIA:	Pastel on paper, framed
CONDITION:	Good/Fair
PROVENANCE:	Cologne, Germany, September 1994, 32 German marks
NOTES:	Signed "Aides Märezden."

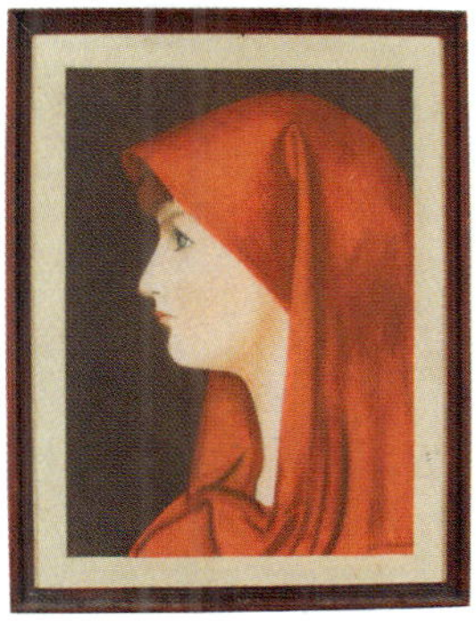

184

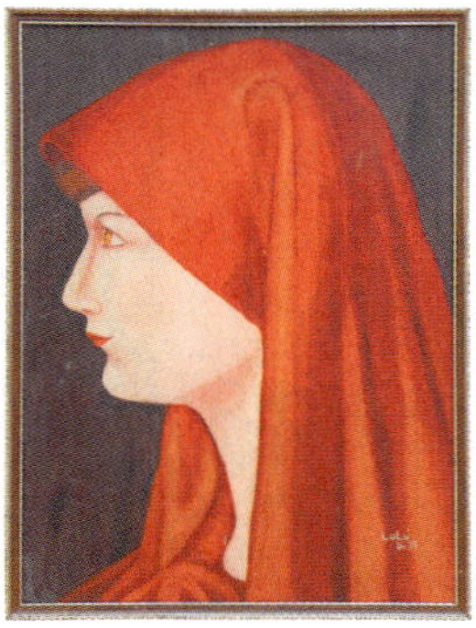

186

DIMENSIONS: 33 ⅛ x 25 ¼ x 1 ¼ inches (84.1 x 64.1 x 3.18 cm)
DATE: 1979
MEDIA: Paint on canvas, framed
CONDITION: Good—There are a few small losses or abrasions in the paint layer.
PROVENANCE: Mexico, 2004, 3000 Mexican pesos
NOTES: This painting shows a closer view of the subject than is typical. The composition places the top of the subject's head at the uppermost point of the image plane. Signed "Lulú Dic. 79."

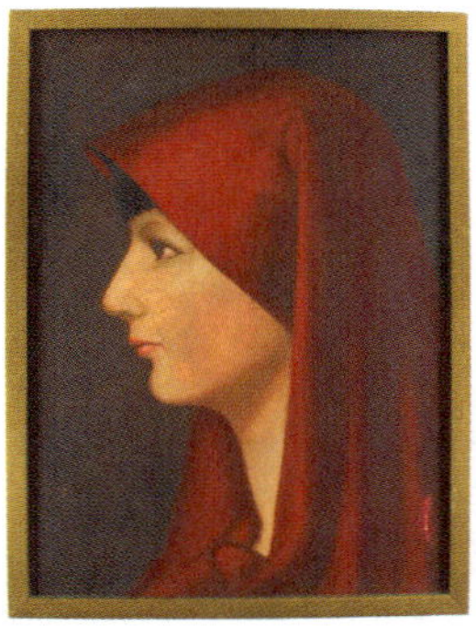

187

DIMENSIONS: 22 ⅞ x 17 ⅜ x 1 ½ inches (58.1 x 44.1 x 3.81 cm)
DATE: Unknown
MEDIA: Paint on panel or board, framed
CONDITION: Good—Slight discoloration and/or accretion in lower proper left corner.
PROVENANCE: Unknown

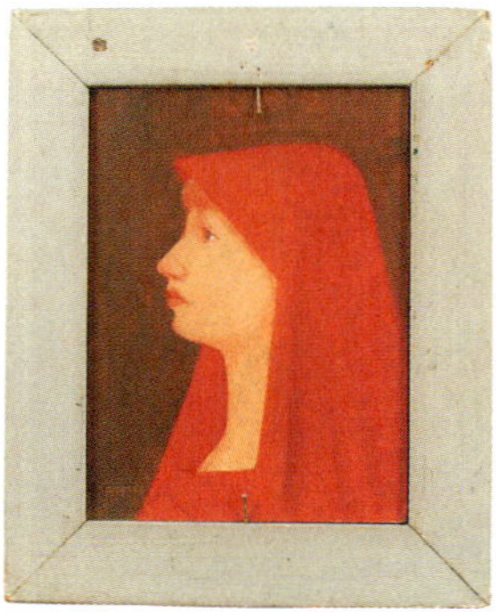

188

DIMENSIONS: 9 ⅞ x 8 x ⅞ inches (25.1 x 20.3 x 2.22 cm)
DATE: Unknown
MEDIA: Paint on panel or board, framed
CONDITION: Good
PROVENANCE: Mexico, 2003
NOTES: Panel is inserted into the frame in a backward position. Signed "Kaufman."

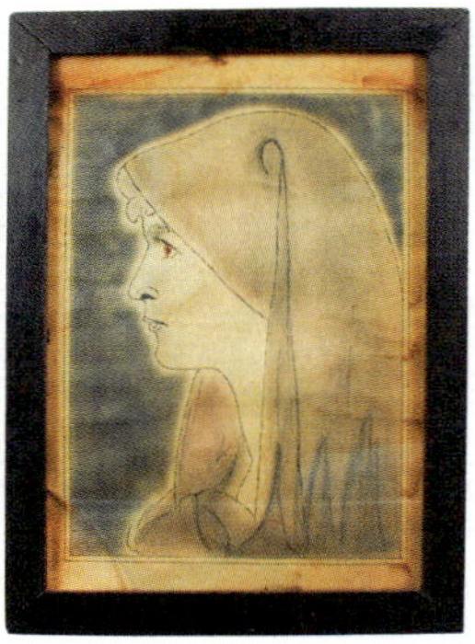

189

DIMENSIONS: 14 ¾ x 10 ⅞ x ½ inches (37.5 x 27.6 x 1.27 cm)
DATE: Unknown
MEDIA: Ink and pencil on paper, glazed and framed
CONDITION: Fair/Poor—There are numerous areas of stains and surface soiling on the piece. There is a small hole or tear that was likely the result of a prior mounting or hanging method.
PROVENANCE: Brussels, Belgium, 1995, 20 Belgian francs
NOTES: Glazing is broken with a missing section at the lower proper right corner. Backing board for frame appears to be a remnant of flooring material. Signed "HB" in lower proper left corner.

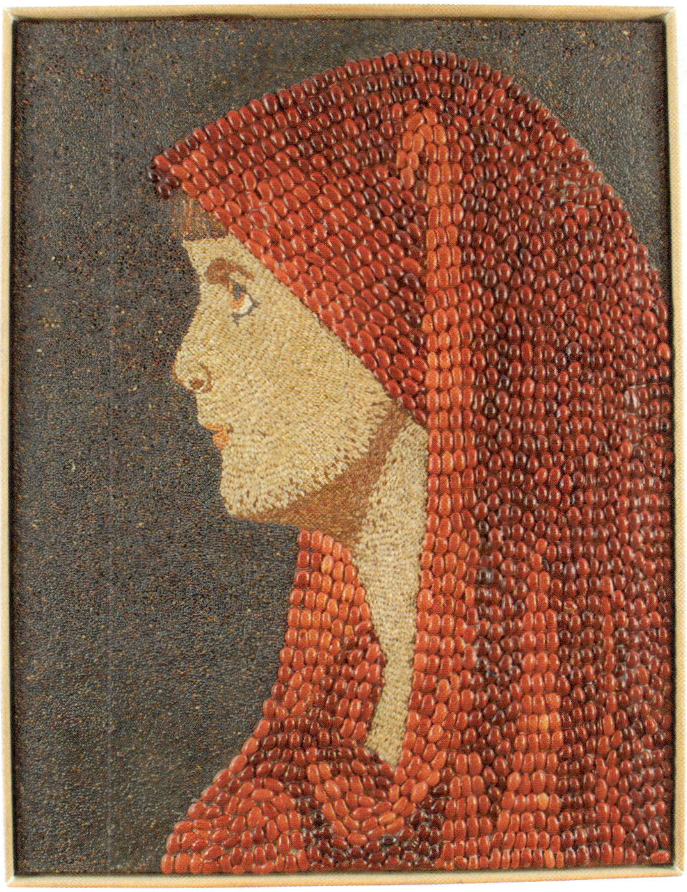

185

DIMENSIONS:	22 ¼ x 17 ¼ x 1 ⅜ inches (56.5 x 43.8 x 3.49 cm)
DATE:	Unknown
MEDIA:	Grains, seeds, and legumes mounted on wood composite panel or board
CONDITION:	Good
PROVENANCE:	Mexico, 2004, gift
NOTES:	This Fabiola is noteworthy in its use of foodstuffs. Given the unconventional media, it is nonetheless a stunning achievement in portraiture.

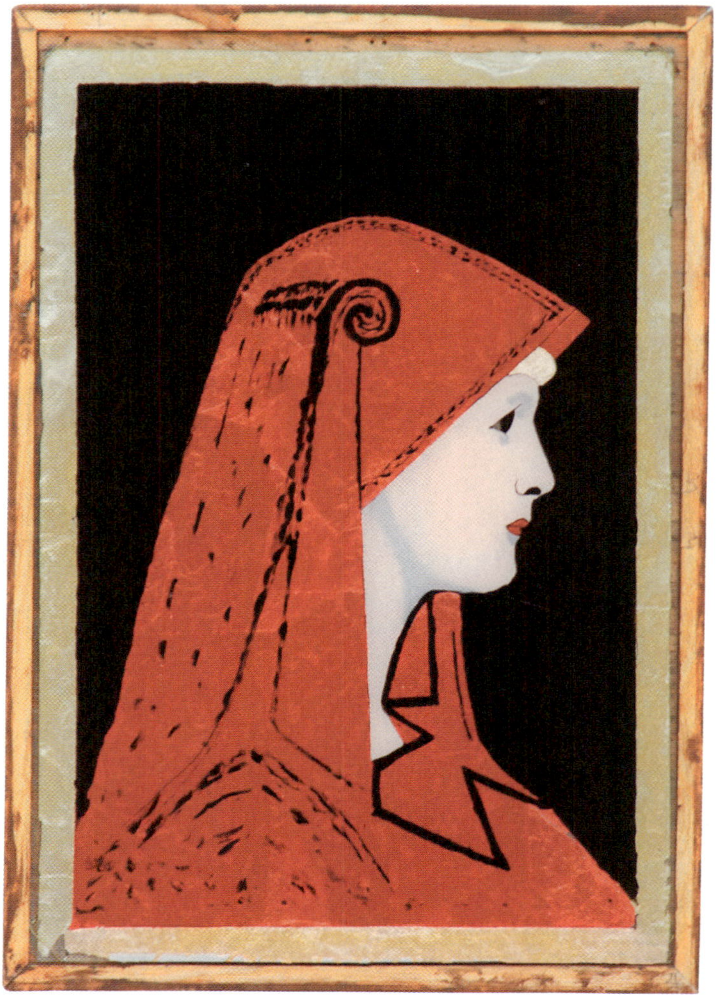

190

DIMENSIONS:	16 5/8 x 11 3/4 x 3/4 inches (42.2 x 29.8 x 1.91 cm)
DATE:	Unknown
MEDIA:	Foil and paint on glass
CONDITION:	Good
PROVENANCE:	Brussels, Belgium, November 1993, 200 Belgian francs
NOTES:	Subject is facing the proper left as opposed to the right, which is typical. This Fabiola is unusual and distinctive, mostly owing to the spiral shape at the top of the prime vertical fold of the hood. Also, there are heavy geometric lines at the base of the subject's neck to indicate folds in the hood and cloak. Subject's hair is depicted using gold foil.

DIMENSIONS: 10 ½ x 8 ¼ x ½ inches (26.7 x 21 x 1.27 cm)
DATE: Unknown
MEDIA: Paint on canvas
CONDITION: Good—Surface has overall layer of soiling.
PROVENANCE: Mechelen, Belgium, March 1998, 1000 Belgian francs
NOTES: Signed "L. Marco."

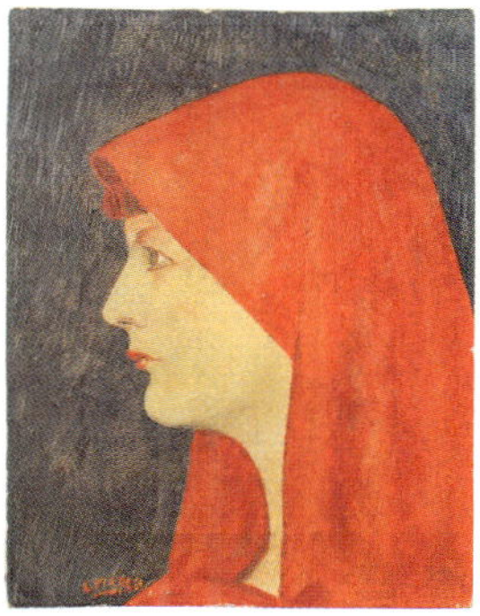

191

DIMENSIONS: 11 ¼ x 8 x 1 ½ inches (28.6 x 20.3 x 3.81 cm)
DATE: Unknown
MEDIA: Wood carved relief
CONDITION: Good
PROVENANCE: Netherlands, 2002
NOTES: Carved texture has been created for the ground plane.

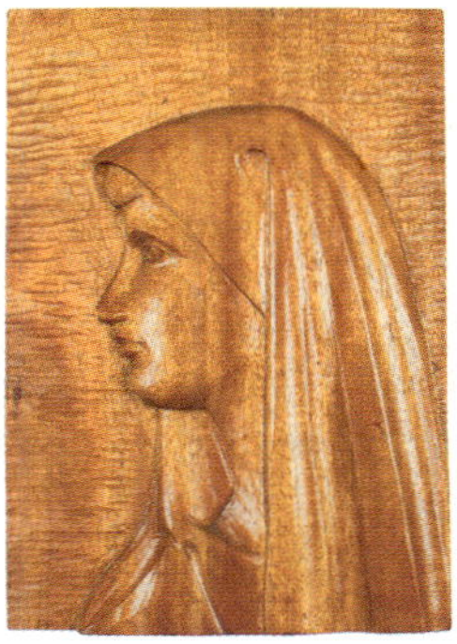

192

DIMENSIONS: 17 ⅝ x 12 ½ x ⅛ inches (44.77 x 31.75 x 0.32 cm)
DATE: 1941
MEDIA: Paint on canvas mounted on paperboard panel
CONDITION: Fair—Varnish layer has discolored significantly, and there are numerous cracks throughout paint layer. Very soiled overall.
PROVENANCE: Enghien, Belgium, November 6, 2005, 15 euros
NOTES: Owing to severely yellowed varnish, subject is without tonal difference. Signed "Stilmant 1941."

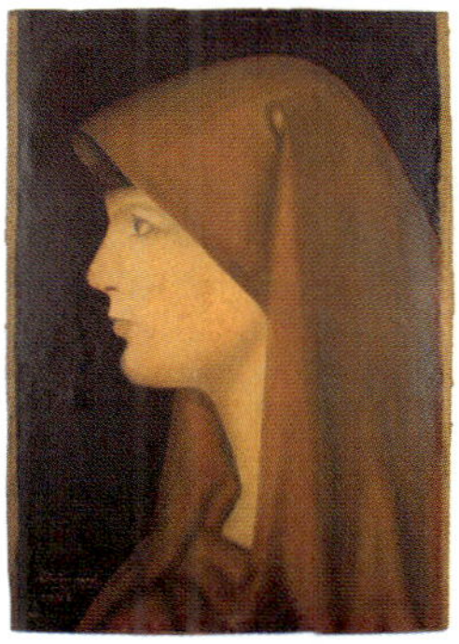

193

DIMENSIONS: 8 ⅛ x 5 ⅝ x ⅞ inches (20.6 x 14.3 x 2.22 cm)
DATE: Unknown
MEDIA: Embroidery on mesh suppport with encaustic or wax coating
CONDITION: Fair—Two small white accretions at lower region of painting. Mesh support has sagged so that edges of stretcher are visible from the front and cracks appear in the wax layer along these lines.
PROVENANCE: Brussels, Belgium, January 1993, 150 Belgian francs
NOTES: Rescued from Estonia in 1997. Wax coating obscures the texture of the embroidered surface, thereby creating a closer resemblance to a painting.

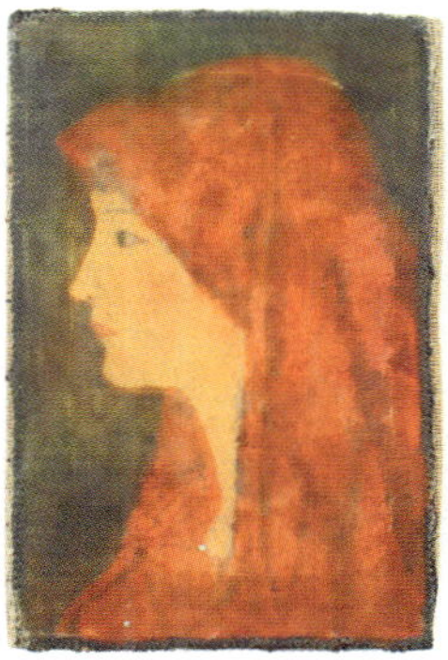

194

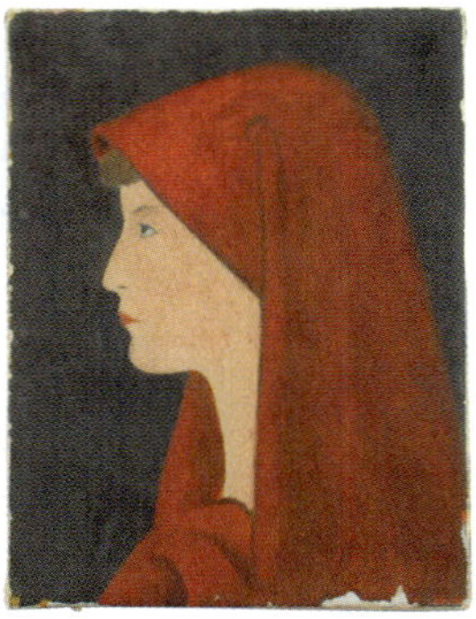

195

DIMENSIONS:	8 1/8 x 6 1/8 x 1/2 inches (20.6 x 15.6 x 1.27 cm)
DATE:	Unknown
MEDIA:	Paint on canvas
CONDITION:	Fair—Surface is very soiled and appears to have a coating. There are losses along the bottom edge.
PROVENANCE:	Mexico City, Mexico, February 1994, 20 Mexican pesos
NOTES:	Rescued from Estonia in 1997. This Fabiola is distinctive because the only depiction in the hood is the articulation of the prime vertical fold.

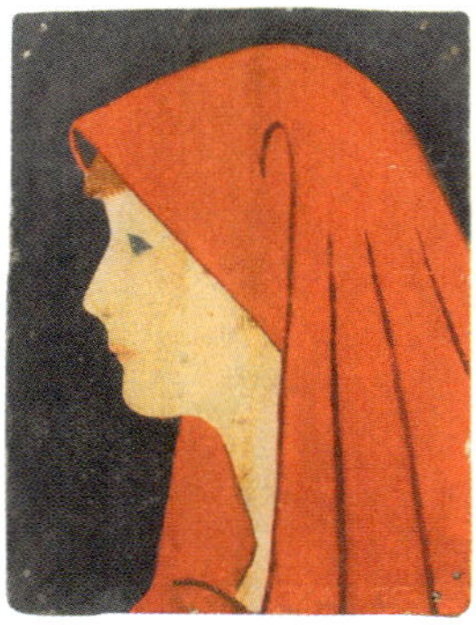

196

DIMENSIONS:	8 x 6 1/8 x 3/4 inches (20.3 x 15.6 x 1.91 cm)
DATE:	Unknown
MEDIA:	Paint on panel or board
CONDITION:	Fair—Surface is soiled throughout, although there is an unsoiled section—approx. 1" wide—that runs vertically down the center of the painting which could be related to a cleaning test or packing materials.
PROVENANCE:	Lille, France, June 1994, 30 French francs
NOTES:	Rescued from Estonia in 1997. The folds of the hood are articulated in a fanlike array of lines; the face appears flat and cartoonish.

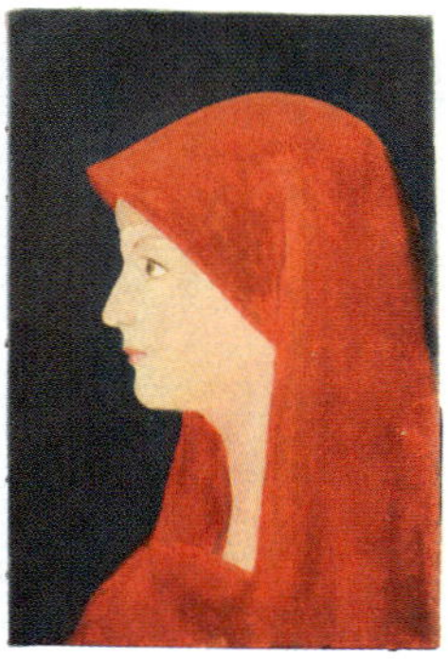

198

DIMENSIONS:	11 5/8 x 7 7/8 x 1/2 inches (29.5 x 20 x 1.27 cm)
DATE:	Unknown
MEDIA:	Acrylic on canvas
CONDITION:	Good
PROVENANCE:	New York City, United States, October 1995, 60 U.S. dollars
NOTES:	Rescued from Estonia in 1997.

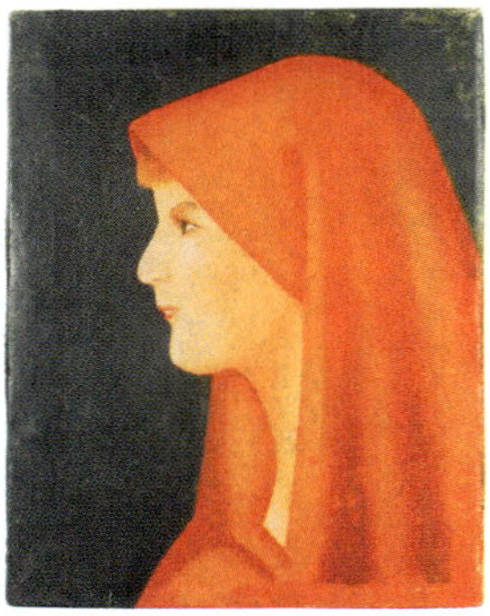

199

DIMENSIONS:	9 1/2 x 7 5/8 x 3/4 inches (24.1 x 19.4 x 1.91 cm)
DATE:	Unknown
MEDIA:	Paint on canvas, mounted on panel board
CONDITION:	Good—Slight surface cracking and soiling throughout paint layer.
PROVENANCE:	Paris, France, July 1994, gift
NOTES:	Rescued from Estonia in 1997.

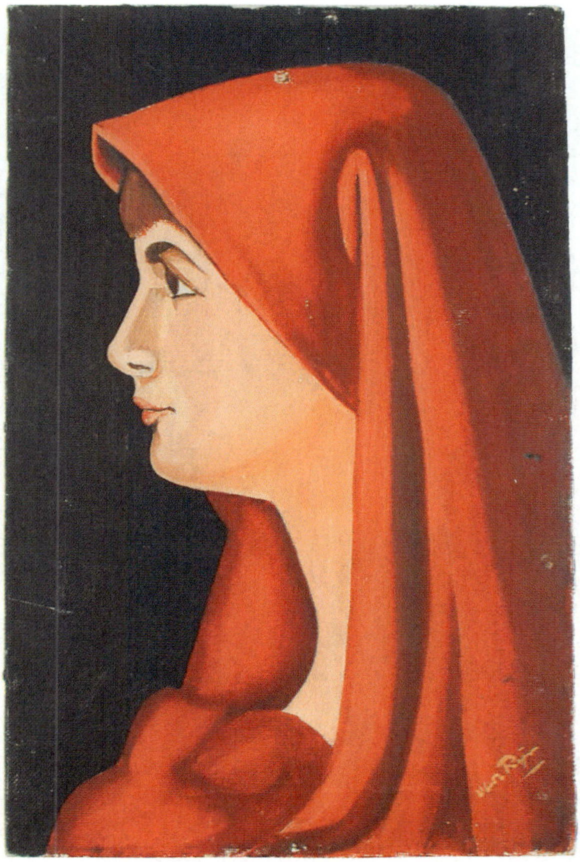

197

DIMENSIONS:	7 ⅞ x 11 ¾ x ⅜ inches (20 x 29.8 x 0.95 cm)
DATE:	Unknown
MEDIA:	Paint on canvas
CONDITION:	Poor/Fair—There is a ¼ inch tear/loss at the top edge of the hood. Numerous losses, abrasions, and accretions are present throughout the surface of the painting.
PROVENANCE:	Unknown
NOTES:	Rescued from Estonia in 1997. Signed "van Rijn" on proper left lower corner.

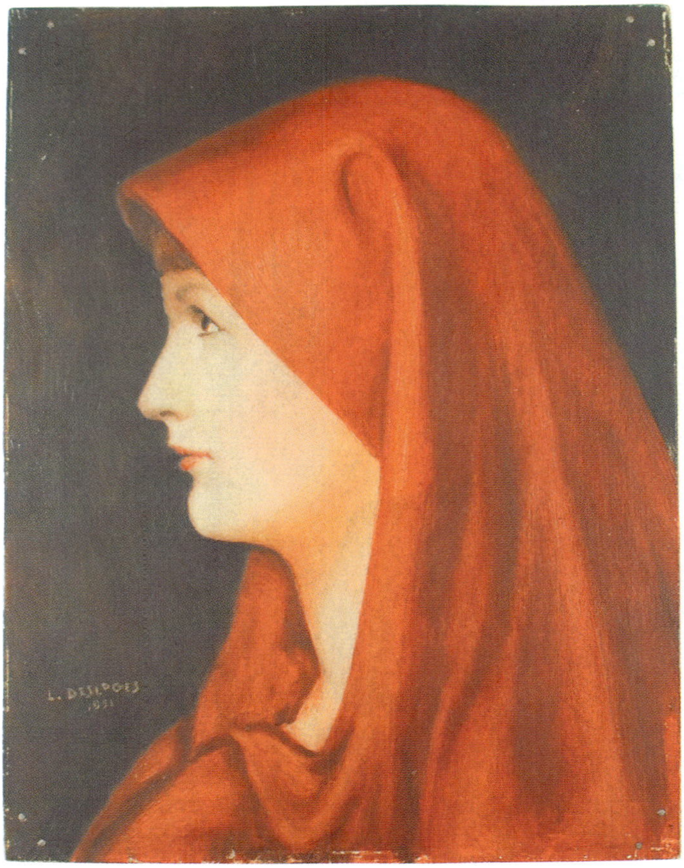

204

DIMENSIONS:	11 ¾ x 9 ⅜ x ¾ inches (29.8 x 23.8 x 1.91 cm)
DATE:	1951
MEDIA:	Oil on wood composite board
CONDITION:	Good—There are slight surface accretions in proper left lower corner and small cracks in support along bottom edge.
PROVENANCE:	Brussels, Belgium, October 1992, 450 Belgian francs
NOTES:	Rescued from Estonia in 1997. Signed "L. Desloges 1951."

DIMENSIONS: 9 7/8 x 7 7/8 x 7/8 inches (25.1 x 20 x 2.22 cm)
DATE: Unknown
MEDIA: Acrylic on canvas
CONDITION: Good
PROVENANCE: Los Angeles, United States, thrift shop, December 1995, 45 U.S. dollars
NOTES: Rescued from Estonia in 1997.
Signed "Huls"or "Luis."

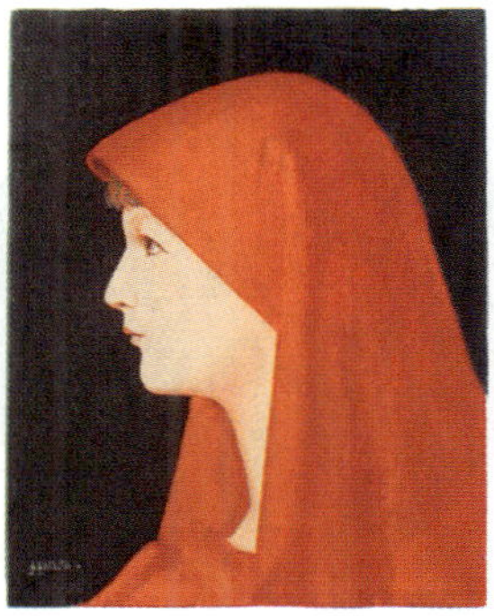

200

DIMENSIONS: 9 5/8 x 7 1/8 x 1/2 inches (24.4 x 18.1 x 1.27 cm)
DATE: Unknown
MEDIA: Oil on canvas
CONDITION: Fair—There are numerous surface cracks throughout painting, although they appear stable.
PROVENANCE: Copenhagen, Denmark, 1996, 65 kroner
NOTES: The prime vertical fold in the hood is painted as a discrete abstract form in the composition. Rescued from Estonia in 1997. Signed "Mars Haeperson."

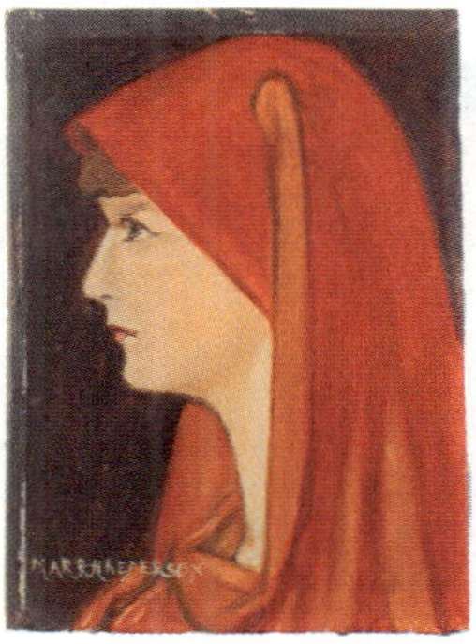

201

DIMENSIONS: 11 x 7 1/4 x 5/8 inches (27.9 x 18.4 x 1.59 cm)
DATE: Unknown
MEDIA: Paint on panel or board
CONDITION: Good
PROVENANCE: Brussels, Belgium, November 1993, 300 Belgian francs
NOTES: Rescued from Estonia in 1997.

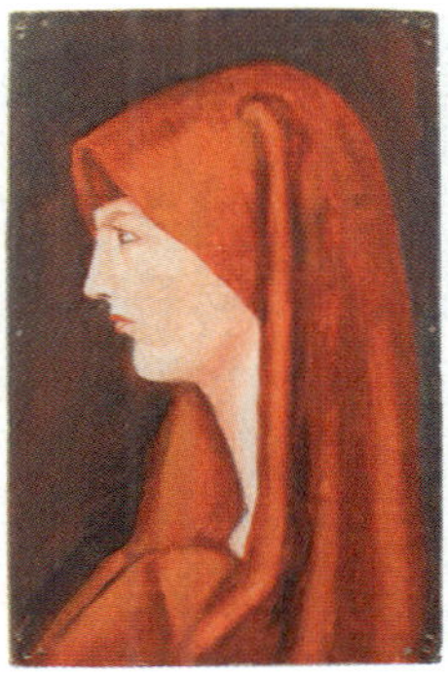

202

DIMENSIONS: 12 x 9 3/8 x 1/2 inches (30.5 x 23.8 x 1.27 cm)
DATE: Unknown
MEDIA: Paint on canvas
CONDITION: Fair—There is a tear/loss at top of subject's head and numerous losses in paint layer throughout.
PROVENANCE: Oostende, Belgium, 1994, 300 Belgian francs
NOTES: Rescued from Estonia in 1997. Signed "J. Viss."

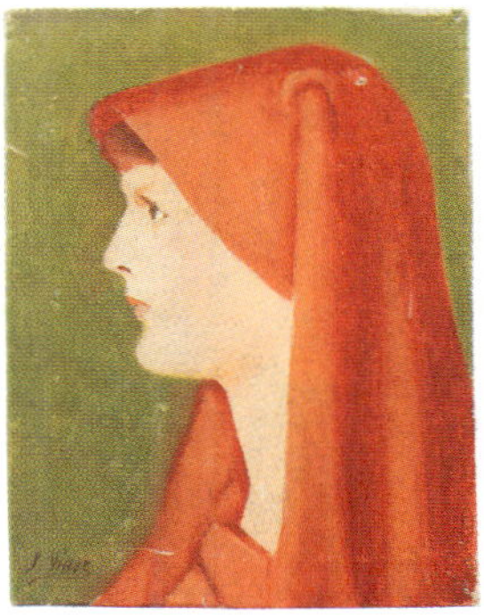

203

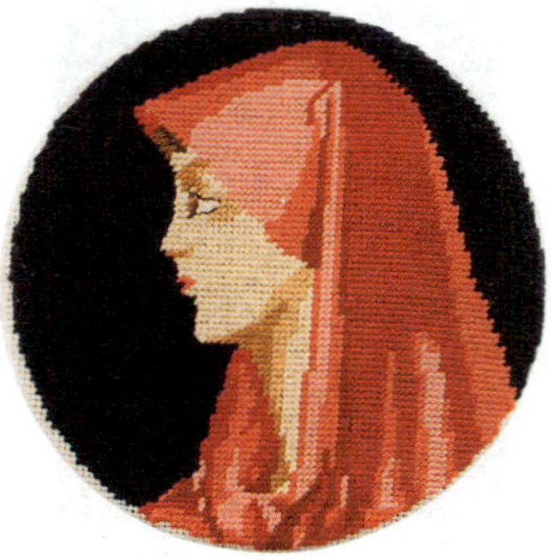

205

DIMENSIONS:	7 ½ inches diameter x ⅞ inch (19.05 cm diameter x 2.22 cm)
DATE:	Unknown
MEDIA:	Needlepoint on mesh support mounted on circular form
CONDITION:	Good
PROVENANCE:	Lille, France, 1994, 40 French francs
NOTES:	Rescued from Estonia in 1997. This is the only needlepoint in the collection that is not square or rectangular in shape. "Fabiola d'après Henner" in pencil on verso along with other writing in French.

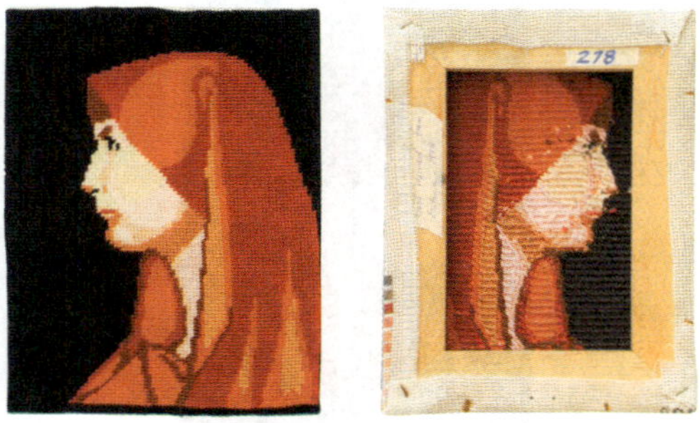

207

DIMENSIONS:	11 ½ x 8 ¾ x ⅞ inches (29.2 x 22.2 x 2.22 cm)
DATE:	Unknown
MEDIA:	Needlepoint on mesh support stapled onto wood stretcher
CONDITION:	Good
PROVENANCE:	March 1997, gift of Laurent Diercxsens
NOTES:	Rescued from Estonia in 1997.

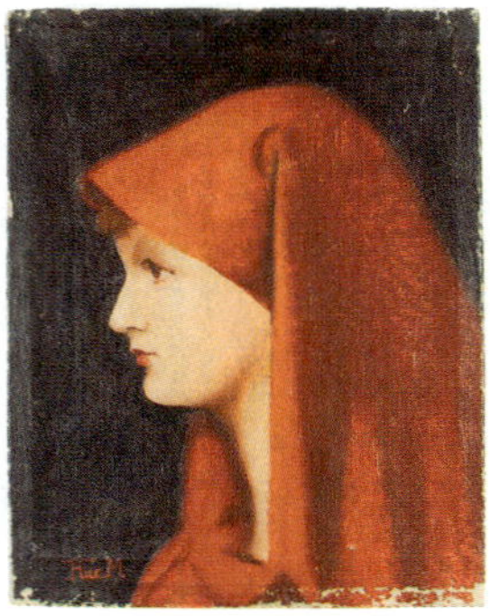

208

DIMENSIONS:	11 ⅞ x 9 ⅜ x ¾ inches (30.2 x 23.8 x 1.91 cm)
DATE:	Unknown
MEDIA:	Oil on canvas
CONDITION:	Poor—The surface of the painting is very friable, and there are significant areas of losses along the bottom edge and proper right edge.
PROVENANCE:	Brussels, Belgium, September 1992, 50 Belgian francs
NOTES:	Rescued from Estonia in 1997. Signed "Hue M."

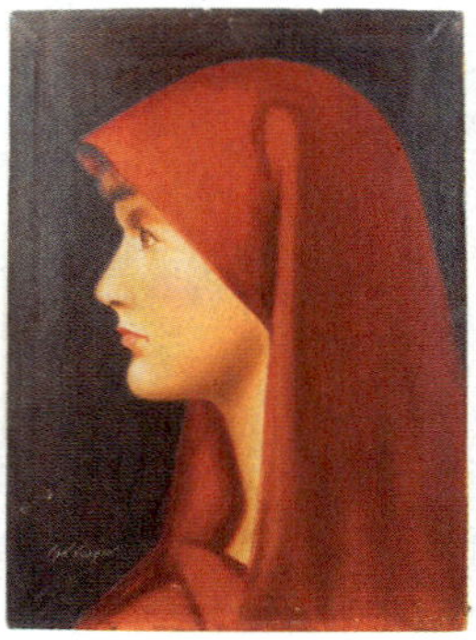

209

DIMENSIONS:	15 ¾ x 11 ¾ x ⅜ inches (40 x 29.8 x 0.95 cm)
DATE:	Unknown
MEDIA:	Oil on canvas
CONDITION:	Good—With a few small accretions.
PROVENANCE:	Antwerp, Belgium, May 1993, 300 Belgian francs
NOTES:	Rescued from Estonia in 1997. Signed "Van Vooren."

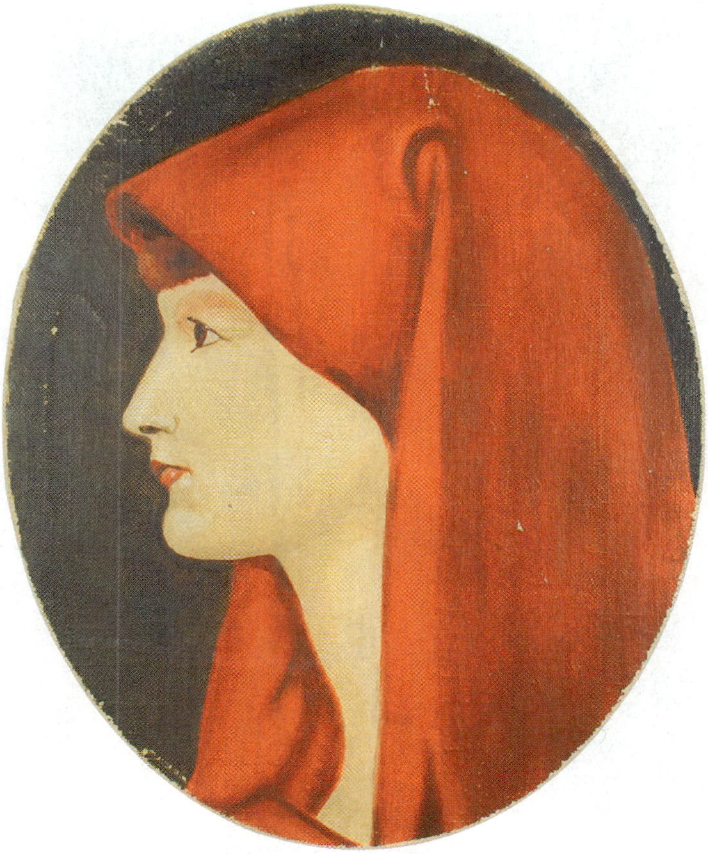

206

DIMENSIONS:	11 ⅛ x 9 ¼ x ⅞ inches (28.3 x 23.5 x 2.22 cm)
DATE:	Unknown
MEDIA:	Paint on canvas mounted on oval-shaped wood support
CONDITION:	Fair—Various losses and cracks throughout entire surface.
PROVENANCE:	Paris, France, November 1995, 50 French francs
NOTES:	Rescued from Estonia in 1997.

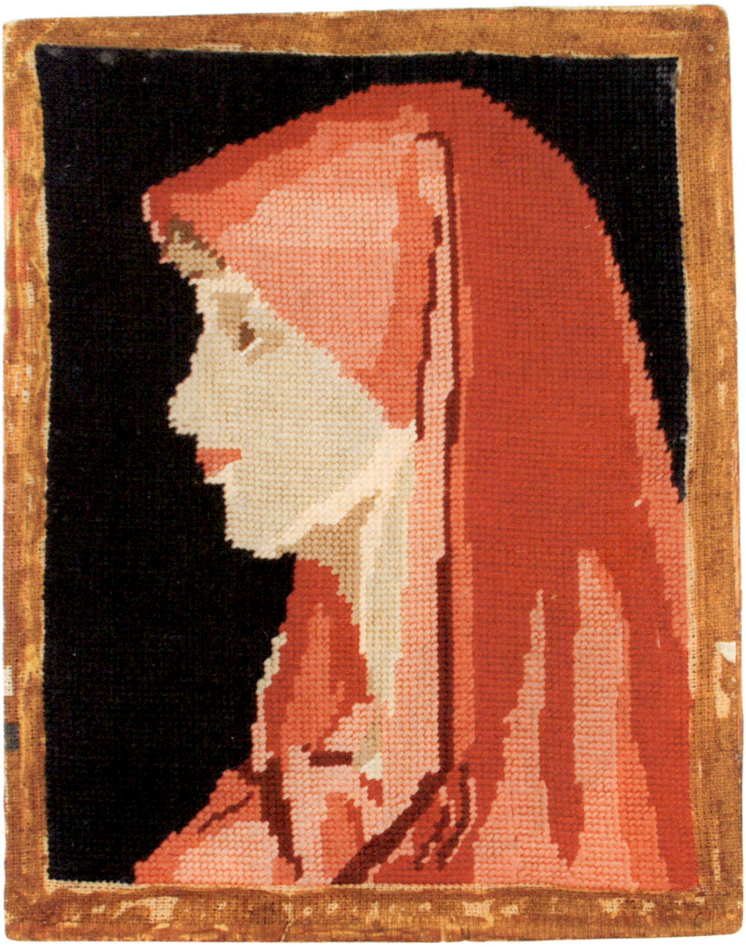

210

DIMENSIONS:	12 ⅜ x 9 ¾ x ¾ inches (31.4 x 24.8 x 1.91 cm)
DATE:	1933
MEDIA:	Needlepoint on mesh support mounted on wood composite panel or board
CONDITION:	Good—Slightly soiled surface.
PROVENANCE:	Tournai, Belgium, March 1993, gift of Edith De Kindt
NOTES:	Rescued from Estonia in 1997.

DIMENSIONS: 12 5⁄8 x 1 1⁄4 x 1 inches (32.1 x 26 x 2.54 cm)
DATE: Unknown
MEDIA: Needlepoint with cotton embroidery thread on mesh support, framed
CONDITION: Good
PROVENANCE: Belgium, October 1994, gift of Paty Blake
NOTES: Rescued from Estonia in 1997. Unlike other needlepoint Fabiolas, this does not appear to be made from a commercially available pattern.

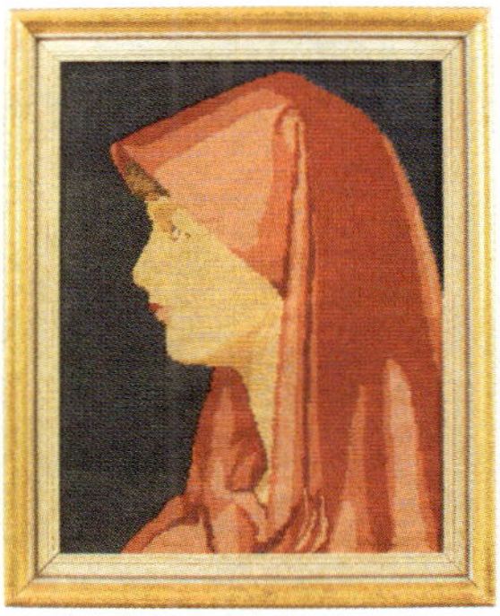

211

DIMENSIONS: 13 1⁄4 x 10 3⁄4 x 1⁄2 inches (33.7 x 27.3 x 1.27 cm)
DATE: Unknown
MEDIA: Pastel on paper, framed and glazed
CONDITION: Good
PROVENANCE: Brussels, Belgium, November 1995, 20 Belgian francs
NOTES: Rescued from Estonia in 1997. Subject's gaze and appearance suggest sadness. Signed "Farezijn Rene."

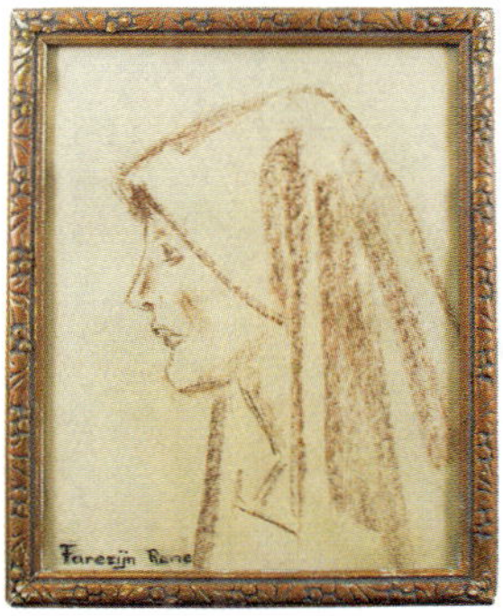

212

DIMENSIONS: 2 1⁄8 x 1 3⁄4 inches (5.4 x 4.44 cm)
DATE: Unknown
MEDIA: Brooch/cameo with image of Fabiola. Paint on unknown support within a brass setting.
CONDITION: Good—Paint and setting are in good and stable condition.
PROVENANCE: Belgium, 30 euros
NOTES: Signed "L. Lachenal d'après Henner."

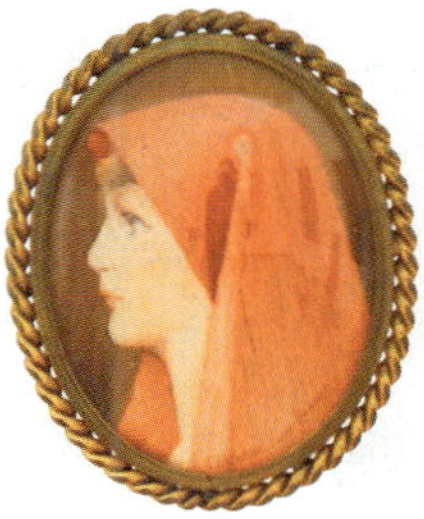

213

DIMENSIONS: 17 5⁄8 x 15 5⁄8 x 1 inches (44.8 x 39.7 x 2.54 cm)
DATE: Unknown
MEDIA: Paint on canvas
CONDITION: Good
PROVENANCE: Unknown
NOTES: Fabiola is depicted in a painterly manner.

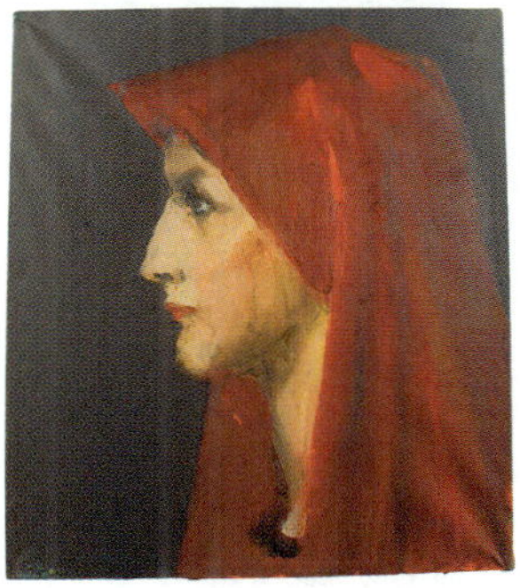

214

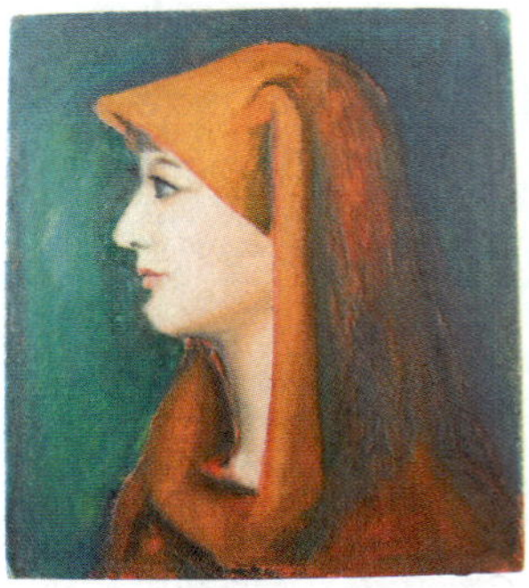

215

DIMENSIONS:	17 ¾ x 15 ⅞ x 1 inches (45.1 x 40.3 x 2.54 cm)
DATE:	Unknown
MEDIA:	Acrylic on canvas
CONDITION:	Good
PROVENANCE:	Brussels, Belgium, October 1992, 450 Belgian francs
NOTES:	Fabiola's drapery is distinctive in the hood and cloak areas.

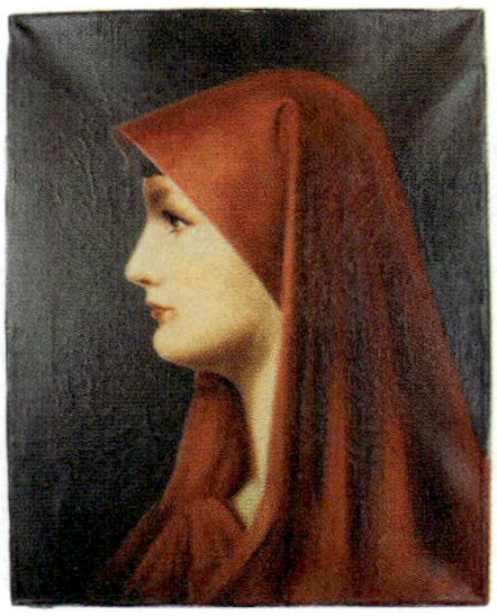

216

DIMENSIONS:	19 ¾ x 15 ¾ x ¾ inches (50.16 x 40 x 1.9 cm)
DATE:	Unknown
MEDIA:	Paint on canvas
CONDITION:	Poor—Severe cracking throughout paint layer and discoloration from aged varnish.
PROVENANCE:	Unknown
NOTES:	Signed "R. Deleu."

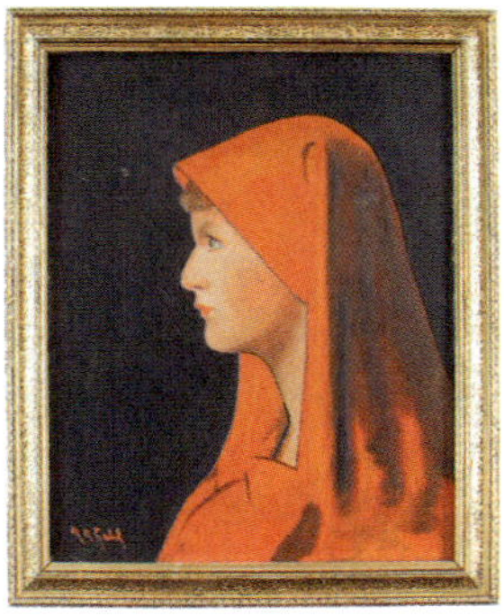

218

DIMENSIONS:	15 ⅝ x 12 ⅞ x 1 ¼ inches (39.7 x 32.7 x 3.18 cm)
DATE:	Unknown
MEDIA:	Paint on canvas
CONDITION:	Good/Fair
PROVENANCE:	Unknown
NOTES:	Signed "M. R. Gabriel."

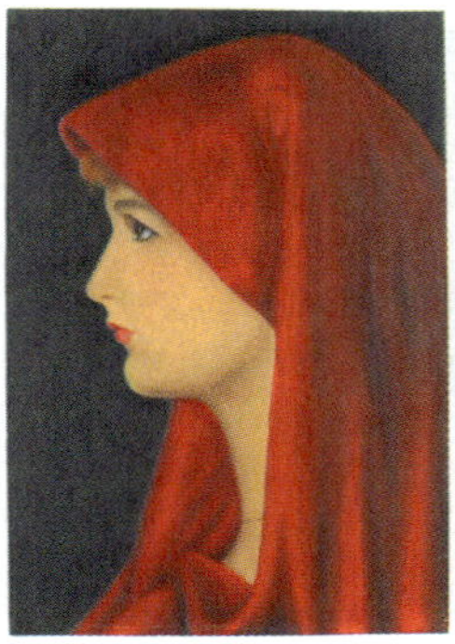

219

DIMENSIONS:	16 ½ x 11 ⅝ x ¾ inches (41.9 x 29.5 x 1.91 cm)
DATE:	Unknown
MEDIA:	Paint on wood composite panel or board
CONDITION:	Good
PROVENANCE:	Mexico City (Pecos), Mexico, January 2005, 200 Mexican pesos
NOTES:	Subject's gaze is distinctly upward.

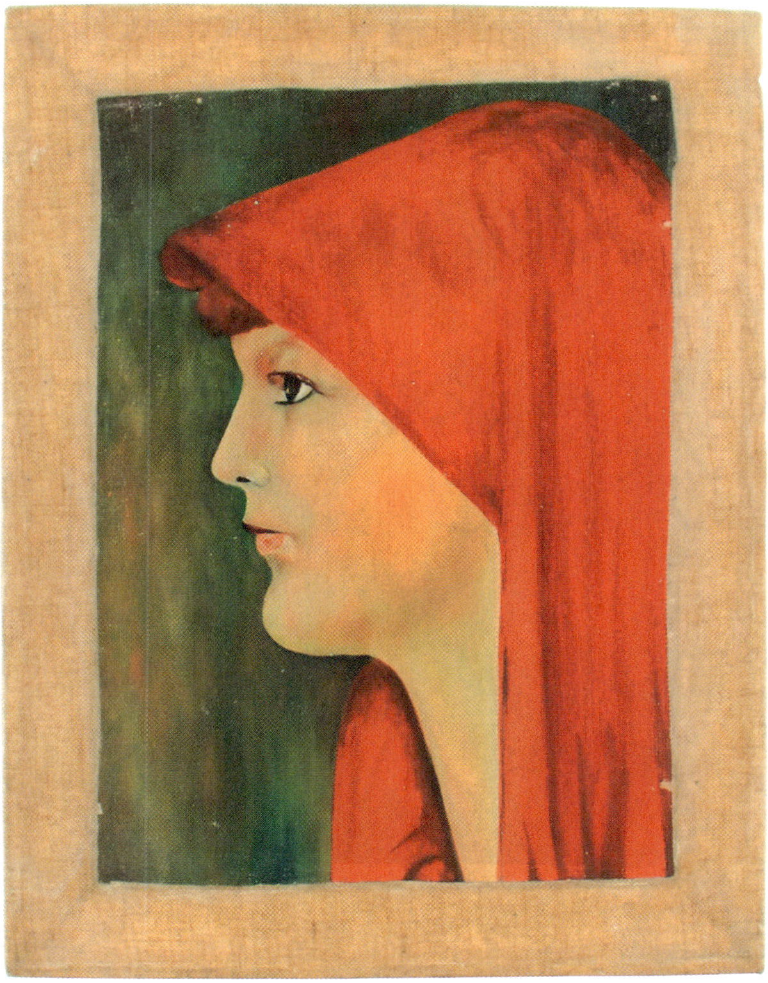

217

DIMENSIONS:	16 ¾ x 13 ⅛ x ⅞ inches (42.5 x 33.3 x 2.22 cm)
DATE:	Unknown
MEDIA:	Oil on canvas with unknown coating
CONDITION:	Good/Fair
PROVENANCE:	Unknown
NOTES:	Illegible writing in pencil on verso of stretcher.

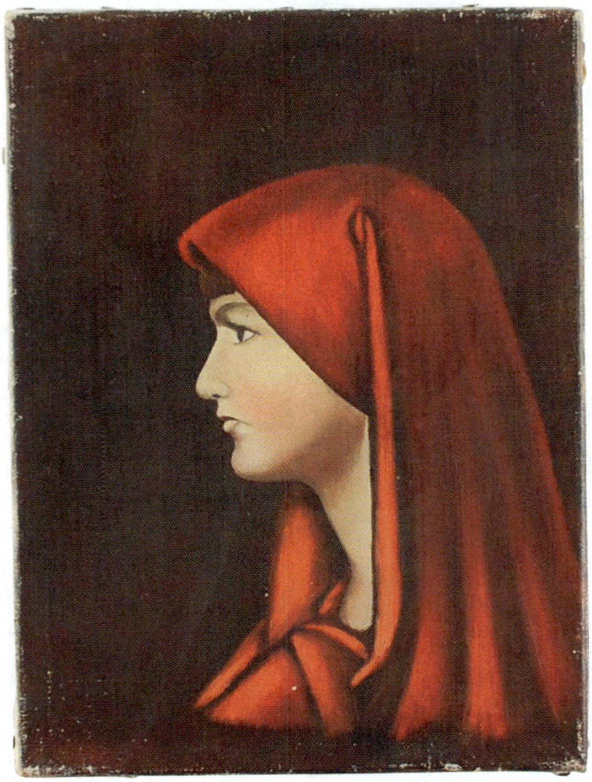

224

DIMENSIONS:	9 ½ x 7 ⅛ x ⅝ inches (24.1 x 18.1 x 1.59 cm)
DATE:	Unknown
MEDIA:	Paint on canvas
CONDITION:	Good
PROVENANCE:	Oostmalle, Belgium, December 1996, 700 Belgian francs
NOTES:	Rescued from Estonia in 1997.

DIMENSIONS:	9 ½ x 10 ¼ x ½ inches (24.1 x 26 x 1.27 cm)
DATE:	Unknown
MEDIA:	Needlepoint on mesh support mounted on stretcher
CONDITION:	Good
PROVENANCE:	Mexico City, Mexico, 2005, gift of Señora Toxqui
NOTES:	Fabiola is depicted in a backward-leaning posture.

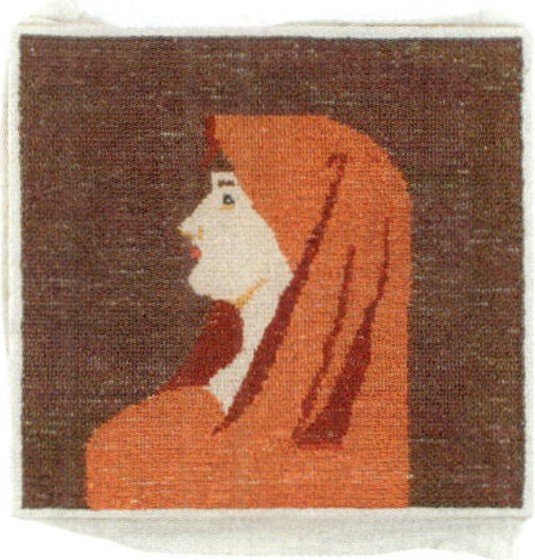

220

DIMENSIONS:	7 ⅞ x 11 x ⅝ inches (20 x 27.9 x 1.59 cm)
DATE:	Unknown
MEDIA:	Paint on canvas
CONDITION:	Good/Fair—There is a prior restoration between the heads of the center figure and the figure on the proper left.
PROVENANCE:	Mexico City, Mexico, 2004, gift of Angel Toxqui
NOTES:	This painting is noteworthy in its composition, which includes three Fabiola figures. None of the three figures assume the typical profile position. In addition, the painting is executed with more sophisticated technique, especially evident in the eyes and the draping garments.

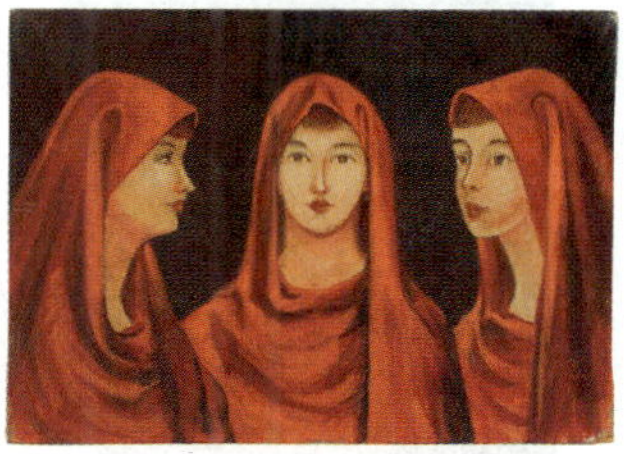

221

DIMENSIONS:	5 ⅜ x 4 x ¾ inches (13.7 x 10.2 x 1.91 cm)
DATE:	Unknown
MEDIA:	Paint on canvas mounted on wood composite panel or board
CONDITION:	Fair/Poor—There are numerous losses and abrasions in the paint layer.
PROVENANCE:	San Telmo, Buenos Aires, Argentina, May 2004

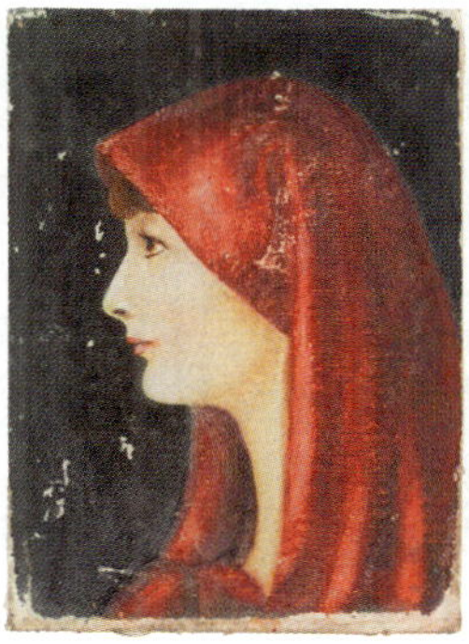

222

DIMENSIONS:	5 ⅝ x 4 ¾ x ½ inches (14.3 x 12.1 x 1.27 cm)
DATE:	Unknown
MEDIA:	Paint on unknown support in faux-tiled frame
CONDITION:	Good
PROVENANCE:	Unknown
NOTES:	Signed "M. Henner." Backing is a newspaper clipping, and there is a small stamp/label on verso that says "Elfenbein—Miniatur aus Elfenbein."

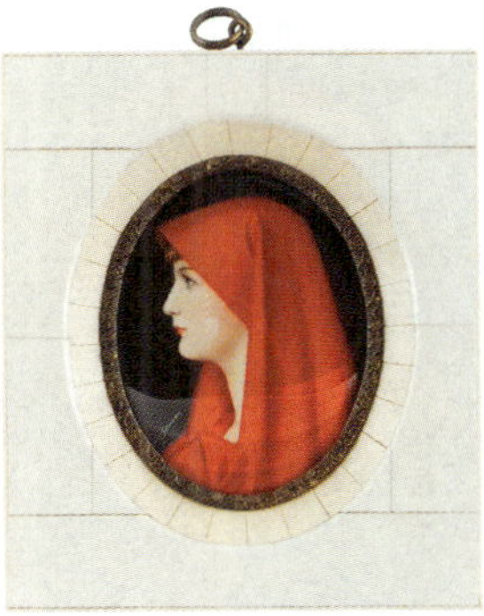

223

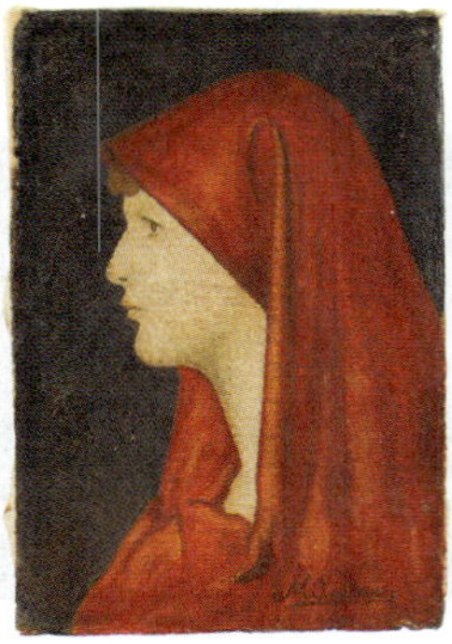

225

DIMENSIONS:	9 ½ x 6 ⅝ x ⅝ inches (24.1 x 16.8 x 1.59 cm)
DATE:	Unknown
MEDIA:	Paint on canvas
CONDITION:	Fair
PROVENANCE:	Mexico City, Mexico, May 2002, 1200 Mexican pesos
NOTES:	The black background in this portrayal has extensive and elaborate brushwork. "Fabiola J. J. Henner" on verso of canvas. Signed "Mifolloger."

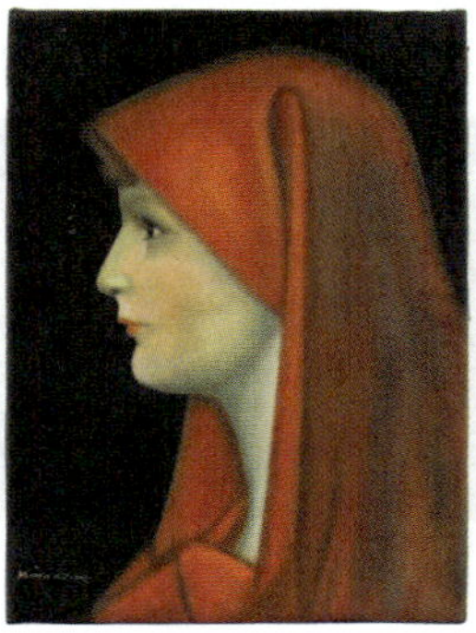

227

DIMENSIONS:	16 x 12 x ⅞ inches (40.6 x 30.5 x 2.22 cm)
DATE:	1985
MEDIA:	Paint on canvas
CONDITION:	Good
PROVENANCE:	Unknown (Belgium?)
NOTES:	Signed "Martin M. P.—1985."

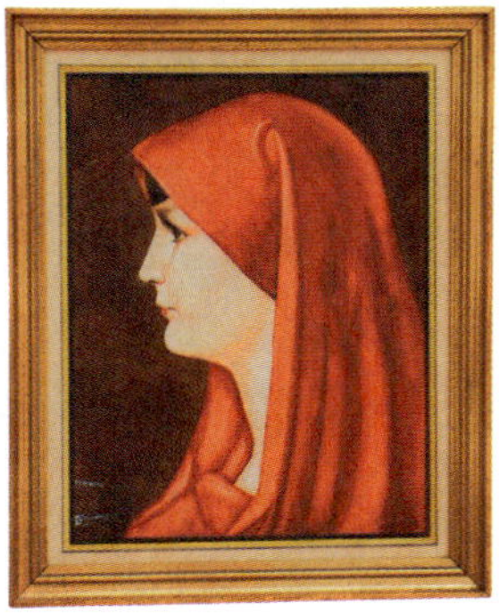

228

DIMENSIONS:	19 ½ x 16 x 1 inches (49.5 x 40.6 x 2.54 cm)
DATE:	Unknown
MEDIA:	Watercolor on paper, glazed and framed
CONDITION:	Good
PROVENANCE:	2005, gift of Louise
NOTES:	Signed "J. J. Henner L Vauwenberghe."

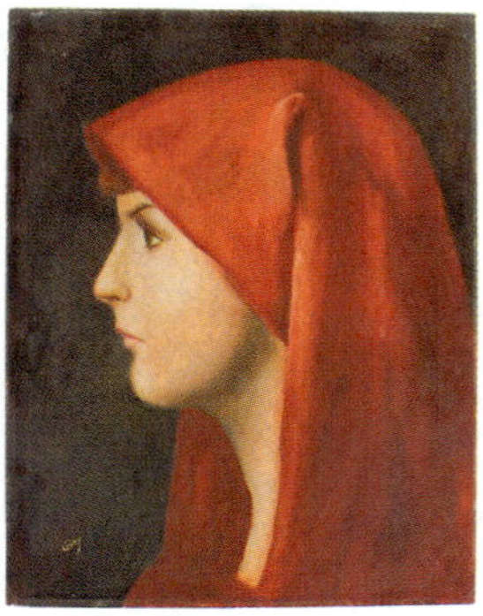

229

DIMENSIONS:	19 ¾ x 15 ¾ x ¾ inches (50.2 x 40 x 1.91 cm)
DATE:	Unknown
MEDIA:	Paint on canvas
CONDITION:	Good
PROVENANCE:	Mexico City (Raul), Mexico, April 2005, 1500 Mexican pesos
NOTES:	Signed "Giny."

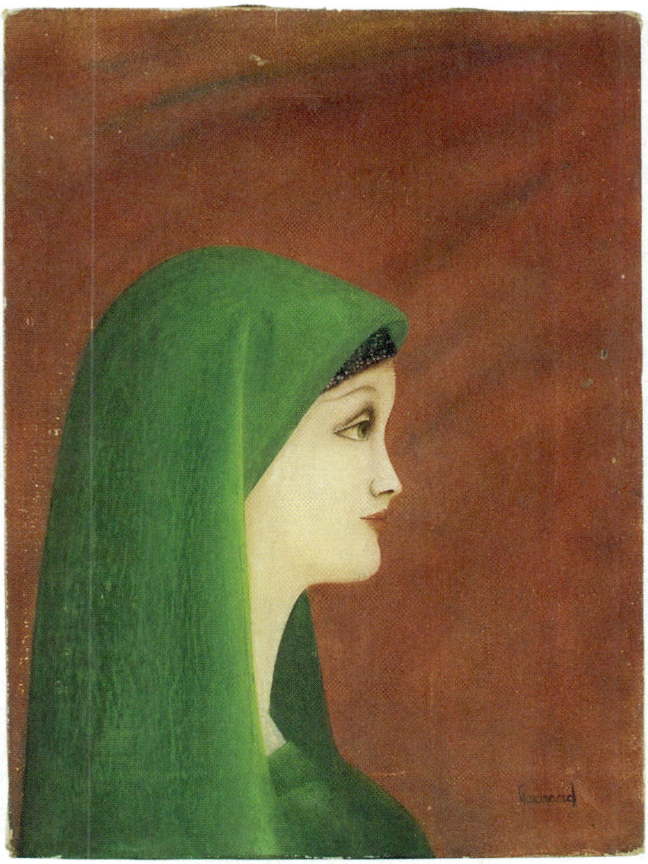

226

DIMENSIONS:	15 ¾ x 11 ⅞ x ¾ inches (40 x 30.2 x 1.91 cm)
DATE:	Unknown
MEDIA:	Paint on canvas
CONDITION:	Good/Fair—There is a prior restoration and patch to the canvas support.
PROVENANCE:	Mexico, 2006
NOTES:	"Designo Espanol Original y autentico" in pencil on verso of canvas support. Figure is wearing green hood, as opposed to red, which is typical of Fabiola depictions. Also, figure is facing the proper left as opposed to the right as is typical. Signed "Harmand."

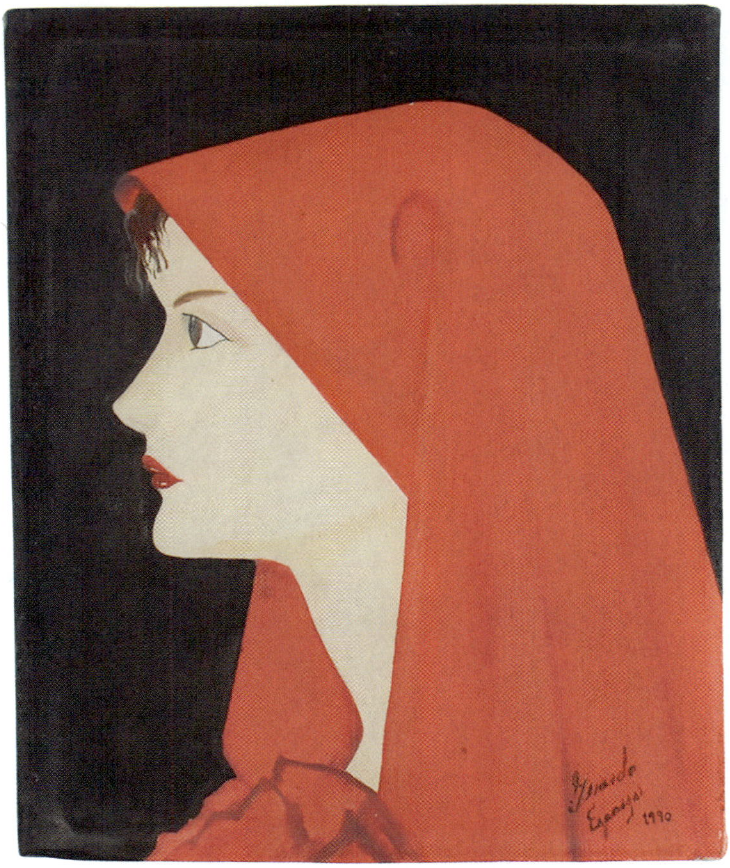

232

DIMENSIONS:	11 7/8 x 9 3/4 x 3/4 inches (30.2 x 24.8 x 1.91 cm)
DATE:	1990
MEDIA:	Acrylic on canvas
CONDITION:	Good
PROVENANCE:	Mexico City (Raul), Mexico, November 2005, 800 Mexican pesos
NOTES:	Fabiola has sparse bangs, however the visible hair appears styled. Signed "Gerardo Egansga."

DIMENSIONS:	19 ¾ x 16 x ¾ inches (50.2 x 40.6 x 1.91 cm)
DATE:	1992
MEDIA:	Paint on canvas
CONDITION:	Fair—There are abraded areas along the inside line of the stretcher and losses and abrasions at the corners.
PROVENANCE:	Unknown
NOTES:	Signed "O. Erosa Camara 8–92 Cob."

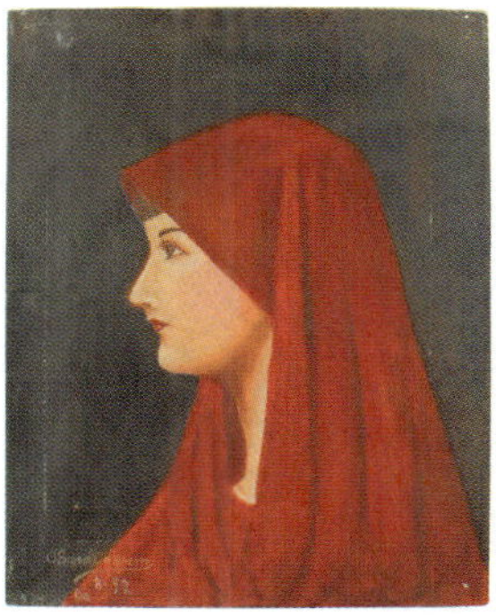

230

DIMENSIONS:	11 ¾ x 10 x ½ inches (29.8 x 25.4 x 1.27 cm)
DATE:	1915
MEDIA:	Paint on canvas
CONDITION:	Poor—There is a large loss with a tear in the canvas support to the right of the subject's head. There are also numerous losses and surface abrasions throughout, and the paint layer is very soiled.
PROVENANCE:	Mexico City (Pecos), Mexico, May 2005, 1200 Mexican pesos
NOTES:	The subject's hood is depicted here with three angles, as opposed to one curved line. Signed "HM. Bonilla. XI–XX–XV."

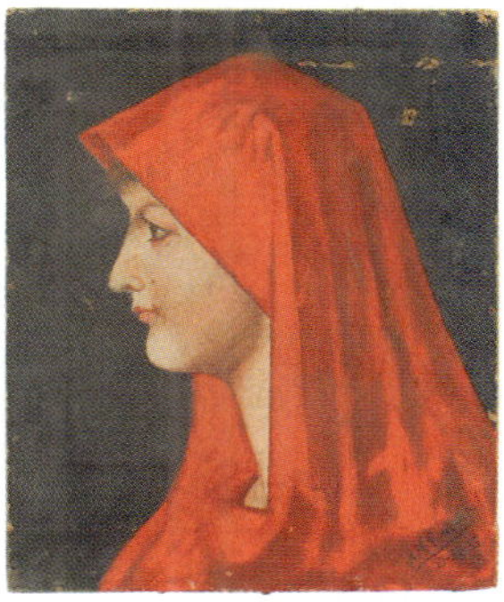

231

DIMENSIONS:	11 ¾ x 10 x ¾ inches (29.8 x 25.4 x 1.91 cm)
DATE:	Unknown
MEDIA:	Paint on canvas
CONDITION:	Good
NOTES:	Mexico City (Angel), Mexico, November 2005, 450 Mexican pesos

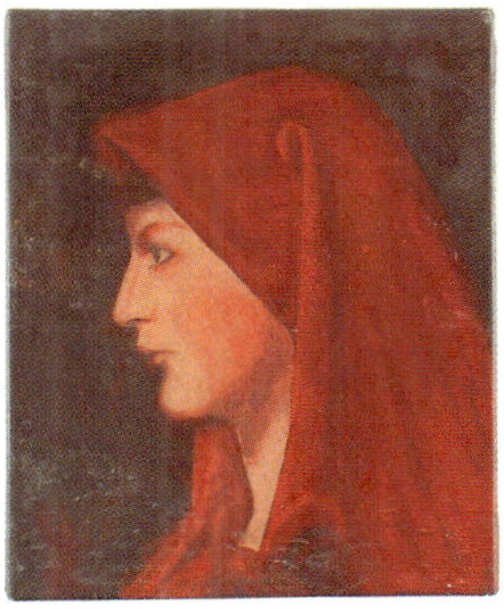

233

DIMENSIONS:	4 ¾ x 4 ⅞ x ¾ inches (12.1 x 12.4 x 1.91 cm)
DATE:	Unknown
MEDIA:	Painting in wood frame
CONDITION:	Good
PROVENANCE:	Douai, France, 400 French francs
NOTES:	Backing is covered with a newspaper clipping with French writing. Signed "J. Henner."

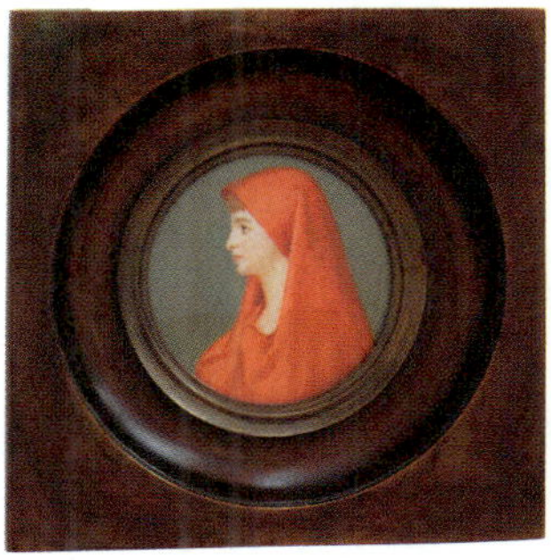

234

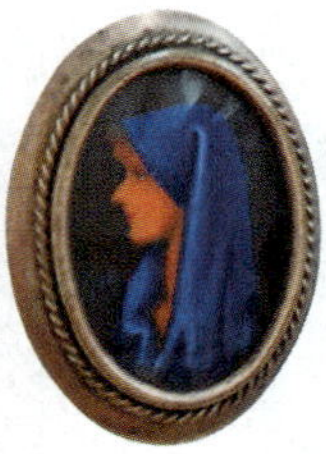

235

DIMENSIONS:	1½ x 1⅛ x ¼ inches (3.8 x 2.9 x 0.64 cm)
DATE:	Unknown
MEDIA:	Brooch/cameo. Painting on unknown support within a silver setting.
CONDITION:	Good
PROVENANCE:	Unknown
NOTES:	Fabiola figure is wearing a blue veil, as opposed to red, which is typical of Fabiola depictions.

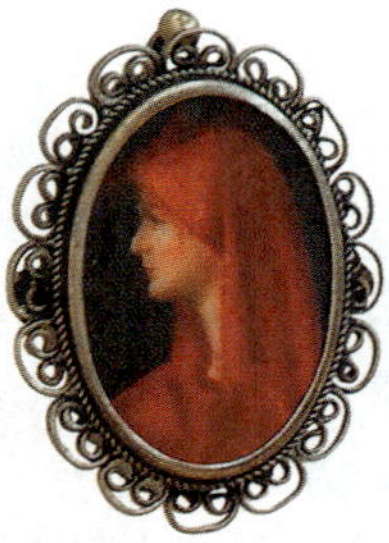

236

DIMENSIONS:	1⅝ x 1⅜ x ⅜ inches (4.1 x 3.5 x 0.95 cm)
DATE:	Unknown
MEDIA:	Brooch/cameo. Painting on unknown support within a silver filigree setting.
CONDITION:	Good/Fair—There are slight stains or accretions on the painting.
PROVENANCE:	Unknown
NOTES:	This Fabiola's posture is in a forward-leaning position and suggests a determined purpose.

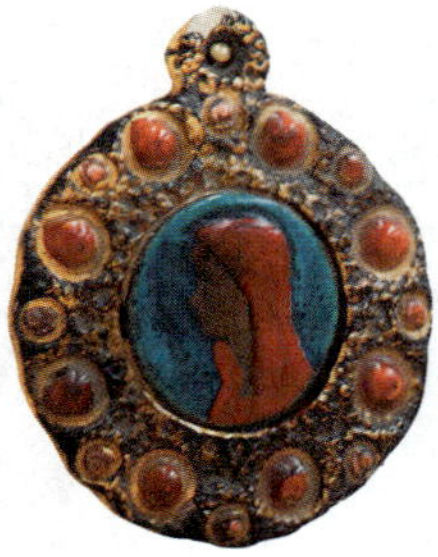

237

DIMENSIONS:	3⅝ x 3 x ¼ inches (9.2 x 7.6 x 0.64 cm)
DATE:	Unknown
MEDIA:	Ceramic pendant
CONDITION:	Fair—There are small losses and chips in the paint or glaze layer.
PROVENANCE:	Unknown
NOTES:	The style of this object seems related to non-Western traditions.

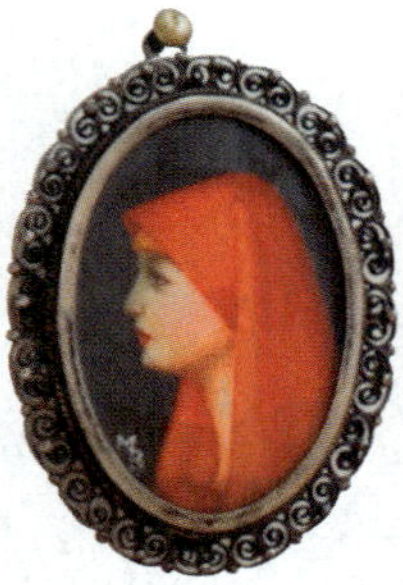

239

DIMENSIONS:	1¾ x 1⅜ x ⅜ inches (4.4 x 3.5 x 0.95 cm)
DATE:	Unknown
MEDIA:	Brooch/cameo. Painting on unknown support within a silver filigree setting.
CONDITION:	Good
PROVENANCE:	Unknown
NOTES:	Signed "MB."

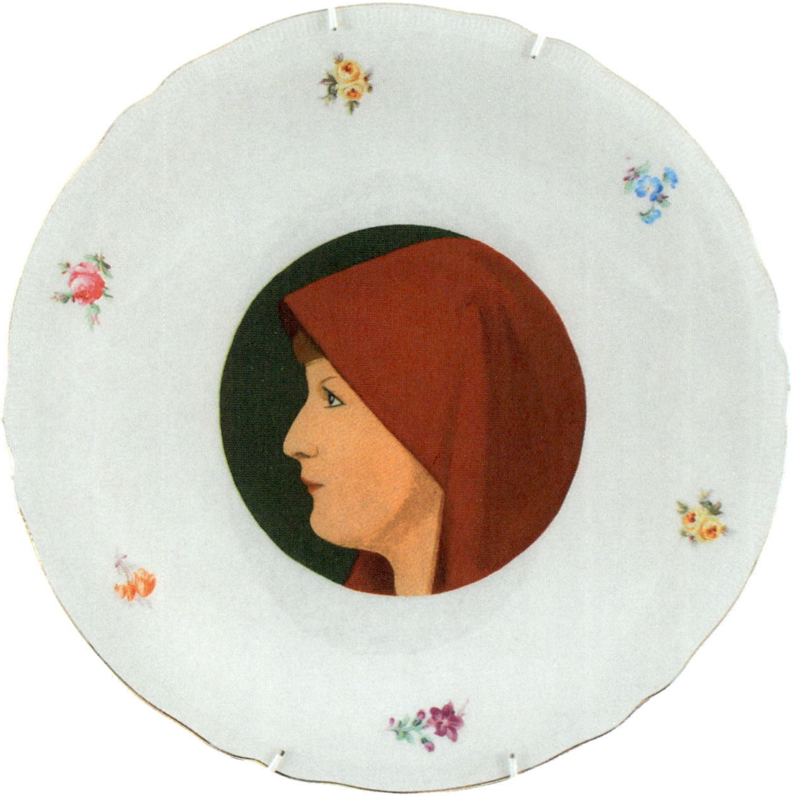

238

DIMENSIONS:	10 ⅝ inches diameter x 1 ½ inches (27 cm diameter x 3.81 cm)
DATE:	Unknown
MEDIA:	Painted ceramic or porcelain plate
CONDITION:	Good
PROVENANCE:	Brussels, Belgium, September 1995, 500 Belgian francs
NOTES:	Rescued from Estonia in 1997.

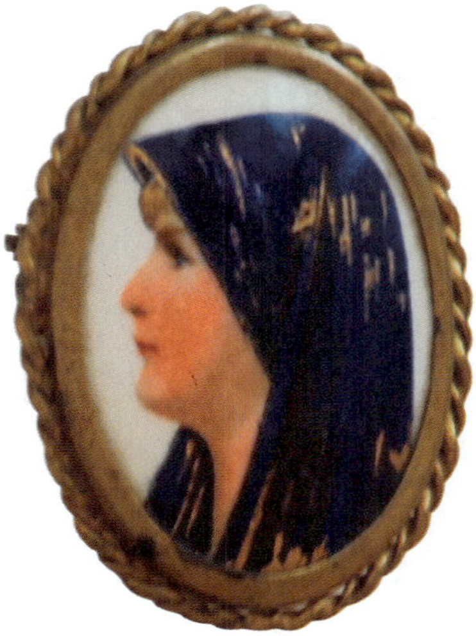

244

DIMENSIONS:	2 1/8 x 1 3/4 x 3/8 inches (5.4 x 4.4 x 0.95 cm)
DATE:	Unknown
MEDIA:	Brooch/cameo. Paint on porcelain within a brass setting.
CONDITION:	Good/Fair
PROVENANCE:	Paris, France, July 1997, 750 French francs
NOTES:	Fabiola figure is wearing a blue veil as opposed to red, which is typical of Fabiola depictions. Stamp of maker reads "Limoges France."

DIMENSIONS:	1 ¾ x 1 ½ x ⅜ inches (4.4 x 3.8 x 0.95 cm)
DATE:	Unknown
MEDIA:	Brooch/cameo. Painting on unknown support within a silver filigree setting that includes four red semiprecious stones (likely carnelian).
CONDITION:	Fair—There is a band of soiling or staining along the bottom edge of the painting.
PROVENANCE:	Unknown

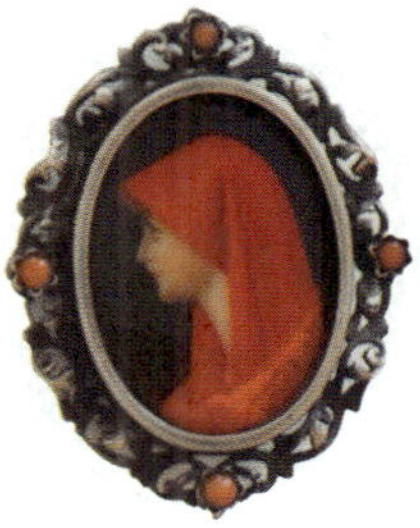

240

DIMENSIONS:	1 ¾ x 1 ½ x ⅜ inches (4.4 x 3.8 x 0.95 cm)
DATE:	Unknown
MEDIA:	Brooch/cameo. Paint on unknown support within a silver filigree setting that includes four red semiprecious stones (likely carnelian).
CONDITION:	Fair—There are large losses and abrasions in the painting in the subject's veil.
PROVENANCE:	Unknown
NOTES:	Signed (illegible). There is an illegible jeweler's stamp on the verso.

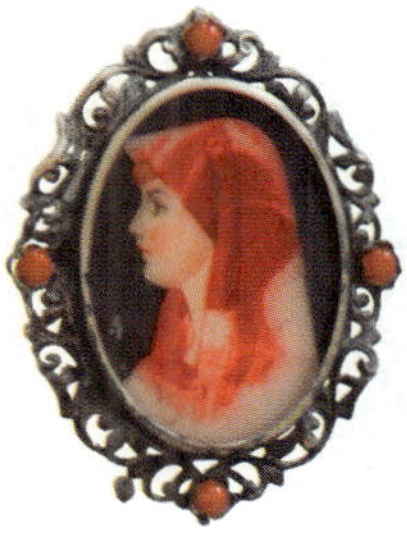

241

DIMENSIONS:	1 ⅛ x 1 x ⅜ inches (2.9 x 2.5 x 0.95 cm)
DATE:	Unknown
MEDIA:	Brooch/cameo. Paint on unknown support within a silver filigree setting.
CONDITION:	Fair/Poor—Face of figure is obscured owing to moisture and or losses in the paint layer.
PROVENANCE:	Unknown

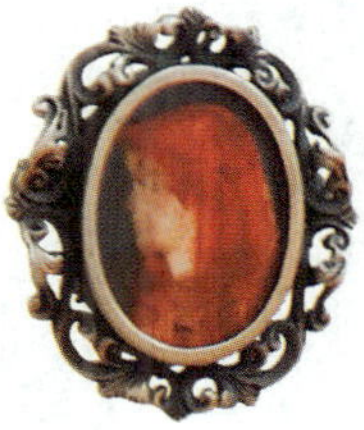

242

DIMENSIONS:	1 ⅝ x 1 ⅜ x ⅜ inches (4.1 x 3.5 x 0.95 cm)
DATE:	Unknown
MEDIA:	Brooch/cameo. Paint on unknown support (possibly bone or ivory) within a silver filigree setting.
CONDITION:	Poor—Figure's face is entirely obscured by abrasion—perhaps related to devotional use.
PROVENANCE:	Unknown

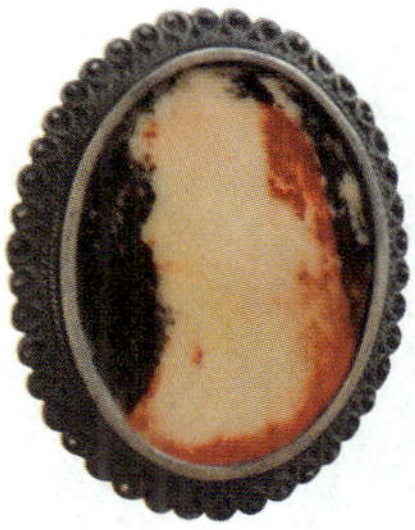

243

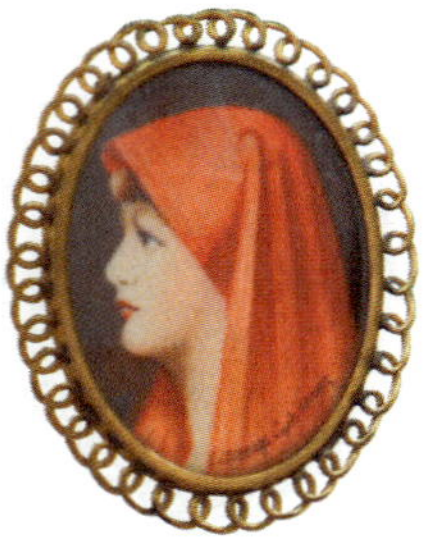

245

DIMENSIONS: 2 ¼ x 1 ⅞ x ⅜ inches (5.7 x 4.8 x 0.95 cm)
DATE: Unknown
MEDIA: Brooch/cameo. Paint on unknown support within a brass setting.
CONDITION: Good
PROVENANCE: Unknown
NOTES: Signed "L. Lachenal d'après Henner."

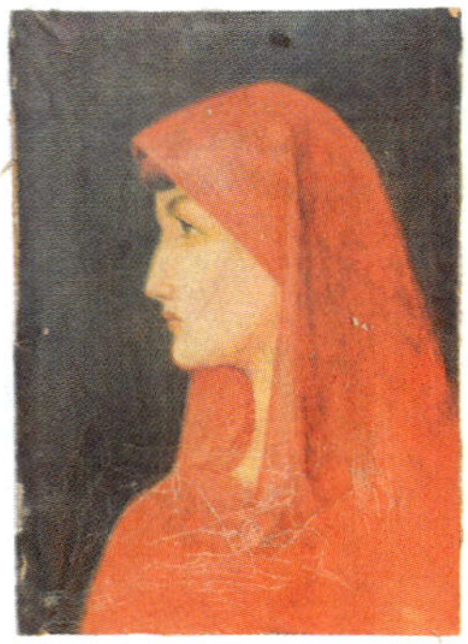

247

DIMENSIONS: 38 ½ x 27 ½ x ¾ inches (97.79 x 69.85 x 1.91 cm)
DATE: Unknown
MEDIA: Paint on canvas with backing board and polystyrene insert
CONDITION: Poor—There is severe cracking throughout the surface with significant areas of lifting paint. There are also losses in the subject's hood and along the edges and corners.
PROVENANCE: Unknown
NOTES: Size is substantially larger than that of other Fabiola portraits. "Christina" written on verso.

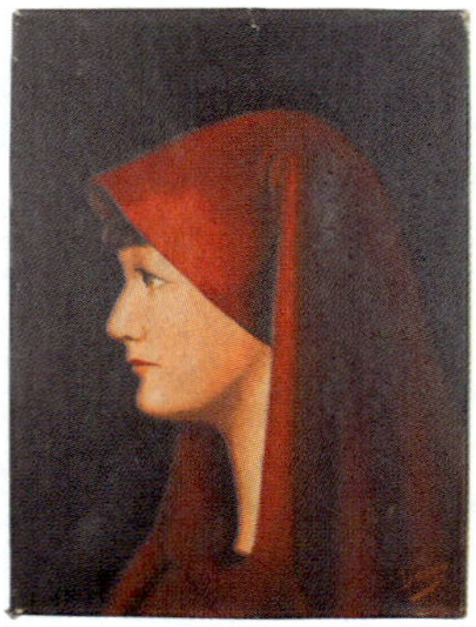

248

DIMENSIONS: 15 ¾ x 11 ⅞ x ⅝ inches (40 x 30.16 x 1.59 cm)
DATE: Unknown
MEDIA: Paint on canvas
CONDITION: Fair—Numerous small losses, especially at corners and along edges. Splatter pattern of an accretion or inconsistencies in the varnish layer.
PROVENANCE: Crisnée (Liège), Belgium, May 1, 2007, 25 euros
NOTES: Signed "Darolo."

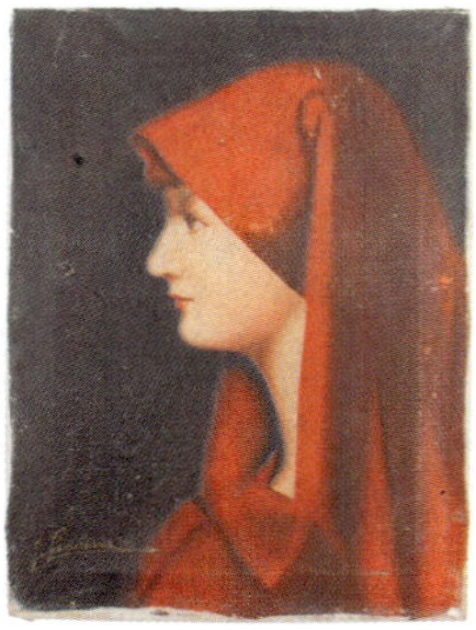

249

DIMENSIONS: 15 ¾ x 11 ⅞ x ⅝ (40 x 30.16 x 1.59 cm)
DATE: Unknown
MEDIA: Paint on canvas
CONDITION: Poor—Severe cracking throughout paint layer. Canvas is practically transparent in some areas from deterioration. Losses throughout and numerous unknown white accretions, especially in the lower proper right region. There are also punctures and severe tears in the canvas along the proper right edge.
PROVENANCE: Belgium, 2005, gift of Tante Aline
NOTES: Inscribed "de la part de Florence (+), fille de Tante Aline, pour Freid[??], avec loute ma Tante Aline" on paper taped to verso of canvas. Signed "J. Vérulpens."

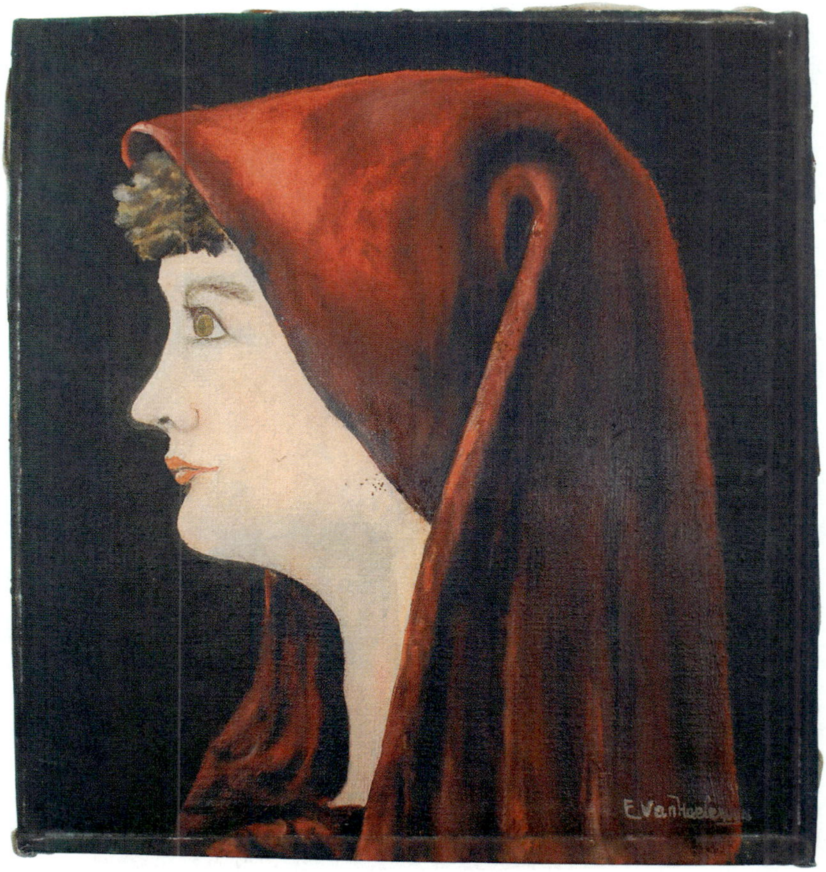

246

DIMENSIONS:	15 ¾ x 14 ⅞ x ⅝ inches (40 x 37.78 x 1.59 cm)
DATE:	Unknown
MEDIA:	Paint on canvas
CONDITION:	Poor—Paint layer is relatively stable; however, surface is very soiled with fly specs and accretions throughout. Losses and abrasions along edges and sides.
PROVENANCE:	Maldegem, Belgium, July 26, 2005, 5 euros
NOTES:	Prime fold in subject's hood departs from the norm, as it descends at an angle toward the proper right. Subject is depicted with prominent, curled bangs. The lack of the pupil in the subject's eye contributes to her blank stare. Signed "E van Haelewyn."

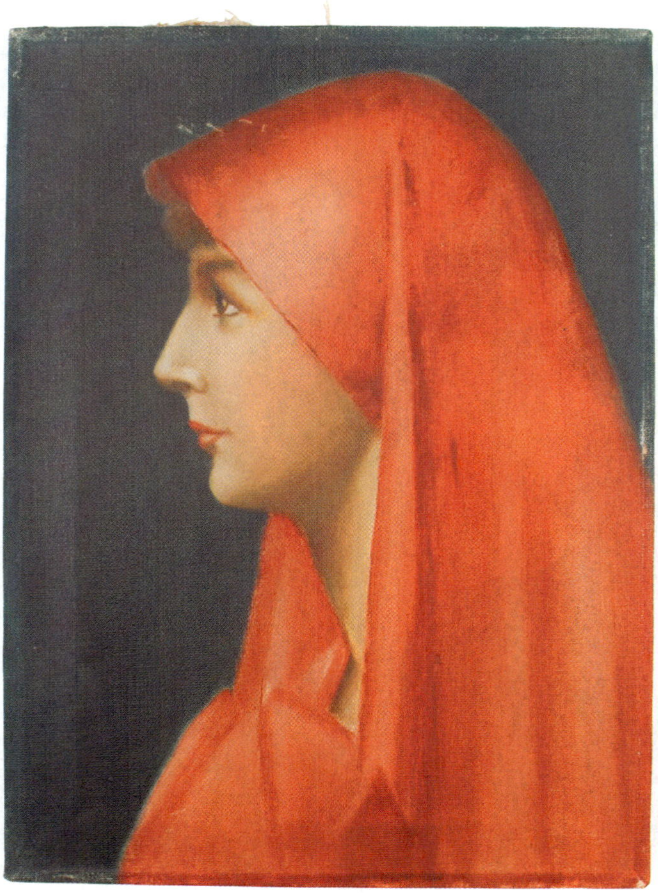

251

DIMENSIONS:	15 ⅞ x 12 x ¾ inches (40.32 x 30.48 x 1.9 cm)
DATE:	1955
MEDIA:	Paint on canvas.
CONDITION:	Good/Fair—Abrasions and/or losses at upper hood area and along edges and sides.
PROVENANCE:	Unknown
NOTES:	"Florence LE 20 Juni 1955" in ink on verso. "Fabiola di Hener—E. Bianchini" in crayon or black paint on verso of canvas.

DIMENSIONS: 11 ⅞ x 9 ¾ x ¼ inches (30.16 x 24.76 x 0.64 cm)
DATE: 1960
MEDIA: Paint on wood panel (panel is composed of individual slats of wood)
CONDITION: Fair—Network of cracking throughout panel and paint layer, which is primarily horizontal in orientation. Otherwise paint layer appears stable. Horizontal bands of losses and/or abrasions at the top and bottom of panel, likely where paint surface came into contact with a prior frame.
PROVENANCE: Crisnée (Liège) Belgium, May 1, 2007, 12 euros
NOTES: Signed "Léon. Cilissen. 1960."

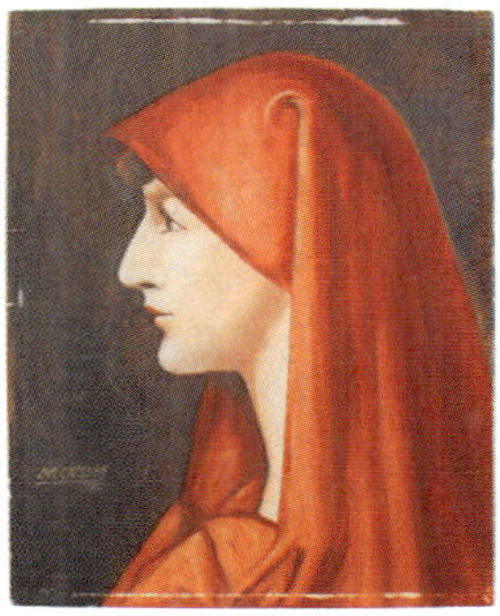

250

DIMENSIONS: 16 ⅝ x 13 ¼ x ¾ inches (42.22 x 33.65 x 1.9 cm)
DATE: Unknown
MEDIA: Paint on canvas
CONDITION: Fair—There is a tear in the canvas and paint layer adjacent to the subject's nose. Overall the paint layer is stable, although there are slight losses along the edges.
PROVENANCE: Unknown
NOTES: Subject's hood is depicted with four angles, as opposed to one curved line. The prime vertical fold in the hood slopes toward the lower proper right corner.

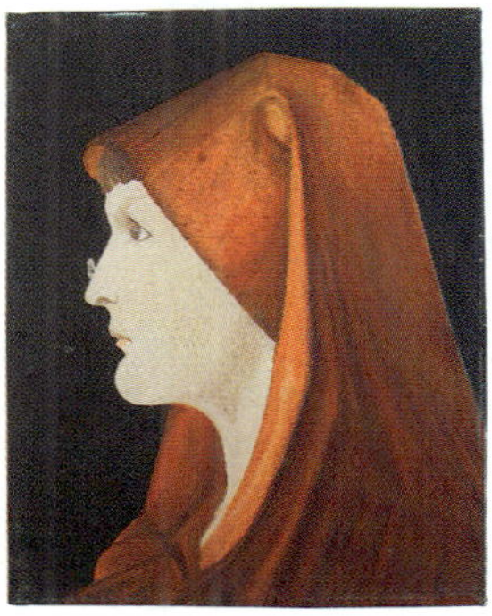

252

DIMENSIONS: 10 ¼ x 7 ¾ x ¼ inches (26.03 x 19.68 x 0.63 cm)
DATE: Unknown
MEDIA: Paint on wood panel
CONDITION: Good—There are a few vertically positioned losses or scrapes in the paint layer. There are two cracks at the upper center of the panel and numerous accretions throughout.
PROVENANCE: Wonck (Liège), Belgium, July 21, 2007, 10 euros
NOTES: Subject exhibits a childlike appearance. "Fabiola Musée du Louvre Paris" on blue bordered label on center top of verso. This work is virtually identical to no. 017. Signed "F. Heyden."

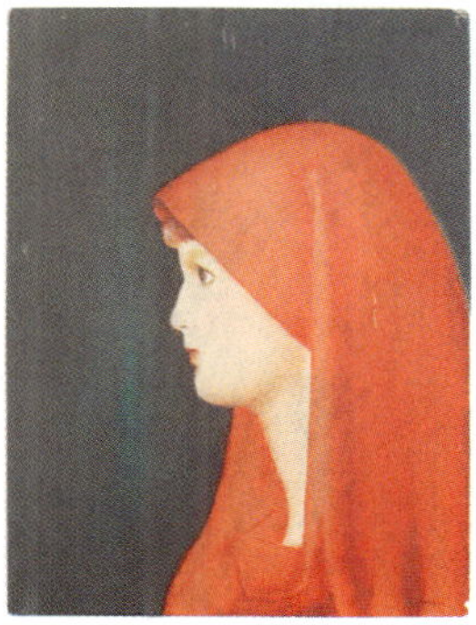

253

DIMENSIONS: 15 ½ x 11 ¾ x ¾ inches (39.37 x 29.84 x 1.9 cm)
DATE: Unknown
MEDIA: Paint on canvas
CONDITION: Fair—There is a T-shaped tear in the canvas support in the lower proper left corner. This tear has been modestly repaired using pressure-sensitive tape on the verso. Minor surface abrasions and scuffs in the paint layer throughout.
PROVENANCE: Utrecht, Netherlands, November 19, 2005, 15 euros
NOTES: Signed "FvHout."

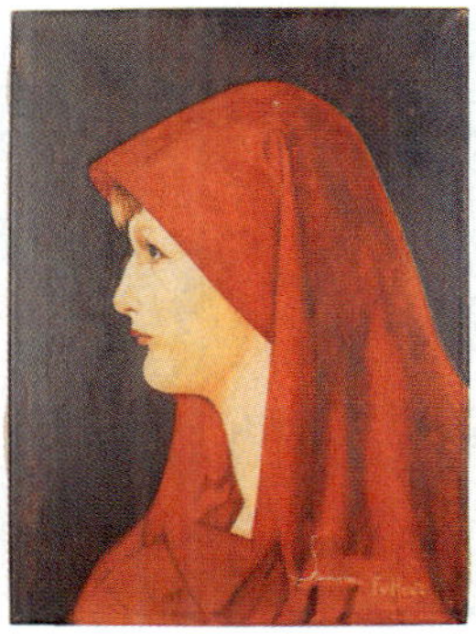

254

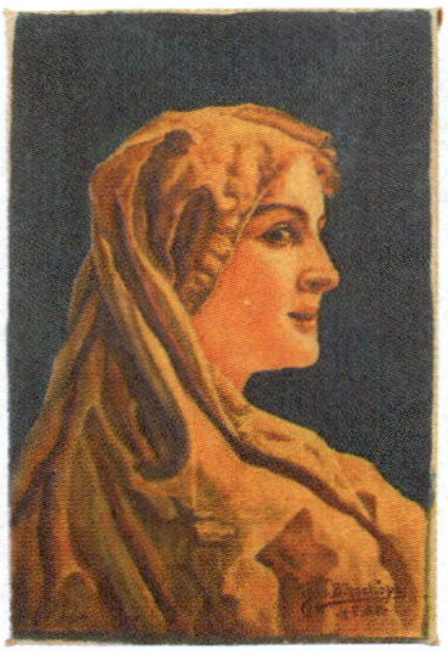

256

DIMENSIONS: 12 x 8 x ½ inches (30.48 x 20.32 x 1.27 cm)
DATE: 1922
MEDIA: Paint on canvas
CONDITION: Good—Paint layer is stable, although soiled overall. There is an indentation in the canvas support and paint layer at the subject's forehead.
PROVENANCE: Unknown
NOTES: "H693 29 †" on white label on verso. Subject faces the proper left of the composition, as opposed to the right as is typical. Also, it is not a strict profile since a small portion of the subject's other eyebrow is visible. This is the only Fabiola whose teeth can be seen. Signed "Jos Bissehops 4–6–22."

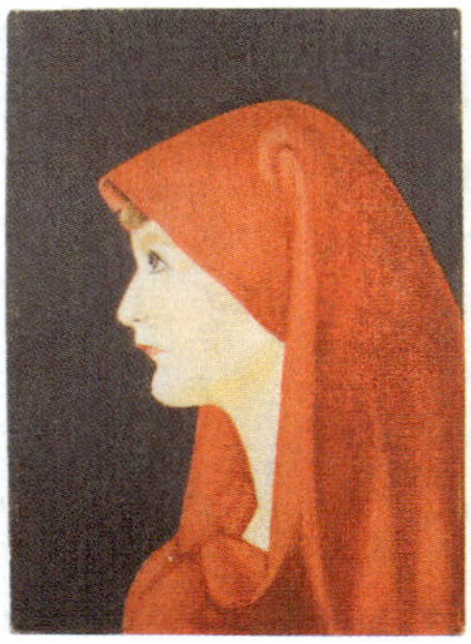

257

DIMENSIONS: 13 x 9 ⅜ x ⅛ inches (33.02 x 23.81 x 0.32 cm)
DATE: Unknown
MEDIA: Paint on preprimed canvas board
CONDITION: Good—There are a few slight abrasions in the paint layer.
PROVENANCE: Belgium, August 2006, gift of Edith De Smedt
NOTES: Commercial label for preprimed canvas board on verso.

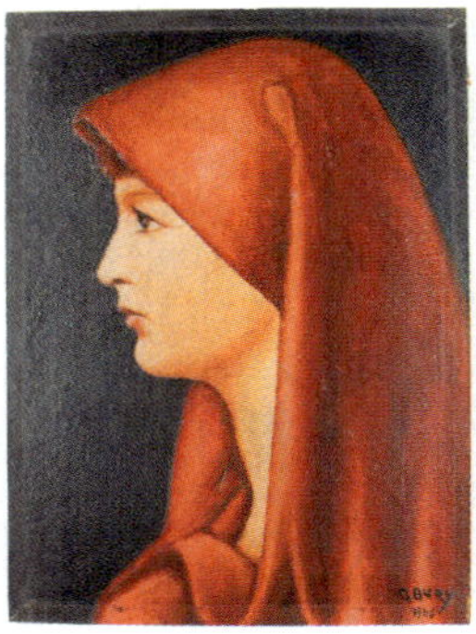

258

DIMENSIONS: 12 ¾ x 9 ½ x ⅛ inches (32.38 x 24.13 x 0.32 cm)
DATE: 1946
MEDIA: Paint on paperboard or Masonite panel
CONDITION: Fair—Paint layer is in stable condition, although there is severe soiling and discoloration throughout and in the varnish layer. Slight losses and abrasions along edges and sides.
PROVENANCE: Esneux (Liège) March 24, 2007, 15 euros
NOTES: Signed "C. Bury 1946."

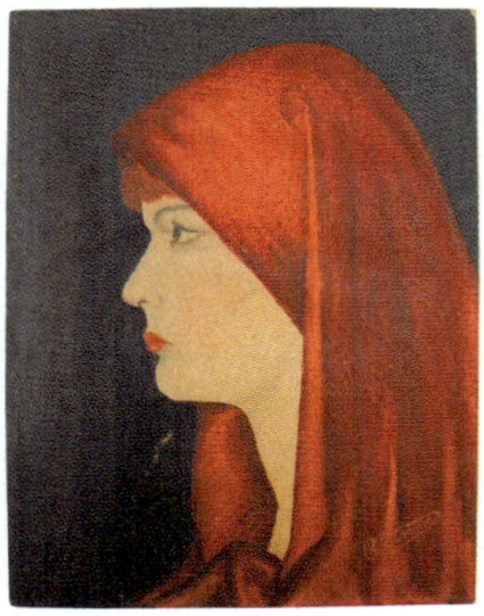

259

DIMENSIONS: 19 ⅝ x 15 ½ x ⅛ inches (49.85 x 39.37 x 0.32 cm)
DATE: Unknown
MEDIA: Paint on paperboard or Masonite panel
CONDITION: Fair—Paint surface is stable; however, there are heavy dust layers and overall soiling and small abrasions and losses throughout.
PROVENANCE: Brussels, Etterbeek, Belgium, June 2, 2007, 15 euros
NOTES: Signed "R. [illegible]."

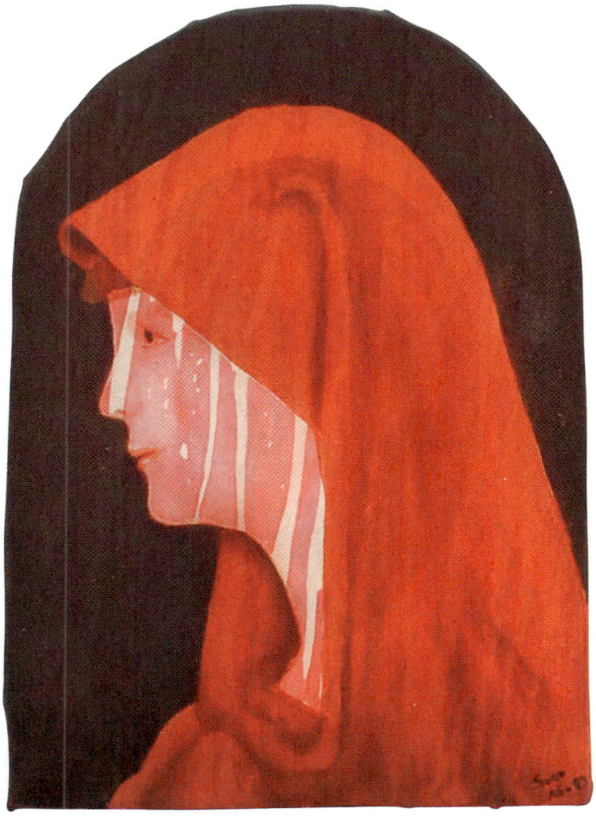

255

DIMENSIONS:	8 x 5 ¾ x ½ inches (20.32 x 14.6 x 1.27 cm)
DATE:	1983
MEDIA:	Paint on white textile (satin?) with unknown support (likely wood) and unknown padding material
CONDITION:	Fair—Structurally the object is in good and stable condition; however, severe staining has occurred and discolored the figure and ground throughout in a pinkish/reddish tone and in a striped pattern.
PROVENANCE:	Mexico, 2007
NOTES:	Signed "Soca 10–83."

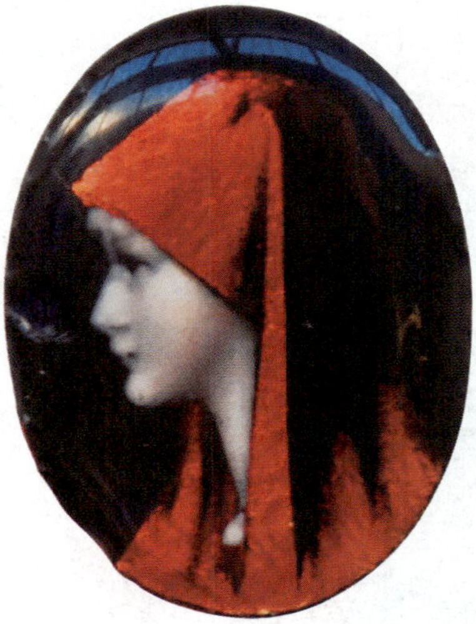

262

DIMENSIONS:	¾ x ⅝ inches (1.9 x 1.6 cm)
DATE:	Unknown
MEDIA:	Enamel or glass cabochon with foil on oval-shaped copper support
CONDITION:	Fair—Numerous small losses and chips in the enamel or glass layer around the edges.
PROVENANCE:	Flea market, Marché Vernaison, Porte de Clignancourt, Paris, France, October 2007, 80 euros
NOTES:	It appears that this Fabiola has white or gray hair, which is unique to this collection of Fabiolas.

DIMENSIONS: 19 ⅞ x 15 ¾ x ¾ inches (50.48 x 40 x 1.9 cm)
DATE: 1972
MEDIA: Paint on canvas
CONDITION: Fair—Paint layer has a condition of unknown cause. Blisterlike areas near subject's ear related to accretion on verso of canvas. Canvas support is slack and wrinkled especially at corners.
PROVENANCE: Unknown
NOTES: Signed "M. Hooyhe 72."

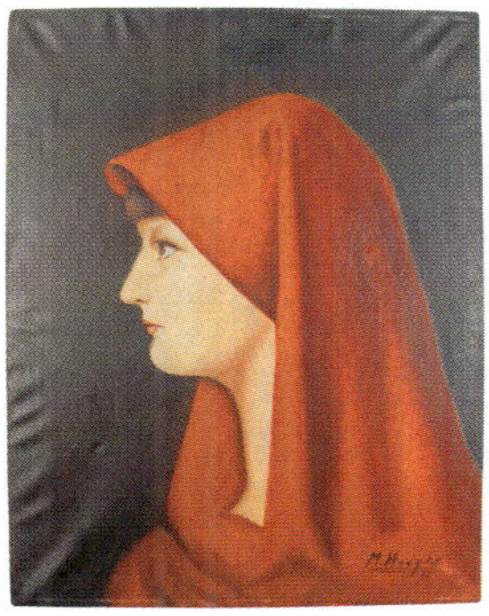

260

DIMENSIONS: 2 ⅝ x ⅜ inches (6.66 x 0.95 cm)
DATE: Unknown
MEDIA: Enamel on metal oval-shaped support
CONDITION: Good—Exposed metal surfaces demonstrate mild tarnishing or oxidation. Mild evidence of loss and wear along edges of enamel as is typical with the age and function of this object.
PROVENANCE: Flea market, Marché Vernaison, Porte de Clignancourt, Paris, France, October 2007, 50 euros

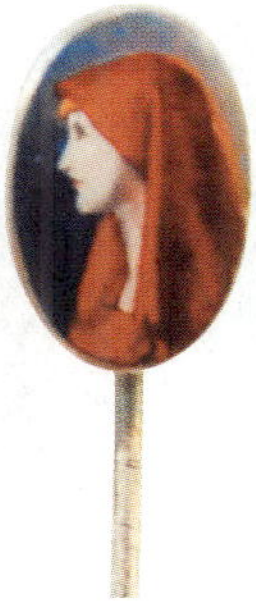

261

DIMENSIONS: 1 ⅝ inches diameter (4.1 cm diameter)
DATE: Unknown
MEDIA: Enamel brooch on circular copper stamping with gold frame and clasp
CONDITION: Good
PROVENANCE: Flea market, Marché Vernaison, Porte de Clignancourt, Paris, France, October 2007, 90 euros
NOTES: "L. Jonbert Limoges" on verso of brooch.

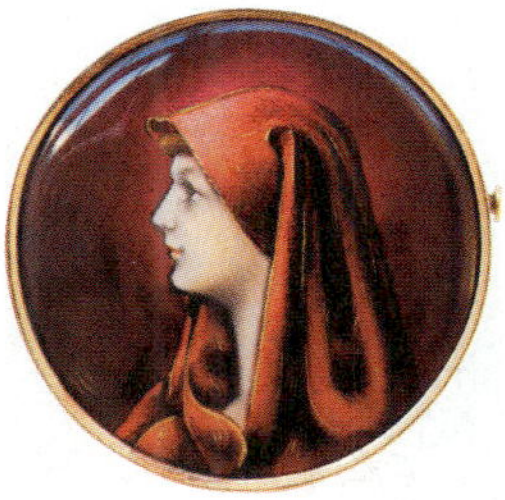

263

DIMENSIONS: 1 ⅜ x 1 inches (3.5 x 2.54 cm)
DATE: Unknown
MEDIA: Enamel pendant on triangular-shaped copper support with gold frame
CONDITION: Fair—There is slight pitting or soiling in the area of the subject's face.
PROVENANCE: Flea market, Marché Vernaison, Porte de Clignancourt, Paris, France, October 2007, 80 euros
NOTES: "Emaux de Limoges" on verso of pendant. All other depictions of Fabiola on jewelry or decorative objects in this collection could be described as delicate or pretty, however, this Fabiola does not share that quality.

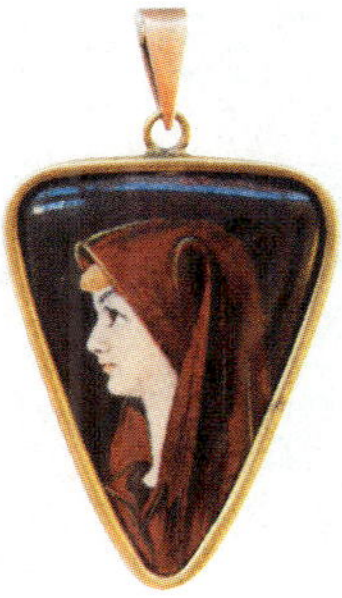

264

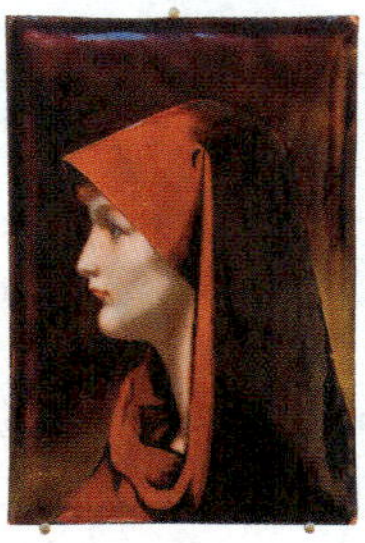

265

DIMENSIONS:	6⅜ x 4⅜ inches (16.2 x 11.11 cm)
DATE:	Unknown
MEDIA:	Enamel with foil on copper support
CONDITION:	Good/Fair—There are small scratches in the enamel layer, especially along the edges.
PROVENANCE:	Flea market, Marché Vernaison, Porte de Clignancourt, Paris, France, October 2007, 250 euros
NOTES:	Inscribed "Limoges" on the lower right-hand corner.

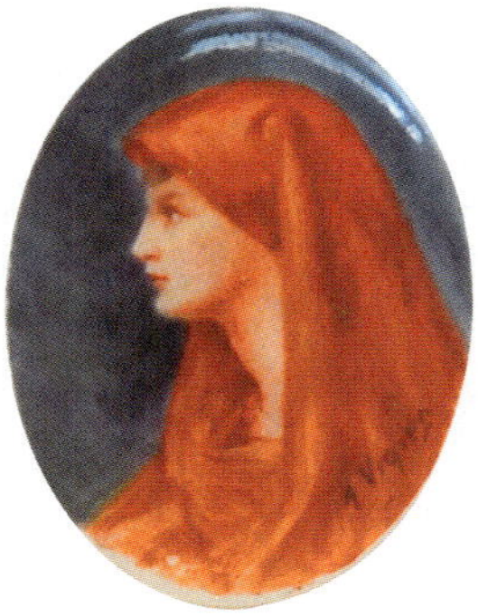

267

DIMENSIONS:	1⅝ x 1¼ x ¼ inches (4.13 x 3.15 x 0.64 cm)
DATE:	Unknown
MEDIA:	Painted cabochon of unknown support
CONDITION:	Fair—Small areas of abrasion are present along top and bottom edges.
PROVENANCE:	Flea market, Marché Vernaison, Porte de Clignancourt, Paris, France, October 2007, 80 euros
NOTES:	Signed "A. Vigien" on recto. "A. Vigien" inscribed on verso.

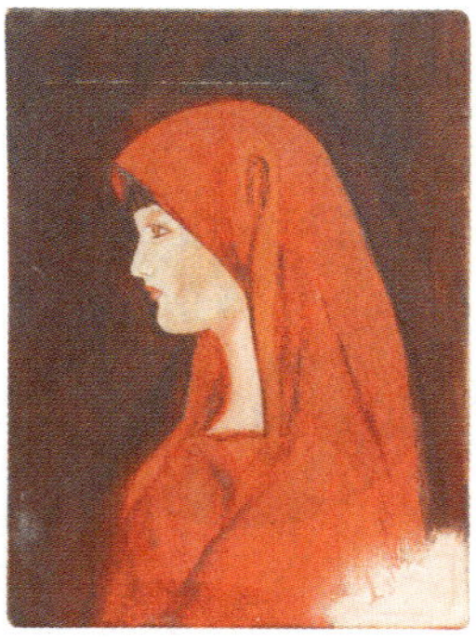

268

DIMENSIONS:	8 x 6 x ⅝ inches (20.32 x 15.24 x 1.59 cm)
DATE:	Unknown
MEDIA:	Painting on canvas
CONDITION:	Fair—There are areas of accretions and/or discolorations in the area of subject's cheek. There is a horizontal scratch or loss in the paint layer at the top edge of the canvas. Proper left lower corner has an area of abraded or removed paint.
PROVENANCE:	Tianguis Cuauhtémoc, Mexico City, Mexico, 1979, 1000 Mexican pesos
NOTES:	Abraded or removed paint layer at lower proper left corner seems to suggest an intent to obscure or erase a signature.

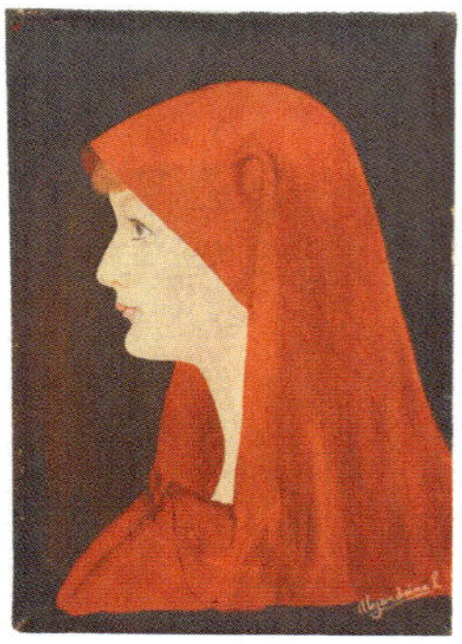

269

DIMENSIONS:	13¾ x 9⅞ x ¾ inches (34.93 x 25.08 x 1.9 cm)
DATE:	Unknown
MEDIA:	Painting on canvas
CONDITION:	Fair—Unknown accretions in the area of subject's chin, jawline, and neck.
PROVENANCE:	Lagunilla, Mexico City, Mexico, 1984, 3000 Mexican pesos
NOTES:	Signed "Alyandrinal" at lower proper left corner of recto.

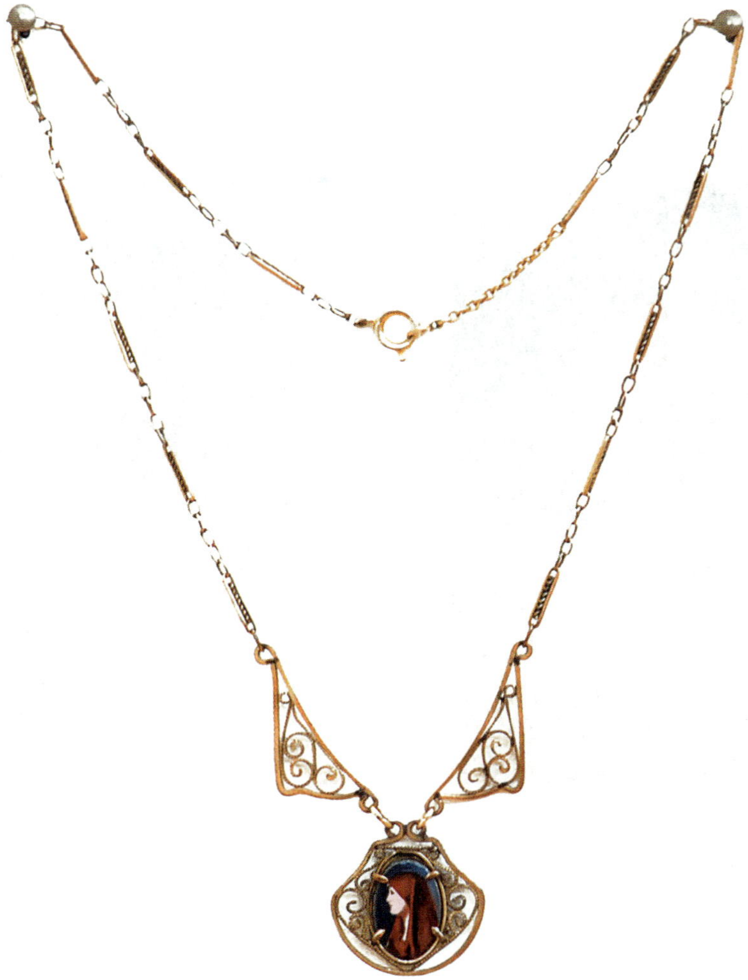

266

DIMENSIONS:	14 ½ x 1 x ⅛ inches (36.83 x 2.54 x 0.32 cm)
DATE:	Unknown
MEDIA:	Necklace with enamel cameo portrait in gold filigree setting
CONDITION:	Good.
PROVENANCE:	Flea market, Marché Vernaison, Porte de Clignancourt, Paris, France, October 2007, 100 euros
NOTES:	This is the only example of a necklace in this collection. A small section of gold chain (approx. ½ inch [1.27 cm] long) has been added to extend the necklace's length.

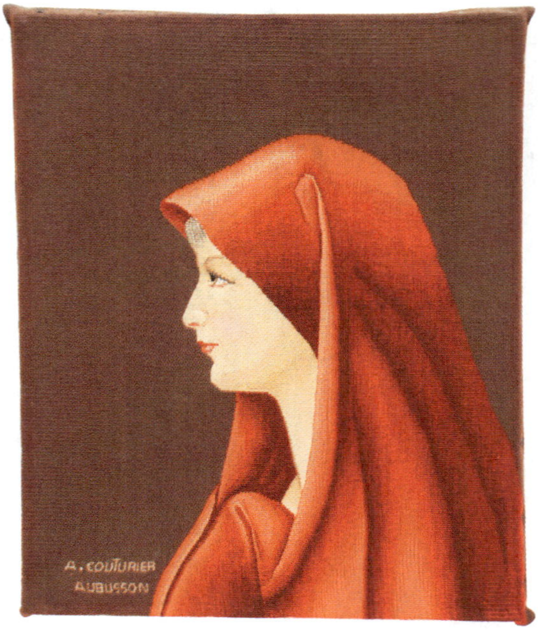

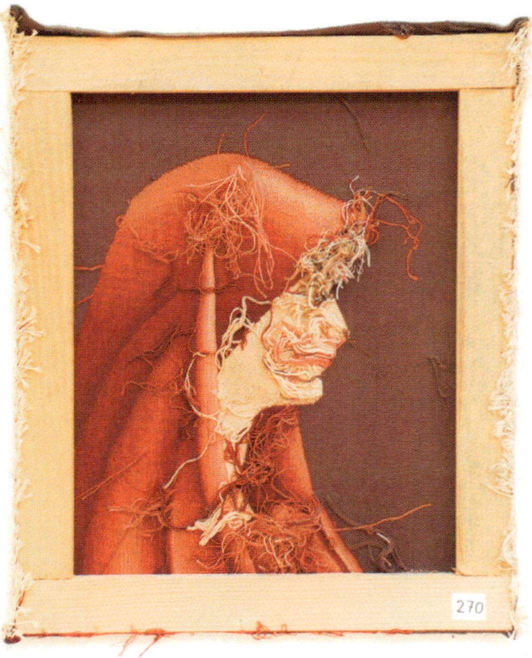

270

DIMENSIONS:	16 ⅜ x 13 ¾ x ⅝ inches (41.59 x 34.93 x 1.59 cm)
DATE:	Unknown
MEDIA:	Woven and/or embroidered textile of indeterminate method or technique
CONDITION:	Excellent
PROVENANCE:	Flea market, Marché Vernaison, Porte de Clignancourt, Paris, France, October 2007, 250 euros
NOTES:	Signed “A. Couturier Aubusson” at the lower proper right corner. Quality of portraiture and technique is exquisite. Hood exhibits luminosity or lightness.

DIMENSIONS:	23 5/8 x 19 3/4 x 7/8 inches (60 x 50.16 x 2.22 cm)
DATE:	Unknown
MEDIA:	Painting on canvas
CONDITION:	Good—There is a small deformation in the canvas support in the area of the subject's cheek.
PROVENANCE:	Iztapalapa, Mexico City, Mexico, 1987, 7000 Mexican pesos
NOTES:	Subject has a green hood, as opposed to red, which is typical of other Fabiola portraits.

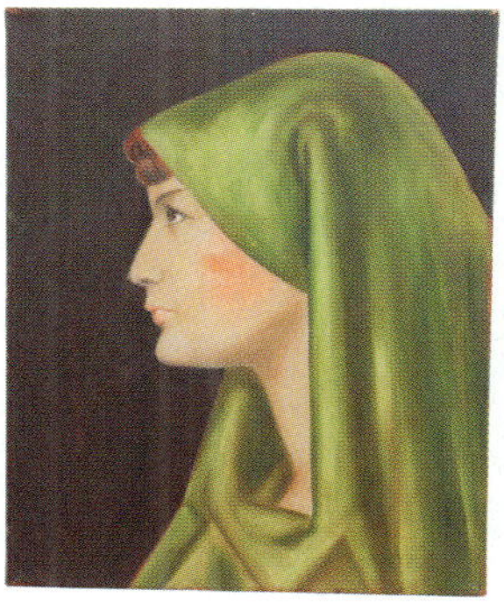

271

DIMENSIONS:	5 7/8 x 4 7/8 x 1/8 inches (14.92 x 12.38 x 0.32 cm)
DATE:	Unknown
MEDIA:	Painting on textile mounted on paperboard support
CONDITION:	Fair—Edges of textile are slightly frayed. There is a linear, horizontal area of discoloration at the lower center edge.
PROVENANCE:	Tianguis Cuauhtémoc, Mexico City, Mexico, 1979, 1000 Mexican pesos
NOTES:	Signed "O. Agala C."

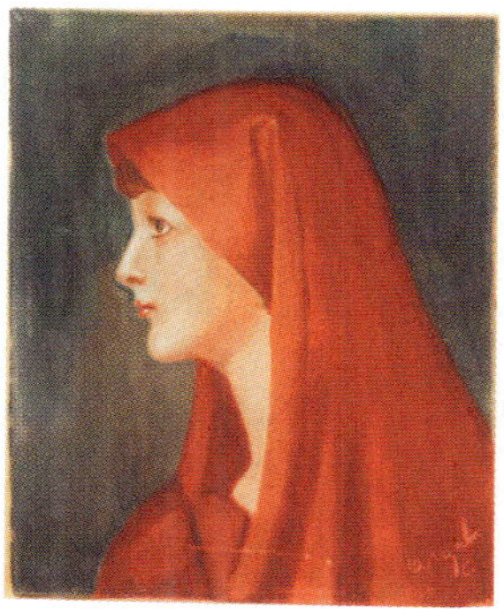

272

DIMENSIONS:	3 1/2 inches diameter x 1 5/8 inches depth, closed (8.89 cm diameter x 4.13 cm depth)
DATE:	Unknown
MEDIA:	Sterling silver filigree circular hinged box with enamel portrait in lid
CONDITION:	Good—Surfaces on silver appear to be slightly tarnished, and enamel portrait is loose but secure in its bevel setting.
PROVENANCE:	Flea market, Marché Vernaison, Porte de Clignancourt, Paris, France, October 2007, 750 euros
NOTES:	The prime vertical fold in subject's hood is articulated in metallic gold, as well as the edge of the hood along subject's face. "Leonard Limoges d'apres Henner" inscribed along top edge. Three dessicated coffee beans are present in the interior space of the box.

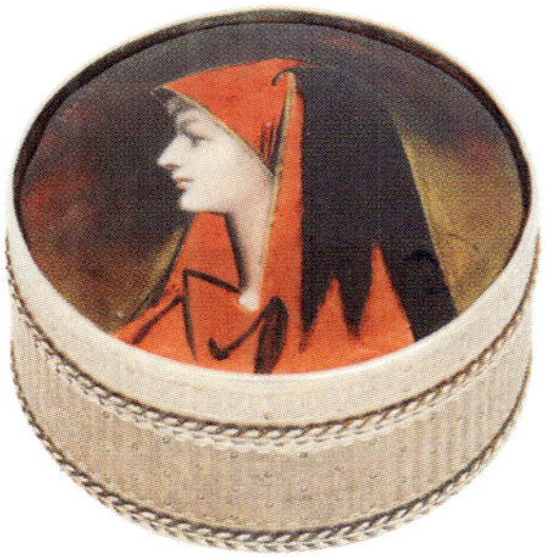

273

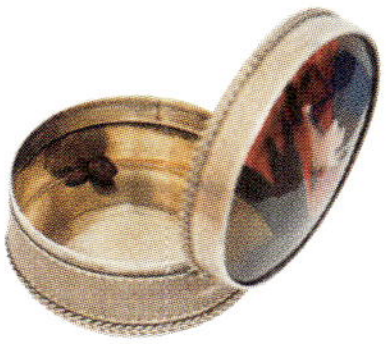

In 1997, Francis Alÿs sent sixty-two Fabiolas to an exhibition in Estonia. When the works were shipped back to him, he discovered that twenty-six had been replaced with substitutes, crude versions made to simulate the "originals," which had mysteriously vanished en route. Wishing to conceal rather than acknowledge the disappearance, the Estonian organizers seemingly hoped to fool him into believing that the substitutes—the copies they commissioned of his copies—were the works Alÿs had collected. The following images and records document the fakes, which have remained in Alÿs's collection.

DIMENSIONS:	5 ⅛ inches diameter x ⅝ inches (13 cm diameter x 1.6 cm)
DATE:	1997
MEDIA:	Paint on textile adhered to circular wood support
CONDITION:	Good
PROVENANCE:	Fake, Estonia, 1997

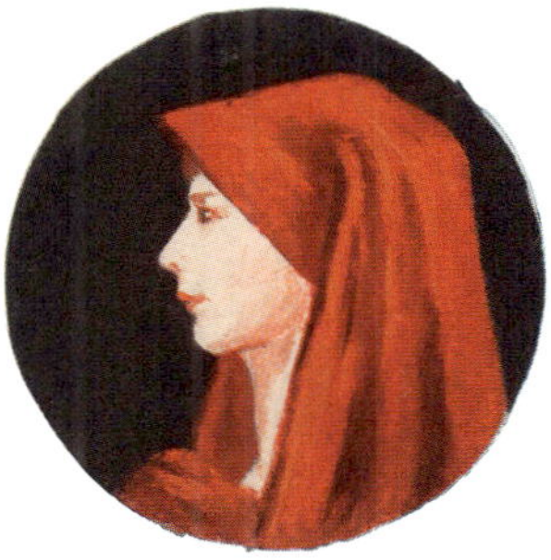

A

DIMENSIONS:	7 ⅞ x 5 ⅞ x ½ inches (20 x 14.9 x 1.27 cm)
DATE:	1997
MEDIA:	Paint on canvas mounted on oval-shaped wood block
CONDITION:	Good
PROVENANCE:	Fake, Estonia, 1997

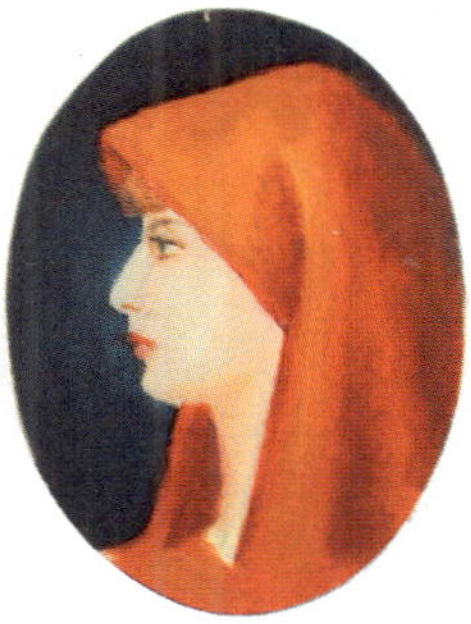

B

DIMENSIONS:	7 ⅞ x 5 ⅞ x ½ inches (20 x 14.9 x 1.27 cm)
DATE:	1997
MEDIA:	Paint on canvas mounted on oval wood support
CONDITION:	Good
PROVENANCE:	Fake, Estonia, 1997

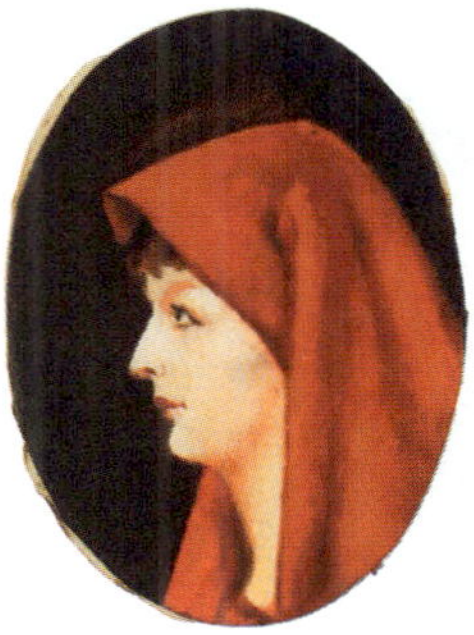

C

DIMENSIONS:	6 x 5 x ⅝ inches (15.2 x 12.7 x 1.59 cm)
DATE:	1997
MEDIA:	Paint on canvas mounted on oval-shaped wood block
CONDITION:	Good
PROVENANCE:	Fake, Estonia, 1997
NOTES:	Subject's head is listing slightly outward toward the viewer, softening her stance. This portrait demonstrates a classic feature, in that the hood is depicted with three angles, as opposed to one curved line.

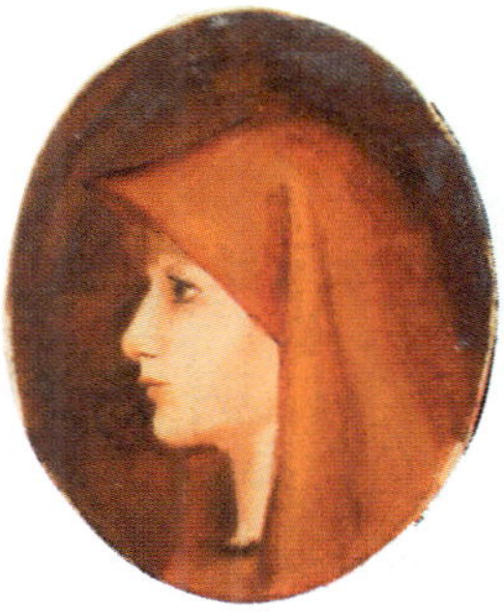

D

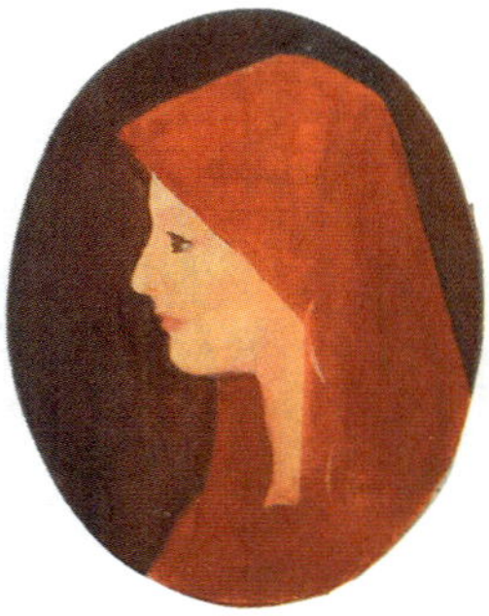

E

DIMENSIONS:	6 ¾ x 5 ⅜ x ⅝ inches (17.1 x 13.7 x 1.59 cm)
DATE:	1997
MEDIA:	Paint on canvas mounted on oval-shaped wood block
CONDITION:	Good
PROVENANCE:	Fake, Estonia, 1997

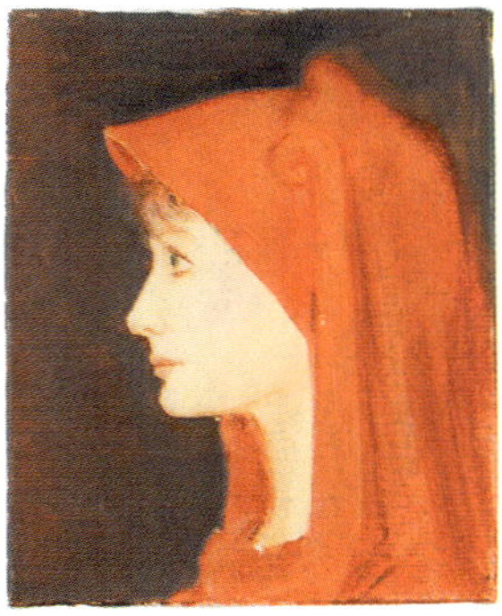

F

DIMENSIONS:	10 ¾ x 8 ¾ x ¾ inches (27.3 x 22.2 x 1.91 cm)
DATE:	1997
MEDIA:	Acrylic on canvas
CONDITION:	Good
PROVENANCE:	Fake, Estonia, 1997
NOTES:	There is a hornlike shape at the top of Fabiola's head.

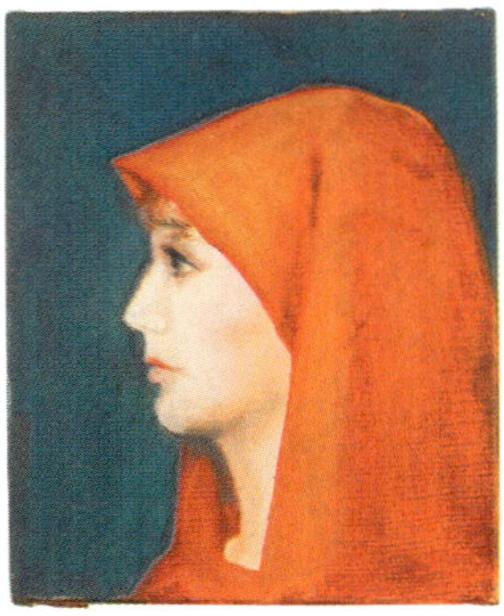

G

DIMENSIONS:	10 ⅝ x 8 ¾ x ¾ inches (27 x 22.2 x 1.91 cm)
DATE:	1997
MEDIA:	Acrylic on canvas
CONDITION:	Good
PROVENANCE:	Fake, Estonia, 1997

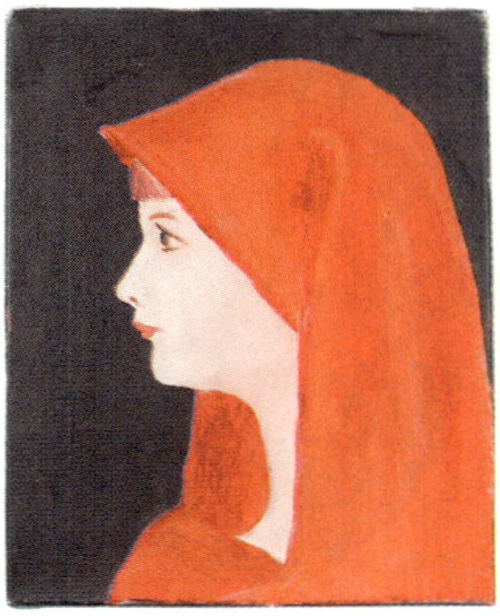

H

DIMENSIONS:	10 ⅝ x 8 ¾ x ¾ inches (27 x 22.2 x 1.91 cm)
DATE:	1997
MEDIA:	Acrylic on canvas
CONDITION:	Good
PROVENANCE:	Fake, Estonia, 1997

DIMENSIONS:	10 ¼ x 8 x ¾ inches (26 x 20.3 x 1.91 cm)
DATE:	1997
MEDIA:	Paint on canvas
CONDITION:	Good
PROVENANCE:	Fake, Estonia, 1997

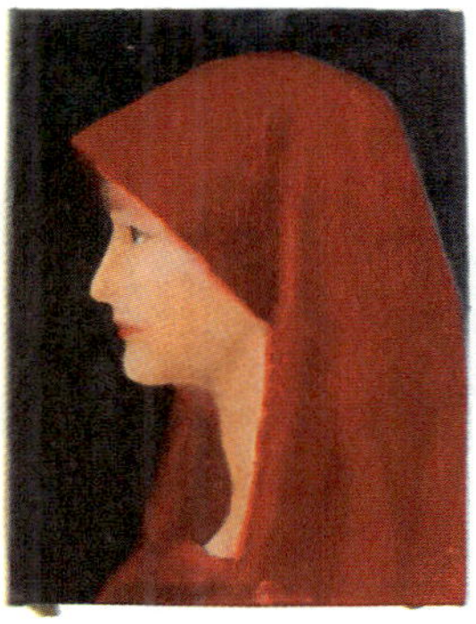

I

DIMENSIONS:	10 ⅝ x 8 ¾ x ¾ inches (27 x 22.2 x 1.91 cm)
DATE:	1997
MEDIA:	Acrylic on canvas
CONDITION:	Good—Small blue accretion.
PROVENANCE:	Fake, Estonia, 1997

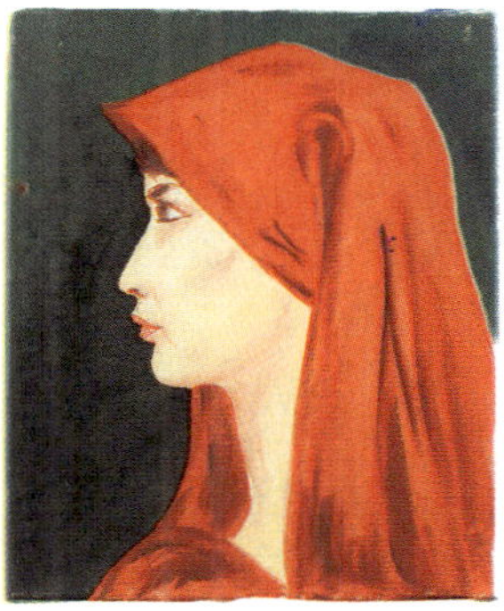

J

DIMENSIONS:	10 ¾ x 8 ¾ x ¾ inches (27.3 x 22.2 x 1.91 cm)
DATE:	1997
MEDIA:	Acrylic on canvas
CONDITION:	Good
PROVENANCE:	Fake, Estonia, 1997
NOTES:	As in several examples, this Fabiola has dark coloration throughout face, which could possibly suggest bruises or injury.

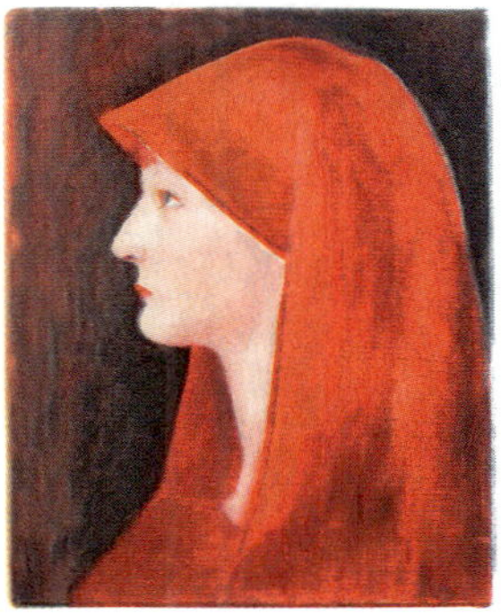

K

DIMENSIONS:	10 ⅝ x 8 ⅝ x ¾ inches (27 x 21.9 x 1.91 cm)
DATE:	1997
MEDIA:	Acrylic on canvas
CONDITION:	Fair—There is a slight indentation in the canvas on the proper right side near the subject's eye level.
PROVENANCE:	Fake, Estonia, 1997

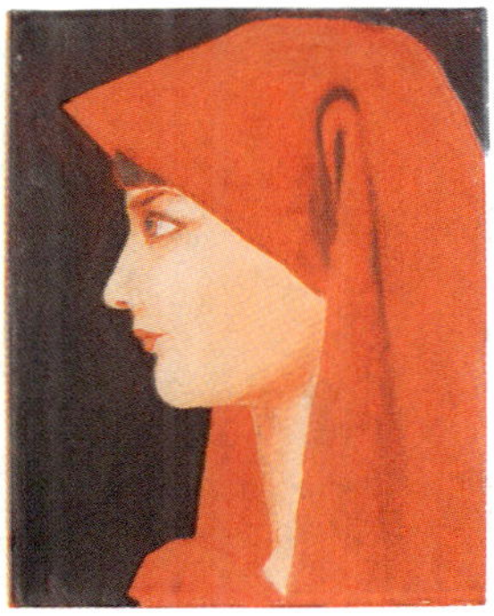

L

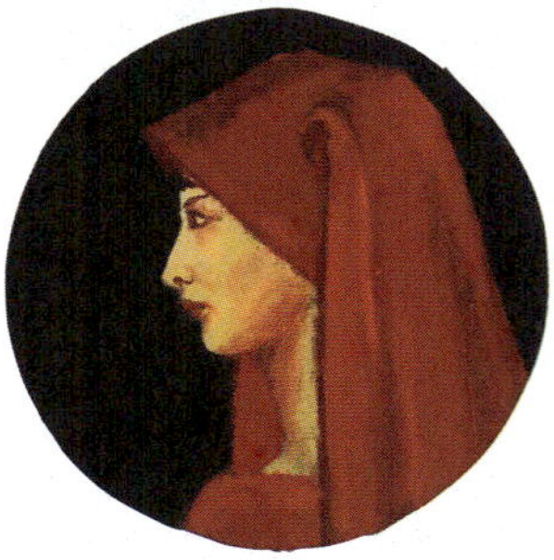

DIMENSIONS:	5 ⅛ inches diameter x ⅝ inches (13 cm diameter x 1.6 cm)
DATE:	1997
MEDIA:	Paint on textile adhered to circular wood support
CONDITION:	Good
PROVENANCE:	Fake, Estonia, 1997

M

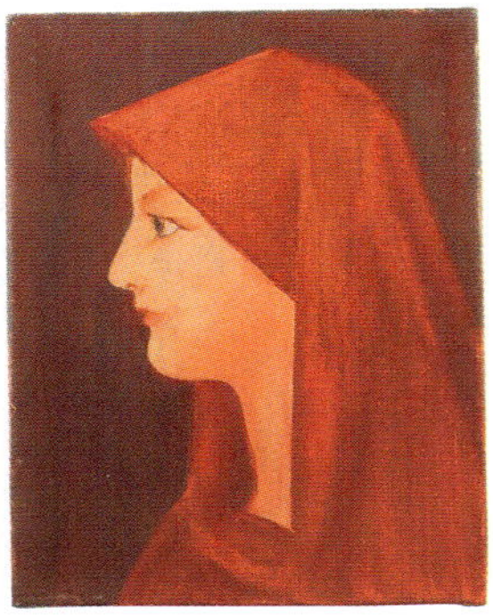

DIMENSIONS:	8 ⅝ x 6 ⅞ x 1 inches (21.9 x 17.5 x 2.54 cm)
DATE:	1997
MEDIA:	Acrylic on canvas
CONDITION:	Good
PROVENANCE:	Fake, Estonia, 1997

N

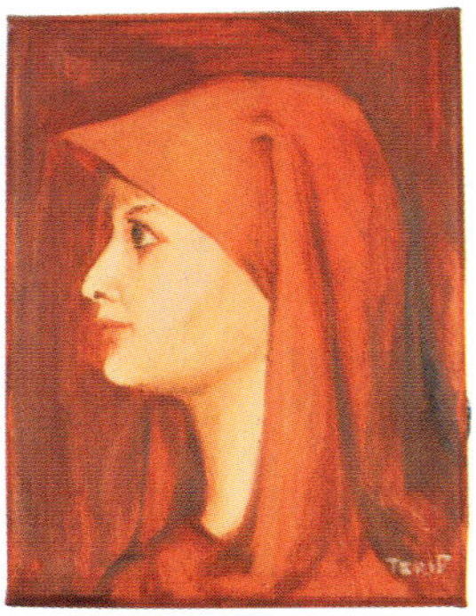

DIMENSIONS:	10 ¼ x 8 x ⅝ inches (26 x 20.3 x 1.59 cm)
DATE:	1997
MEDIA:	Acrylic on canvas
CONDITION:	Good
PROVENANCE:	Fake, Estonia, 1997.
NOTES:	Signed "Teri P." This is among only a few examples of a signature in the collection of fake Fabiolas made in Estonia.

O

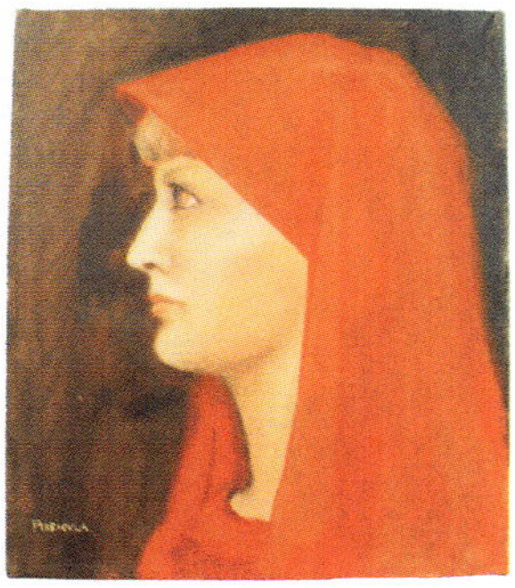

DIMENSIONS:	17 ⅝ x 15 ⅝ x 1 inches (44.8 x 39.7 x 2.54 cm)
DATE:	1997
MEDIA:	Acrylic on canvas
CONDITION:	Good
PROVENANCE:	Fake, Estonia, 1997.
NOTES:	Signed "Pirriqola." This is among only a few examples of a signature in the collection of fake Fabiolas made in Estonia.

P

DIMENSIONS: 8 ⅝ x 6 ⅞ x 1 inches (21.9 x 17.5 x 2.54 cm)
DATE: 1997
MEDIA: Acrylic on canvas
CONDITION: Good
PROVENANCE: Fake, Estonia, 1997

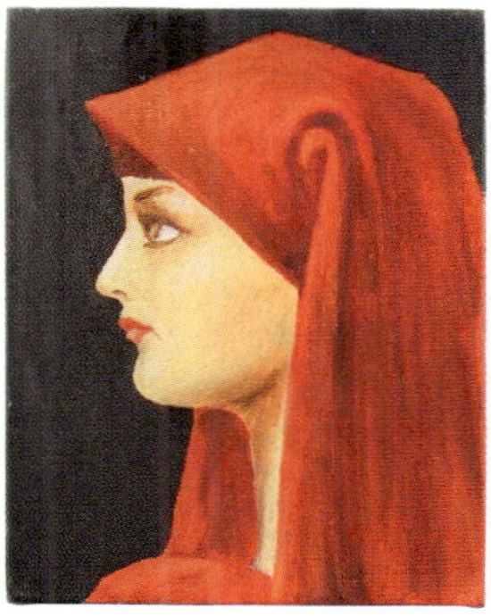

Q

DIMENSIONS: 13 ⅞ x 10 ¾ x ¾ inches (35.2 x 27.3 x 1.91 cm)
DATE: 1997
MEDIA: Acrylic on canvas
CONDITION: Good
PROVENANCE: Fake, Estonia, 1997

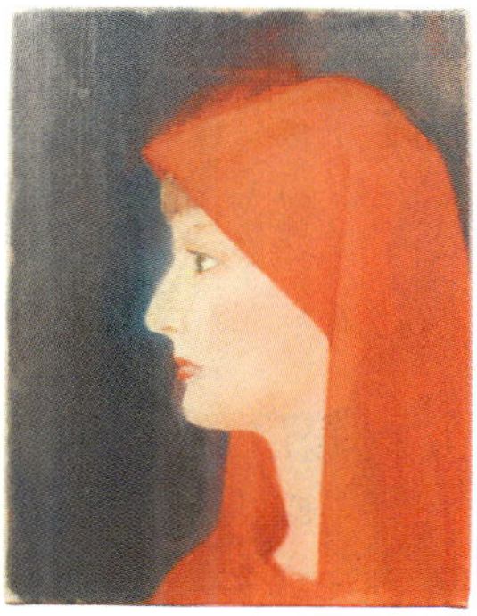

R

DIMENSIONS: 8 ⅝ x 6 ⅞ x ⅞ inches (21.9 x 17.5 x 2.22 cm)
DATE: 1997
MEDIA: Acrylic on canvas
CONDITION: Good
PROVENANCE: Fake, Estonia, 1997

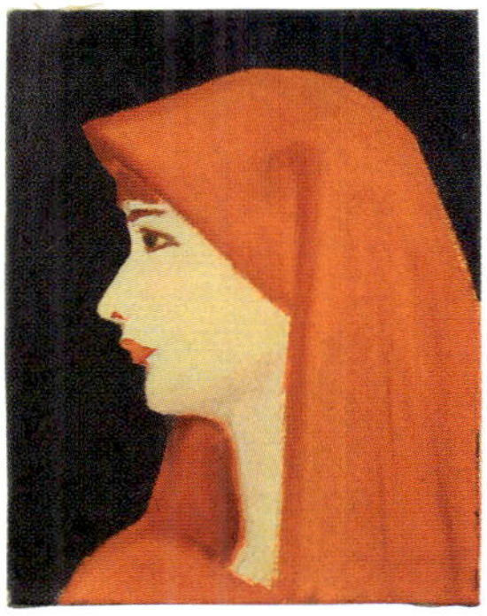

S

DIMENSIONS: 8 ½ x 6 ⅞ x ½ inches (21.6 x 17.5 x 1.27 cm)
DATE: 1997
MEDIA: Acrylic on canvas
CONDITION: Good
PROVENANCE: Fake, Estonia, 1997
NOTES: Subject has unusually large nose. Also, the hood is depicted with three angles, as opposed to one curved line.

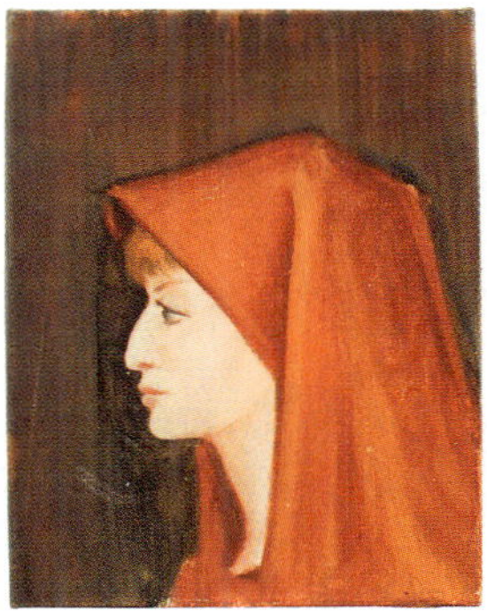

T

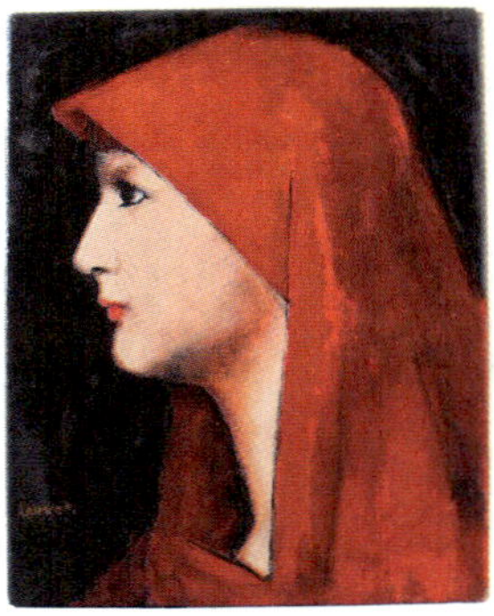

U

DIMENSIONS:	15 x 12 x ¾ inches (38.1 x 30.5 x 1.91 cm)
DATE:	1997
MEDIA:	Acrylic on canvas
CONDITION:	Good
PROVENANCE:	Fake, Estonia, 1997
NOTES:	Signed "Laimra 97." This is among only a few examples of a signature in the collection of fake Fabiolas made in Estonia.

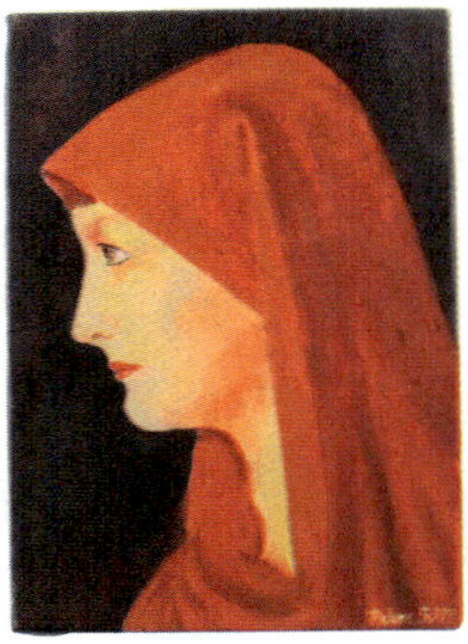

V

DIMENSIONS:	13 ⅞ x 10 x ¾ inches (35.2 x 25.4 x 1.91 cm)
DATE:	1997
MEDIA:	Acrylic on canvas
CONDITION:	Good
PROVENANCE:	Fake, Estonia, 1997
NOTES:	Signed "Pebre 5.997." This is among only a few examples of a signature in the collection of fake Fabiolas made in Estonia.

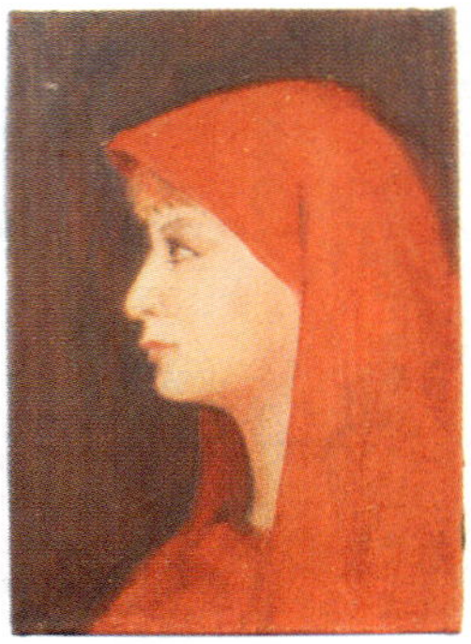

W

DIMENSIONS:	13 ¾ x 9 ⅞ x ¾ inches (34.9 x 25.1 x 1.91 cm)
DATE:	1997
MEDIA:	Acrylic on canvas
CONDITION:	Good
PROVENANCE:	Fake, Estonia, 1997

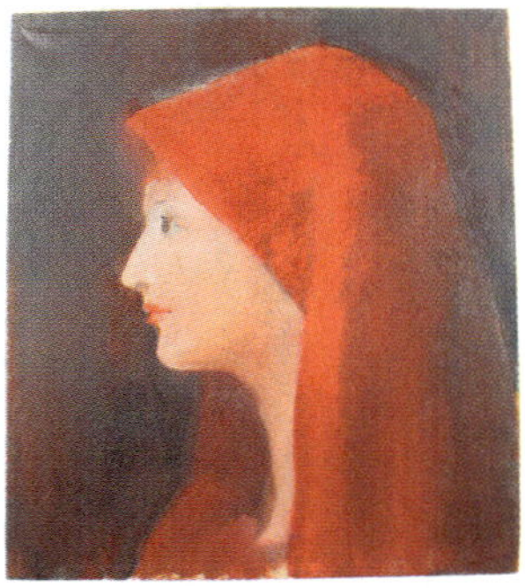

X

DIMENSIONS:	17 ¾ x 15 ⅞ x 1 inches (45.1 x 40.3 x 2.54 cm)
DATE:	1997
MEDIA:	Acrylic on canvas
CONDITION:	Good—Although there is an area of slight accretion or bloom along top and back of hood. Also, the surface has apparently had a treatment to force a false "craquelure" pattern, and this is of unknown consequence for the condition of the painting in the future.
PROVENANCE:	Fake, Estonia, 1997

DIMENSIONS:	17 ¾ x 15 ¾ x 1 ¼ inches (45.1 x 40 x 3.18 cm)
DATE:	1997
MEDIA:	Acrylic on canvas
CONDITION:	Good
PROVENANCE:	Fake, Estonia, 1997

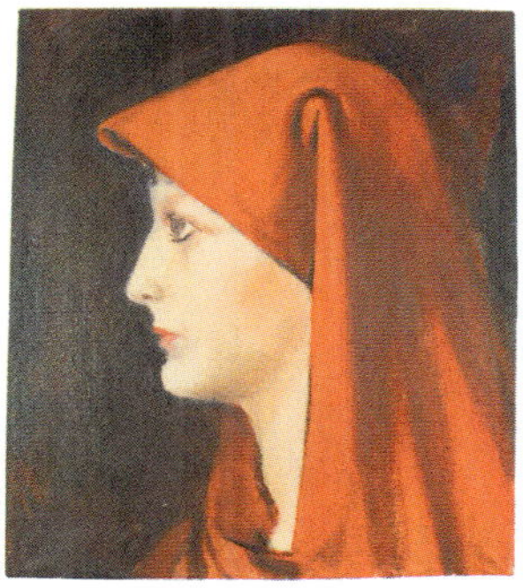

Y

DIMENSIONS:	17 ¾ x 16 x 1 inches (45.1 x 40.6 x 2.54 cm)
DATE:	1997
MEDIA:	Acrylic on canvas
CONDITION:	Good
PROVENANCE:	Fake, Estonia, 1997

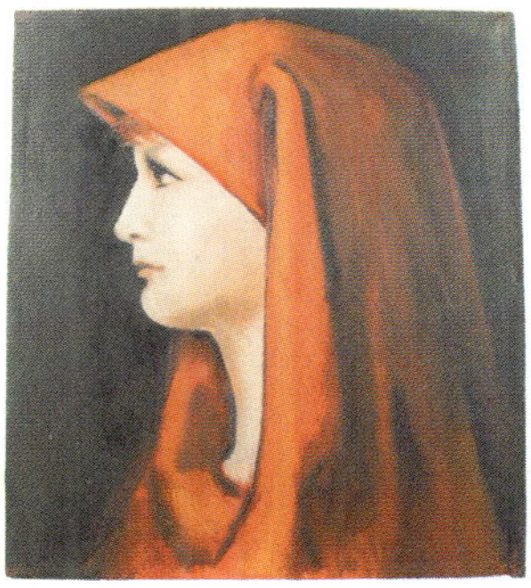

Z

ADDENDUM

Postcards and other printed reproductions of Jean-Jacques Henner's *Fabiola* (1885) have long been produced. A few of these materials are shown in the following pages. Because the painting disappeared before the advent of color photography, the true colors of the work can only be assumed. In addition to the standard reproduction, Henner's painting has also appeared in "negative"—that is, facing in the opposite direction and with a green, as opposed to red, cloak and hood. Reproductions of painted copies of the original have been misattributed to Henner. Captions indicating that the Henner work is in the collection of the Louvre, Paris, are inaccurate.

Muy queridos Bertha y Román:

Importé d'Italie - Printed in Italy

N. 1018 - FABIOLA - J. J. Henner

Museo del Louvre - Parigi

Eliocromia ZENO ZACCHETTI
Via L. Bissolati, 31 - Milano

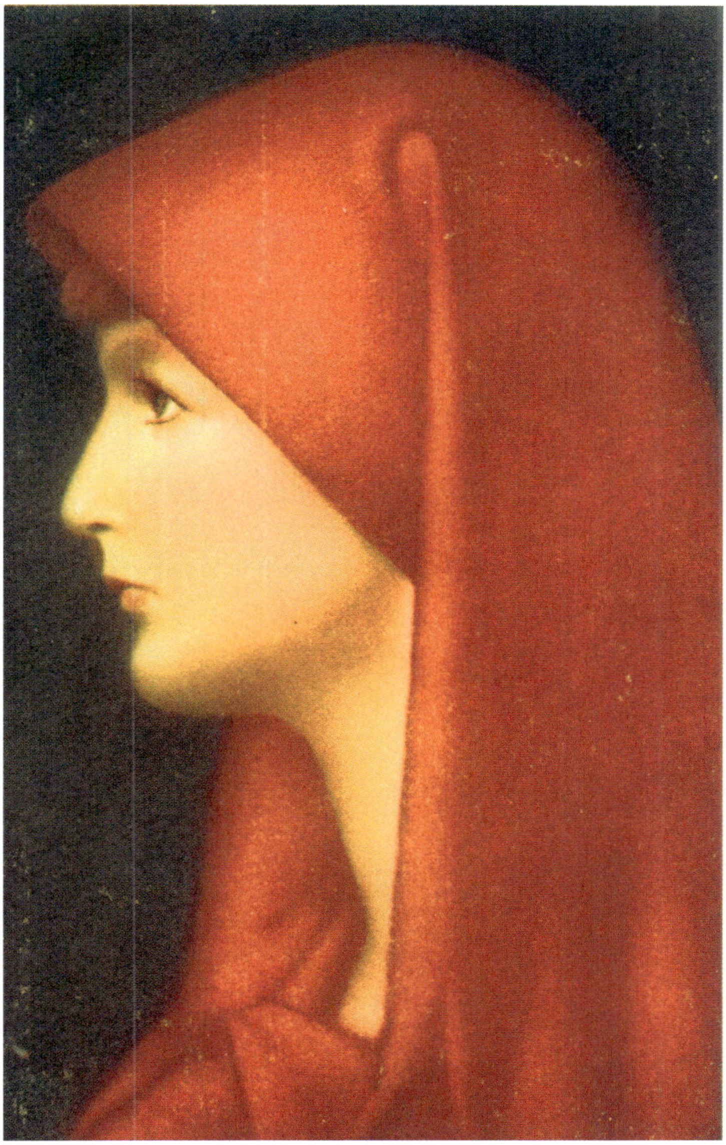

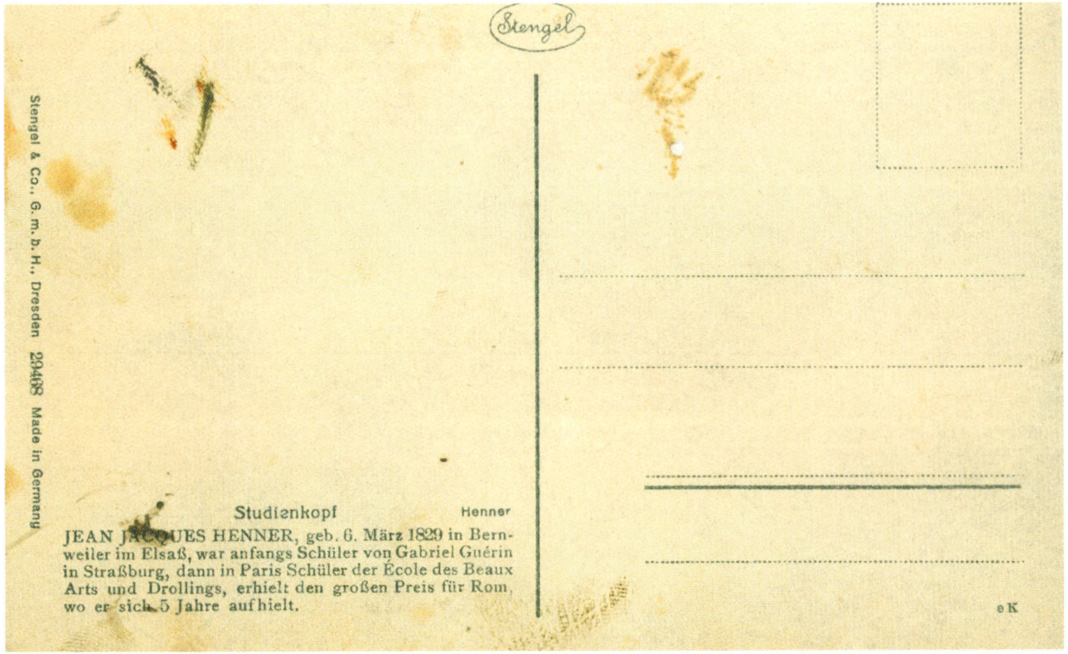

Stengel
Stengel & Co., G. m. b. H., Dresden 29468 Made in Germany
Studienkopf
Henner
JEAN JACQUES HENNER, geb. 6. März 1829 in Bern-
weiler im Elsaß, war anfangs Schüler von Gabriel Guérin
in Straßburg, dann in Paris Schüler der École des Beaux
Arts und Drollings, erhielt den großen Preis für Rom,
wo er sich 5 Jahre aufhielt.
eK

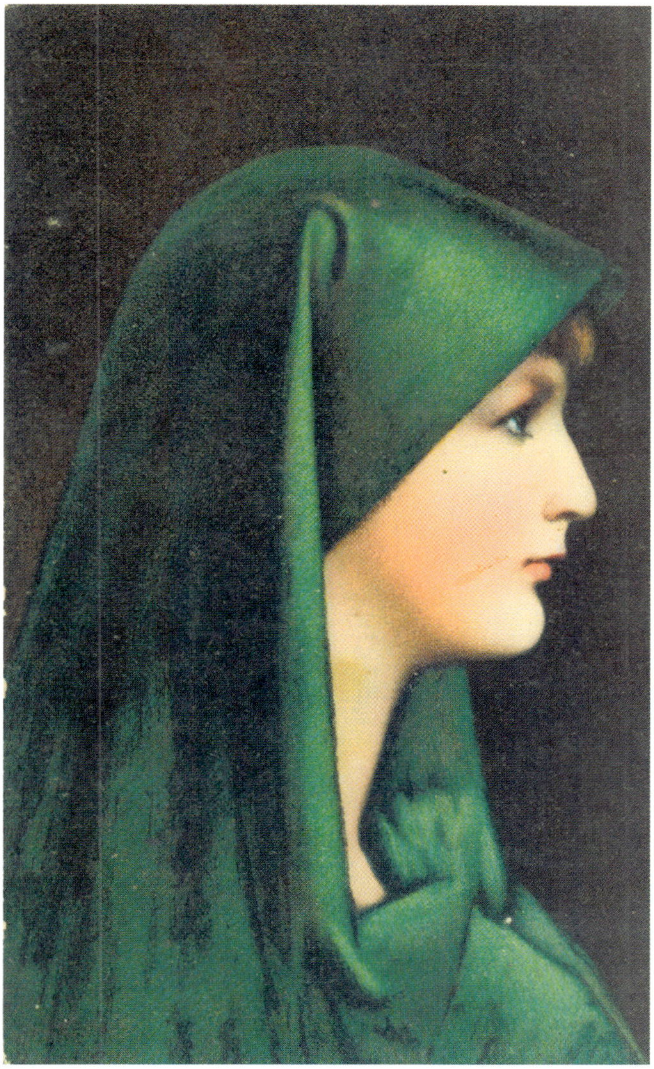

CHEFS D'ŒUVRES
DE LA
PEINTURE

LA FABIOLA
J.-J. Henner 1829-1905
École Française
Musée du Louvre - Paris

PRINTED IN FRANCE

023

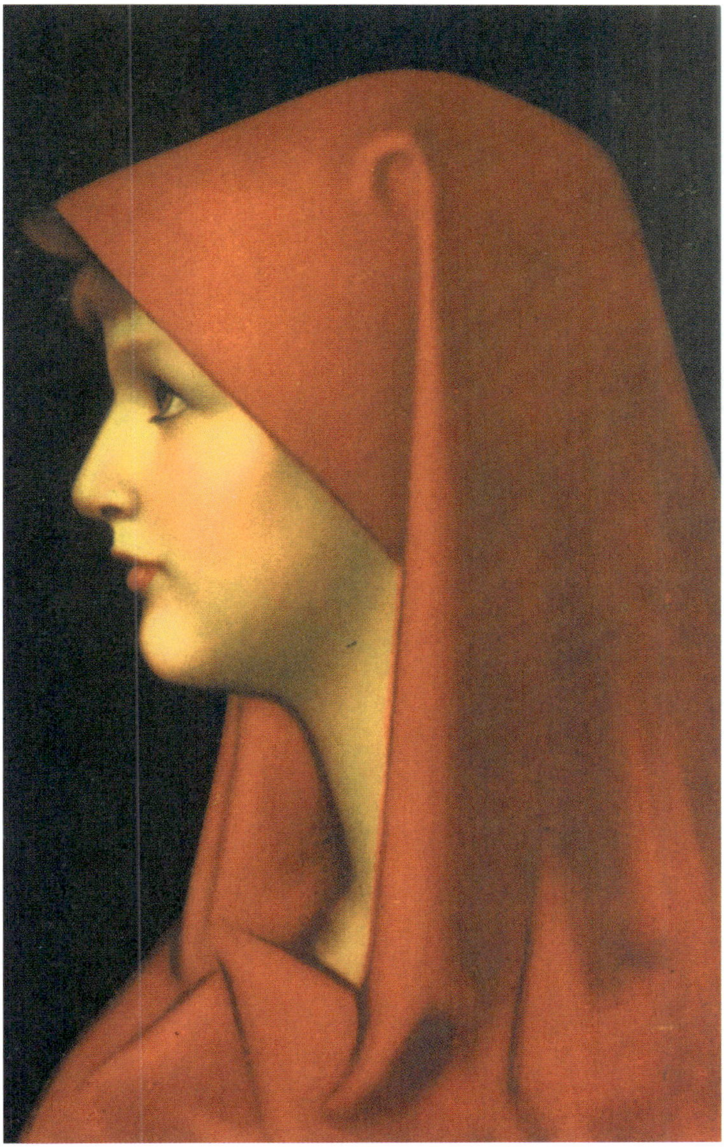

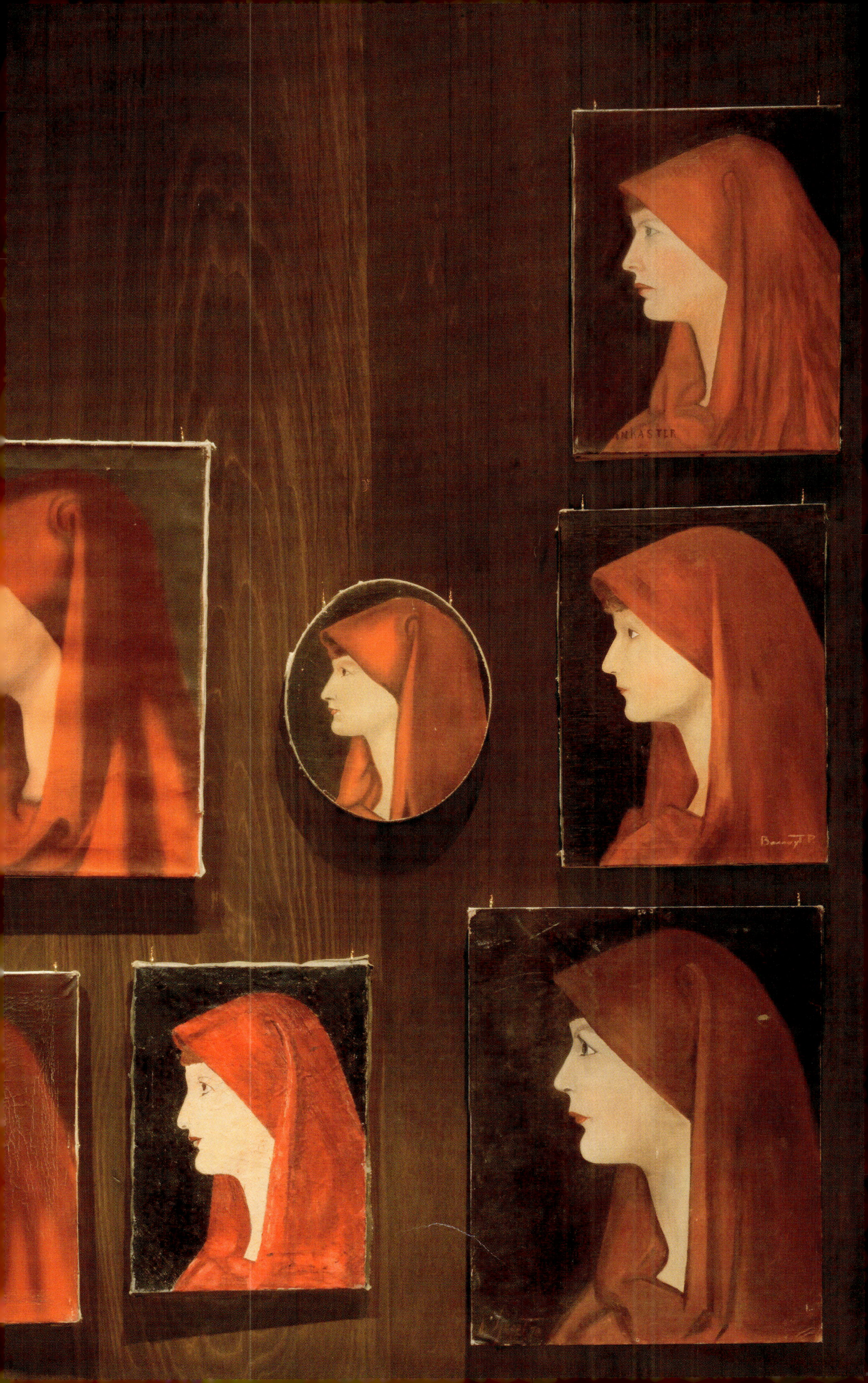

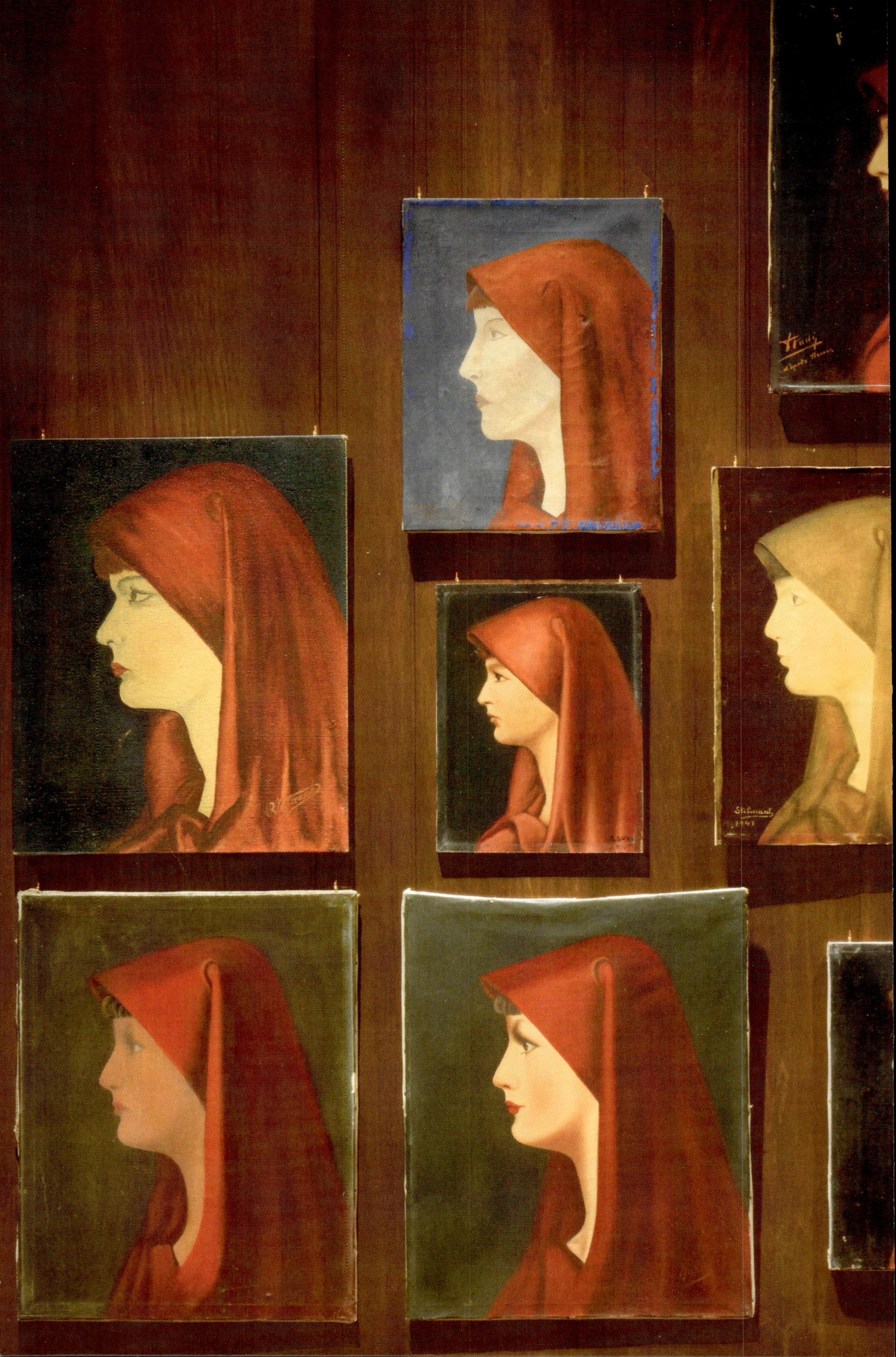